Alison Britton

Seeing Things

CW01622452

Collected Writing on Art, Craft and Design

Occasional Papers

Contents

Preface

Glenn Adamson

The first time I met Alison Britton – this was about 2005, when I first moved to the UK – I remember feeling *watched*. Her eyes were filled with curiosity, focus, and a degree of challenge. It was not an unpleasant feeling: I understood it immediately as the way she looked at things in general.

An intense, pervasive curiosity can be felt in every aspect of Britton's work. It is abundantly there in her pots, no two the same, each invested with its own persona. They often lean forward, as if shaped by her eagerness to explore new possibilities. Curiosity is there in her teaching, too; students of every stripe speak of her incisive and sensitive responses to their efforts.

And it is there, of course, in Britton's writings. As you read through this selection of her essays, collected here in chronological order, you can feel the persistent intensity of her looking, the prospecting intelligence that I experienced when I first met her. It is a compelling document on many levels: historical, critical, and personal. The urgency of each successive moment is there. Objects made many years ago seem crucial. She is vigilant.

In this sense, it is appropriate that Britton's anthology begins with an essay from the exhibition *The Maker's Eye*; for her method is always to look carefully, and then to think deeply about what she has seen. Like many artist-critics, an important point of reference is her own work. Notice how she registers her sensibility as a potter even as she writes about furniture, turned wood, glass, textiles, and avant-garde lighting. Notice, too, how she sometimes quotes previous writings, as if to test the continued validity of her thinking: *I believed that then, do I still believe it now?* She is a profoundly self-aware writer.

I love the passage in 'The Manipulation of Skill on the Outer Limits of Function' (1991) where she contrasts the differing pleasures of her two *métiers*: 'The only representational work that I do is writing. I notice that finishing a piece of writing can give me an acute thrill quite unlike finishing making a pot... perhaps I allow myself the thrill because it is not my real work.' Maybe not, but there is real work in the texts. Some writers gush. You have the sense that the words flow from them, almost unbidden. Britton is not like this. You feel that each sentence is the product of serious consideration and editing. Even if you don't agree with her positions, you will invariably respect the means by which she arrived at them.

That integrity has come in useful over the years, particularly on those occasions when Britton has been drawn into combat over the perennial debates of her subject. This happened principally in the 1980s – the time of the postmodern culture wars. Intelligent art critics and truculent traditionalists alike attacked Britton and her peers for falling into a 'no-man's land between art and craft', lacking the conceptual ambition of the former and the social ethos of the latter. Britton refused this Manichean logic. She proclaimed the virtues of a hybrid, in-between space: 'the only satisfactory, if draughty, home'.

In this book, one can feel her exploring the consequences of this choice more and more widely. The essays of the 1980s center firmly on objects, about which she writes beautifully. When she looks at Ken Eastman's pots, she says, 'Italian whitewash is brought to mind – somehow these are building colours, faded in bright light.' Walter Keeler's technique is described in a few words, her prose as decisive as his process: 'Keeler throws a pot on the wheel, cuts it off like a loose sleeve, then ovals it and puts it on a new base.' The recycled plastics used by furniture maker Floris van den Broecke are 'like multi-coloured Spam'. (As I said, it was the time of postmodernism.)

When the 1990s came, Britton by no means left objects behind, but she also began to articulate the moral dimension of craft more fully, grappling with the consequences of feminism and writing on the socially progressive current that lay under the 'little gestures of advance' made in individual studios ('Gender and Art', 1990; 'Craft: Sustaining Alternatives', 1991). At the same time she was getting older, and sounding the changes. It is poignantly funny when, at 50 years old, she realises she is the same age as Contemporary Applied Arts: 'I now know I am as old as an institution' ('The Open-Minded Eye', 1998). Once a young Turk, she was gradually becoming a village elder. She can now see her interests refracted – and perhaps vindicated – in the work of younger artists like Clare Twomey and Keith Harrison, who are taking up the challenge of working with clay in a medium-specific but post-disciplinary way.

Perhaps it is this thinking about new currents – on artists who rely on external fabricators, found objects, and other 'hands off' means of production – that has caused Britton to revise her opinion on the importance of skills. Asked by *Ceramic Review* to remark on her own early career in hindsight, she replied, 'I wish I'd known that skills really matter; I rather took them for granted because of the emphasis on them in the way I had been taught, and in my teaching over the past decades I have seen them slipping away from the norms of people's lives' (2007). Lest we forget just how skilled Britton herself is, she has included here a 2001 interview with BBC journalist Michael Rosen. As he asks one basic technical question after another, and she offers matter-of-fact replies that only scratch the surface of her process, we begin to realise just how much Britton knows that she typically leaves tacit in making her critical assessments. Yet that repository of knowledge is present throughout. To my mind, that lends her judgments an undercurrent of authority, of a sort that the untrained can never have.

The decision to assemble her past thoughts was not necessarily a straightforward one for Britton. Many other texts might have appeared here, and the process of anthologising one's own writing is inevitably personal. It is interesting that only late in her writings do we get much of Britton's back story – her youthful encounter with the ceramist William Newland, from whom she first understood 'a different, more mysterious set of values about clay shapes and vitality and touch, and learned to hit my pots with a stick while coiling them'; or her visit to Scandinavia in the early 1970s, which briefly seemed a paradise of modernist balance between art and industry until her 'over-developed notions of freedom' made this seem constraining ('The Open-Minded Eye', Bodil Manz, both 1998). But what is personal, for Britton, has not necessarily to do with biographical detail. It is more elusive, more experiential than that. Describing that reality is, I think, what has kept her writing all these years. She has wanted to bring her ideas to the surface by reacting to the objects around her.

Here is a simple exercise: try flipping through the book, reading only the last paragraph of each essay. Sometimes you will find a miniature manifesto:

> Two-faced objects such as I have described are giving more than was demanded of them. That seems to be worth doing. ('The Maker's Eye', 1981)
>
> Public art, above all, is out in the open and inherently sociable. It can only do harm to the progress of alienation. Perhaps all art that aspires to the relation of meaning is public anyway. ('Scale and Meaning', 1992)
>
> Letting the everyday shape thought, the slight subversion in thinking of the house as a place of practice, it is only a small step further to recognise and celebrate the intrusion of living into work. ('Things and Work', 2012)

What is 'worth doing'? That is the question Britton has constantly asked herself. In these writings, as surely as in the 'real work' of her pots, she has been finding the answer.

Glenn Adamson took up the Directorship of the Museum of Arts and Design, New York, in October 2013, following eight years at the V&A, where he was Head of Research, and active as a curator, historian, author and theorist. He is also the co-founder and editor of the *Journal of Modern Craft*.

Introduction

Alison Britton

Through my working life I have wanted to mix practices. My work in one material, clay, and the continuity of making different pots for forty years, has run alongside other things. Pots are my métier, but I have also chosen to write, teach and curate. I have always been writing over these decades and published mainly in the ephemeral forms of exhibition catalogues and magazines, therefore almost all the texts have been commissioned, which is unlike my work in clay. The slightly random nature of what I have been *invited* to write about in more than three decades, and my situation in London at the start of a craft surge in the 1980s, are conditions that shape what is here. I have selected a body of these writings to reprint.

In deciding to call this book *Seeing Things* I want to imply an open-ended array of possibilities. Almost all this writing has been about looking at objects, though the word *thing* is more vague and elastic than the word *object*, which posits a concrete presence. 'Seeing things' literally, observing the appearance of objects, has been necessary in order to write from their visual promptings, but I am also happy with the other meaning, the illusory connotation of that pair of words: seeing what *isn't* there, imagining or hallucinating. The process of investing sight and thought into the meanings of form and visual manifestation creates a speculative response that may open doors for some readers and provoke others, in an investigation with the eyes that opinion makes into words.

The essays in this book consider objects across the spectrum of art, craft, and design. Craft, as I hope to convey, is brought to life in a wider context, as most things are. As I wrote in a gallery leaflet for the British Crafts Centre in 1985:

> Craft is a means to an end and is not really anything in itself.
> It consists of doing something properly, and it is a basis of recognition of values and skills and methods and knowledge of materials.
> It has no real substance or meaning without one or other of these leanings: the design world and the art world have equal need of it.
> Craft is a substratum not an entity.

My own curiosity about the high and low ratings of visual culture was there from the beginning of my art school education, even on my foundation course, coming from clay-filled sixth form years at school into the course at Leeds staffed by fine artists. I could see that there was a kind of class system where ideas about function seemed pedestrian, if not completely disqualified from 'arthood'.

Where is the border? I wondered, until some years later I stopped looking for the border and enjoyed the uncertainty.

Craft is absorbing and stimulating and weird because it is marginal, unfenced and up for grabs. It gets interesting, it seems to me, when things and disciplines cross over or slip out of their conventional category, and open to various readings. If craft is not a definable kind of practice with its own rules, but insinuates itself across the fields of art and design, it is more dynamic and complex than is often assumed. The overlaps, transgressions and experiments, especially clear in the rapid evolution of the 1980s, chewed up past definitions and brought new ideas to light.

Ambiguity became the mainstay of my pot making and is an undercurrent in my appraisal and reading of other people's work as well as the scene as a whole. Like a good poem, any interesting object has layers of possible meaning to a keen eye, and they may contradict each other. Intimacy with the fluid categories and blurred edges of the crafts can make you a connoisseur of allusion and ambiguity.

Why write? I have always liked using language as another medium, one that stretches across all aspects of living and thinking. I was brought up to write comfortably in different ways for different reasons, and to play with words. In the process of making things I have always put words in sketch books as much as drawings of ideas and shapes and diagrams of the kiln packing. My mixed occupations also drew me further into verbalisation and thence text.

My interest has been in writing as an *insider*, having a dual voice as artist and commentator, which seemed from early on to be something to pursue as a contribution and a kind of translation. Many critics don't make things and many artists don't write; aesthetic response to new things is hard to put into words, and a different reading of art objects may come from a person who makes them.

With a blend of subjective and objective, physical experience and opinion, writing as an insider involves thinking through the workings of something, to see where senses of material and process, for instance, have played a part in the form and presence of an object. Being an insider means understanding things with head and hands, for their ideas, their specifics, and for their feel. It involves the capacity to look in detail, to examine and preferably touch what is in front of you and compare it with the memory of dozens of other objects, built up from the habit of looking analytically at stuff. Trawling in the streets and museums wherever you find yourself is part of the practice of being an artist and builds the basis of personal aesthetic reaction and response.

Despite being versed in ceramics I have gladly written about a lot of other things within and beyond craft. Knowing the constraints of one material assists the translation from visual to verbal with others; you can conjecture the negotiations with stuff and skill involved in bringing the work into being.

And from a comparative material understanding you might react in a side-step, an interjection across fields, a sliver of another kind of expertise that offers a new perspective. The possibility of shifting the expectations of the onlooker is something I have saught in pot making and also in writing. As did the sculptor Richard Deacon, writing about ceramics by Jacqui Poncelet:

> ... there is, I suggest, a clear invitation for active engagement with the pots as objects of use. However, that invitation, once recognised, is almost immediately cancelled or confused by the complex discussion of colour, form, pattern, interior and exterior with which one is as quickly engaged.[1]

Writing about how objects worked as ideas and enquiries, as well as material facts, developed significantly in the 1980s in what might now be seen as the progressive phase of the Crafts Council and *Crafts* magazine that encouraged an avant-garde.

In the construction of this book, what I have *not* done is define the major themes of the last three decades observed in the crafts, and their place in the wider visual world, and then found the essays in my files that reveal my ideas on those themes at the time. Instead, I have been intrigued by the diversity of what editors and gallerists and curators and artists have asked me to write about, and raked through all my texts – this is my raw material. I have picked less than a quarter of them with a range that seems to hold good for a number of half-intuited reasons. Reflecting on the choices does bring up signs of a changing history, covert threads and symptoms, from within the whole. These are explored in a postscript for each decade, that finds a focus in an event, person, or idea.

The essays have been left as they are and I am publishing the printed version, not always what I originally wrote as some were edited and some, particularly in the gallery leaflets, hardly at all. I also decided to keep the chronological order of the essays as a system against which the new ideas that emerge in bringing the book into a whole, from my current viewpoint, can be floated. Trying to inhabit the reader's ear, I have picked different kinds of writing, essays for catalogues and exhibition handouts, reviews and articles in magazines, and introductions to other people's books. I have also chosen pieces to vary the verbal tones of arguing, describing, and explaining, critically or enthusiastically, formally or casually; and chosen texts of different lengths and densities to change the pace of reading. The subjects also range across media and international scope, and I have included less known artists and practices as well as the established, and also critics.

With the decision to go for more than an anthology, to review the old essays in some new writing, the prospect of constructing the book lit up. If there is a key to it, it is in this double exposure of the original commentary on new work through many years, and the recent reconsideration of the long period of seeing craft practice and its place on the borders and overlaps of visual culture. This is consistent with the dualistic thinking that is usually apparent in my pots.[2]

Most of these written pieces were about a recent phenomenon: a new book, an exhibition, a summation of a person's work to date, or a recent museum display. I have had a close relationship with two main galleries in London, showing with Contemporary Applied Arts until 1995, and since 1998 with Barrett Marsden Gallery, now called Marsden Woo. In both these places I have written introductions to new work by many artists in the form of the 'gallery leaflet'. I have been able to walk into an artist's studio, perhaps someone I have never met, and got straight into talking about what they are trying to do and the way they think. Doing this frequently, as I did in the adventuring craft world of the 1980s and 1990s, allowed me to explore some of the inner arguments and connections that animated the field. Because it responds to the newly made, the writing, perhaps hurriedly, catches the tensions and actualities of the moment in a way that it would not if I sat down to write a retrospective history. I am much more interested in combining these first reactions with recollection and my age-altered, built-up understanding. In using what was written when the work was just made, and then picking over the perceptions of that time through new commentary, the book is both immediate and distant; the coal-face and the bird's eye view.

It is surprising that the crafts have remained a kind of off-beat hidden art world that many people do not come across. This collection of writing relates craft not as a discrete category in a closed box, enmeshed in tradition, but suggests that ideas of the hybrid and ties to the material physical world are the life in it. Craft practices can be stretched and played around with, seen in other contexts, detached from function as a norm, and propose objects made for a variety of reasons. Craft's separation from ordinary and habitual purposes is at the same time a loss, the downside, which has become more visible to me in recent years.

Is this an assembly of random fragments, or a revealing of essential themes? Does it add up to a kind of history? I hope it is both a book of essays and an episodic narrative tracking some of the new ideas in objects made in this postmodern period. The structure of the book lets me reflect on the evolution of craft in the continuum of art and design, and what people thought about it, but also on how my own ideas have changed over time.

1. Richard Deacon, catalogue introduction, *Jacqui Poncelet, New Ceramics*, Crafts Council, 1981. See also my 1983 essay *Sèvres with Krazy Kat*, see below.
2. See for example *Double Green Pot*, 1995, see below.

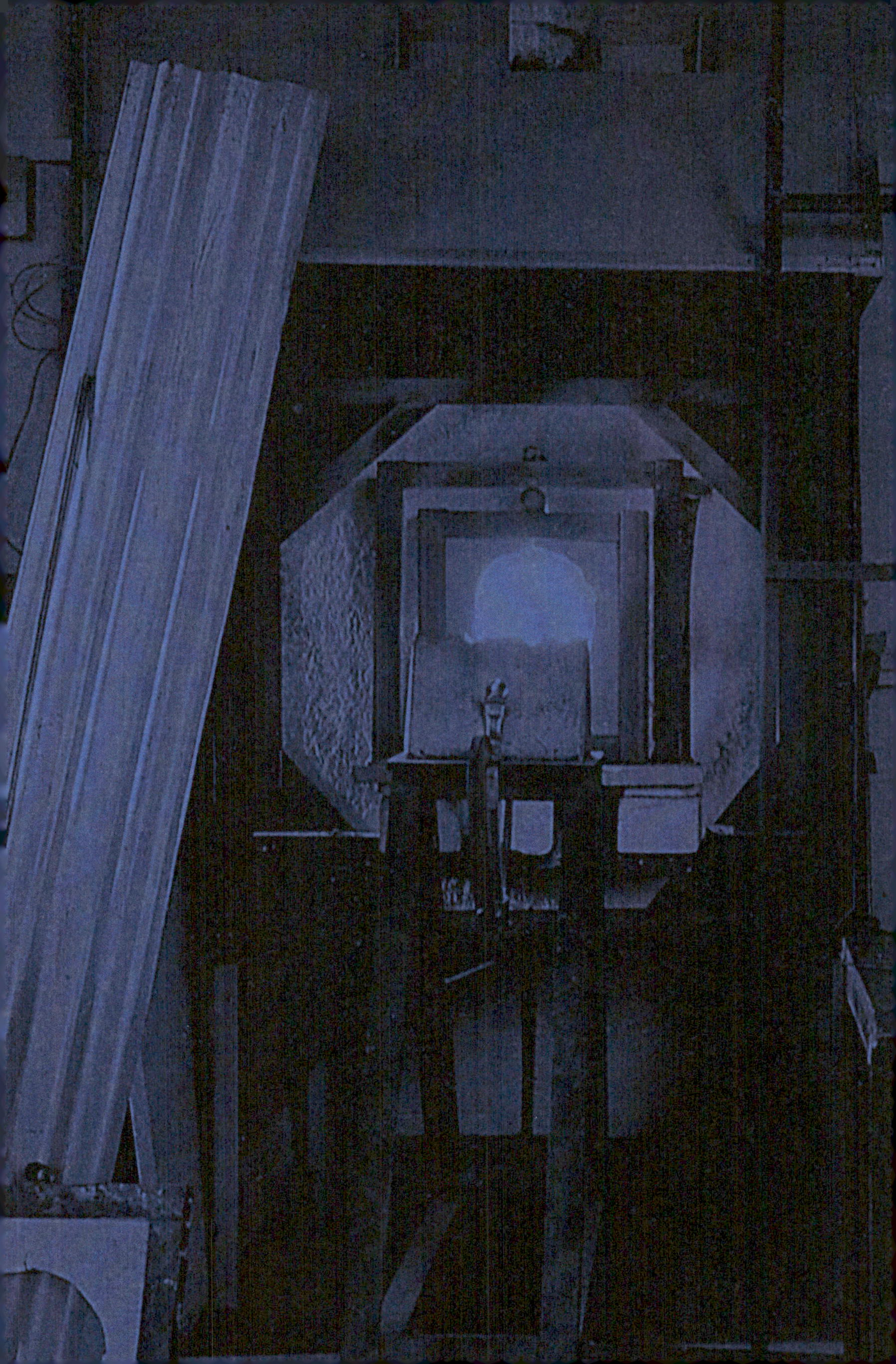

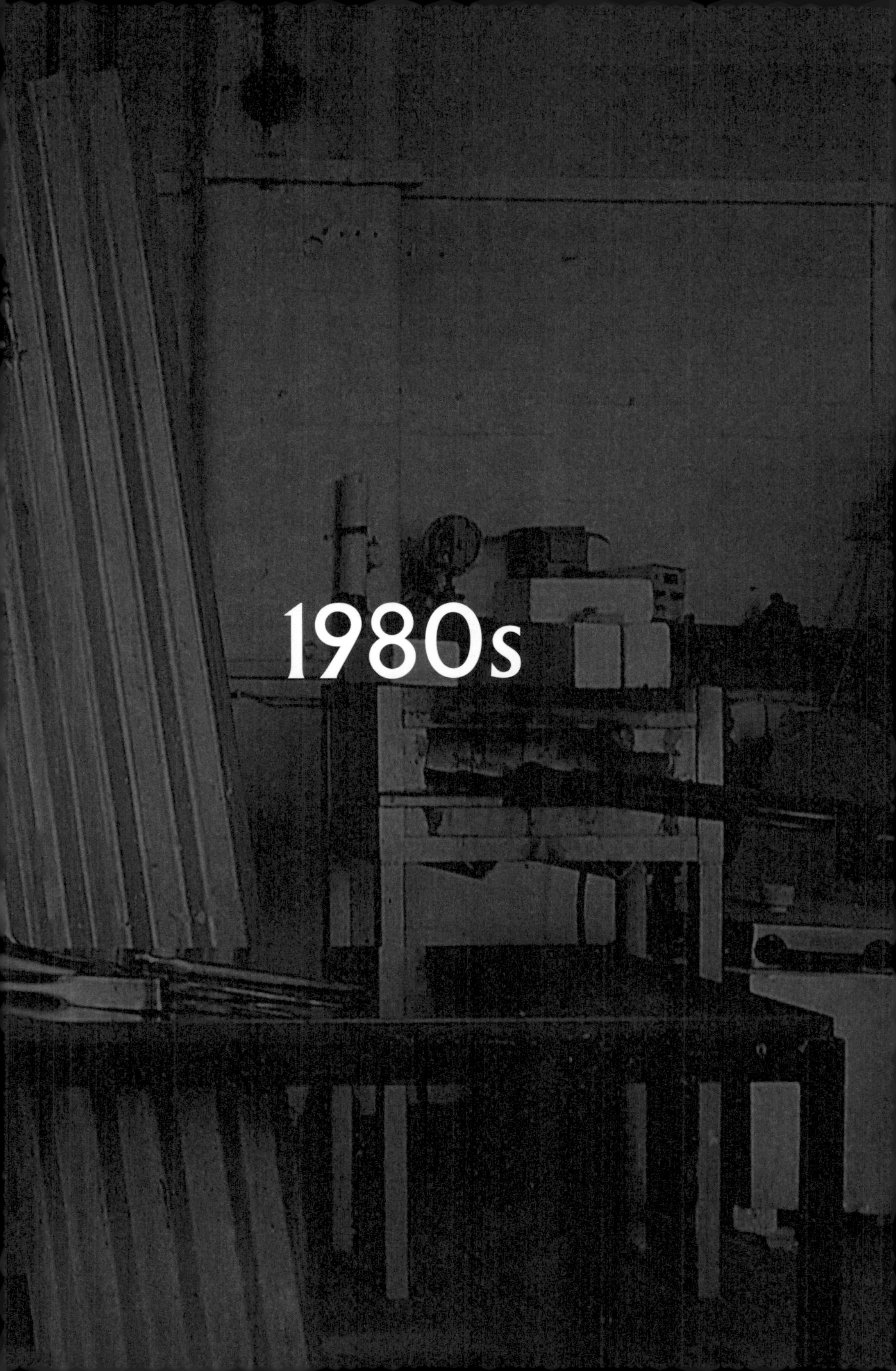
1980s

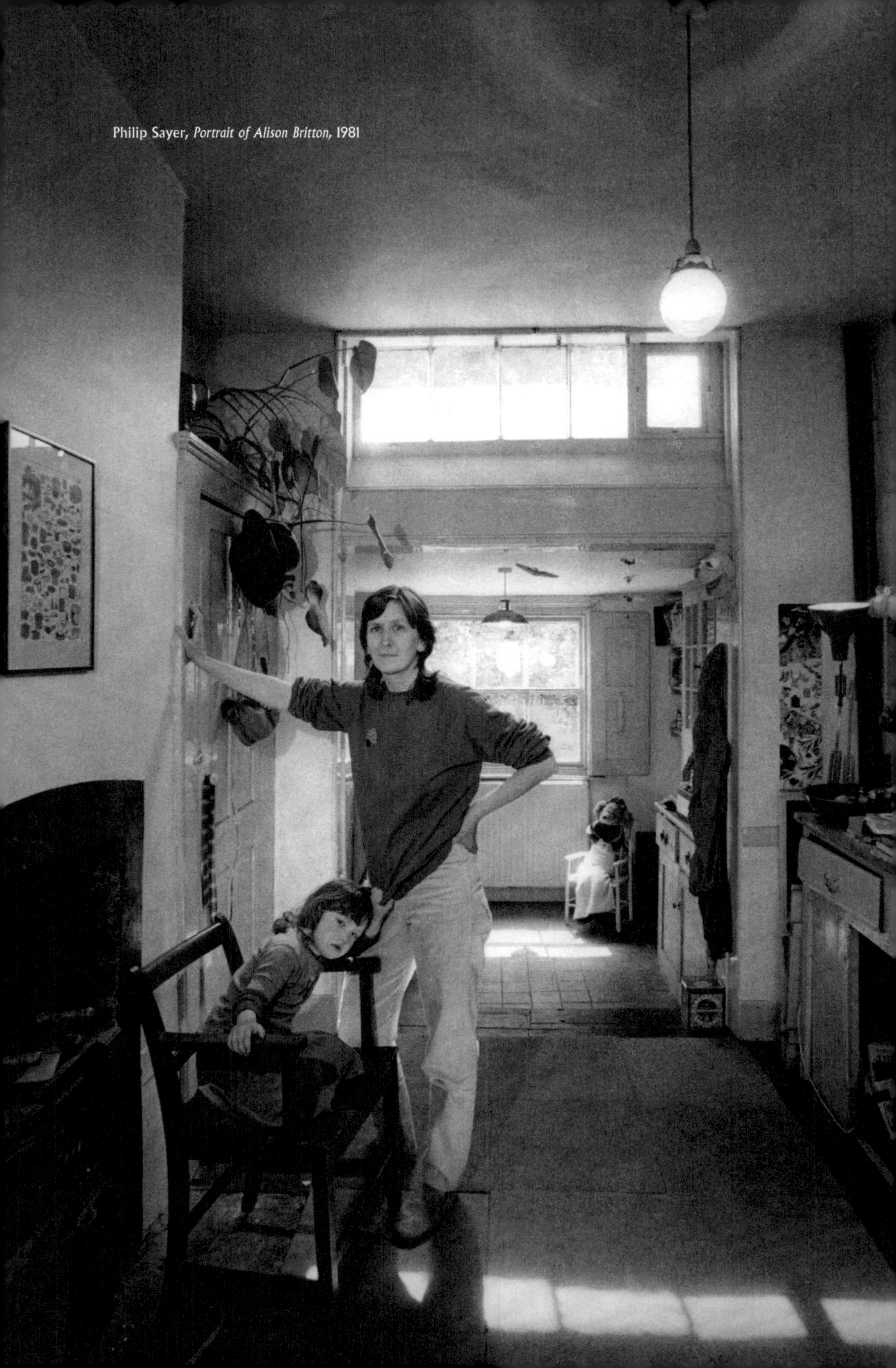

Philip Sayer, *Portrait of Alison Britton*, 1981

The Maker's Eye

Exhibition catalogue, Crafts Council Gallery, London, 1981, p.16. *The Maker's Eye* was a major exhibition (13 January–28 March 1982) showing more than 500 objects chosen by 14 selectors, from all generations and all kinds of craft practice. The range of objects I chose reveal what I still think, namely that ignoring the borders of a category, such as craft, brings more meaning to all of it.

Many of the objects that have had a powerful effect on me and my work have been ancient, foreign, or outside the definition of 'craft', and so it has been something of a shock to have to choose mainly from what has been made by craftspeople in Britain during this century. I find, to my surprise, that within these confines what seems to me to be most important reveals a narrow and specific interest: almost all vessels are in my own material, ceramics, and produced in the last few years.

My work may in the future be seen to have belonged to a 'group', and I think that the objects I have chosen reinforce this idea of a hypothetical group of artist craftspeople, having certain trains of thought in common, whether or not these have been articulated or brought to the surface. I would say that this group is concerned with the outer limits of function; where function, or an idea of a possible function, is crucial, but is just one ingredient in the final presence of the object and is not its only motivation. I think that this preoccupation, which can be perceived in various fields and materials, stands out as a distinct contribution of the last ten years: something has happened that is only gradually being described and recognised. Some people will certainly feel that it represents the last decadent throes of an artistic crafts movement of dwindling relevance, where over-self-conscious makers turned in on themselves for want of a real sense of necessity. But perhaps to others it will be seen as something closely in line with 'modernism' in other arts, in painting or literature for example. A 'modern' novel (i.e. following such writers as Marcel Proust and James Joyce) is both made of, and about, language. Some of the objects I have chosen are similarly self-referential, that is, they perform a function, and at the same time are drawing attention to what their own rules are about. (As Michael Rowe, in the notes for his 1978 exhibition at the Crafts Council, says: 'The boxes are purely about their own space and the characteristics of the sheet metal that they are made from.') In some way such objects stand back and describe, or represent, themselves as well as are. In this analogy 'function' stands for 'story', as the central content.

However, I am not only concerned with this rather elusive category in my selection. I have chosen vessels or containers that are 'ordinary' too, and to me supremely and powerfully so. I would like to make a comparison evident between 'prose' objects and 'poetic' objects; those that are mainly active and those that are mainly contemplative. To me the most moving

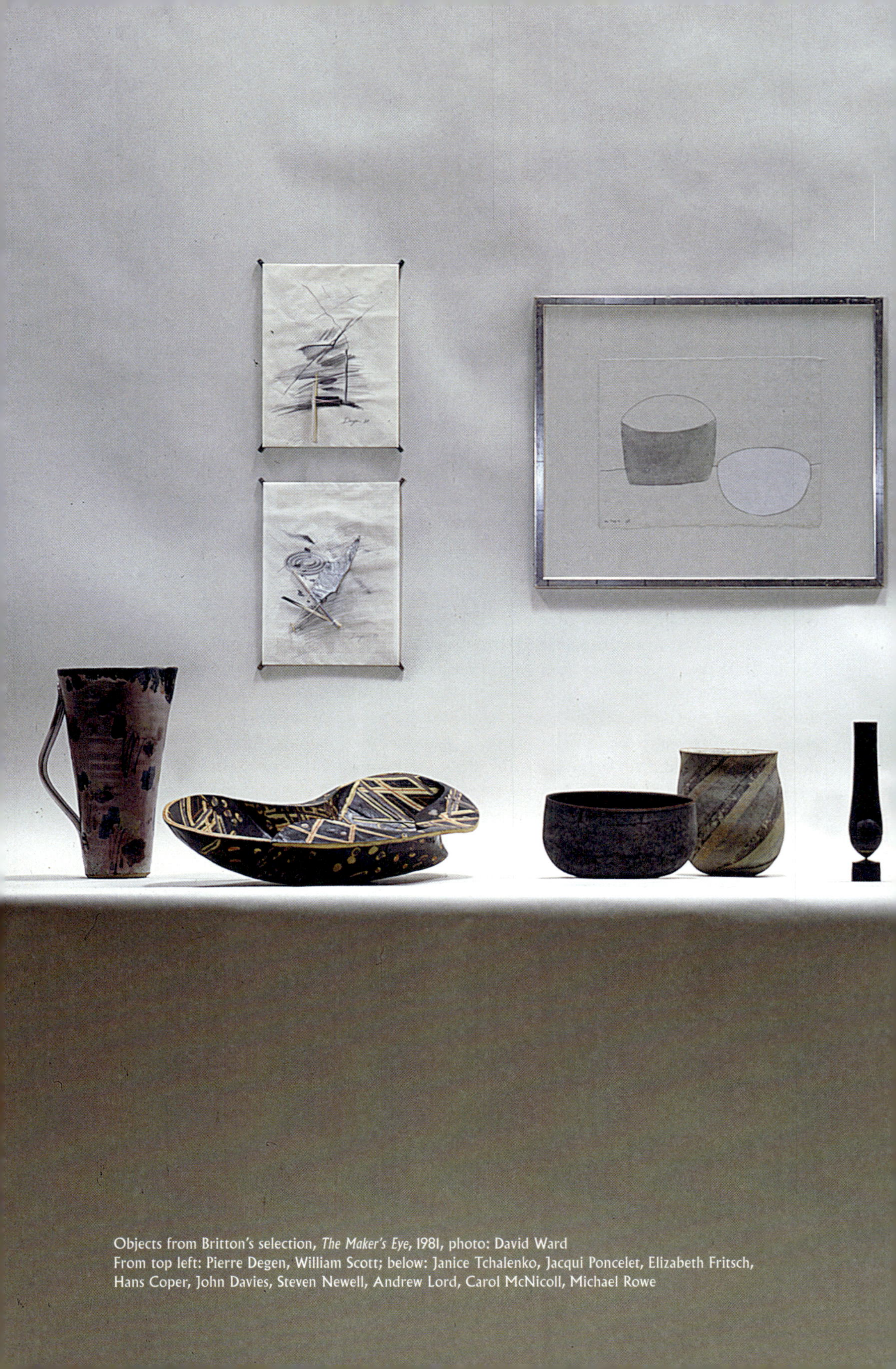

Objects from Britton's selection, *The Maker's Eye*, 1981, photo: David Ward
From top left: Pierre Degen, William Scott; below: Janice Tchalenko, Jacqui Poncelet, Elizabeth Fritsch, Hans Coper, John Davies, Steven Newell, Andrew Lord, Carol McNicoll, Michael Rowe

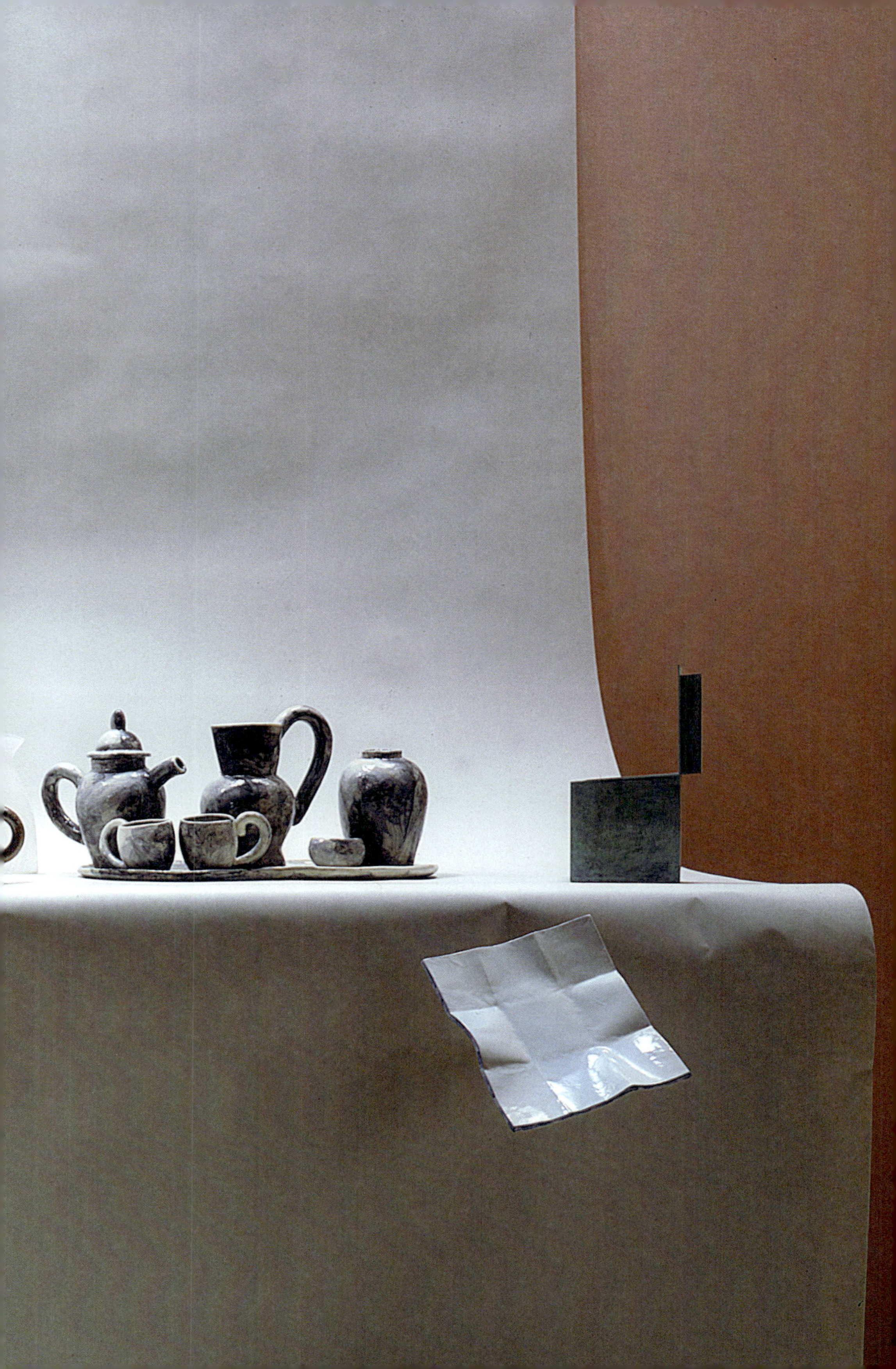

things are the ones where I experience in looking at them a frisson from both these aspects at once – from both prose and poetry, purpose and commentary. These have what I call a 'double presence'.

I would like now to focus on my own subject, ceramics. Clay is a material that has been prone to metaphor for centuries. It is such a malleable, versatile, simulatory substance, that practical objects have been formed in some guise or other for probably as long as clay has been used. The first vessels to use clay are thought to have been woven reed containers plastered with a layer of sticky clay to make them waterproof. Even here there is an ambiguity between 'pot' and 'basket'. Being a vessel is not very demanding. Once the functional requirements of holding are fulfilled, there is still plenty of room for interpretation and variety of outer form. Chronologically, my selection begins with a Martin Brothers jar; a striking example of object that is not what it seems, where decoration is carried to dominating extremes. A jar becomes a bird – and a Carol McNicoll plate becomes a piece of origami – function unimpaired. I am suggesting that what I have been trying to define is a descendant of this tradition. A jar can also be a representation of a jar, function unimpaired.

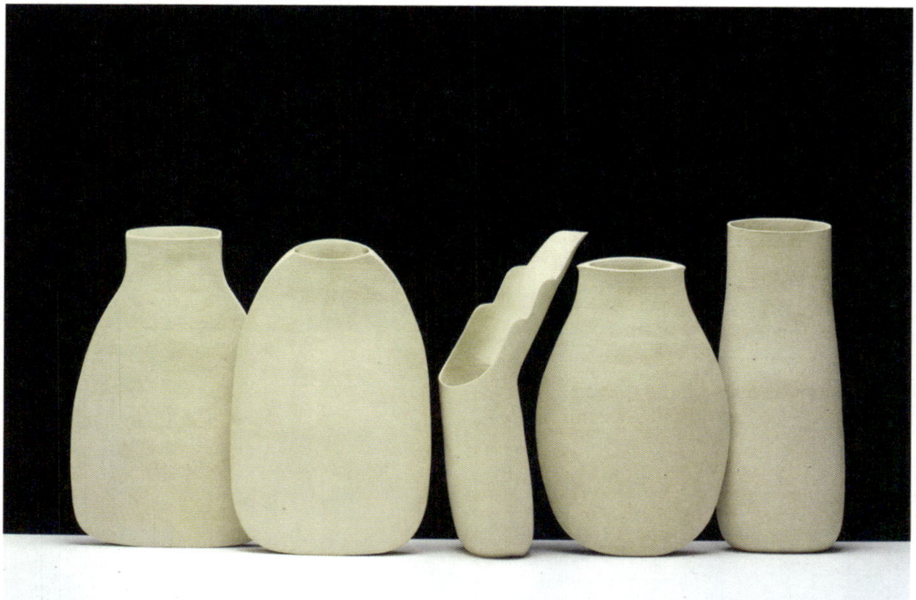

Raw pots by Elizabeth Fritsch, 1979, photo: David Cripps

Many of these objects have been made, it seems, in the light of modern painting. Still life painting is such a strong tradition, at its most seductive perhaps with Henri Matisse and Giorgio Morandi. Why have painters cared so much about depicting pots and pans? What do they stand for – slices of life? Symbols of domestic or intimate selves? I find myself aware of a sequence here: from ordinary everyday objects, to painting, and to a re-depiction in three dimensions of not-so-ordinary objects. Andrew Lord, working in ceramics, reconstructs the objects that might have been the subject of a painting. They are presented in prescribed groups. He concerns himself with the way light falls on objects, and builds in clay with a painter's eye on the transmutations of light and tone. Physically, his objects retain some of the imprecision and loose, impressionistic quality of a two-dimensional representation. Function is hardly a characteristic at all – though they are still hollow and waterproof, and more than that, eloquent about the relation between inside and outside. Life has been translated through still life and beyond into some ghostlier, more ambivalent form of object. Lord's work stands at the far edge of my spectrum from ordinary to magical. The objects in the middle, my main concern, are about life and still life at once. They can be used, but their function is partly frozen in reflection about themselves.

Technically, I think this effect is usually achieved through some kind of physical distortion, some thwarting of our expectations of form, and has perhaps particularly to do with flattening of form. A Steven Newell jug, for instance, simply by being flattened (and helped by being transparent) moves towards being a representation of a jug as well as being a jug in fact. An Erik de Graaff chair (could a chair be described as a container?) gives a similar jolt to expectations, and is at once business-like and questioning. Objects such as these fill the gap between prose and poetry, between ordinary and breathtaking, combining both. These are the things that matter to me most.

It is hard to explain my own inability to stop making vessels. It could somehow be inherent in the training of a potter, something one is lumbered with as part of the equipment. Or it could be that the inclusion of function is a crutch for one lacking the courage to make a piece of work that is entirely aesthetic; I may be clinging to the residue of use as a justification. Or I may have an irresistible (and fairly abstract) preoccupation with something very deep-rooted. Vessels are basic, archetypal, timeless. A container is a fundamental prop (and symbol) of civilisation. A container is an object made with a specific relation to people in mind. Two-faced objects such as I have described are giving more than was demanded of them. That seems to be worth doing.

Sèvres with Krazy Kat

Crafts magazine 61, March/April 1983, pp.18–23. For my first commission from *Crafts* magazine, I was asked to review recent work that explored the decoration, humour, and visual contradiction that was in the air. Some of these artists had been colleagues at the Royal College of Art a decade earlier.

I am embarking here on an investigation of some of the issues that have interested me in decoration during the span of my professional life, which is the last ten years. I am going to refer only to ceramics, and mainly to things that I have seen in this country. I mean to include not simply decoration as it lies upon an object, collaborating with its form, but also the decorative object itself (whether adorned or not); to look at the ornamental status of my kind of quasi-functional object.

Most pictorial pots that I have seen have been, I think, to some degree unsuccessful – it seems nearly impossible to keep a good form and a good painting in balance. Clearly Pablo Picasso could do it, but in looking at more contemporary work, I think that when the decoration more actively becomes part of the form it works best. A series of goldfish bowls made by Jill Crowley in 1977 are a good example. Ruth Franklin, too, has done some very fluent and witty illustrative pots but her images have now been carried away from the objects and become freestanding cut-outs. I have often felt that surface drawing and painting are much more exciting than the shape underneath; early work by Jane Osborn-Smith and Rachael

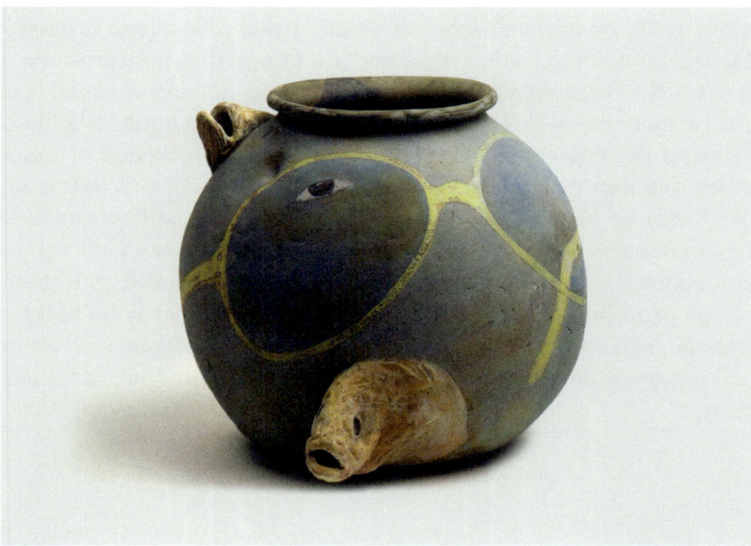

Jill Crowley, *Goldfish Bowl*, 1979

Mellor comes to mind. The use of relief can make an important bridge from decoration to form. Carol McNicoll, the boldest and most spontaneous of the slip-cast-and-assemble school, is pictorial in a more outspoken way. She made a fish plate several years ago where the plate adorned the fish as much as the other way around, and without loss of function.

Work like this relates I believe to some splendid Americans – I am thinking particularly of a collaboration between Robert Hudson and Richard Shaw that led to an exhibition of cups, bottles, teapots and jars at the San Francisco Museum of Art in 1973 that were complex, witty, and striking as well as beautiful in a new and disturbing way. They were usable objects wearing the disguise of their decoration to the extent that the decoration had become the thing itself. I think that we owe a lot to the sight of such work in this decade. The West Coast American potters, above all, have offered us glimpses of previously forbidden fruit – both their strength and their weakness lie in their freedom from, and ignorance of, a clear line of tradition. Our line of pot precedents, from Peasant to Industrial to Arts and Crafts to the Oriental Drift, is unavoidable and unforgettable for most, fencing ourselves around with taboos and truth to materials.

West Coast American ceramics grew out of the 1950s with a group of disenchanted painters, headed by Peter Voulkos, looking for a new mode of less abstract expression that could include humour and irreverence. Their work is radical because it is visualised so strongly without the confines of a technical background. These artists invented a sophisticated technology uninhibited by ceramic conventions. And so succeeding generations have

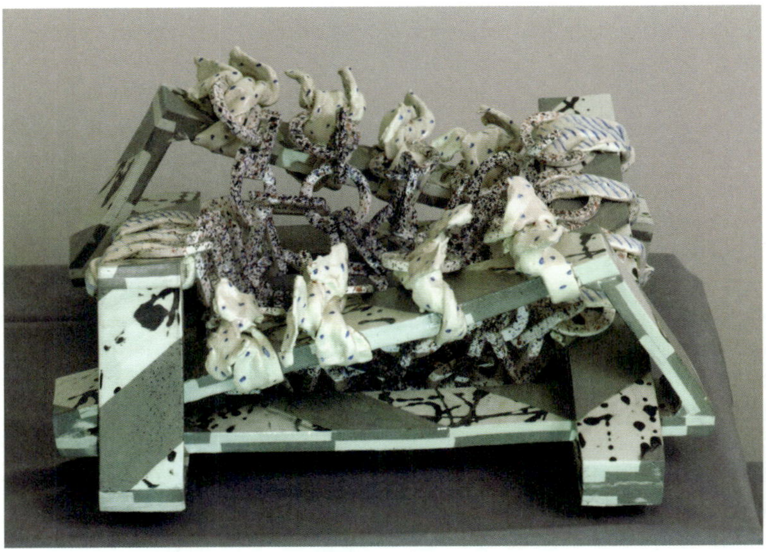

Carol McNicoll, *Dish*, 1983, photo: David Cripps

a better chance of making sculpture out of clay that makes no reference to vertical growth from a base, or of using colour as colour without knowing what it is made of; and will pursue much larger and more brazen pioneering plans. The threshold for success and failure is a very wide one. The best work is breathtaking. With my own predilection for the vessel, Kenneth Price and Ron Nagle, Voulkos and, from further East, Betty Woodman, are all important for me. As is Andrea Gill, whose figurative pots I enjoy very much, and who brings us back to discussing pictures.

Generally, then, I find pictorial pottery a bit sweet and lacking in edge. I was involved with it myself for several years. Ten years ago I was in my last year at the Royal College of Art. I was not feeling confident or potent at all, but it seemed that other people around me were, and there was change in the air. I wrote an essay then on the difference between art and decoration, and it is curious to see that I was treading around in the theory of applying decoration to objects, and the status and context of different kinds of artifacts, before making any pots. My work at the time was almost entirely flat, and was, I now suppose, an attempt to separate off the surface to deal with it by itself before returning to object making. When I did make things again, I had to start from scratch with developing a sense of form. Painting on these cautious surfaces was irresistible, and I played around a lot with strengthening formal weakness via painted emphasis. Wanting to stay on the more recognisable side of vessel making, I found that as my shapes got better, and more thoroughly three-dimensional, the pictures had to go. The forms got tougher when I stopped making jugs in 1980, and could no longer lean on lips and handles for animating charm. At least that is part of the reason for the shift to painting abstractly on my recent pots. I also have shifted my sources of inspiration out of the British Museum and into the 20th century.

My old concerns were not just with portraying, but with mixing imagery and pattern. Dualism is a constant feature of my thinking, and is an aspect of the argument about function, actual and referred. I am now considering the 'decorative object' rather than just decoration. The exploration of the 'outer limits of function' was the subject of my selection for *The Maker's Eye* exhibition at the Crafts Council in 1982, where I showed hybrids of various kinds, not just ceramic ones, but mainly vessels ranging from ordinary to metaphorical. The effort of selecting, and commenting, has left me with a stronger sense of being part of a peer group, with various levels of common ground. We have in common the choice, by most, of urban life, a certain self-consciousness, and a formal preoccupation with the articulating aspects of pots. Much catalogue space has been expended on lips and rims, feet, hollow space, a sense of volume or capacity (often illusory), containing, positive and negative forms, front and back planes, relation to horizontal surface, of inside to outside, flatness and roundness, and aperture and depth. What all this adds up to is a shifting of function in the old sense.

Elizabeth Fritsch was the first I came across to put it in writing in a set of boldly scrawled notes for her show at the British Crafts Centre in 1974. She made a poetic list of the pertaining parts of a pot, and on coming to function she presents the paradox of kitchen and temple: utilitarian and realistic, besides playful and surrealistic. Later in her catalogue essay for the Leeds Museum in 1978 she writes, 'I suspect that pots do not have to function for cooking, eating and tea-making either, but that they can be allegorical objects in which the only essential physical function is the minimal one of containing.'

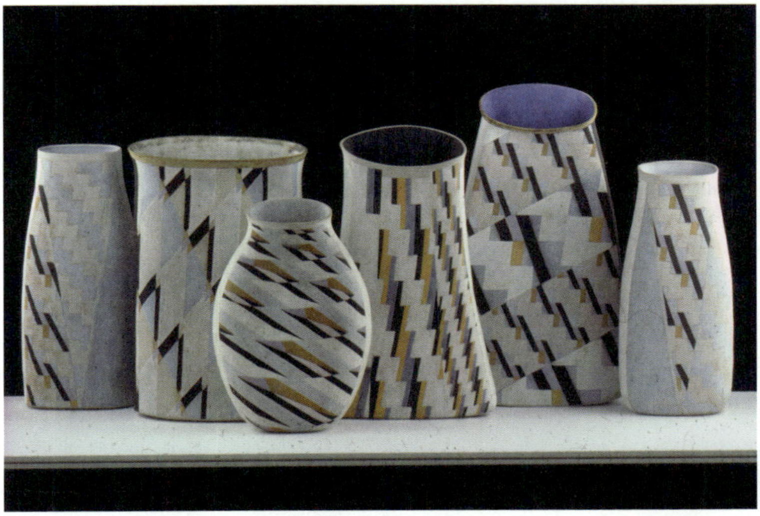

Elizabeth Fritsch, *Piano Pots*, 1978, photo: David Cripps

Richard Deacon also writes clearly and well about the contradictions that raise themselves about use and/or contemplation in his catalogue essay for Jacqueline Poncelet's exhibition at the Crafts Council in 1981. He says that her pots first of all invite you to take them on as things to be used, but that then the invitation is almost immediately complicated by the number of other levels on which the pots function as objects, the different formal claims of colour, dense pattern, intricate shape, visual metaphor, etc. And in *The Maker's Eye* essay I argued, 'Being a vessel is not very demanding. Once the functional requirements of holding are fulfilled, there is still plenty of room for interpretation and variety of outer form.' I am suggesting that I and my peers continue to hang around on the fringes of making usable things because it is tantalising to try and take up the slack in so many different ways.

Another thing the peer group has in common is a strong regard for tradition, but on the whole a quite separate channel of tradition from the Oriental one which has sustained the majority of pots made here in the last 40 years. When I was a student at the Central School in the late 1960s, I remember that part of our sense of corporate pride and college rivalry was expressed in the fact that we made blue and yellow things whereas at Camberwell they were still green and brown. Anti-Orientalism (in our inspiration though not our appreciation), and divergence from the Bernard Leach line, is a stance held in common. Useful sources are varied; though great respect for ancient and primitive and very different cultures is a binding factor. Richard Slee lists influences that range from Pre-Columbian vessels to Krazy Kat cartoons through Sèvres porcelain and the Surrealists, and is entirely convincing. I, like Angus Suttie, have found great riches in primitive textiles – and indeed in the Japanese sense of asymmetric pattern as applied to textile. Only the pots are unusable as sources, the ground around them being well-trodden.

The members of this hypothetical group need and recognise tradition, not in order to follow it, as perhaps the Orientalists have been inclined to do, but to mix it all up and try to invent freely on top of it. How else could Krazy Kat and Sèvres contribute to the same piece? Some sort of distortion, or visual deception, and non-symmetry, are other usual features of these new vessels. Even those who throw now muck about with the shapes afterwards. Both my favourite throwers, Walter Keeler and Betty Woodman, are expert at this.

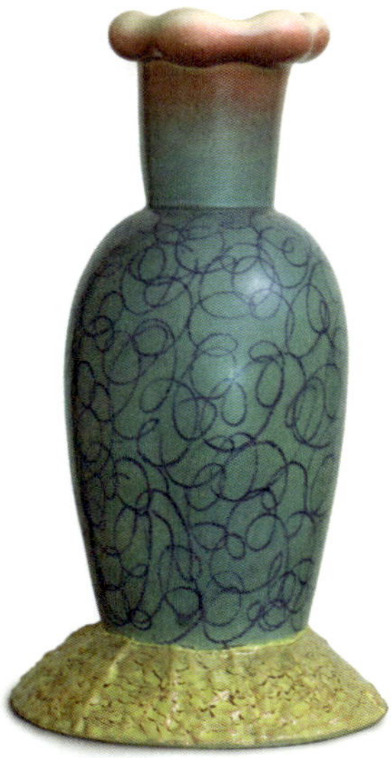

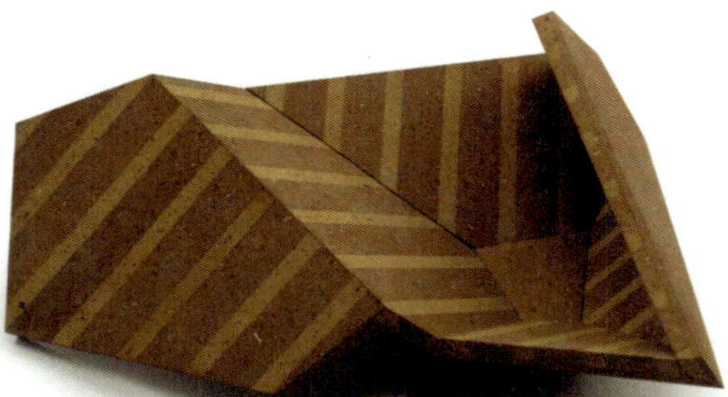

Richard Slee, *Bottle*, 1983, photo: David Cripps
Martin Smith, *Dish*, 1984, photo: Martin Smith

Keeler's pots are very restrained and subtly deviant, with taut leather or metallic qualities, where Betty Woodman's are exuberant and almost reckless, with their great stretched forms and splashed and strapped decoration. The tendency to trust spontaneous improvisation, by which I don't mean accepting what chance brings, but rather 'shaping at the point of utterance,' is clearly shown in such pots.

It is evident then that some different kinds of object have appeared in the last ten years, and they have made a certain kind of impact. Some people have been made very angry by the slippery slope into uselessness, and into expensive one-off artiness. Others have been excited by what seems to be pioneering work, and the levelling of some absurdities in the conventions of evaluating different kinds of art. The debate is not new. Last century saw disputes in the decorative arts, caused largely by the effects of mass-production. Some of the issues are still with us. Ruskin denounced machine-made decoration for displaying 'all the short, and cheap, and easy ways of doing that whose difficulty is its honour,' which is a sentiment echoed by the crafts today. But whereas we have only trends to argue about, the Victorians were all for laying down laws and values and morals of decoration as distinct from art, which was pictorial. Illusion and imitation in decoration were dangerously seductive and corrupting. (I think that unusable pots for looking at would have been an outrage to one such as Mr Gradgrind in *Hard Times*: '... You must discard the word Fancy altogether. You have nothing to do with it. You are not to have, in any object of use or ornament, what would be a contradiction in fact. You don't walk upon flowers in fact; you cannot be allowed to walk upon flowers in carpets.' And the architect Adolf Loos, in an essay written in 1908 called *Ornament and Crime*, went so far as to say that all art was erotic and that decoration must be eliminated from all useful objects if culture was to evolve at all.)

Will the decorative products of this decadent decade go on developing, or are the formal definitions of vesselness losing their appeal? Some edges of all this will continue, I expect, to be pushed about, but the results will soon need to look different. I cannot say what lasting difference it may have made. The boundaries between art and decoration, and art and craft, are perhaps vaguer than they were. Pots can be many things, and can contain multiple intentions as well as any poem. Liz Fritsch makes pots to deflect the tide of over-washable and over-disposable products of our society with these more hard-wearing values: 'It is this that drives me to turn each pot into something improvised and different and to squander days, even weeks, on the making and painting of one vessel. I suspect that the making of art at all in this society has to be in defiance of economic pressures and psychic repressions; a kind of insistence on some measure of freedom and of magic.'

We can be going on with that.

Stephenie Bergman
Work On Canvas: Dyed and Painted

Gallery leaflet, solo exhibition, Crafts Council Gallery, London, 6 June–15 July 1984. Bergman's work had moved from painting to constructing with sheets of dyed and painted canvas sewn together, and she later worked with clay. We had a joint exhibition, *Jugs and Aprons*, at Aberdeen Art Gallery, in 1979.

Stephenie Bergman makes ambiguous things and it is their 'between-two-stools' quality that is attractive. She is a painter with a sewing machine. These are not paintings in the conventional sense, though paint is applied with a brush to canvas in considerable acreage. But the sheets of canvas are subsequently washed (by hand or by machine for varying effects), cut up and sewn together, and finally stretched on the wall with staples. The deliberately chosen colour (of which she has an exquisite sense) plus the scale, and the form that the cloth dividing takes, ensure that this is not patchwork either. The colour sings, louder than any wrangling between art and craft.

The work has recently got much bigger and braver, and where in previous smaller pieces she relied on holding in the loosely floating coloured shapes with a sewn surround, like framing strip, these new large paintings are unrestrained, and divisions of colour run right through and off the edge. Expanses of one colour are enlivened by the seams that carve through them, and disrupt their edges. The uneven edge is very important. It suggests stress and excitement, where coloured pieces are combined in complicated ways with perfect passive co-operation within the painting, but seem to erupt in ragged rebellion on reaching the outer extremity. The coloured 'motifs', often long and oblong, float calmly in their field, but the evidence of their insertion, physically as well as visually, is revealed at the edge. Really they are not floating at all, their inclusion has cut the ground apart, and the reconnection is tracked by long seam lines. These lines, almost always straight, are the 'drawing' equivalent.

Besides being a painter Bergman clearly has urges towards utility – the first work of hers I saw was a series of aprons, some pastiches of her own paintings, equally at home on the wall or on the body. The formal requirements of waistband, bib front, and straps, were played with most inventively without loss of function. They were beautifully made, and similarly when she turns to armchairs, the upholstery is thorough and beautiful. There is a quest here I think for a massive three-dimensional gesture as well as the application of art – and if the craft element of so much tugging and tacking has conquered the uneven edges, there is both wit and luxury still in sitting on a painting.

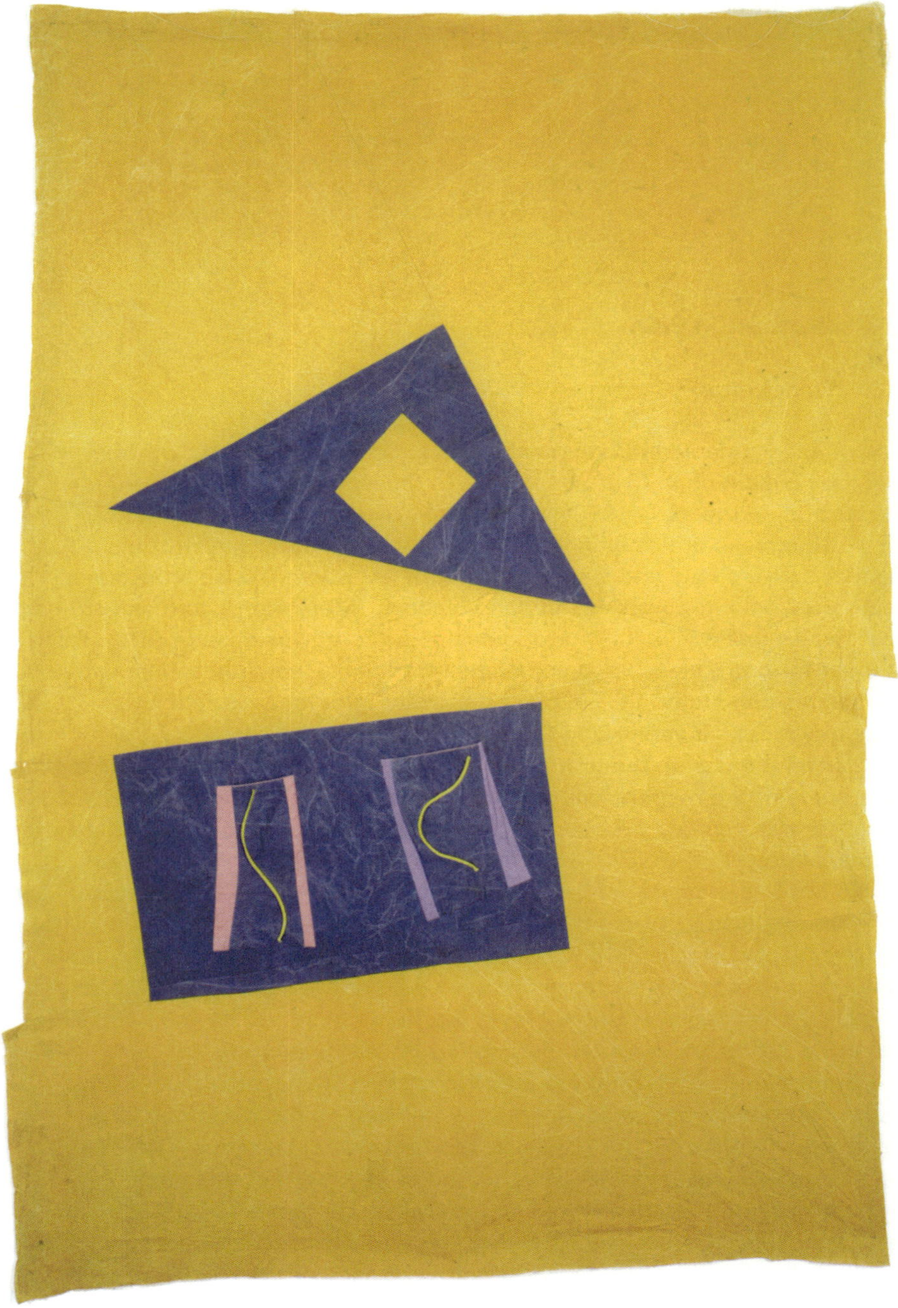

Stephenie Bergman, *Untitled*, 1983, photo: David Cripps

Correspondence

Crafts magazine letters page, John Fletcher's letter in issue 69, June/July 1984, p.59; my response in issue 70, August/September 1984, p.59. Letters were given headings by the magazine. Fletcher, the playwright, wrote to *Crafts* magazine to express his fears that the craft world would be overtaken and spoiled by theory and critical analysis. As he used me as an example of the new constraint, I replied.

Serpent in Eden

Dear Editor,

Could I please comment on recent developments in the crafts world, and their reflection in *Crafts* magazine? I think most people involved in the 'Crafts' in the early 1970s would admit that they were great 'fun'. (A word to make critics blanch!) The work of such as Alison Britton, Candace Broadhead and Caroline Bahouth (all women) unselfconsciously celebrated colour, power, beauty and humour. (More words to make critics blanch!) An instinctive flair for originality and form was mixed with a strong respect for craftsmanship in sometimes traditional, sometimes innovative techniques and materials. No one asked why, everyone just did it. Bright-eyed imagination ruled OK in Albion.

And then came the first fatal mistake, for which *Crafts* magazine must bear some of the responsibility. The term 'Artist Craftsman', in all its awful ugliness, was coined.* The serpent had entered this particular Eden. Various critics, alerted to the word 'Artist', raised their heads from the loveless, sterile deserts of modern fine art – which they had grazed to extinction – and beheld fresh lush pastures they might enter and lay waste, stocked only by strange, exotic, inarticulate creatures known as Artist Craftsmen (a cross between a giraffe and a hedgehog), who did not have one critical 'theory' to rub together between them. Poor, deprived creatures! By the late 1970s and early 1980s critics were pouring into the field; theories and punch-ups proliferated. This is not the place to go into the appalling sterilising affect that critical and academic theory has had on the traditional arts – whole areas of fine art, architecture, modern music, literature and theatre have been laid waste, flattened beneath the dead weight and pomposity and power of non-practising, university-trained theorists. Critics made a comfortable living from theory, artists died from it. But suffice it to say that by the early 1980s, with a glut of university-honed critical faculties on the loose and a downturn in the fine art market, the critics were pouring into the crafts world – and *Crafts* magazine – bristling with self-important dvice, instant analysis, and absolute, unremitting imperatives.

To begin with this was quite good 'fun', watching two critics drawing attention to themselves (and away from the craftsmen) and establishing their territories by knocking the stuffing out of each other. I mean, it appealed to that secret love of good old-fashioned blood sports in all of us! But gradually it became appalling. *Crafts* magazine started to silt up with long, cross, and incomprehensible articles filled with jargon, its arteries hardened with rigid poses and inflexible dogma and definitions. One had to peer through the persiflage to still discern the odd craftsman or two, quaintly pottering about in their obscure and reactionary old trades.

The disease is spreading. One notices the younger generation of craftsmen, brought up under the harsh regime of führeristic theorising teachers at their art schools, are much more hesitant and apologetic in discussing and practising their work. It's almost as though the production of objects ceased to be an end in itself and has become a rather nervous appendage to and illustration of some all-powerful, all-inclusive theory.

I mean, just take a look at Britton these days. All right, so we're all older and wiser than we were ten years ago, and the world we live in is a much more sombre place, but in the greyer, more hesitant tone of her work, isn't there just a hint of self-doubt, of apology even for the fact that she is still actually producing the odd pot as opposed to coining a theory and writing a book about it. I ask myself, 'Is there still a meaningful place for mere craftsmen in the crafts world?'

Sorry for all the wild exaggerations in my letter, but, then, exaggeration is so much more 'fun'!

Yours sincerely,
John Fletcher

Pilton, Somerset

* The phrase 'artist craftsman' is nothing new – see Bernard Leach's *A Potter's Book*, Faber, 1940.

Fair Criticism

Dear Editor,

In response to John Fletcher's letter in the last issue, which immediately drew him into the sort of controversy that he so objects to for weighing down the pages of *Crafts* magazine, I would like to raise the following points.

It cannot be denied that there is all manner of quality in criticism as in everything else, but to say that criticism in itself is sterilising in effect is naïve and romantic. Good criticism is stimulating to the maker and the viewer alike, and can facilitate rather than suppress creativity. Debate and controversy expose very varied opinions, and such variety cannot be said to be rigid or dogmatic; alternatives are being put forward to provoke individual reaction and thought. I find it surprising that a writer should so underestimate the value of language in articulating and elaborating our visual perceptions.

Furthermore, I fail to recognise his picture of the current situation in art schools. You can't teach without language, but in the range of colleges that I visit there is no 'führeristic theorising' going on and students are still wending their own self-absorbed ways as ever.

And as for Fletcher's nostalgia for the 'fun!' of the 1970s – time passes; and craftsmen, artists, and other hybrids can only reflect what they are immersed in. The 1970s were expansive and optimistic, the 1980s are recessive and pessimistic. It does not follow that better work was produced then or now, the best was appropriate to its own time. Perpetual enthusiasm went out with flowerpower before the 1970s began, and Eden was not built to last – a few serpents can be a fruitful challenge.

The work that I made in the 1970s looks mainly soppy and formless to me now and I would be glad to have it forgotten. There is neither doubt nor apology in my decision to make abstract rather than figurative pots, and my working processes are as intuitive and untheoretical as always. My purpose in writing as well as potting is to sharpen my own, and hopefully others, views of what I and my contemporaries are up to. Writing can reflect and enhance as well as impose restrictive judgements. Also I think that Fletcher and I would agree that there is a need for some of the words to come from the practitioners. In my opinion, as a non-university-honed critical faculty, *Crafts* magazine is vastly more enjoyable for having got off the coffee-table and become something to read as well as look at. When he asks 'Is there still a meaningful place for mere craftsmen in the Crafts world?', is Fletcher suggesting that mere craftsmen are all supposed to be illiterate?

Yours,
Alison Britton

Philip Sayer
The Face of Craft

Gallery leaflet, solo exhibition of portrait photographs by Philip Sayer, British Crafts Centre, 5–27 October 1984. Philip Sayer and David Cripps are photographers who consistently conveyed the new ideas, objects, and world of modern craft practice although both have done many other things as well. They initially did this through working for the magazine and catalogues of the young Crafts Council, though in this instance a group of Sayer's portraits were shown in the British Crafts Centre.

It may well be asked: what is to be gained by those interested in the hardware of crafts – in the objects themselves, and in the ideology of craftsmanship – from the sight of a selection of the practitioners portrayed by a well-known photographer? Is it just a display of narcissism and public relations by the British Crafts Centre? The proposed exhibition could bring to mind an array of bright young things posing artfully, like the 'professional-woman-of-the-month' featured in some glossy magazines, whom we know was chosen more for her good teeth than her professionalism. But Philip Sayer's portraits are not at all like these. They are strong images, subtle and sensitive, intriguing, revealing sometimes, and with a wry edge, such that they are objects in their own right and not merely descriptive shots that enhance object makers and glamorise work.

Sayer is not an art school trained photographer, and his background in the trade has given him a very acute sense of the importance of printing one's own pictures, and of the specific nature of real print quality, as well as a sound knowledge of how prints will appear in reproduction, and a journalistic sureness of appropriate images. He is happiest working in black and white because of the fine control of printing as well as I suppose the satisfaction of an aesthetic restraint. He is autocratic with clients – they are never allowed to see contact sheets and are shown at the most two prints to choose from. Pictures are printed as taken, and not cropped in the darkroom; the compositions stand as they were perceived in the second they were taken.

Being photographed by him is, I find, memorable; and I am normally a very uncomfortable sitter. The process of being photographed, by amateurs or professionals, is not unlike being netted as a butterfly. It is awful mainly because it seems so important to present on the outside how you think you are on the inside, and the anxiety and the effort freeze-dries the expression and tenses every muscle. In childhood one was so often forcefully arranged by a dominating adult as if each shot was too precious to leave anything to chance. Sayer manages to make an event of a situation but it is not a daunting event, even for the self-conscious. This I think is his great skill. He has written: 'I find that much of the time available to photograph is taken

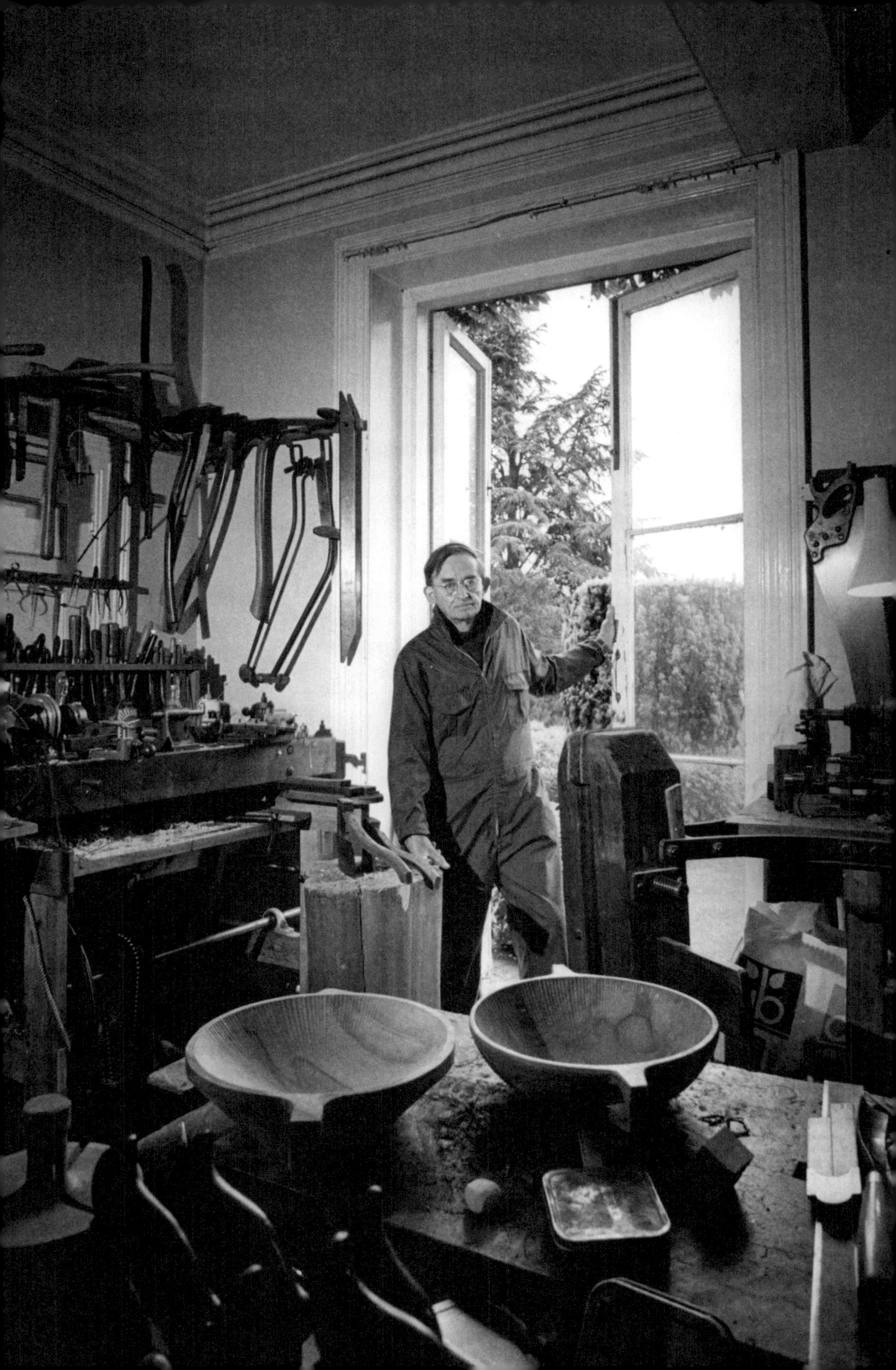

up with giving the subject a sense of occasion that is appropriate to the difference between a formal portrait and a snapshot.' And this distinction is very delicately maintained – he is neither sneaking, catching you off guard; nor predatory, like photographers who shoot without communication; but draws you gently into collusion with the camera and him. Drinking tea and chatting empathetically, one is half-conscious of an initiatory procedure, but it is startling to discover suddenly that he has decided, in detail, where you should stand, how to rearrange the furniture, what you should do, and which lights should be on or off. It is a fait accompli, and you have been given a straightforward part to play. This kind of management is a relief and not an oppression. With quiet businesslike charm he sets about achieving an idea. He shoots a lot of pictures, and says that he usually arrives at what he wants with the last few frames. He has a strong selective eye, that can unexpectedly reveal a 'subject' in its field. It is a curious triangle – the eye, backed by imagination and the power to choose; the sitter, full of self-conceptions and with no control but with an urge to join in; and the camera, a precious machine, between them. Sayer orchestrates this trio with perfect timing because he is both decisive and expressive, communicative and directive. These are photographs that will keep.

Philip Sayer, *Portrait of David Pye*, 1981

Taking up the Chair

Crafts magazine 76, August/September 1985, pp.32–37. This article was commissioned as Floris van den Broecke became Professor of Furniture at the Royal College of Art. His collaborative instincts, Dutch modernist background, and his fascination with words and materials, brought new insights to his colleagues and to those he taught.

Quite soon Floris van den Broecke will have lived in England for as long as he lived in Holland. Whether or not this turns an outsider into an insider is uncertain; he seems rather to have reached a state of 'foreignness' in both countries. The switch of countries was also the switch of disciplines: he came in 1966 from the Department of Painting in the Akademie voor Beeldende Kunst, Arnhem, to the School of Furniture, Royal College of Art, London. He finds it still a pleasure to have feet in two camps or more aptly to be still sitting on the fence, between art and design, England and Holland.

His first notable exhibitions in England were under the art umbrella. In 1974 he was one of *Five Dutch Artists* at the Serpentine Gallery, London, where he showed a series of drawings; and had in the same year an exhibition called *Fantastic Furniture* at the Whitechapel Gallery, also in London. The subsequent establishment of the Crafts Council, which began to pick up some of the loose ends and hybrids between art and design, made a great difference to him, and others like him, and his next solo show was in 1980 at the Crafts Council. Ann Hartree of the Prescote Gallery, Banbury, which ran from 1979 to 1983, also contributed to the shaping of a feasible career in the production of furniture.

Art, design, and craft require three feet, and van den Broecke is evidently well equipped. In his working process there is always a search for the underlying concept and other intuitive gropings that are artistic more than designer-ish, and precede the systematic work on the drawing board. He says that the conceptual stage of a design must be stretched out as long as possible; consequently his furniture is invariably made on adrenalin, at the last moment, and in a state of panic. An attempt to define some of the 'underlying' aspects, concepts of seating and sitting, for instance, in gallery notes for the Whitechapel exhibition landed him in 'Pseuds' Corner' in *Private Eye*. In a leaflet for his *Aspects* exhibition in 1983 he described the triple complexities of his attitude. 'As an artist one is free to comment upon the human condition. As a designer one should be involved with experiment without direct pressure from practical or economic motivation, at least some of the time. As a craftsman one could observe and develop those conventions that define a well-made object fit for a purpose.'

But how much of a craftsperson is he? He claims not to be especially skilful – except perhaps in upholstering which is tackled quite rarely by independent makers – so it is hard to make comparisons, yet there is a

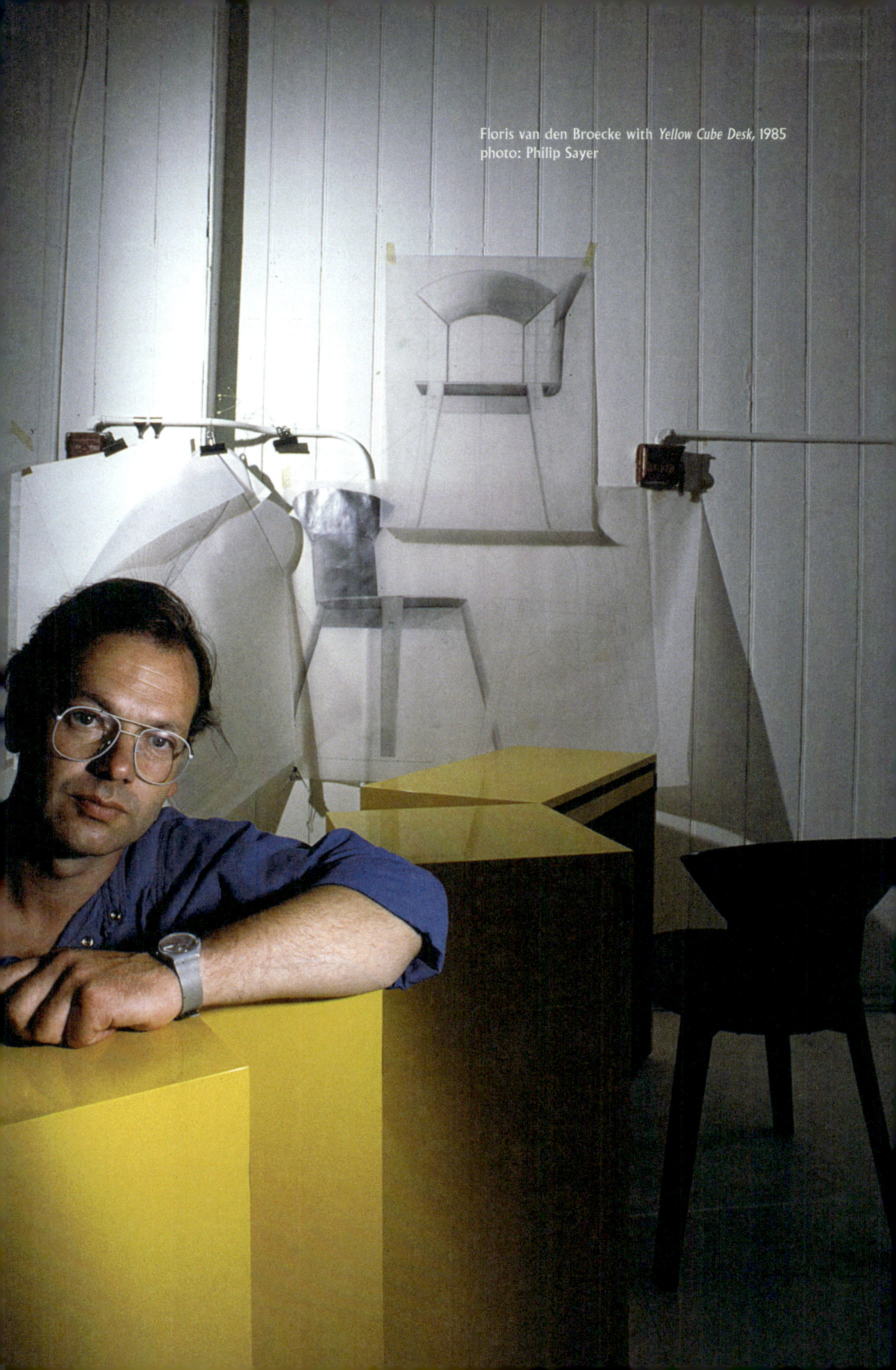

Floris van den Broecke with *Yellow Cube Desk*, 1985
photo: Philip Sayer

need to make every piece himself whether they are one-offs or ultimately for production. An idea is only brought to fruition in the final construction; there is always many a potential slip between project and actuality. The increasingly plastic, modelled three-dimensional forms that interest him now need much more than drawing to be properly conceived – though he has the advantage of both objective (arty) and technical drawing up his sleeve. Now he makes full-size models or maquettes quite early on in the designing process. There is more emphasis on material; he used to think that colour and shape would carry him through, now material details and textures are mattering more. But his work is not tied to particular materials; he likes to range widely amongst the natural, the traditional, the synthetic and exploratory. The series of tables that he made for the *Aspects* exhibition, which I shared with him in 1983, were made of a variety of substances – three different ones in every table – running from mahogany through oxidised iron and glass to a recycled industrial plastic like multi-coloured Spam.

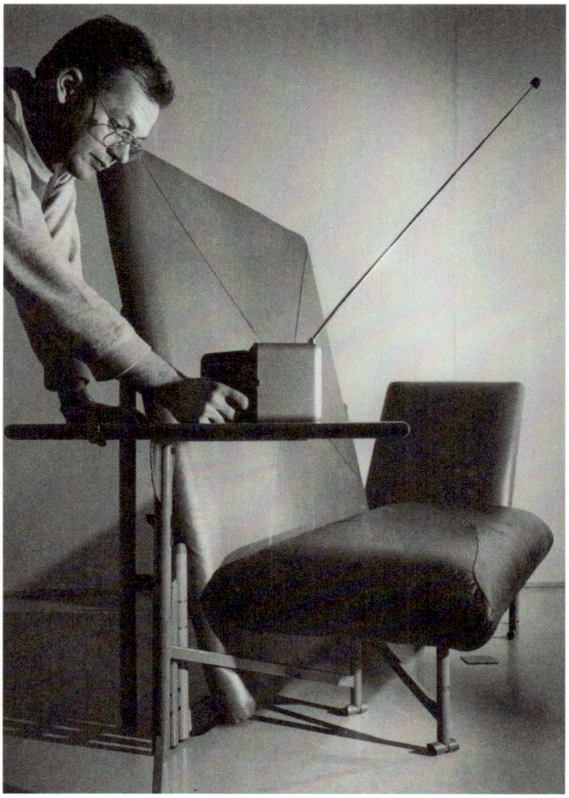

Floris van den Broecke with *S.E.T.T.L.E,* 1985, photo: Philip Sayer

Some of his work is soft and some is hard. He seems at ease with both and can work in both veins at once. His upholstered work, in particular, stands out: it is fluid and sculptural, with poised irregularity. I remember most a blue sofa, now in the Birmingham Museum, that is like a suspended skate (fish), having the profile of an upright chair at one end, flowing through to a reclining dental (or something more sensual) position at the other. Another sofa strews itself on the floor like a dropped hanky, rippled into a bit of back support at one corner. Memorable 'hard' pieces have been the severe and perfectly proportioned black stools that were seen in the *Maker's Eye* exhibition at the Crafts Council in 1982, and the yellow cube desk that unfolds. The 'hard' work, he says, has more to do with materials and technique, and the 'soft' is anthropomorphic, more to do with the human body and its relation to surface and surroundings.

For Le Corbusier in the 1930s the house was a machine for living in and the chair was a tool. These definitions still hold interest; van den Broecke is more absorbed by the chair than anything else. (I see an echo of my own preoccupation with the jug in this; there is a mixture of formal, practical and symbolic concerns that is exciting.) First of all the chair is a form; vertical and horizontal must be brought into conjunction in some appealing way. Then it could have the image of a body, an absent sitter. A chair makes contact with all of a person, it involves the whole of a user, takes their weight. It is a prop for a variety of human activities, and it is the smallest piece or unit of tectonic form in the living space, the smallest containing, protecting, supporting territory.

Language is important for van den Broecke. Having spent the last 19 years using a foreign language, perhaps he is able to see words as objects, tools, playthings, in a way that also stimulates the visual in him and promotes ideas for work. The gap between a thing and the name we give it is alterable – it can be extended or tightened, tugged in, and the fluidity of this is inspirational. Batting words around can be a trigger to the visualisation of an idea.

The 'Settle' he made in 1985 to show at the British Crafts Centre, London, his most ambitious piece of furniture so far, was jolted thus into existence partly out of verbal intrigue, with a foreigner's pleasure in the corners of the English language. ('Truckle' chairs came first in 1980; both words seem lodged in the heavy oak and roaring fires of medieval England.) It arrived with a paragraph of wordplay, evolved during and after its construction, but definitely *part* of the process and the motivation.

> *S:E:T:T:L:E: (British Crafts Centre 85)* The title of this piece refers to its type, which is an acronym of the functions, namely: Sleeping, Eating, Telewatching, Teadrinking, Lovemaking – *id est* EXIST.

The subtitle is a description, also of its place and time, and stands for Big, Comfor(table) and Completed in nineteen hundred and eighty five.

I described it at the time as a complicated substructure of coloured metal pipes, which can be shunted into different positions that will support the upholstered slabs in different relationships. 'He is not just redefining the sofa, he is incorporating a bed, a table, a chaise longue, and an upright seat. A rich and varied life could be sustained on a sole piece of furniture.' (British Crafts Centre Leaflet, January/February 1985). It is the first mechanical piece he has made, things move, slot and relocate. The proportions are necessarily very subtle.

This and other pieces seem to convey thoughtfulness and understanding about changing lifestyles, about fragmented families, living alone, small rooms, working lives. Perhaps the chair is a particularly potent vehicle for expressing new uses and contexts, new needs for versatility.

Design in England, or at any rate in London, is on the up, van den Broecke feels, and the existence of the Crafts Council, paradoxically, has helped to bring about this feeling of 'something in the air'.

Paradox is one of the things he enjoys about England, and quirkiness, and some specifically anti-modernist things. He has assimilated modernism from his Dutch background, and feels a great debt to Piet Mondrian and Gerrit Rietveld. The Dutch, he says, make a principle out of design, and consistency is the ultimate virtue. There is still for him 'a lot of inspirational stuff going on' when he is in Holland. Like other Dutch people he finds flatness incomprehensibly (to me) beautiful, and cherishes the light and the sky, the only natural thing in Holland.

Modernism sums up the differing aesthetic legacies of Holland and England: we never really took to it. This difference is of crucial interest to one in van den Broecke's position, straddling the divide, and he has much to say on the subject. William Morris and the Arts and Crafts movement, and John Ruskin (soon translated into German) were the seeds of modernism; they were the beginnings of Design History, and the first to comment on the Industrial Product. It is significant, he thinks, that Morris was a two-dimensional designer, typically English, the English being better at surface than form. (Which is why we have so much enthusiasm for postmodernism). Consistently the best art and design criticism has come from England, he says, which is an anomaly. Perhaps it is the spectator role we have as an island overlooking the continent. Modernism is art/design made in the light of the bald facts of industrialisation. It is about stripping away narrative, which the English are very reluctant to do, he suggests, because the language is so richly developed.

Finally, he is an excellent teacher. His presence here is making a considerable difference. His next major show of furniture will be at the British Crafts Centre in the spring of 1987, and should not be missed.

Studio Glass

Gallery leaflet, group exhibition, British Crafts Centre, 12 July–10 August 1985. *Studio Glass* could include glassblowing in craft practice after Harvey Littleton and Dominick Labino in America developed a small glass furnace in the early 1960s. In studio glass in the 1980s in Britain it was normal to use blowing for 'functional' vessels, and casting for sculpture. It did not remain so clear-cut.

In a potter's view there is both envy and relief in looking at glass. Transparency is an extraordinary characteristic for a solid material to have, and in allowing light to pass through it, it exchanges one kind of mystery, that of hidden depths, for another, which is the ambiguity of near and far, and outside and inside surfaces, added to the uncertainty of whether one is confronting coloured light or a coloured substance. Such subtleties are enviable. The relief the potter feels is this – clay has its problems but at least you can touch it with your bare hands, it is malleable and versatile and prods into shape responsively. Not like molten glass, which must be remotely manipulated at the end of a metre of iron with a crucial sense of timing and choreography, or cast in premeditated moulds.

The studio glass world is of much more recent origin than studio pottery. Its development has been very rapid in the last decade, from modest beginnings in the 1960s when Sam Herman came from America and taught at the Royal College of Art and set up the original Glasshouse in Neal Street. The costs of producing glass are inhibitive, but gradually more courses have started and more studios have opened, and British glass is now having an impact in Europe, Japan and America. This exhibition contains the work of over 30 practitioners and spans a range of techniques and styles that is impressive after such a relatively short history.

There are two kinds of work in glass, useful and useless, or sculptural, just as there are in pottery, and it seems as though the sudden expansion of the field has been too fast for gulfs and hostilities: there is no longstanding establishment trying to keep out the tide of innovation. Currently it can be said that the Glasshouse is the centre of blowing, and Keith Cummings at Stourbridge College is the nucleus of kiln-formed sculptural work (interestingly in the midst of traditional utilitarian factory glass production).

There is not the space to go into much detail about the exhibitors but I would like to point to a few remarkable things. Evidence that British studio glass is not developing in self-congratulatory isolation can be found in the fact that both Arlon Bayliss and Charlie Meaker have done design work for Rosenthal in Germany, and Simon Moore for Venini in Italy. Diana Hobson has worked out a method of producing exquisitely thin pâte de verre vessels by herself with very little technical or historical information to draw on (see *Crafts* no 64). Anna Dickenson has evolved a way of electroplating a layer of patinated metal onto the surface of the glass, while still a student

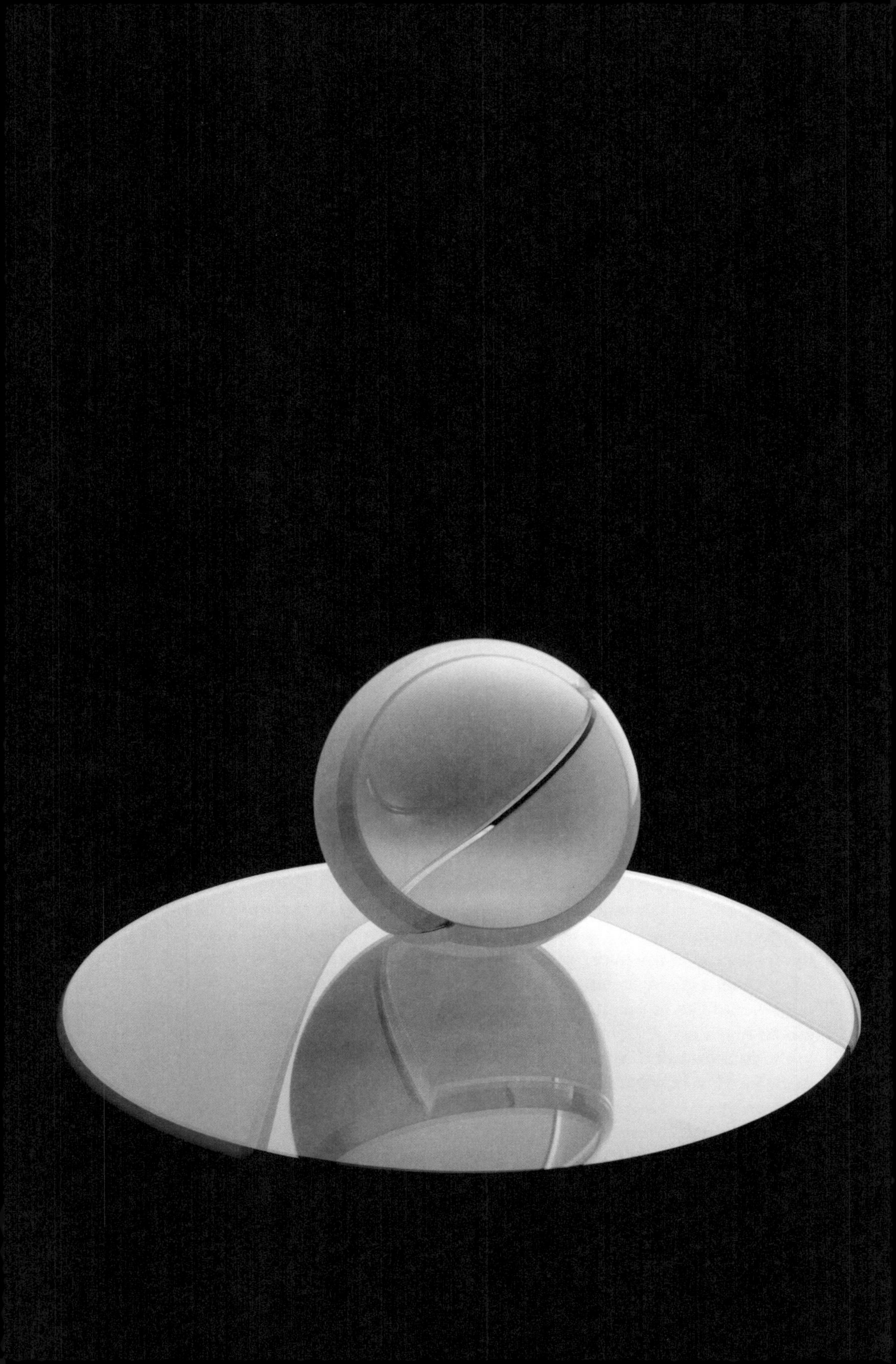

at the Royal College of Art. Ronald Pennell came from a background of gemcutting and his drawings are deeply carved, robust and witty, unlike the expected wispy foliage and ethereal glades of conventional glassengraving. Stephen Procter started as an engraver but found it essential to learn to blow as well. The need to make larger and larger work has led him to Swiss and Austrian factories, where it is easier to produce the big blanks for his pieces of sculpture that are composed from cut and polished sections. Colin Reid makes sculptural work that juxtaposes machine-perfect outer planes with gritty natural textures on inner surfaces. He comments in an American catalogue on the danger of glass's seductive transparency, and explains why he makes plaster models first: 'The piece must work as a form in a bland material like plaster and not rely on the beauty and magic of glass to enhance it and make it work.'

The studio glass world is poised between innocence and expertise: glass is a simply wonderful material, and the temptation was there in the early days to lean heavily on its intrinsic qualities. This exhibition shows how much more complex and diverse and experienced today's practitioners are.

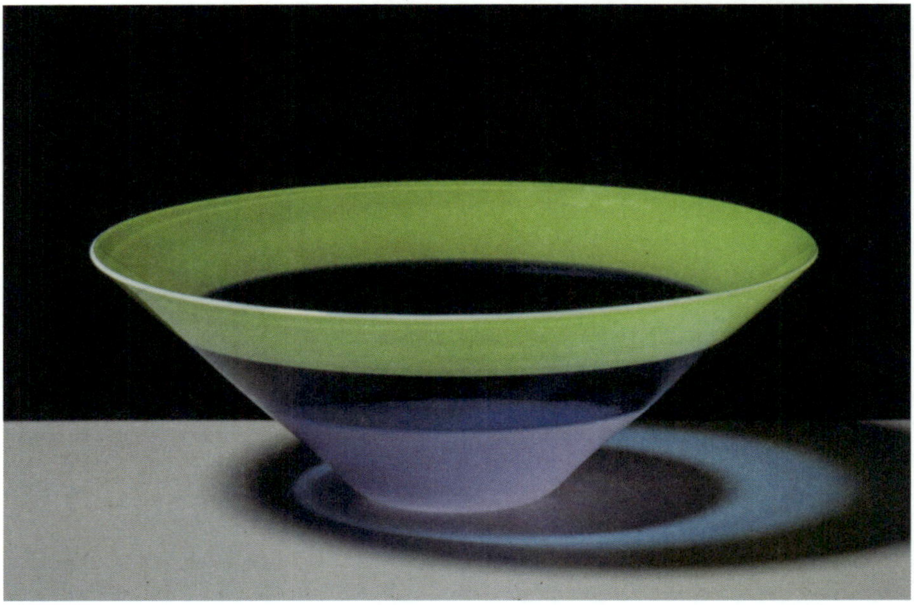

Above: Simon Moore, *Three Striped Bowl*, 1985, photo: Karen Norquay
Opposite: Stephen Procter, *Momentum*, 1985, photo: David Cripps

American Potters Today

Ceramics magazine 3, May/June 1986, pp.36, 37. Preview of the major American donation to the V&A ceramics galleries, shown at the V&A, 14 May–31 August 1986. The differences between Bernard Leach and Peter Voulkos, both so influential in the directions taken in ceramic practice in Britain and the United States, are marked. Voulkos said 'I like to handle materials I can't quite control. When I can control it too much … I start contriving.'

Peter Voulkos is as important a figure for the development of American studio ceramics as Bernard Leach is for Britain. It is hard to imagine two more different ceramic characters; Leach's work being genteel, refined, restrained and understated, backed up by bookfuls of philosophy and advice, where Voulkos's is exuberant, loud, challenging, hyper-masculine, and promoted by a kind of teaching that was more mutually felt than ever articulated – an experimental atmosphere. The times were of course different. Leach's pottery was set up between the Wars, and Voulkos began working in clay in the expansive confident years after World War Two, when American art took the lead with Abstract Expressionism and all the gusto of the winning side, in a country where the War had barely taken place. The new spirit was pervasive; there did not appear to be any trouble with works made in clay being seen in art galleries. Voulkos's work, massive in scale but still largely based on the assemblage of thrown parts, was unproblematically sculpture. In 1959 the critic Jules Langsner said Voulkos 'heads for the front ranks of West Coast abstract artists.' Since these early days of big work and big reputations, Americans have been less hampered than the British by categories and definitions ('Is it art?' etc.). This is not to say that there is no distinction drawn between pots and sculpture, but it does not seem to matter as much; things are more open, more can be risked; pioneering is a national characteristic. Garth Clark runs galleries for ceramics in New York and Los Angeles, writes and lectures extensively across the country, and has set up the 'Institute for Ceramic History' which initiates international conferences. Over the last few years he has drawn together a collection of American work and organised its donation, by a large number of extremely generous people, to the V&A. The collection will be on show for the first time in May, and there will be a two-day symposium with visiting American artists to celebrate. We have a great deal to thank him for.

The collection consists of more than 40 pieces mostly made in the last few years. They are all pots, which reflects Clark's own interests as well as those of the V&A. Many of the pieces could be described as *sculptural*, but none fall entirely over the fence, unlike much of the work seen in the last exhibition of American ceramics in London (the Stedelijk Museum collection from Amsterdam shown at the Crafts Council in 1982), which was largely sculpture. The V&A collection includes a large Voulkos plate with jagged holes in it, and several other massive dishes that aptly straddle the ambiguity between pictorial and purposeful, painting and pot. Viola Frey's, for instance, is cluttered with brilliant and nostalgic hardware fused together with glaze, quite clearly for the wall rather than the table. Another fine large plate is by Ken Ferguson and is salt glazed with a slashed drawing of Adam and Eve and a robust inscription round the rim comparing the evils of drink and women (pioneering masculinity again).

The range of work represented in this group is impressive, though we should expect great diversity from an enormous country. That the studio pottery world in Britain is only a small pond is brought vividly to mind by the statistic from a survey done around 1980, when 100,000 people in the United States claimed to be potters. The figure for those living largely by making rather than teaching would be smaller, and smaller still in 1986 it seems. But if you add to the sheer numbers the hotchpotch of different cultures and traditions, then the potential is vast.

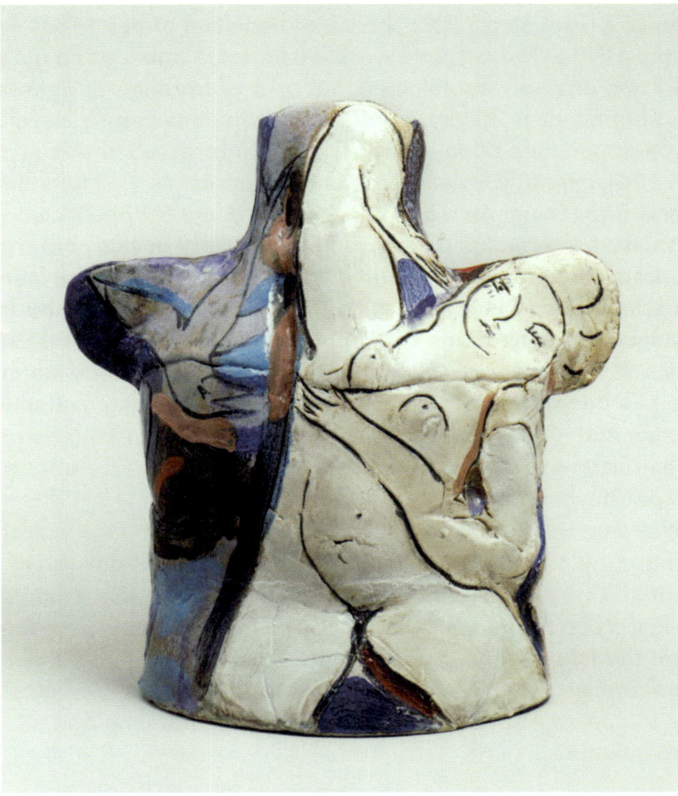

Rudy Autio, *Two Ladies Averting the Angry Swallow*, 1983
photo: Christine Smith, courtesy V&A

The aim for early waves of immigration from different corners of the world was to blend into a 'melting pot' rather than hold onto national differences. This means, in the end, a loss of history and of cultural continuity. Habits that belonged to the old context fade out. There is something lost but freedom is gained – freedom from the constraints of inherited techniques and fixed ways of going about things – and this applies to aesthetics too. Are American artists lucky or unlucky to be allowed a fresh start? Potters can choose their own strands of history, and are not lumbered with orthodoxy. (Though orthodoxy in ceramics in Britain for much of this century meant the acceptance of a graft of Oriental tradition onto our own.) Seeing this breadth of approach across the Atlantic, I think, made a big difference to artists of my generation, trained in the 1960s, and we are beginning now to appraise where it has led. I expect this point – whether independence from tradition is a blessing or a deficiency – to be discussed at the symposium.

Clark in his excellent catalogue introduction describes the 1980s as a period of new maturity for potters, a period of strong growth from a smaller number of ceramicists, after the sensationalism of the 1960s and the illusionism of the 1970s. The ceramic world in America does, to an outsider, look beautifully and enviably established, led by a wide range of figures who have been working for over 20 years and have been consistently developing. Large studios, and bunches of collectors who are interested in things made now and not a 100 years ago, seem to be their support, as well as more plentiful university teaching, on a basis that leaves time for one's own work.

Although studio ceramics is very long established in this country, we do not, or cannot afford to, take risks or take bulls by the horns as much as they do in the US. The results are work that looks often too neat and tidy, and lacks the vigorous poise of many of the splendid pots in the new V&A collection. The pot *Two ladies averting an angry swallow* by Rudy Autio from Montana, who has been at work since the 1950s, is a stunning example. It is both massive and lyrical, quite rough in construction but fluently painted in a way that half refers to the form of the pot, and half departs from it, stretching the pot beyond itself.

Betty Woodman, Art Nelson, Richard Notkin, William Daley, and Akio Takamori are my other preferences and display a great diversity, the 'vast potential' that I have mentioned. In an ideal world there would be a Kenneth Price cup in the collection as well, and if it were up to me, something from the joint Robert Hudson and Richard Shaw exhibition of cups in San Francisco in 1972. But let us hope that the V&A can make such additions in due course to what is already an outstanding and comprehensive selection.

Five Pots on the Horizon

Domestic Landscape, Your Home – Whose Choice?, exhibition catalogue, Cornerhouse Gallery, Manchester, 29 November 1986–18 January 1987, pp.24, 25. Five designers and makers chose five things each in their material: glass, clay, wood, metal and plastic. The exhibition was conceived, and more objects selected, by Peter Dormer, John Houston and Ib Bellew – two critics and a publisher. This was the first craft and design exhibition to be held at Cornerhouse.

If I were thinking only of my own domestic landscape, and making this selection more for myself, I would probably put together a collection of five plain industrially made white cups, because in my life this is one level at which choice seems very important. I like the fact that I don't have whole sets of anything, and that porcelain is produced all over the world (though little in Britain), and you can find cups with different national design characteristics in different countries in a consistently appealing material. Some of the cups hanging currently on the hooks in my home are from Denmark, Germany, Spain, Italy and Japan. Some are anonymous and second-hand. The material is constant but the shapes are very varied, though all are straightforward and clear. This is porcelain used for strength rather than prestige, everyday and durable, not 'best china' with frills and rococco leanings. It is curious to me that my cups are mostly foreign – I haven't wanted them as exotic souvenirs but for their appropriateness to my needs, both functional and aesthetic – and it is still very hard to find plain, white, hard, beautiful cups made in this country. The need for such things seemingly puts one at odds with one's own culture, or at odds with the manufacturers. (Feeling at odds with one's surroundings is often what motivates artists – there is a need to make up for deficiencies, to fill in the gaps, to provide the previously unthought of.)

With my selection of cups I would reveal myself as a consumer, a discriminating recipient. But I am also a producer, an artist and an optimist, a filler of other people's spaces, and I have decided, instead, to put forward something that is both more and less personal. With a broader view, I have chosen five things that I value, though I might not live with them myself, and that I think would be rewarding landmarks in other people's lives. What you can produce and how you live are interestingly separable. That I should care so much about plain white cups, and make things in ceramics that are so far removed from them, is another curiosity.

The landmarks I have chosen are for looking at, primarily, though use is not out of the question with some of them, and they are of an engaging scale that is both domestic and challenging. They are also complex, non-passive, not to be taken in at a glance and grown weary of, and not so calm and retiring, like in the old virtuous days of craftwork, that you hardly notice them. Hopefully there is a prolonged relationship between viewer and object in which views change but do not fade. Loosely speaking, all these objects are pots, or the offspring of pots.

I was drawn to ceramics in the first place by its range of possibilities. Clay is a splendidly versatile material; it makes drainpipes and sinks as well as ornamental clockcases and monumental sculpture. As experience proceeds, both in making and looking, the field of interest narrows and more detailed distinctions become remarkable. This is true of acquiring sophistication in any sphere. It could not be said that the five objects I have chosen say anything about the great array of possibilities in ceramics. They are all the products of a rather small world – the studio pottery world whose ideals have grown from the turn-of-the-century Arts and Crafts movements which were daunted by the great sweep of industrialisation. My five choices, furthermore, belong to an even narrower band within studio pottery, to those that have remained outside the Orientally inspired line of development that has dominated the craft for half a century. A strong sense of history, combined with a contemporary flexibility about function, and some aspect of commentary on pots and their issues, also links my selected pieces. But beyond this, and acknowledging that mine is a specialised, or biased, and close-range vision, I have chosen these pieces for their contrast and individuality.

A lot of pots made in the last 30 years have been 'organic'. Clay is earth, and nature has been their inspiration. On the whole I have found these very boring – for me I think the dramatic metamorphosis of sticky clay into hard pottery needs to find some echo in form, in a duality of theme and substance; a little more resistance and tension. Ewen Henderson is a painter of landscapes and a builder of craggy powerful pots that cut through my doubts. In all good potters I think there is the ability to balance control and

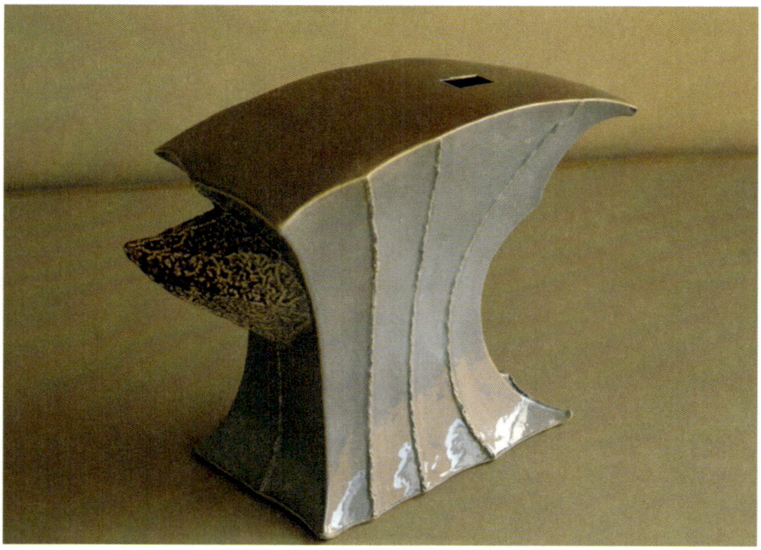

Richard Slee, *Anvil*, 1986, photo: Richard Slee

spontaneity, and this balance is life or death to a pot. Henderson's pots of the last few years seem to have contained more – more volume, more vigour. Very strong forms emerge from these amalgamated surfaces that are like jumbled rock faces.

The greatest contrast in my group is between Henderson and Richard Slee. Slee's pots are slippery and urbane where Henderson's are rugged. They are full of commentary about pots and art and other objects. They have a very English humour to them that is affectionate and based on the juxtaposition of incongruities. His work has been often misunderstood, and seen at a distance as slick and fashionable. The reality is a pondering English wit and great subtlety of colour and glaze surface.

Betty Woodman is one potter who really makes me wish I could throw. The ease with which she dismembers thrown forms and reassembles them, building composite pots that take on so much more than verticality and symmetry (which is what thrown pots generally consist of), is something I greatly admire. The sense of speed, fluidity, and softness, is enviable. Her pots are welcoming and exuberant – there is a lot about The Good Life in them, not in an ostentatious way, but she seems able to incorporate a thorough sensual enjoyment of sights and tastes and experiences, and a need to celebrate them. She did a collaboration recently with a chef in New York, and one glorious meal was the outcome rather than an exhibition.

Jacqui Poncelet's work has changed more than anyone else's I can think of in the relatively short span of her career; she is always questioning and stretching definitions and moving on. She has done more than anyone

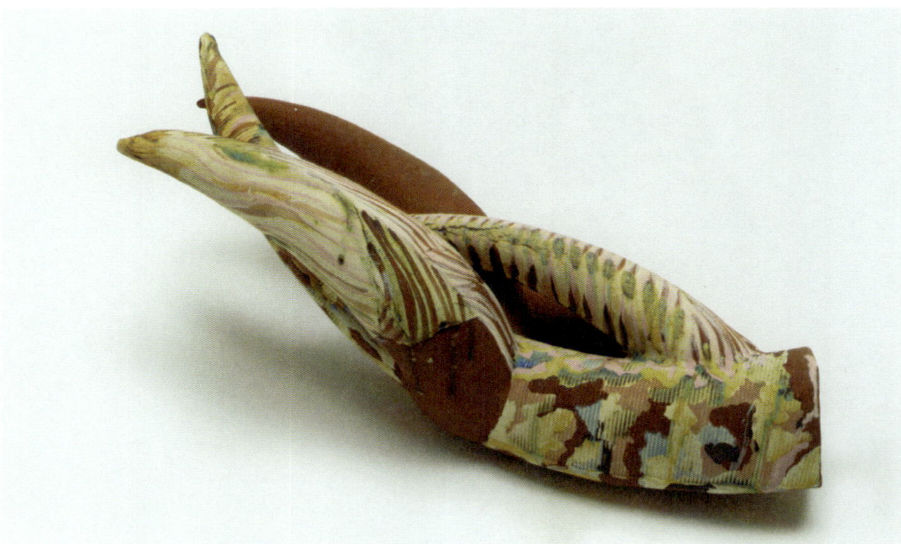

Jacqui Poncelet, *Bunch*, 1985, photo: David Ward

in studio pottery to disgruntle and confront our assumptions about the nature of pots. But meteors pass through the atmosphere; the work she is making now is to be seen in the much broader context of sculpture that is not tied to a particular material. The piece I have chosen to show belongs to me, is part of my surroundings, and is very important to me.

The blue pot that I made is one that I would like to have kept. I think it is down to earth, conventional and yet unconventional, it is *about* jugs without actually being one. References and allusions are to me more pleasurable than bald statements. The pot belongs to Floris van den Broecke, who designs furniture, and it went to him in part-exchange for a sofa. I can change my own domestic landscape by bartering.

All these five pieces are quite demanding – which is something else I value about them; they are for sticking out rather than fitting in. I would only want one of them at a time in my own environment. But landmarks are like that: they have to have solitary splendour or they become meaningless.

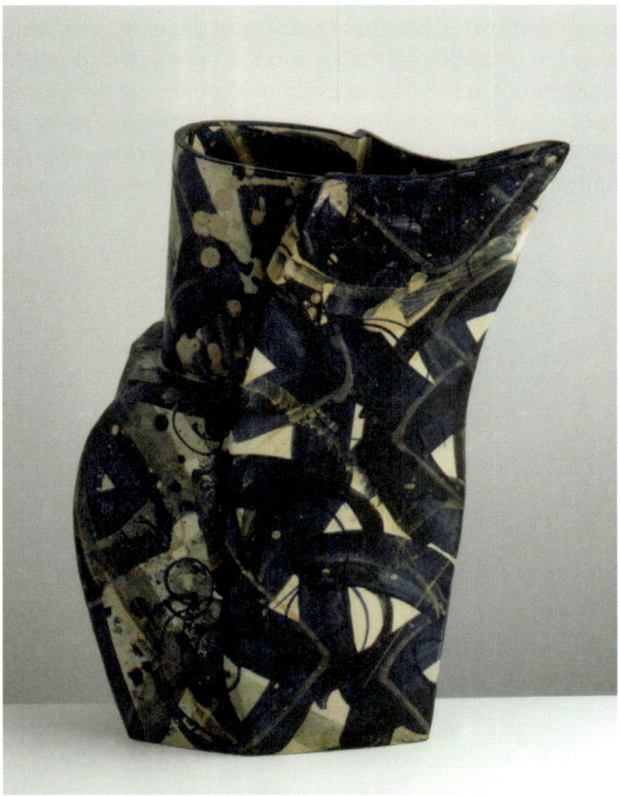

Alison Britton, *Blue and Black Pot*, 1985, photo: David Cripps

Eastern Approaches

Crafts magazine 83, November/December 1986, pp.32, 33. Article previewing the opening of the Toshiba Gallery of Japanese Art, V&A, 18 December 1986. I had been to Japan for the first time the year before to install an exhibition. I was full of images of things I had seen in museums in Tokyo and Kyoto, and so the way museums communicate, and the planning and ideas behind this new display, meant a great deal to me.

The fashion in which we are presented with the past is a progressive thing. The last century's more gluttonous approach, when we were imperial conquerors and know-alls, was still apparent when I was first a student; in the British Museum's Greek Pottery room, for instance, where hordes (or hoards) of pots crammed the cases, showing 'how many' at the expense of 'how beautiful'. This attitude has been erased. What it has taken me longer to become aware of is that a museum cannot always show us a complete picture if how things were – they can show us what they have. Collections are built up over the decades from a sequence of individual perceptions, by successive curators, of what they see as important, as well as what lands on them from bequests and donations. What we experience in a museum is not a simple interaction with the history of our own or foreign lands, but a double-take, particularly with regard to foreign artifacts. We are seeing one culture, whose historical objects remain as facts, through the changing and partial eyes of another culture.

The development of the Japanese collection at the V&A is a good case in point. Buying from Japan began in the very early days of the museum (then the South Kensington Museum) with some contemporary lacquer and porcelain. Then a large consignment of pots that had been selected by the Japanese government, from a variety of periods, was bought in 1877. The early didactic aims of the museum to inspire a richer sense of design during the industrial boom, and to enlighten 'manufacturers, artisans, and the public in general', were born out in the Japanese acquisitions, which were largely of contemporary applied arts, where other factions had quickly turned to a more academic and historicist approach. But there was, as yet, no 'Japanese Department'. The pots would have been categorised with other pots from everywhere else; the textiles (samples mainly rather than complete garments) with other textiles. The Japanese collection expanded greatly around the turn of the century with several large donations from private collectors, which are both an advantage and an anomaly. They now possess thousands of sword fittings, *inro* (little containers that dangled over the belt) and *netsuke*, the little toggles that enabled them to dangle, and other fiddly things that do not feature so largely in the Japanese perception of their own history. They were the passion of English collectors in the 19th century. They *are* exquisite, and revealing of the Japanese aesthetic, and do thoroughly belong in a museum of decorative arts, but one wonders what other kinds of passion we may have missed. I myself would prefer to see a vast array of padded workmen's kimonos, worn by firemen and fishermen.

After the World War Two, the V&A began to reshuffle its possessions and established the 'Primary Galleries', which displayed their finest things defined by date and style rather than medium. Sensitive perhaps to postwar feeling, no Japanese 'Primary' was planned and the Japanese collection hung about on the fringes of Chinese galleries for decades. In 1970, a curatorial Japanese Section was started, and in 1981 a temporary Japanese Gallery was opened in a smallish space next to the restaurant. The V&A is now embarked on another major upheaval, redefining everything in terms of 'Art and Design' or 'Materials and Techniques'. A new Japanese Gallery was a clear priority this time, and with generous support from the Toshiba Corporation it comes into being in December, in a large ground floor gallery that has been beautifully restored to Victorian splendour in the upper regions. Paul Williams has designed the display in the classical Japanese idiom as regards lighting and proportions and colours and surfaces, without any pretence to replicate an authentic interior. The sense of 'museum' is not lost. (If in any doubt, look up at the ceiling.)

Joe Earle and his colleagues in the V&A's Far Eastern Department have published an excellent book to coincide with the Gallery's opening[1]. In his introduction, he describes the different aspirations that have been held for the collection at different periods. In the 1960s, it was hoped that some major medieval and 17th-century masterpieces might be acquired, to establish painting and sculpture in the collection as well as the applied arts (somewhat in envy of the major American museums). But, Earle says, 'limited funds concentrate the mind wonderfully... The prices of such things have soared, purchase grants have been cut... As a result new ways of giving extra significance to the inherited collection have had to be found. The answer has been to buy a small number of high-quality pieces in areas where there is something to build on.'

The collection is presented to us not just chronologically or materially, but in a variety of ways that best reveal its strengths. Ceramics and metalwork are the only two 'early' sections, pre-16th century; at the other end of the spectrum, the Meiji period (one of supposed decline after the splendours of Edo and the fall of the Tokugawa regime in 1868) and the 20th century are both presented chronologically. In between times, we focus mainly on different crafts – lacquer, armour, prints, dress, and so on. There is a special section for tea ceramics, objects associated with the tea ceremony, which was an important middle-class activity from the 16th century; and for folk craft, which was a movement called 'Mingei', similar to our own Arts and Crafts movement, initiated by Yanagi Soetsu in the 1920s (and in which Bernard Leach played a significant role). 'Accessories to Dress' covers the *netsuke* and *inro*, and swords and their affiliated bits, to which several pages

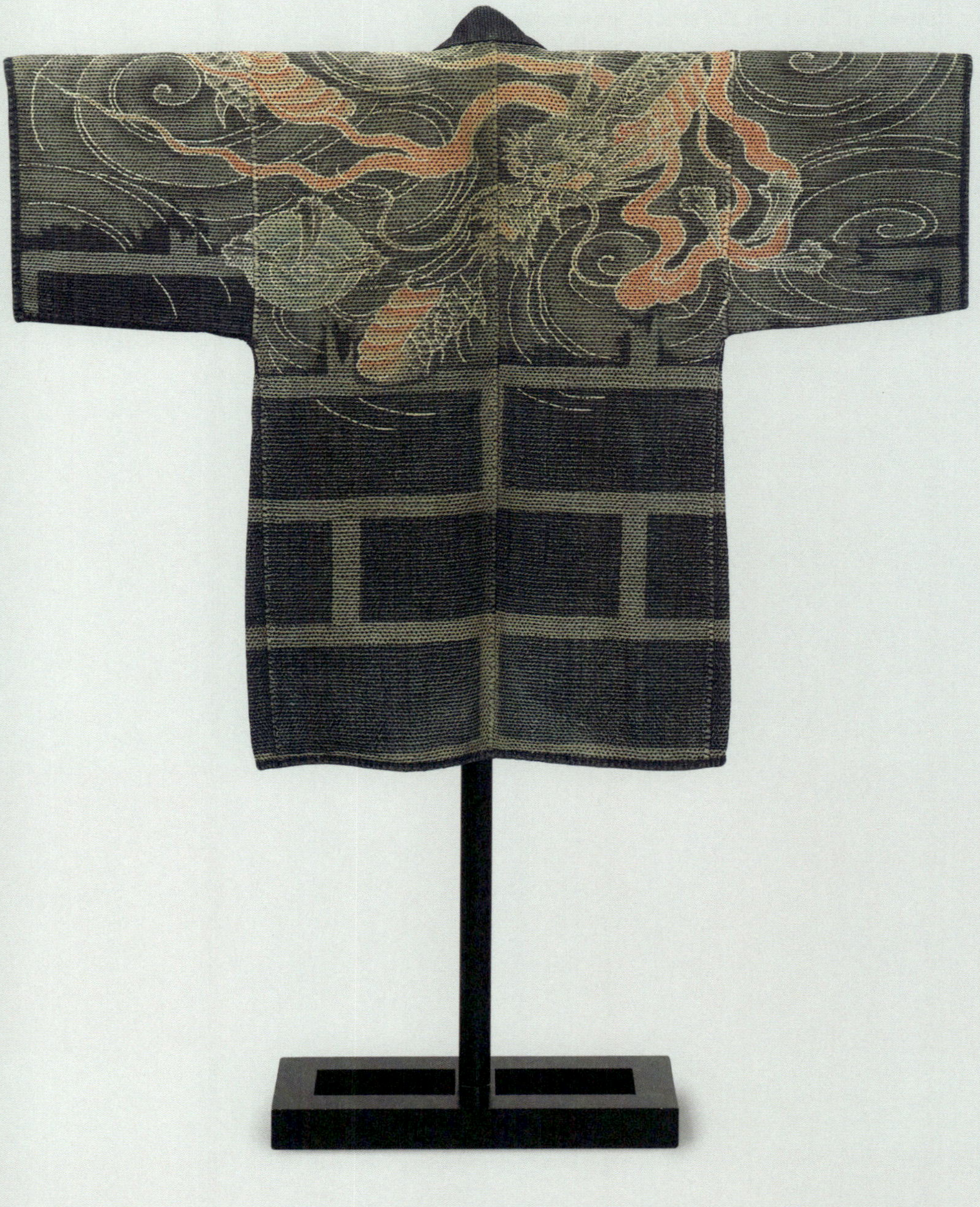

Unknown craftsman, *Fireman's Jacket*, late 19th/early 20th century
courtesy V&A

of the glossary are devoted, have their own section. Both the 'Porcelain' and 'Lacquer for Export' sections raise interesting questions about the impact of East on West and vice versa.

The V&A are showing us the best of what they have; no claims are being made for the presentation of a whole picture. The collections will grow and the displays will change. They own 10,000 woodblock prints, for instance; only the tip of the iceberg can be on view. The 20th-century collection has more pots in it than anything, and I was interested to learn that the current state of the independent studio potter in Japan is not too different from here. My own attachment is to the work of Kamoda Shoji from Kyoto, who died too young in 1983. Seeing his work in the full context afforded by the new Toshiba Gallery will be a great delight, among many delights, and well worth waiting for.

1. *Japanese Art and Design*, ed. Joe Earle, Trefoil/V&A, London, 1986.

Bryan Illsley
Souvenirs of St Ives

Gallery leaflet, solo exhibition of Bryan Illsley's work, Contemporary Applied Arts, London, 15 April–10 May 1988. This exhibition of painting and sculpture was Illsley's first solo show in London since he left St Ives in 1986. He had settled there as a young man and among many jobs, had been a packer for the famous Leach Pottery, and shared a studio with Breon O'Casey, where they also had a forge.

A title such as this conjures up an image of seagulls and sails against the clear blue of sea and sky, perhaps seen through the cultivated frame of Bernard Leach and Barbara Hepworth, Ben Nicholson and Alfred Wallis. The reality of this exhibition is different. It is much more about enduring struggle than holiday spirit. There *is* a cheerful side to Bryan Illsley's work, roughly carved and brightly painted figures, mirror frames and so on, with the primitive vigour of the fairground. But there is a non-festive kind of work too. This show consists of the 'main' work, the basic and essential stuff, all produced between 1978 and 1986, when he left St Ives for London.

The work is not about landscape, it is not rural, particularly, in feeling. He could have made it in other environments. It results from a period of quiet graft and concentration in a location that happened to be a Cornish barn near St Ives. A two-storey barn with a floor for painting and a floor for making, and a forge outside. Wood and iron and painted canvas are the materials of this basic work. The wood is bare and untreated, hewn and pegged. The iron is rusted or painted black. The metal forms are economically assembled, forged, not welded, with the purist's pleasure in working with only heat, and contending with a set of severe restrictions. Techniques are always basic and solitary and largely self-taught. Canvases are sombre in colour, sand and blood and black against black. Brighter colours burst in occasionally. The surface of the paint varies, usually very matt, sometimes gritty or glossy. Most of it is acrylic, with the sudden fattiness of oil paint in a few corners.

In all forms the work is about abstraction. The business of approximating feeling with form; giving an indirect shape, or a visual gesture in the right direction, to complicated notions and experiences of life. There is a lot about gender in this work, sex without misogyny, and procreation as a parallel to art. Intuition, traditionally a feminine aspect, is what drives these paintings and sculptures into being. The harshness of their form is perhaps contradictorily masculine – the ruthless simplicity of shapes, great spikes of wood or metal piercing space and skewering things together, reminiscences of butchers's hooks. Most of the parts are made from scratch, with difficulty, but occasionally an oblong scrap metal or a piece of a builders plank is incorporated just as it came. More often, though, the found object is remade before it can be used – understood and claimed by manufacturing it himself (like the enormous boat-builders's nails, for instance, that inspired the iron spikes in several works).

Many of the sculptures are heads that rest on the floor. Titles are short, descriptive and wry. *Head – Mobile Features* has the iron outlines of a nose and eyes dangling suggestively from hooks inside the empty hoop of the face. *Tree with Hanging Limbs* has in it both upward growth and swinging carcasses, and a reference to crucifixion. Surging up, and hanging dead, and holding in tension; three kinds of movement animate this piece.

Bryan Illsley, *Black, Black and White,* 1979, photo: Tim Hill

The paintings in this exhibition are even more abstract than the sculpture. The habitual centre of the eye's attention in a painting, about where the head would be in a portrait, is generally empty. Nothing much is happening in the usual places. Instead the eye is drawn into the corners, with expectations thwarted, and is rewarded by the more eventful borders of the painting. Scanning the whole surface again reveals other scrawls and marks and messages, a scribbled date, or the letters HV, meaning Higher Vorvas where he lived. The paintings ask for a broad gaze, not a narrow and specific search for recognisable things. They create a context rather than a commodity. Illsley liked making mirrors for this reason – there was definitely nothing, or even less than nothing, in the middle, and the beholder had to provide it. He talks of 'poverty', as a positive quality in describing the paintings, and talks of this necessary wide awareness being more important than a quest for individual detail also in other spheres of life, perhaps in all of them. Like the difference in scope of zoology and ecology; one studies species in depth, separately, whereas the other spans the complicated interrelationships among species and the spaces in between. Illsley is more comfortable with the breadth and complexity of ecology than with the narrow focus of zoology.

A modern view, from a man who rates modernism as the most important phenomenon of this century. His work is rooted in respect for early abstraction, Cubists and Constructivists. Nothing that has happened more recently in art touches him as deeply, and indeed he is dismayed by what he feels is a loss of nerve in moves away from the abstract, back to representation and tighter focus on the individual. It is striking and significant for him that Vladimir Tatlin, in pre-revolutionary Russia, made small abstract reliefs to hang in the home across the corner of the room, in exactly the place that the icon would have hung. Abstract or figurative, the general or the particular, aesthetic or dogmatic, free association or specific content: different kinds of art evoke different kinds of engagement and relationship. The open-ended relationship between the viewer and the abstract is the only one worth pursuing for Illsley.

Bryan Illsley began his working life as an apprentice stone carver and started going to classes at art school as a way of deferring National Service. The idea of being an artist was not one that came to him on a plate. The work is evidence of a long and independent battle, and is powerfully expressive of humour as well as anguish. It is tough but never bleak. William Blake wrote:

> Man was made for joy and woe
> And when this we rightly know
> Thro' the world we safely go.

Which I think Bryan Illsley would appreciate.

Michael Rowe

Gallery leaflet, solo exhibition of Michael Rowe's work, Contemporary Applied Arts, 21 October–19 November 1988. Rowe's research into the surfaces of metal in the early 1980s extended the scope of his work. This exhibition showed the start of Rowe's great series of objects playing with ornamental additions to sheet metal containers, and the relationships between form and decoration that were his focus for some years under the title 'Conditions of Ornament'.

Michael Rowe writes: 'The function of vessels will determine the kind of regard we have for them. For example, a tin bucket will receive a different kind of attention than a reliquary, and this difference will be apparent in the appearance given to them. Vessels are more or less "visible" according to our regard for them.'[1]

His own vessels are very 'visible', and need to be looked at long and hard. Paradoxically enough, they have some of the overall simplicity, at first glance, of the tin bucket, but closer attention reveals subtleties of proportion, ornamental ventures into space, veiled references and layers of meaning, that are much more in line with the reliquary. Both reliquaries and buckets have a specific function, the bucket merely to carry something, probably liquid. The reliquary's job is to impart significance, through ornament, and make certain that the mouldering fragment contained within is not regarded as ordinary. The things Michael Rowe makes have no such specific role, and it is form rather than function that interests him, though formal excellence has its own right to existence, and is necessary enough. He is manipulating simple forms with such aesthetic precision, like poems with every word and simile and metaphor in its place, that what is produced cannot be regarded as ordinary.

I first saw his work soon after he left the Royal College of Art in the early 1970s, when he made things that were witty and elaborate, scaled-down architecture and games with perspective. I remember a piece that was ambiguously like a chest of drawers and a staircase, drawers spilling out in sequence, and meant I think to hold dried rose petals. Then in 1978 he had an exhibition at the Crafts Council of a series of boxes, all based on the cube, that were breathtakingly simple. They were not boxes that opened and shut, though they had lids; the lid and the box had a fixed relationship, and the conventional cube form had been slightly altered so that the piece offered itself with a particular viewpoint. This sudden stillness, the calm of an object frozen, as it were, for an aesthetic pause, a deeper scrutiny, a reappraisal of its objectness, was an important essence of what was in the air at the time, and not just in metalwork. Across the board the makers of objects were reassessing the rules, and the vessel in particular is a nice vague subject that one could rummage about with for a long time. In 1981 I was asked to be one of the selectors for an exhibition called *The Maker's*

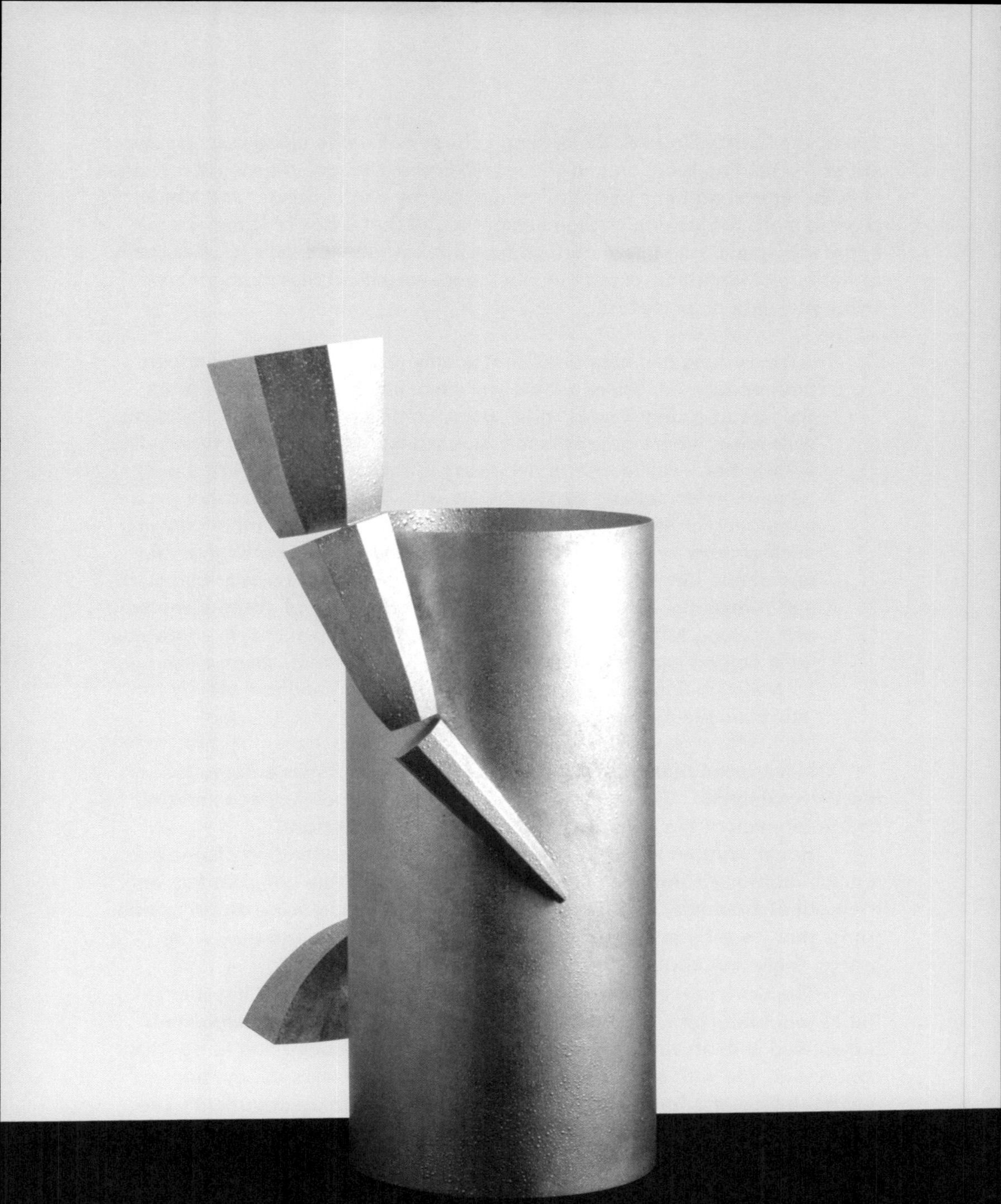

Eye at the Crafts Council. Everything I chose had some place in a discussion about the holding function and the art/life ratio, though some were drawings, still-life representations of pots, some everyday useful things, and some objects more for looking at than using. I found that a box of Rowe's, an apparently plain green patinated copper box with its lid stuck up, was really at the hub of what interested me most, and expressed that moment and these realisations perfectly.

> ... something has happened that is only gradually being described and recognised. Some people will certainly feel that it represents the last decadent throes of an artistic crafts movement of dwindling relevance, where over self-conscious makers turned in on themselves for want of a real sense of necessity. But perhaps to others it will be seen as something closely in line with 'modernism' in other arts, in painting or literature for example. A 'modern' novel (one following such writers as Marcel Proust and James Joyce) is both made of, and about, language. Some of the objects I have chosen are similarly self-referential, that is, they perform a function, and at the same time are drawing attention to what their own rules are about. In some ways such objects stand back and describe, or represent, themselves as well as being. In the analogy with the novel 'function' stands for 'story' as the central content.[2]

I illustrated that analysis with a sentence from Rowe's notes for his 1978 exhibition: 'The boxes are purely about their own space and the characteristics of the sheet metal that they are made from.'

Rowe went on to work on the bowl form, with extending planes and a much more horizontal emphasis. These pieces became complicated, and I felt out of sympathy with them. Then in 1984 he made some larger upright forms that were by and large cylindrical, with additions, and they were staggeringly beautiful.

The work in this exhibition is a further development of that theme: the cylinder interfered with, enhanced, sealed off, resituated, explained, juxtaposed with attendant forms. These things have something to do with containers, and with a discussion of ornament. What links the outside and the inside of a form, and what links an object with its ornament? The recognition of resonance with familiar forms like fruit, spoons, handles, parts of the face, bits of buildings, is part of the pleasure of these things alongside an appreciation of their pure form. Features recur – faceted areas, always the same perfect, even intervals – that can undermine the smooth cylinder wall, or wrap around into a solid form like a geometric lemon, that is perched provocatively somewhere as decoration.

Everything here is made of sheet metal, and it is tempting to compare the sheet form to both folded paper constructions and to slab building in ceramics. What Rowe has to do is a lot more arduous than either of these. Metal is very stiff compared with paper, and a metal wall is springy, tense and thin compared with clay. Particular forms are radiant and strong and surprising when made in metal. Rowe is materially fluent and what he makes is both surprising and straightforward, simple and magical. All pieces here are made of brass with various different final surfaces. Rowe is an expert on the patination of metals and co-wrote a book on the subject that is used by metalsmiths internationally.[3] The purpose of patination, which is a chemical treatment of the surface, is to extend the palette of colours and to alter the surface quality of the metal and make it more interesting. To this end Rowe also uses other finishes such as gold leaf and tinning. With the latter, particles of tin are fused onto the surface of the brass to give it a glistening silvery texture. He uses it as a decorative finish in its own right, extending the traditional purpose of providing a protective coating for cooking pans or indeed buckets.

This exhibition comes a decade after the metal boxes were seen at the Crafts Council. It is a rare thing to see so many of Rowe's pieces together in one room, the nature and time-scale of the work making frequent exhibitions impossible. With such drama in the forms, and such subtleties of colour and surface, and echoes both of architectural grandeur and domestic simplicity, these objects make their own strong context, and should not be missed.

1. Gulbenkian Craft Initiative, Vessel Forum, Birmingham, 1987.
2. *The Maker's Eye*, exhibition catalogue, Crafts Council 1981.
3. Richard Hughes and Michael Rowe, *The Colouring, Bronzing and Patination of Metals*, Crafts Council, 1982.

The Critic's Eye

Crafts magazine 98, May/June 1989. Ken Eastman has worked with the sheet of clay, building with slabs, for most of his working life. Architectural references can readily be seen in clay objects, and are found throughout the history of ceramics around the world – clay is a basic building material, after all.

One of the things that I like about pottery is the fact that a pot consists of the clay that it is made from; plus something else, a surface of slip or glaze, or both. So there are two strands to the work: first, building the pot in three dimensions and then dealing with the surface, which will probably involve painting, and a composition with colours that will change in firing. This treatment aims at a link between two- and three-dimensional ideas; between skin and body. When pots are not wheel-made and are irregular in form, the two- to three-dimensional relationship becomes especially interesting. I have chosen a pot where the painting is very important to its success and its beauty.

The pot is straight-sided and roughly cylindrical; it reads easily as a pot, though not one that makes you think of a use for it. Its pleasures are abstract. It provides a place for the eye to wander in, to compare and contrast different aspects of the form and colour, and to make imaginary connections with other forms. It is a pot with two halves: looking down on it, it consists of a thin and a fat semicircular arc that lap over each other in an unexpected and asymmetrical way where they meet to enclose a wide flat floor. The duality is further emphasised by colour: dark brown on the thin arc against bluish white on the fat one. The outside shape of the pot is very severe and flat – no organic swelling of the form from foot to lip, as straight as a drainpipe.

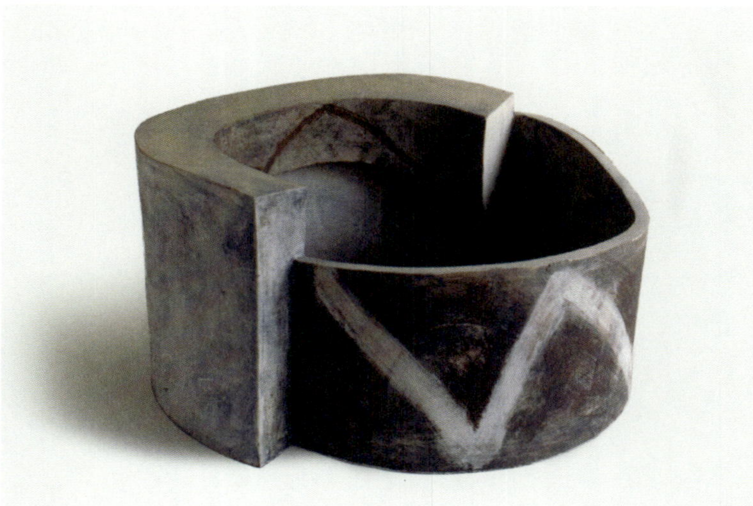

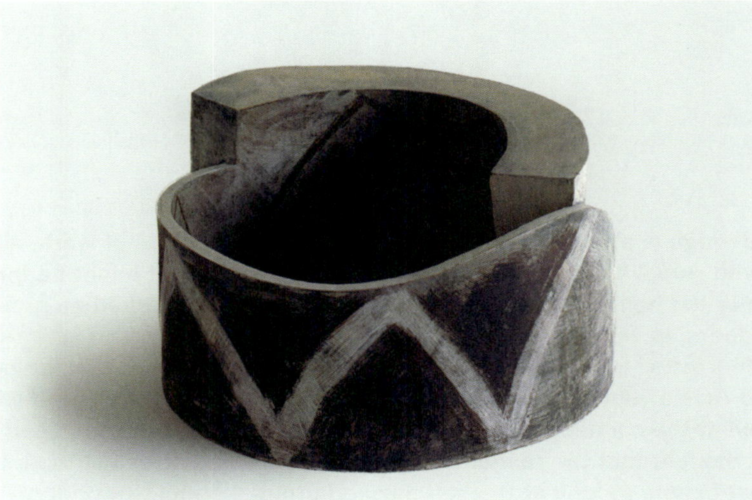

The main focus of the form is inside the pot, where the inner wall of the fat arc is cut away in a big arch under the rim, which casts strong shadows. This arch is mysterious and compelling, and draws the eye into its darkness. It gives the pot an architectural reference, and an ambiguous sense of scale. We might be looking into a secret courtyard, or a stage in an amphitheatre, instead of into a lap-sized basin. The pot succeeds against the odds, for it is hard to give a feeling of large, light and airy architectural space in a form that still remains quite clearly a pot: there is a fine distinction to be maintained, or else something that is simply a little clay model of a building will result.

The severity of the form is enriched by the way it is painted. The surface is very dry and matt and soft-looking, built up with thinly brushed layers of slip that are reminiscent of deteriorating fresco, or old walls where one layer of paint is partly visible through another. Italian whitewash is brought to mind – somehow these are building colours, faded in bright light. The only surface decoration (the main source of decoration is the form itself with its complimentary arcs) is in the two bold zigzag lines that run around the curves. The large scale of this pattern against the form is just what brings it back to pottery, away from architecture, in a highly satisfactory way. Glaze would have killed this pot, for it would have overstated the allegiance to ceramics. It has been apparent how important matt surfaces are to the success of many of the more sculptural pots. I admire this pot for its simplicity, and its subtle way of encompassing aspects of stiffness and sensuality, ancient and modern qualities, architectural and intimate scale. Above all, it is a calm but stimulating thing to have around.

Left and above: Ken Eastman, *Untitled Pot,* 1988, photo: Derek Lomas

The Work of Jim Partridge

Catalogue, solo exhibition of Jim Partridge's work, Crafts Council Gallery, London, 2 August–8 October 1989. This was Partridge's first major solo exhibition, and was unusual in including so many kinds of work. The range from indoors to outdoors covered a great variety of scale; the woodland projects being represented in the gallery with James Ravilious's photography.

Jim Partridge is at present involved in three different kinds of work, all of them with wood. He makes bowls; he makes furniture that might be for the garden or the house; and in the last three years he has worked on projects out of doors, in woods and forests.

In a letter to me about a group of work to be shown at Contemporary Applied Arts a year ago – I was about to write the leaflet – he was thinking about what the connections were between his things and wrote: 'I had always thought that the range of work that I did was unusually broad, but now that I come to look at the half finished group, I begin to wonder. There are differences, of scale, function, surface quality, etc. The major concern when making each piece also varies; for the bridge to be strong, for the lights not to be silly, for the bowls to be better than previous ones I have shown at CAA. But the common threads of straightforwardness, lack of interest in technical virtuosity, and directness of handling (both problems and materials) are what stand out to me, anyhow that's what I'm most proud of.'

Partridge was an early graduate of the School for Craftsmen in Wood run by John Makepeace at Parnham. On leaving there he set up a workshop in Wiltshire. The first bowls that I can remember seeing, and being struck by, in about 1981, were of two types. First there were the spiral bowls where a flat disc of plywood was formed into a wide flat-bottomed conical bowl by means of a tight spiraling line cut on a band-saw. The flat sheet drops into a bowl shape and is glued into place. The simple ingenuity of the idea adds to the pleasure of the way it looks. The plywood stripes are in themselves decorative, snaking down the walls, and these were sometimes enriched by the addition of a layer of coloured veneer on the plywood sheet which ended up as a single bright line threaded among the plain wooden layers. Other versions were of plain dark wood, in which case the spiral layering was still apparent in a subtle way, more as a textural than a tonal decoration. The step in the rim, the necessary end of the snake's tail, was also a strong part of the aesthetic – nothing fudged or tidied up. These bowls were extremely popular; they stood out for their direct approach and for not being precious. Using nothing more exotic than plywood, they seemed somehow to be free of 'craftiness', though they were made with skill.

The other early kind of bowl was finely turned on the lathe from green wood, often holly. Green, or unseasoned wood, is softer and juicier to work, cheaper and easier to acquire, and as the turned bowl dries it shrinks and alters its shape. Things made on the lathe will of course come out round, but on drying these thin forms oval slightly and two little points push up on opposite sides of the rim. It occurs in a consistent and beautiful way, and makes the bowl like a boat with two prows.

This represented another sort of freedom, the freedom to consider form beyond the regular circle. An interest in slight deviations of form was in the air at the time, certainly in the ceramic world. The potter's wheel and the woodturner's lathe have much in common. A reappraisal of the alternatives to wheel-made pottery had been going on for some time in Britain, and by the mid-1970s there was a mood not to make wildly diverse shapes, but to make things that were *about* pottery, that defined pottery. Part of the way in which this was achieved was to withdraw from the notion that function was the only arena of worth for a pot. One of the ways of showing that the 'art' quotient was on the increase and the 'modestly useful' quotient was still there but diminishing, was by flattening the forms so that the pots were still pots, but a bit more like the still-life representations of them.[1]

Writing about Elizabeth Fritsch pots – and these are a key to what I have just tried to define – in the *Fast Forward* catalogue, I argued: 'The oval seemed in the late 1970s so much more pert and relevant than the circle, and this sense was an aspect of a new self-consciousness or standing back, to describe rather than to be useful.'

Fritsch hand-builds her pots into their smooth controlled shapes, but Walter Keeler is even more relevant to a consideration of Jim Partridge's bowls. Keeler throws a pot on the wheel, cuts it off like a loose sleeve, then ovals it and puts it on a new base. The discipline of the circular forming method, wheel or lathe, and the subsequent moves that ensure that the form does not remain circular; the extra thinking, controlling or letting be; the search for more subtleties in three dimensions; this is what these two have in common. By the simple device of letting his green holly bowls distort, Partridge joined in the explorations of form and definition that were going on across many fields in the applied arts, and he left, to some degree, the conventions of woodturning.

With a few stunning exceptions, the woodturning fraternity – and it is almost all men – seems less interested in form than one might expect, and more interested in wood, skill, and finesse. The beauty of the material is the main message; different types of wood, often expensive and exotic imports from dwindling supplies, grains, and colours – these speak louder than shapes. For me this makes the role of the maker too passive. David Pye has made a thorough and very impressive investigation of forms through turning in his long working life, but he has not been joined by many with such aesthetic skill. Partridge, and Maria van Kesteren who has worked for the last 20 years in Holland, both seem outstanding in the way in which they are not seduced by their material – they remain able to impose ideas onto it.

Looking through the catalogue of *Lathe-turned Objects*, a large international touring exhibition originating in Philadelphia, there seems to me to be only a handful of people who aren't subdued by the wood itself into making things that are either very safe or fairly vulgar. I want to quote a little from van Kesteren's statement in that catalogue, because it contrasts so vividly with the norm.

> On one thing I am certain: my affinity to form. In my work I concentrate on, and am motivated to develop, round forms in their limitless variation ... Quite secondary to this is the fact that I use wood as a medium. How preferable if a material existed without the disadvantages of wood; discoloration, distortion of form through atmospheric influences, and the sometimes too emphasised grain patterns that interfere with the intended shape. For that reason I use indigenous woods (ash, lime and elm). These have little colour and grain, and can easily be bleached ... Despite the above, I acknowledge a specific feeling that I have for wood as a means or medium of expression.

Partridge and van Kesteren showed work together at Contemporary Applied Arts, then the British Crafts Centre, in January 1986. Their work is very different, but they share a preoccupation with shape and a belief that in turning, the pleasure lies in having the outer form not *always* echo inner form; that the two contours can diverge to be exciting. Both also need to obliterate some of the 'woodiness' of wood by various means – bleach, stain, paint, or in Partridge's case, fire. But I will come back to that.

In 1983, Partridge left Wiltshire and took up a Craftsman in Residence place for a year at Crewe and Alsager College of Higher Education, which was funded by North West Arts. At the end of this year he set up home and workshop not very far away in Oswestry, Shropshire. At Alsager he taught, experimented, took risks, played around with new materials and described himself in that situation as 'part staff, part student, part zoo animal, and part trespasser.' A touring exhibition consisting of furniture and bowls was the culmination of the year.

Partridge bowls had by this time transformed from thin to thick. Earlier he had made some in papier mâché that were small and slightly knobbly, painted black with gleams of red lacquer in them. He achieved a comparable surface texture in the new wooden bowls, which were turned on the lathe from burr elm or oak. Burring is an ailment, a disease or imperfection in the tree where the grain knots up in clumps rather than growing straight. The tightly curled texture of the wood when sliced across the grain is highly priced, and prized, by wood craftsmen for its decorative effect, especially when burring is total and consistent. Partridge tends to use pieces that are less consistent and more surprising, and may have been rejected by the purists. After turning the wood he chars the surface with a blow torch. The spring layers burn more easily because they are softer, and the resulting surface, after scraping off the soot with wire wool and waxing, is gnarled and uneven, a rich dense brownish black, and satisfyingly 'finished'. He still turns the wood green, and though the bowls are much thicker walled than the holly ones, some shrinking and cracking still adds to the upheaval of the smooth turned form that he is seeking.

With this timber and surface he has tried out many different forms. Most turners would start work on the roundish section of wood cut across a tree trunk but Partridge bowls quite often start from a thick square or rectangular plank, into which the concave bowl form is sunk. To do this he has to contend with the corners of the plank whizzing round in front of his eyes as he works. Some of his most successful pieces have been these with the angular outer form. In a few recent pieces the bowl depression has been stained red (a series entitled *Blood Vessels* is touring in the American exhibition), or sometimes gilded.

Bowl making is the core of his work, I believe. Being smaller scale, intimate, easy to get on with whatever else is, or isn't, happening, it has accompanied the development of his thinking over the years – and he has thought a lot about the characteristics of the bowl. He says that he finds writing difficult, but whenever he does the results seem good to me; uncluttered, enlightening and slightly witty. He wrote a short preparatory comment for the Gulbenkian Craft Initiative Vessel Forum that was held in Birmingham in 1987, called *The Dialectics of Inside and Outside*, in which he made tentative and intriguing references to philosophy. And in some notes for a small exhibition in the Wrexham Library in Wales in 1988 he wrote:

> Bowl making is so straightforward that it seems like occupational therapy when compared to my other work – making furniture and larger outdoor things like footbridges designed for specific people and places. But the pleasure does go deeper than just convenience and speed. The relationship between the inside and the outside of a bowl, via its rim, can be used to represent a vast range of experiences; the spiritual relationship of the body to the soul, territorial relationships, the rim separating 'Mine' from 'Yours' (or linking them), the nature of containment, is it protecting or offering up its contents? And all of this takes place (if you want it to) within a simple useful object.

Furniture making, whether or not for batch production, is inevitably a less intuitive process where planning and premeditation are required. Partridge is less comfortable with the mechanisms of designing and promoting, and has yet to push any of his ideas into production by others. Nonetheless, in spite of the frustrations, it is a continuing vein of his work. He has produced mainly chairs, and seating of various kinds, usually made

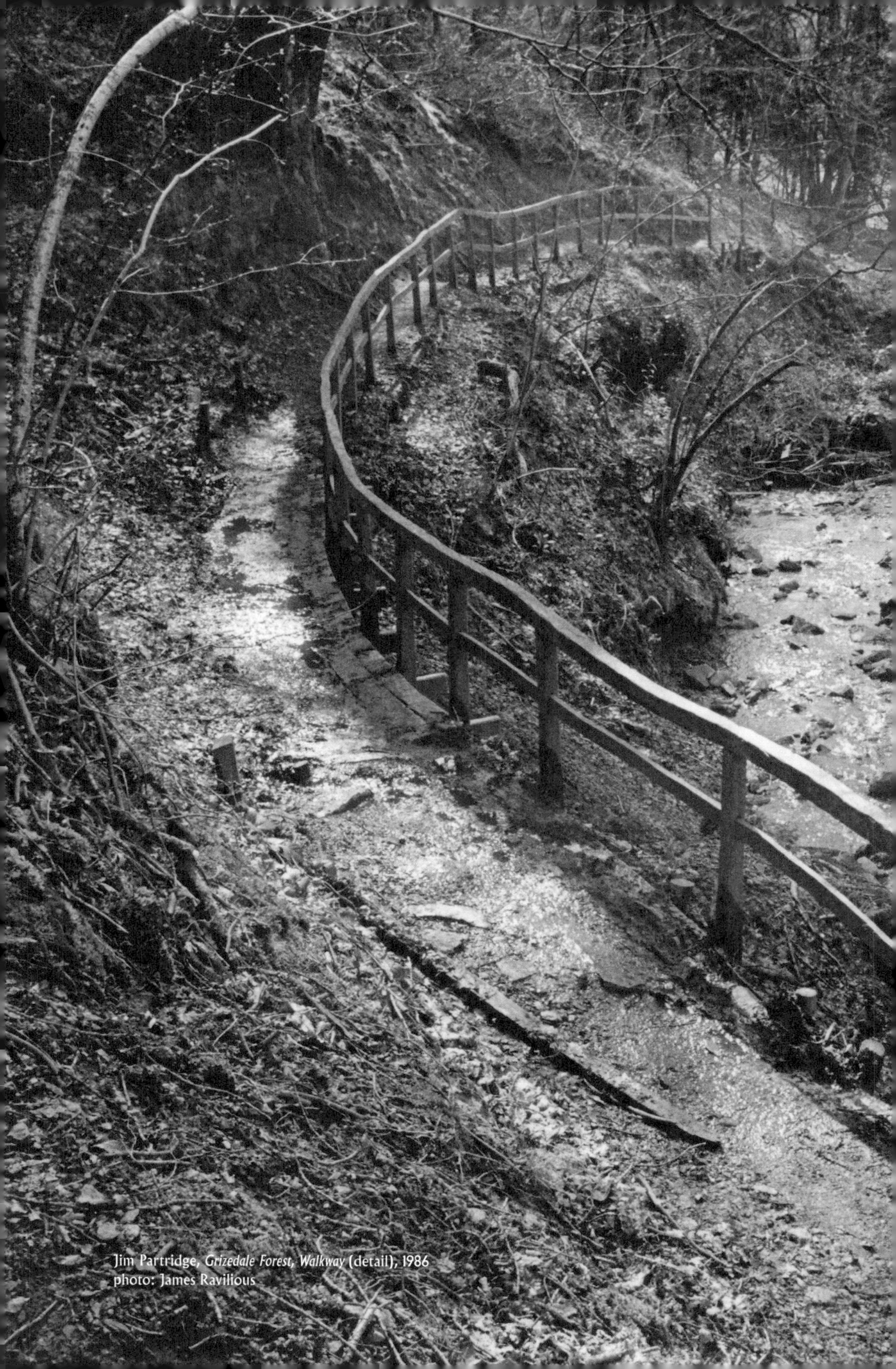

Jim Partridge, *Grizedale Forest, Walkway* (detail), 1986
photo: James Ravilious

from rough-cut blackened planks. These seats are potentially prototypes as well as things in their own right. He makes furniture with the same unwasteful approach that characterises all his work – rectangular pieces are slotted together with economy and sense. The seat for two people, with parallel upright planks slotted into the back of verticals of a long stool form and screwed into a rail near the bottom, is a strong and amiable piece. It has a slightly unnerving anthropomorphic look, as if two people are already sitting down and in conversation, like the Henry Moore sculpture of a seated couple. In my view there is often a disconcerting look about the slab-built furniture, it seems to be a hybrid of indoor and outdoor seating, the medieval settle and the park bench – more Dialectics of the Inside and the Outside, perhaps? I feel surest of the rocking chair that is in this exhibition. It was made at Alsager and is, I think, the most clearly resolved and domestic of the chairs.

In the last few years it has been the outdoor work, three separate projects so far, that has provided the main stimulus for development. In the forest works Jim Partridge is able to be intuitive, to respond, in a way that is much more like the bowl making than the furniture. The woodland seats are fresh and rough, and look like spontaneous gestures with the shape of a particular tree trunk. Using Nature raw, choosing a site and finding the materials, seems to bring out the gut reactions and ingenuity that best suit his working character.

The Grizedale Sculpture Project was set up in 1977 in part of a large forest owned by the Forestry Commission in the Lake District.[2] So far about 30 sculptures have been made there, spread over a wide area such that it would take a couple of days to find everything. I spent the first afternoon walking in the forest in what seemed to be the right direction, getting lost and not reaching any sculpture at all.

Jim Partridge is the first 'non-sculptor' to work in Grizedale. He carried out two separate schemes in 1986–87, one for a bridge over a stream and one for a walkway, a supported path with a handrail, beside a stream. For these outdoor projects Partridge does not work alone – it would be too dangerous for one thing to be chain-sawing away by yourself in the middle of the dark woods – therefore he has an assistant. Liz Walmsley's role has shifted with experience towards that of collaborator, and their next work together will be under both names.

The artists are allowed to use any dead wood they find and any 'non-commercial' timber that is curved by the wind or bent for some reason, and they may be able to fell other trees with permission. The forest has 1,000 acres of hard wood and 8,000 acres of soft wood, and trees of many different types. The scale of the effort involved in merely assembling the raw materials before starting to construct stretches the imagination – a big winch will move a tree trunk only an inch at a time when you pull a huge lever. The foresters help with their tractors where they can, but the timber that was used for the bridge – thin oak logs that had been buried for some years and had young conifers growing on top of them – had to be pulled out by hand.

Some of the sculpture in the forest is wonderful, and some of it is trivial and silly. Partridge's work adds something of worth to the environment because his things aren't trying to be works of art. They are unostentatious and practical, and succeed in being beautiful in their place, rather than as things in themselves. This is particularly true of the walkway; it is very quiet, and does not declaim much about its maker. Only on looking closely do you realise with surprise and pleasure that the handrail is made of just three or four extraordinarily long stretches of curved timber (some 40 foot) which are sections of elongated saplings. The path follows the curve of the hand rail and becomes a semi-bridge crossing a sliding mudbank. It is supported then by stones and heavy planks with gaps between them for the rain and mud to fall through. All the walking surfaces that he has made on planks have deep criss-cross saw cuts in them so they do not become slippery and dangerous.

The bridge at Grizedale is like a pile of logs, or rather a pile of logs with a trough in it. It spans the stream with a small dark arch and carries the track between two thick slices of log pile that form parapet walls. It is reminiscent of a dry stone bridge too, with its neat dense structure. It belongs so thoroughly in its place, blending in with nature, but is evidently the work of someone with doggedness and imagination. It is like a metaphorical bridge between the forest and the sculpture.

The other two outdoor projects, in Kent and in Essex, have been making creative use of hurricane destruction. Common Ground and the Woodland Trust have commissioned several artists to work in various woods, and once again Partridge is the only non-sculptor. In Ashenbank Wood near Gravesend he has made four seats from fallen trees, two of them using the forked 'uncommercial' part of the tree, and another using a great curved trunk lying on its side to make a long bench, enough for a large family to sit on. In a higher part of the wood, where there is a good view, he has made a tall oak throne-like seat with a couple of attendant footstools. These seats are all dedicated to Irene Kathleen Miles and are part of a bequest from her husband to put seats in Woodland Trust woods.

In Essex, Partridge was recommended by Common Ground for a commission from two local Local Councils.[3] In Hockley Woods he has made two very different one-off seats in the children's playground, and using two forked branches he has made an arched entranceway to the playground and an arch for a notice board. Another part of his job has been to develop prototypes for seats and other elements that could be made by the Council's Woodland Staff. And deeper into the wood he has made a jetty and some steppingstones in a pond that are thick sections of tree trunk, heavily criss-crossed in his usual way.

Most of the seats in Hockley are built from very thick planks, unblackened this time, but instantly recognisable as Partridge. But the

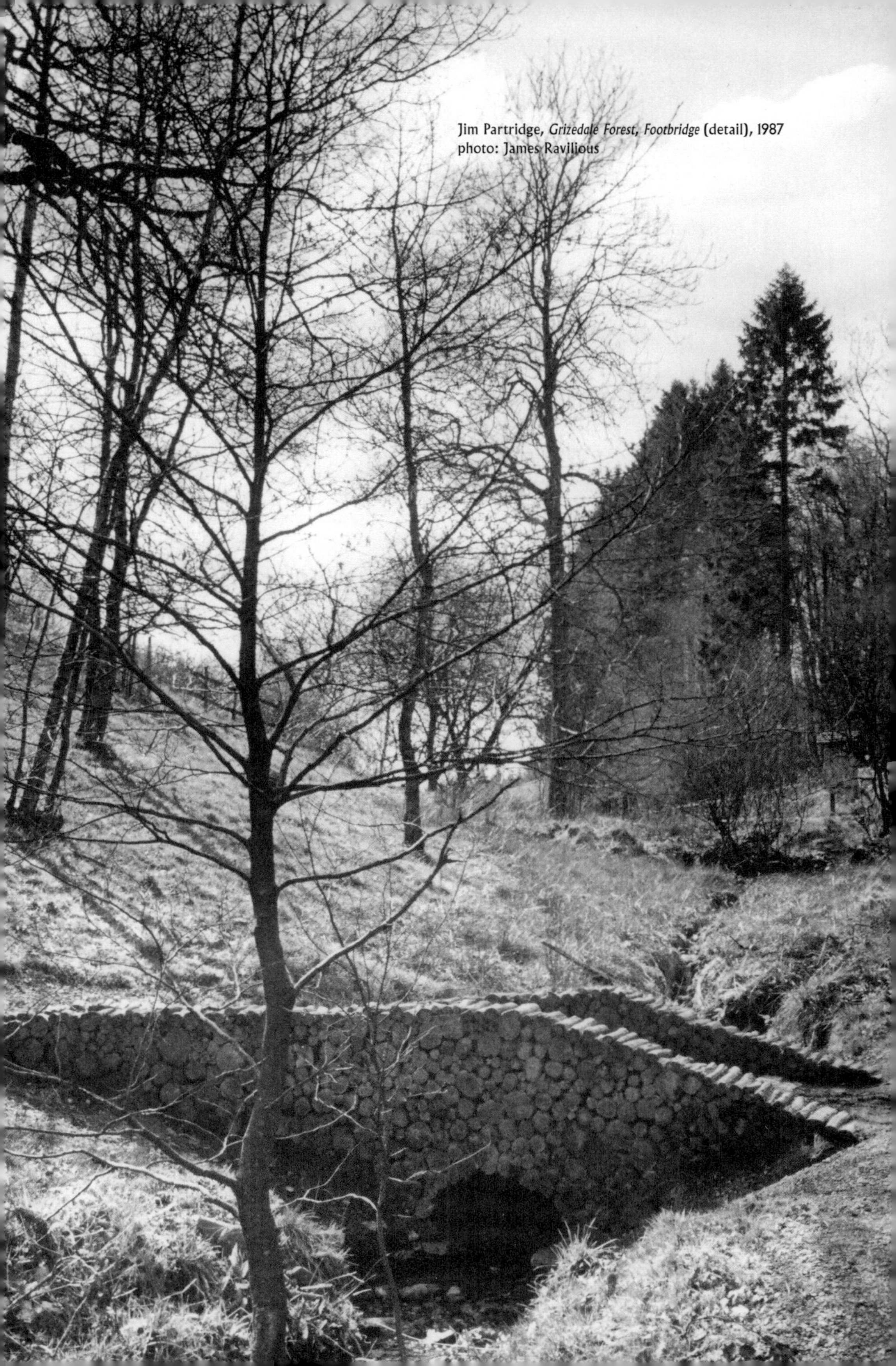

Jim Partridge, *Grizedale Forest, Footbridge* (detail), 1987
photo: James Ravilious

largest seat in the playground is quite different. It is fluid and sinuous and sculptural with a similar feeling to the long curved bench in Kent but with a more complex and ambitious form. It is made from a huge forked tree lying on the ground, and its ambiguous shape tempts one to compare it to things – it is like a wheelbarrow at first sight, and then like a whale. It provides different sorts of seating; children could perch higher up on the two branches of the fork, the handles of the wheelbarrow, and then there is a snuggly enclosed curve that two or three could sit in, at a pinch, and a partition between this and the next seat, angled so that two people could almost sit back to back as in a lovers's seat. It is a thing to climb over as well as rest on, and full of interest; a very communal, and conversational, piece of furniture.

It is to be hoped that these opportunities for working out of doors will continue and multiply, mainly for our benefit, but also because Partridge is so ideally suited to them.[4] He has the capacity to think on his feet, to cope with massive raw material and wield huge chainsaws as well as to plan details like where the rain will drain off the furniture and how things will last. He also likes the life, moving to new places, being out in the wilds and camping in a caravan.

I think that in writing the catalogue in this sequential way I have made the three strands of work seem more separate than they are. The prototype benches at Hockley are offspring of the Double Seat, and one of the outdoor forked tree trunk seats has been charred black and brought indoors as an armchair. Partridge's sensitivity to finish, how much or how little of it is needed, is something that he learned from turning bowls. Making a bowl in the workshop is a quiet, intense, one-to-one relationship. Working in the woods is done in partnership with Walmsley, in public and for the public, exposed to all weather. We owe a lot to organisations like Common Ground and the Grizedale Society, especially at this time when it is apparent that it is almost too late for us all to have a considerate and respectful relationship to the natural world. Making some good of the hurricane damage seems to be a gesture well worth making. Partridge has always worked, and indeed lived, with frugal awareness of his materials and his surroundings. In looking at his work we can learn from his approach.

1. See *The Maker's Eye*, exhibition catalogue, Crafts Council Gallery, 1982; *Fast Forward*, exhibition catalogue Institute of Contemporary Arts, London, 1985; Peter Dormer, *The New Ceramics*, Thames and Hudson, 1986.
2. The Grizedale Society and Northern Arts run the programme. It allows artists to work on long residencies of up to six months, as well as for shorter periods.
3. Rochford District Council and Castle Point District Council, also sponsored by Eastern Arts and the Countryside Commission.
4. Partridge and Wamsley have just been commissioned by Sustrans for a series of seats on a cycle path from Bristol to Bath.

Andrew Greaves
Photographic Work

Essay written in 1989, solo exhibition of Andrew Greaves's work, Lieu Dit 87 & 89, Rouen, France, 13 March–11 April 1992. Greaves studied painting but spent many years making three-dimensional work, as individual objects, as pieces to be photographed, or as installations. In recent years he has been making virtual objects, three-dimensional abstract animated films and prints.

There is nothing spontaneous in Andrew Greaves's work as a photographer. Images are carefully composed of assembled objects, and the objects themselves are chosen in a concentrated and serious manner. The resulting photographs are as far removed from the 'frozen instant' of reportage or documentary photography, the slice-of-life image that gives us a glimpse of another reality, as it is possible to be within the same medium. Such photographs project us into an imaginative reaction to those other worlds; the picture is believed in as a substitute for reality. Commonly we expect this of photography, in art or in journalism.

Photographs in reproduction are constantly consumed by all of us, in the media and in advertising. Most of the time we are scanning photographic images for information, accurate representation, facts. To scan a photograph as if it were a painting, which is necessary with Greaves's pictures, and to be denied facts, is for many people a fresh experience. His photographs hold the attention because they are so strongly composed – form comes first – and they do not obviously reveal their content. The intrigue prolongs the eye's open-minded engagement, and we are cast into an enquiring role. Greaves's photographs are not routes into other worlds, they are objects in themselves. Modernism brought an awareness of a painting as an object; abstraction closed off avenues of interest in the subject matter for its own sake, and preoccupations with verisimilitude. Photography, as practiced by artists such as Man Ray since the early decades of this century, has had an abstract vein in line with painting, but it has not been so apparent to the majority of audiences.

Greaves's background is in abstract painting, not in still-life painting, though his photographs are still lives. But this is their secondary aspect. The objects portrayed, chosen and juxtaposed with such care, are not there being themselves, and what they actually consist of is unimportant and sometimes well disguised. The things that he selects are often abnormal in some way, altered by time and nature if not by him. Fish are frozen solid so that they retain their neat trunk-like section when sliced in half; a balloon is withered and organic looking; lumps of smokeless fuel are painted another colour. He is drawn to objects with modified recognisability, as a way of making them his own, possessing the things before he can contain them

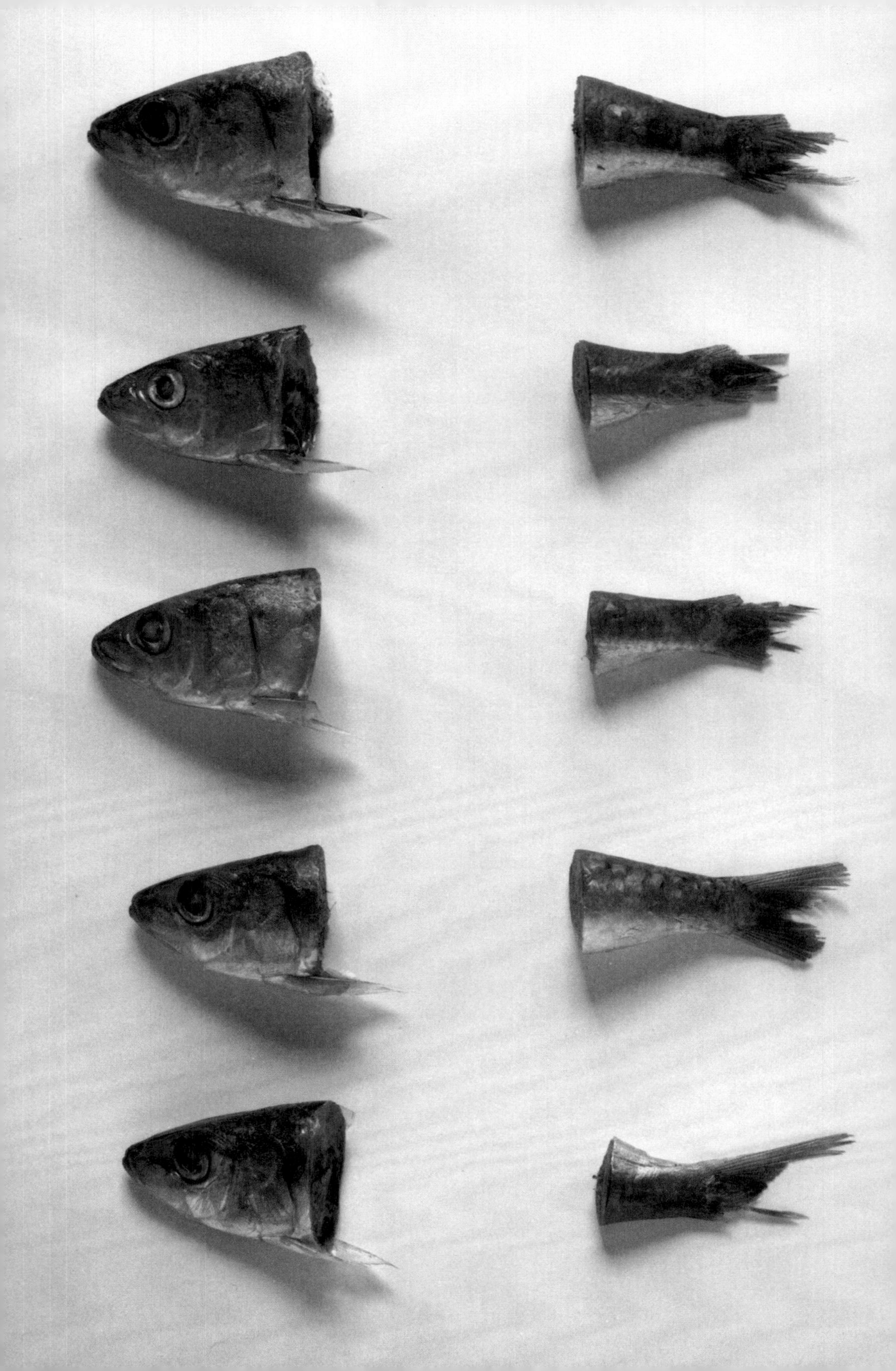

within an image. The first purpose of his photographs is aesthetic, to make an abstract composition of great subtlety and richness, within the constraints of the (usually) black and white form. But photography almost unavoidably brings representation, and he plays with this added dimension of presenting semi-familiar objects, vivid references to reality that coexist with the formalist emphasis. Unlike many painters who turn to photography, he has gone to great lengths to understand and perfect techniques. The quality of the finished object is as important as the content.

A series of pictures made in 1988 all contain a flat painted black image which reads as a frame. This 'frame' has, superimposed on it, a sequence of very different 'still-life' subjects – a pile of sand, textured white paint, dead flowers, severed leads from a hi-fi, broken glass, torn pieces of photographs. They are beautifully portrayed; fish glisten, and petals crumple, with great conviction. But the realness of these things is open to question, as is their three-dimensionality, or lack of it; doubts arise about the existence of these images as upright or as horizontal formulations. The feeling that a picture within a picture evokes is always powerful – the sequential process which creates uncertainty about the flat and the solid, about form and space; at any stage in the series we cannot be sure which parts of the image were 'alive' at that point, and which portrayed. Further play with scale adds to our sense of intrigue and uncertainty. Greaves's pictures are thoroughly ambiguous and engaging, and successfully poised between wit and gravity.

Andrew Greaves, *Frozen Credits*, 1988

Walter Keeler

Gallery leaflet, solo exhibition of Walter Keeler's work, Contemporary Applied Arts, London, 13 October–11 November 1989. Keeler's pots, when he began to play against symmetry and emulate the surfaces of metal, seemed to show a dramatic response to a changing culture. Pots still beautifully made, but not in thrall to the previous conventions of form.

We all know that clay is a pliant and versatile material and that you can do anything with it. But what are its 'natural' forms; where are its true characteristics most vividly expressed? Or is it *so* plastic and forgiving that it is character*less*, and that no one method of forming it is more apt than any other?

Wheel-thrown pots are thought by many to be intrinsically the most suitable. But they are only part of the story: ancient Chinese Han dynasty tomb models of buildings, for instance, testify to a very long history of hand-building too, and demonstrate an equally convincing, and completely different, clay form. I would suggest that it is not that the wheel is 'natural' to ceramics, but rather that it is a quick and practical method of working clay into the vessel shapes that were needed in quantities over many centuries, and the consistent form of a wheel-made pot has become a visual convention.

Keeler still uses the wheel, but alters the thrown shapes afterwards when they are leather-hard, cutting pots off their circular bases and settling them on new elongated ones. The forms are very sharply defined and tense, and diverge with subtlety from the expected upright regularity of throwing. The inspiration for these shapes comes frequently from metal vessels of a simple nature: oil cans, billy cans and watering cans. Keeler suppresses the loose-limbed organic thrown characteristics, the qualities of slipperiness, finger troughs, and essential softness; instead with great skill and pleasurable difficulty he manipulates tightly sprung sleeves and stretched planes, well suited to the beautiful hard lustrous surface of salt glaze, and indeed to the visual references to cans.

I do not wish to convey that the sources for this work are entirely metallic – there is a very strong sense of ceramic history here too, such as the guts and humour of peasant pottery, and the radical early industrial work of the 18th century (Thomas Whieldon and so on). Keeler's ease with clay is powerfully conveyed, and the material makes its own contribution, overriding and softening his control. Clay suits his aims completely.

Getting the pots *off* the circular and tilting them was the first significant move Keeler made in establishing his new territory in the late 1970s, when he began to concentrate on more idiosyncratic work. The additions to the basic slanting forms, the taut limbs zinging off the body in the guise of spouts and handles, were the second. These have a visual importance that is stronger than the practical; they are often exaggerated in scale and are striking, disconcerting, and humorous, while their function is unspoilt. The pots have perfect weight;

not virtuoso lightness, but exactly appropriate thickness and density for their volume. This is derived from their thrown beginnings, and from the longstanding experience of a former production thrower. The teapot, which needs a handle, a spout that pours, and a separate lid with a knob, has been at the heart of Keeler's investigations for some time. It has sufficient requirements and restrictions to thoroughly liberate his skill and his ideas. Keeler, like many artists, thrives on limitations. One of the constraints that he has firmly chosen is function.

> All my pots are functional, it is a fundamental justification and a challenging starting point. If the pots could not be used I would not bother to make them.

He *needs* them to be useful, more perhaps than we do, or the compulsion to make does not get stirring. There has been a lot of talk of 'other' kinds of function in the last decade, symbolic and aesthetic, ritual, or of pots functioning along with interior ornament in general as social signifiers of class, wealth and taste. None of this touches Keeler much, though he says now that he feels it is his job to *provoke* people's interest in functional things. His motivation is still more or less where it was when, in his own words, he was a 'Batterhamesque' domestic potter, and a well-made, harmonious batch-production teapot was £4.50. The cultural climate changed at the end of the 1970s, pots changed, prices changed, our attitudes as audience changed too. Keeler still makes useful pots, but he has developed in the last decade a new language for himself, and thereby initiated a heightened aesthetic expectation for domestic pottery.

In this exhibition Keeler is showing about 30 pots which can be seen singly with clear space around them. He wants to get away from the tendency for functional work to be shown in crowded groups, because it is functional. Some of the pots are 'definitives', particularly striking versions of things he is already known for, like the generous open dish with huge tubular handles, and the flattened bulbous teapot with a macaroni twist on the lid. Some of the forms are simpler than before; there are some severely handsome new large jugs with a sharp back-tilted prow that slides into a pointed lip. Some pieces are becoming more complicated in their precise and elegant details. Simple or elaborate, the pots are powerful, independent, sure of their ground, and unmistakably themselves.

Looking at them brings to mind an interesting recent discussion of the connections between clay and metal objects. In a paper called 'Pottery: Form and Status'[1], Oliver Watson of the V&A began to look at the unrestricted range of forms that clay has taken through history:

> ...from the earliest pots of several millenia BC to contemporary artists's work, we see clay in 'natural' ceramic shapes, but we also see a great number, perhaps even a majority, copying other materials. These 'other

materials' are recognisable by peculiarities of shape or by imitative decorative motifs. We see basketwork, wooden shapes, glass shapes, and even the influence of architectural decoration in stone or plaster. However, metal forms predominate: cast bronze or beaten brass, but particularly worked silver.

Watson refers to a recent conference of art historians which looked at the relationships between precious metal and ceramics in three cultures – Ancient Greece, China, and the Islamic world. It became clear to them that worked silver and gold provided the main source of ideas for ceramic shapes and decoration of high class production in all three locations. 'Did this copying arise just because clay is so versatile and yet somewhat formless in its own substance? Or is clay copying more expensive materials simply to provide a cheap imitation? This latter is bound to be the case.' Watson is asking us to make a dramatic shift in our perception of the art history of these three cultures, in which we were thought ceramics to be highly regarded. He concludes that the pots have merely survived better, conveying the threads of stylistic development, whereas the gold and silver vessels that inspired their manufacture, too precious to be wasted, were melted down and reformed to new tastes and fashions.

I include this fairly startling information as a way of setting a fresh conceptual frame through which to look at the Keeler's work. He is inspired by metal shapes, but non-precious ones; and nothing is further from his mind, or ours, when we confront his pots, than cheap imitation. The metal vessels he feels strongly for are in themselves cheap; mundane, down-to-earth things from railway sheds and engineering works. What impresses him is their straightforward assembly from sheet metal, worked into separate parts, that makes an articulated and 'eventful' whole. Rolled edges and welded seams further animate the shapes, and these have their equivalents too in the way Keeler decorates, divides up and delineates his pot forms.

The device of clay reminding us of metal is rich and enjoyably resonant to the contemporary eye. It is entertaining rather than deceiving. Keeler conveys his affection for the humble originals, and invests his own more precious pots with hints of their appealing ordinariness. At last, in the long history of ceramics, someone is making a *more* prestigious and desirable clay object that derives inspiration from a metal one. The tables are turning.

I wonder if the referential pots of ancient times had any of these double-edged connotations, any metaphorical pleasures that enhanced their visual, if not their monetary, value, for the audiences of the time? What is more certain is that Keeler's pots have a special and contemporary beauty. They are outstanding in our own ceramic history, and they can go on being appreciated through different frames of perception in times to come.

1. 'Pottery: Form and Status' was a preliminary paper contributed to the Vessel Forum held in Birmingham in 1987 and organised by the Gulbenkian Craft Initiative.

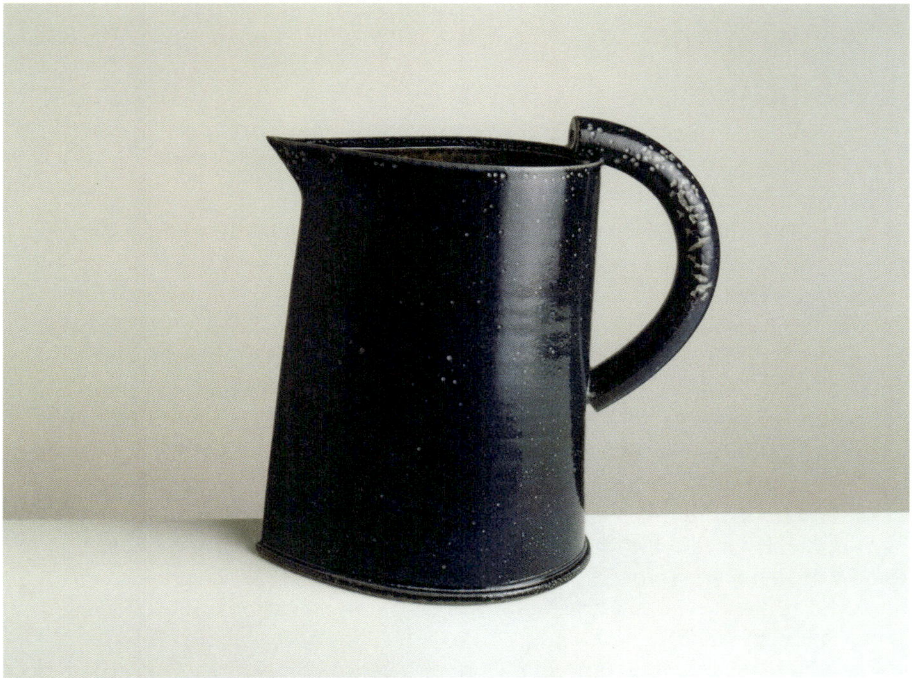

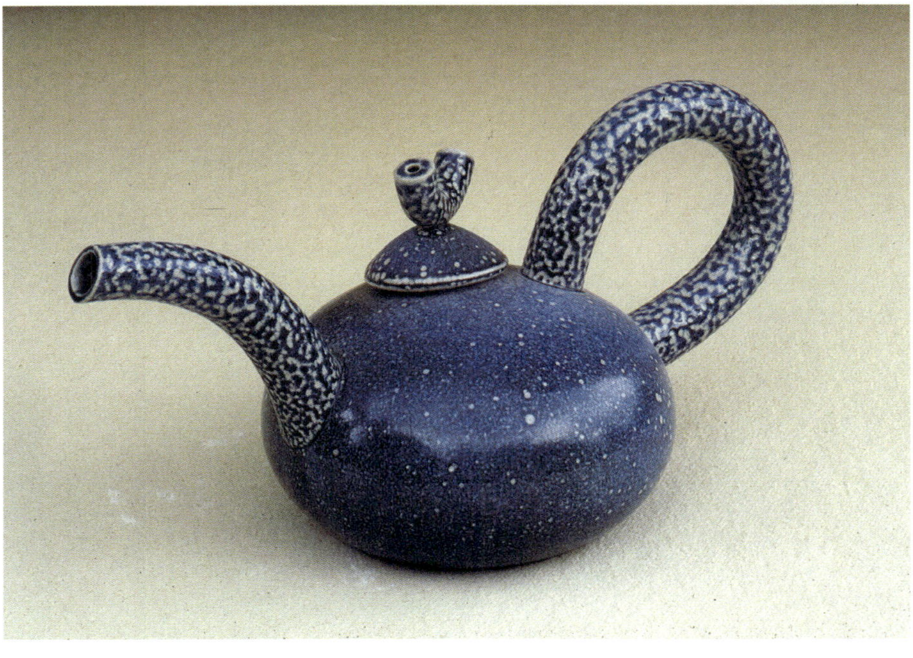

Walter Keeler, *Jug*, 1989, photo: David Cripps
Walter Keeler, *Teapot*, 1989, photo: David Cripps

Postscript
Shifting the Categories

Reading over the 1980s it seems to have been a time full of ideas when people working across the visual arts, in good rapport with each other, were seeking a different cultural space. A lot has already been written about *The Maker's Eye* exhibition, the source of my opening essay.[1] But I will use this event as a focus to look through my first decade in hindsight. I was invited to be a selector in the major Crafts Council exhibition at a point of self-assessment for the institution as well as its expansion into bigger premises in Lower Regent Street in London. The Council, known for the first few years as the Crafts Advisory Committee, had been in operation since 1971, and its first director was Victor Margrie. The exhibition, commissioned by Ralph Turner who led the exhibitions department, aimed at a broad review of ideas within craft practise after a decade of the Council's work. This review was to be seen through the personal selections of a chosen group of craft makers, and amounted to a total of 500 objects. Turner wrote at the time: 'Many people still have a very narrow view of crafts and *The Maker's Eye* is intended to be a crash course'.[2] A sort of landmark, it used the object predilections of 14 'makers'[3] as a barometer of craft understanding of the time. Among those 14 were the very venerable Enid Marx and Michael Cardew, both born at the beginning of the century, and David Kindersley and David Pye. A few selectors were from the interwar and 1940s generations, which included me, and the youngest born in the 1950s, such as Erik de Graaff and Michael Brennand-Wood.

I had run a studio for eight years by then, after leaving college, and due to a considerable extent to the expansive work of the young Crafts Council, its outward-looking ethos and links with the British Council, I had begun to exhibit in the UK and abroad. I had also written a few essays for fellow artists' catalogues.

We were asked to choose objects mainly from the last ten years, and within the 20th century. Marx included a copy of an Eileen Gray table, Emmanuel Cooper a Triumph Bonneville motorbike, David Pye a leather saddle. The selecting task was serious and detailed, and brought not only the chance to represent some ideas about contemporary craft and wider contexts through objects, but was also the beginning for me of a deeper awareness of writing out of practice, of thinking about artworks and categories by writing. Each curator could choose dozens of things, 40 or 50 pieces in some cases, enough to make a statement. In the responsibility of choice, selectors could explore their opinions of a discipline, a generation, a group ideology, or even create a kind of manifesto. In writing the essay after making my selection, I found myself having a position, a discernable stance, through this personal edit of contemporary objects. In the creative patch identified, I felt I was part of something emergent, reflexive and often engaged with ironic enquiry.

The exhibition had a mixed reception. Some Fine Art critics in the papers jibed at the mixture of approaches and the breadth of opinions.[4] Only the oldest curator/makers were generally appreciated, those doing the 'proper work' of the craftsman, in Peter Fuller's phrase.[5] This gave a disappointing impression that the 'proper' art world took no interest in the blurring of categories or any crossover nonsense. Sociologically, it was fascinating, and the long-term impact of the exhibition is impressive. Its ambitious scale and scholarly detail would be hard to repeat, and its catalogue is increasingly a treasure in retrospect. Double-page photographs for each selection, by the artist David Ward, were set up in very different ways in sympathy with each curator's aesthetic. A small image of nearly every object included, per selector, was in the catalogue listing at the back. Turner concluded his preview article with the aspiration that the exhibition '... points the way to a broader definition whereby we recognise craftsmen and craftswomen in factories, drawing offices, street markets, studios and shops.'[6]

In the working environment I knew in the 1980s, it was a confident period of experiment and loosening boundaries. This is very obvious if you flick through the *Crafts* magazines of the time – striking photography, writers commissioned from other critical fields, strong discussion, a lively letters page. Martina Margetts was the editor from 1978 to 1987, and established this more rigorous and enlightened framework of craft discourse. This was supported by the art direction, which for some of this period was by David King, with a Russian Constructivist leaning. Discussion of craft objects had in the past been centred mainly on technique and material, firing temperatures and recipes, furnace building and so on. These had been vital aspects, information and tools, of the modern craft revival.

By the 1980s, a generation of postwar baby boomers had grown up and been through a spacious and well-funded art education. The relative economic ease, low rents and a liberal atmosphere, enabled many people to set up in studios, albeit in spartan conditions. Craft practice flowered in the city in this generation, different from the rurality of much early modernist practice, in the workshops of Ethel Mairet, Bernard Leach, and Cardew for instance. Lucie Rie however stuck to her London atelier that she acquired in 1939, soon after she arrived in England, and lived above it until her death in 1995.

It seems clear that new self-questioning objects appeared in the 1980s in ceramics and in other disciplines, metalwork, textiles, jewellery and so on. One of the preoccupations was an effusion of decoration, *on* things and *as* things. In the wider frame there was also a new positive sense of ornament and *the decorative object*. Decorative Art had long been the museum definition of the crafts. The word itself was being dragged back from modernist disgrace. Decoration (and pattern) seemed vibrant and even daring to articulate, though as a verb I generally found it a better fit to talk about *painting* on the pot surface, rather than decorating it. The significance of this is that conventional decoration both in craft and mass production implied a content-less and subservient (and perhaps feminine) activity, motifs laid on a predetermined form to enhance its value. For my generation this was not good enough, as I discussed in the essay *Sèvres with Krazy Kat*.[7] New thinking about decoration was powerfully evident in Michael Rowe's long series of works in sheet metal, some made in silver, and many in brass with tin or gold leaf finishes. *The Conditions of Ornament*, their common title, was completed over the years 1987–2000,[8] comprising about 30 objects. Early pieces from this series were shown in Rowe's exhibition at the British Crafts Centre, which I wrote about in the essay included above.

It seems obvious now that in these ornamental excursions postmodernism was lapping unacknowledged around our feet while we made decorative decisions about form rather than function, from our modernist art school education backgrounds. But transitions are never simply end-to-end: as was made clear in the V&A exhibition on postmodernism of 2011.

> Postmodernism was both an extension and an intensification of some aspects of modernism, and a conscious departure from it. Moreover, its practitioners consciously played these two aspects against one another. They resisted classification, even running from the label 'postmodernism' itself as if it had turned back to bite them (which indeed it had a tendency to do). Amongst the many artists, designers, architects, performers and makers we have spoken to in the course of organising this project, very few embraced the term with outright affection.[9]

I began my regular essay writing for gallery leaflets for the British Crafts Centre in the 1980s. The breadth of their exhibition programme in this decade made the job a wonderful opportunity, and although wide-eyed enthusiasm was perhaps the norm in my writing in this period, I find I do still like the work of the people I most admired at the time. Though many of the essays are close-ups of a single practice, some of the writing I have included here surveys a wider scene, such as the developing scope of British studio glass, or the donated collection of American ceramics to the V&A, or the museum's new Toshiba Galleries of Japanese Art.

I can see in my 1980s writing some consistent preoccupations that I carry still. These have been with the object as still life, also in photography, and abstraction as a possibility in object making. In thinking about making and materials I find an interest in slippage, cutting up and piecing together, and the ordering of fragments that I often thought were more appealing than wholes. There are juxtapositions of the ordinary and the peculiar, painting and upholstery, metal-smithing and sculpture. Paintings shown in a craft gallery; making bridges in a sculpture forest. This is where I think the energy was, in a rearrangement of the received wisdom. I conclude the 1980s with Walter Keeler, whose approach to throwing pots was transformed in this decade. From his highly skilled traditional making of 1970s counterculture stoneware crockery, he changed during the 1980s both material and shape. Salt glaze and a new elliptical formal vocabulary touched on deconstruction, metaphor, and irony. Clearly at this point we are bridging modernism and postmodernism.

1. On *The Maker's Eye* and the evolution of the Crafts Council, see Tanya Harrod, *The Crafts in Britain in the Twentieth Century*, Yale, 1999.
2. Ralph Turner, 'The Maker's Eye', preview of exhibition, *Crafts* magazine 54, January/February 1982, p.26.
3. 'Maker' was a way of eliding the job descriptions of artist, designer, and craftsman (soon, as gender sensitivity increased, to be a *craftsperson)*.
4. See John McEwan, *The Spectator*, 23 January 1982, p. 24, and *Crafts* magazine 56, May/June 1982, p.49. William Feaver, *Observer*, 24 January 1982.
5. 'The Proper Work of the Potter' was a catalogue essay on the virtues of throwing – 'natural process and natural form' in pottery – by the critic Peter Fuller for the exhibition *Fifty Five Pots and Three Opinions*, The Orchard Gallery, Londonderry, 1983, pp.19–26.
6. 'The Maker's Eye', *Crafts* 54, p.26.
7. See above, p.20.
8. See Martina Margetts's essay in *Michael Rowe*, Birmingham Museum and Art Gallery with Lund Humphries, 2003, pp.14, 24. For images of *The Conditions of Ornament* series, see above pp.75–99, 102–14.
9. Glenn Adamson and Jane Pavitt, 'Curators' Foreword', *Postmodernism Style and Subversion, 1970–1990*, V&A Publishing, 2011, p.10.

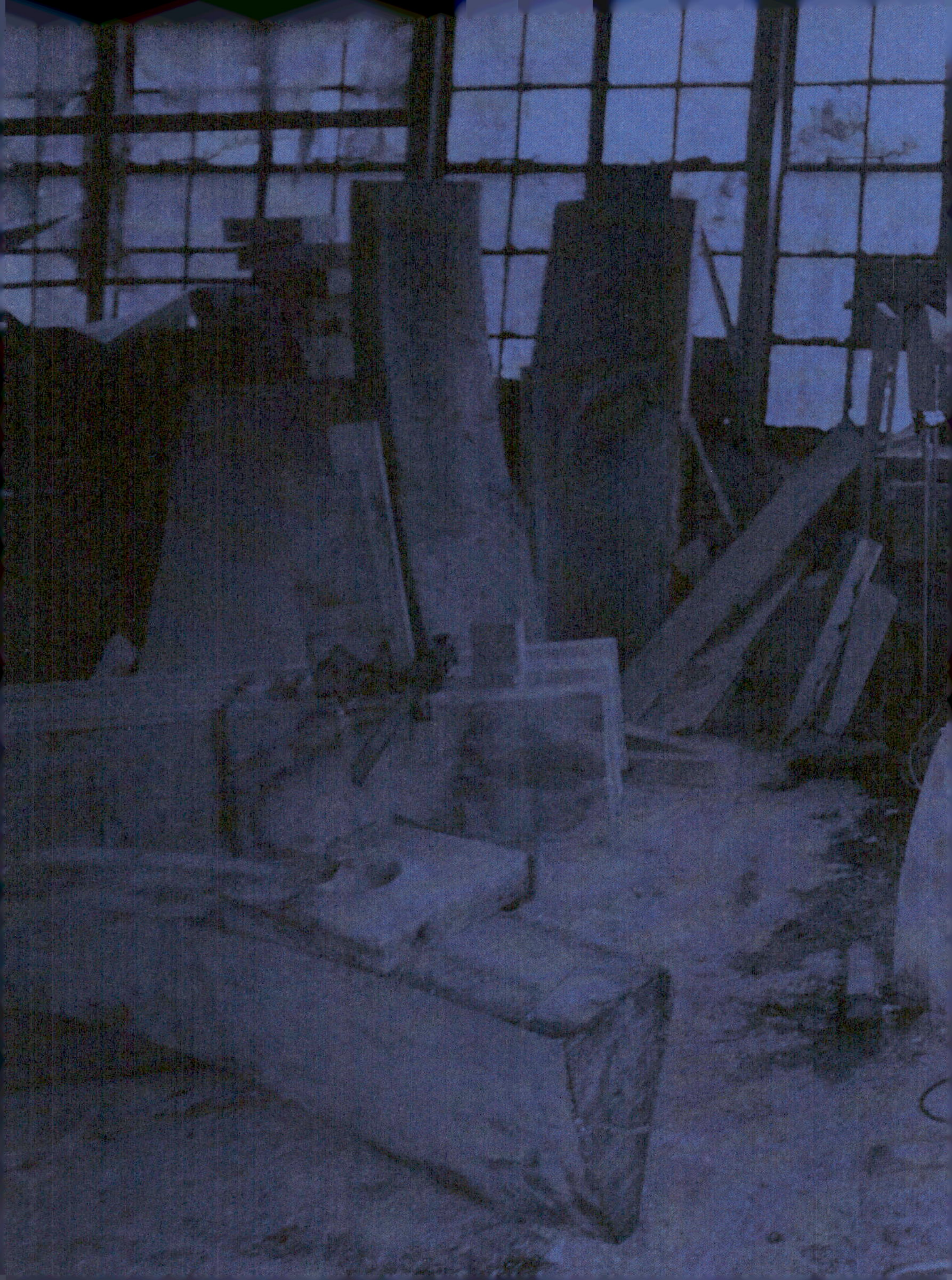

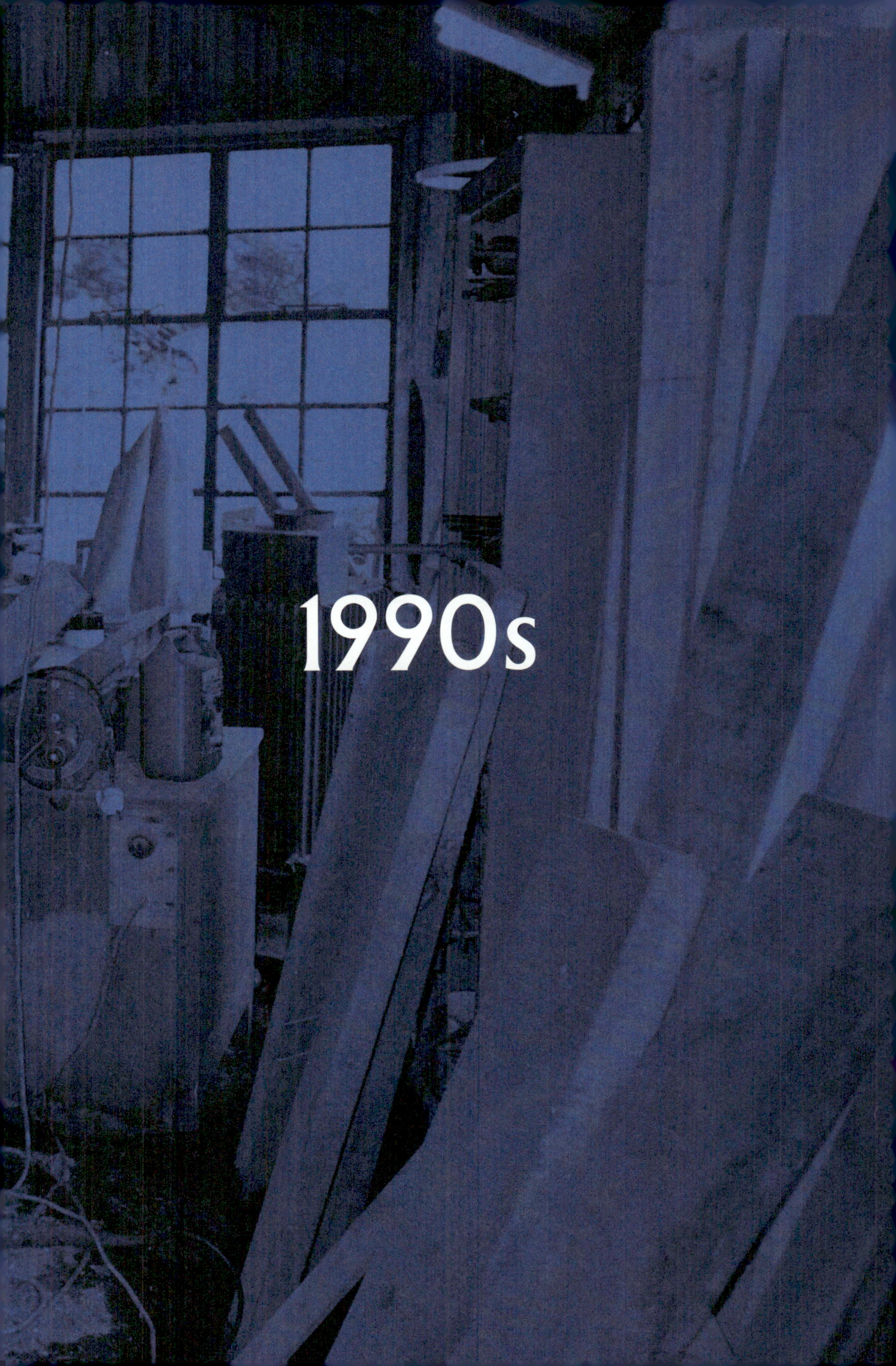

1990s

Gender and Art

Review, *RSA Journal*, Vol.CXXXVIII, No.5410, September 1990, pp.715, 716. Cheryl Buckley, *Potters and Paintresses: Women Designers in the Pottery Industry, 1870–1955*, The Women's Press, 1990; Whitney Chadwick, *Women, Art, and Society*, Thames and Hudson, 1990. Two books published in the same year, one with a focus on the potteries in Stoke-on-Trent, a very specific bit of ceramic history, and the other attempting a view of the whole history of women as artists.

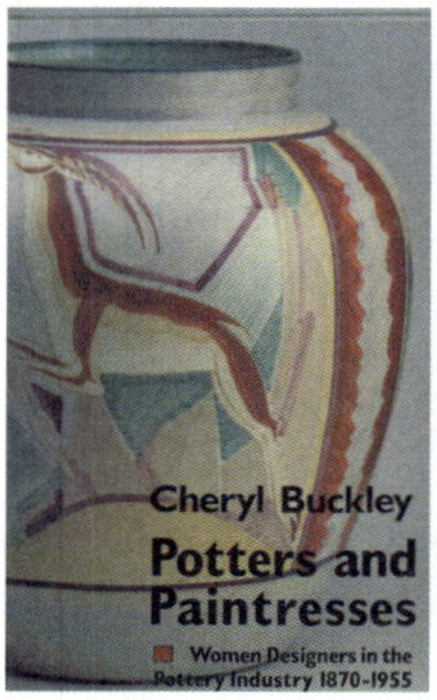

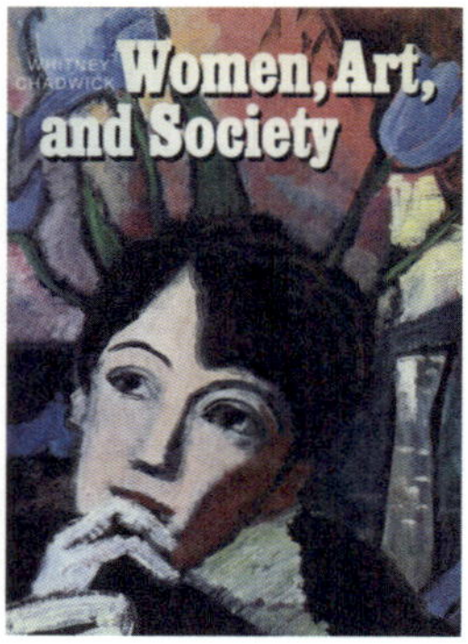

The late 19th century was a time of great debate, definition, and rule-making in the arts as in society. The *Magazine of Art*, in an article by L. Scott, 'Women at Work: Their Functions in Art', declared that 'the instinctive perceptions of woman are often more subtle and finer than those of man; and her heart will guide her to the interpretation of delicacies of sentiment which pass unrecognised by his stronger genius.' In commenting on this quotation, Cheryl Buckley continues: 'Evident in most of these writings is a hierarchical ordering of different branches of art. It was suggested that a woman of great ability (considered a rarity) could work in fine art. But if she combined only intellect and manual skill and lacked the spiritual quality thought to be the distinguishing feature of genius, then she may be said to have talent, and may be a worker in a lower sphere. To her the branches of decorative art are open.'

The decorative, or applied, or lesser arts, have been thought to be the appropriate sphere for women in Western society since the Renaissance. The restricted plan imposed by patriarchal definitions of suitable work for females, is studied in depth in this book which analyses women's role in design in the pottery industry in Britain from 1870 to 1955. The different ways in which some women, from all classes, have pitted themselves against these restrictions, makes inspiring reading. Buckley has made an excellent choice of period, when social change was accelerated by the upheavals of two World Wars, and the subsequent female bias in the population left many women unlikely to marry and in need of the means to live.

The word 'design' had a softer meaning in the 19th century than it holds for us now. I don't think that steam engines were 'designed', and the word could apply very easily to what appeared on the surface of an object, rather than to the object itself. The distinction between shape and surface has been a significant one in the history of the pottery industry in Britain, for with a few spectacular exceptions, up until present times, men have been in charge of shape, and women have provided the surface decoration. Thus, even within the lower-status applied art field of pottery production, the more radical and generative role has been a male one. In the course of this book, which is roughly chronological, Buckley sets out to establish that it is (patriarchal) *ideology* and not *biology*, natural female characteristics, that has prescribed the limitations on what women can achieve in pottery.

Earlier in the 19th century, most women were unskilled slaves in the slip-house, on half the male pay, denied access to apprenticeships. Several factors helped to improve women's chances of interesting work. There were local art schools in the Potteries, where you could study at night after a day in the factory, and some inspired factory owners such as Henry Doulton, who set up an Art Pottery Studio in London as an adjunct to the Stoke-on-Trent works in 1870. The impact of William Morris and the Arts and Crafts movement, with its notions of 'wholeness' in production, as against the division of labour, was also felt. The fact that women were thought to be innately 'dextrous, decorative, delicate, and meticulous' led to them being allowed a stronghold of skill in the decorating departments. This led in the long run to the emergence of Susie Cooper. In the 1930s, she owned her own factory, produced designs that were startling in both shape and pattern, and had a very sound and modern awareness of her changing markets. She is still unique in British pottery history.

Although Cooper is the leading light of this book, she is supported and put in context by many other women designers, including Clarice Cliff. There are others too who deserve to be better known: Hannah Barlow of Doulton, Louise Powell and Millie Taplin of Wedgwood, Freda Beardmore of Foley China, Truda Carter of Poole Potteries in Dorset. Grete Marks was trained at the Bauhaus in Germany, and came to Britain as a refugee, quickly finding work in the Potteries. Dora Billington was a designer in the 1920s, and later taught at London's Central School of Art, where she influenced the generation who turned more to independent studio practice. Jessie Tait worked for Midwinter in the 1950s, responding to the postwar demands for dramatic restyling. This book is clearly and excellently written, and the only improvement I could wish for would be some illustrations in colour that would do more visual justice to the contributions these women made. *Potters and Paintresses* is a close range study of one industry in one country in a specific period. The breadth of material in *Women, Art, and Society* is by contrast immense and encyclopaedic. It covers ten centuries of women's involvement in the visual arts. Chadwick has drawn on existing research, much of which is recent, and often suggests areas that await further investigation.

I used to assume that women's lot in the arts, and in life, had gradually improved over the centuries. It has been most interesting to learn from this book about the downward turns of female fortunes that repeatedly occur through history, new curbs that evolve as society shifts gear. In the Middle Ages, women were involved in mixed guilds, in building and in masonry, in illuminating manuscripts. Respected intellectual women were often leaders of religious orders, some of which were mixed. The Bayeux Tapestry was embroidered by men and women side by side. But the subsequent blossoming of the Renaissance led to a diminution of the artistic role for women. The upgrading of painting and sculpture to heroic status, from being other crafts, and necessitating extensive study of the nude as well as knowledge of mathematics, excluded women's participation.

Ideologically, too, as we have seen from the much later quote above, society was convinced that women were just not cut out for genius. Women were needed as sitters, or subjects, not as protagonists, in the burgeoning secular art. The conflict between active and passive roles in representation is one of the most interesting themes of the book. As with the potters, there have always been some staggering exceptions to convention. In the second half of the 16th century, for instance, Sofonisba Anguissola, an Italian who worked at the Spanish Court, painted a memorable self-portrait that parodies the status quo, painting herself being painted by a fellow male artist, Bernardino Campi. Another dive for female opportunity came in the transition from the 18th to the 19th centuries. The Victorians polarised gender even further, and as recently as the 1940s in America, postwar Abstract Expressionism represented an increase in masculine dominance of art. Lee Krasner was told by a teacher 'this painting is so good you'd never know it was done by a woman'.

Chadwick obviously feels that the Fine Art front is the important one. One might expect her to have given more space to a consideration of post-Renaissance hierarchy, the elevation of painting and sculpture, the notion of the rest being 'lesser' arts. She does argue that 'feminism in the arts has protested against the distinction between "art" and "craft" grounded in their different materials, technical training, and education, and has rejected inscriptions of "feminine" sensibility on craft processes and materials, but it has also pointed out the dangers of sanctifying an artisanal tradition by renaming it "art".' Later on there are examples of 19th-century American quilts and a few pots, and clothes from the daring 1920s, but not very much is made of the points of integration.

The later chapters in the book suffer from overcrowding. Ironically, as more women artists break through the barriers, the text seems taken up with more facts and fewer ideas. Too many hurried biographies are crammed between theoretical points. It is important to put across the expansion of possibilities, but a tighter selection would have been kind to the reader. There is material for several more specialised books in this volume. Perhaps Chadwick will go on to write them.

Rushton Aust

Gallery leaflet, solo exhibition of Rushton Aust, Contemporary Applied Arts, London, 23 February–24 March 1990. Breaking out of the conventions of a material tradition was as apparent in textiles as in any of the craft disciplines in the 1980s and 1990s. This shows in the way Aust was piecing together different fabrics, and arriving at loose outline shapes.

In *The Maker's Eye* catalogue for the Crafts Council exhibition of 1981 – a document that becomes more interesting and valuable with every year that passes – one of the 14 selectors, Michael Brennand-Wood, wrote about the context for his choices: 'There has been an influx of people into the traditional craft-based courses who once might have undertaken a fine art course. A disenchantment with painting courses (especially their incestuousness), and an awareness of the possibilities to be experienced in other areas, has meant that there now exists a group of people with different skills but with a similar desire to make individual pieces of work'.

Rushton Aust is one of these people. And indeed, an early piece of his, before he became a student at the Royal College of Art, was one of the 20 objects selected by Brennand-Wood. It is not anything like the work that he is making a decade later, but it points in the same direction in that it is thoroughly *textile*, using the wax resist process of batik, yet is clearly meant to be hung on the wall and has the size and shape of a painting. It is a single entity, framed by a border. It contains a loose composition of separate striped shapes in beige and grey, like a colony of woodlice heading in many different directions. They are the foreground matter, but the background is broken up with dashes and brushstrokes of much brighter colours, which compete for attention with the main shapes. A strong awareness of the power of colour, and spatial illusion, is already present. The surface still glistens with wax, which has been left in for visual reasons. A well 'crafted' piece of batik would have had it all ironed out. It is evident then that at this early stage, the cloth/painting was a possible area of work for Aust.

He opted at the very beginning, on a foundation course, for the freedom to experiment with new processes in textile printing, thereby avoiding the authoritarian approach and the crowds of people in the fine art room of that particular course. He went on to do a textile diploma in Derby which gave him a sound technical grounding. His 'freedom' has a confident basis in skill and technology. At the Royal College of Art, he took particular trouble to maintain good working relationships with the technicians, and to find out as much as possible about dyes and pigments.

On leaving college Aust worked in a variety of ways, both designing on paper and printing lengths of fabric that were mainly for furnishing. He has designed dress material for Jean Muir, and made costume fabric for the English National Opera. Habitat have commissioned him for one-off furnishing fabric. But over the years he came to realise that he wanted to concentrate on his own independent making, and to get the necessary regular subsistence from teaching two days a week. Now he has a large studio in a Victorian carters' yard with two-storey stable buildings near Elephant and Castle, London. His room is two-thirds filled by the printing table.

I am aware of the need for a better word than 'wall-hanging' to describe what Aust makes. Drab and drooping hessian is conjured up by the term, and these pieces of cloth are ludicrously far from such an image. He has sometimes referred to them as tapestries, though they are not woven or embroidered, because tapestry has a known place: that of being ornamental and serious, wall-mounted, and somewhere between a painting and a carpet. (Carpets, when they are beautiful enough, and indeed camel blankets, are often hung on the wall as if they are too good to use.) These pieces of Aust's certainly *function* as paintings – that is, they are deliberately made to hang, to feed the eye and stimulate the imagination – but they are not paintings, and the ways in which they differ are important to our appreciation.

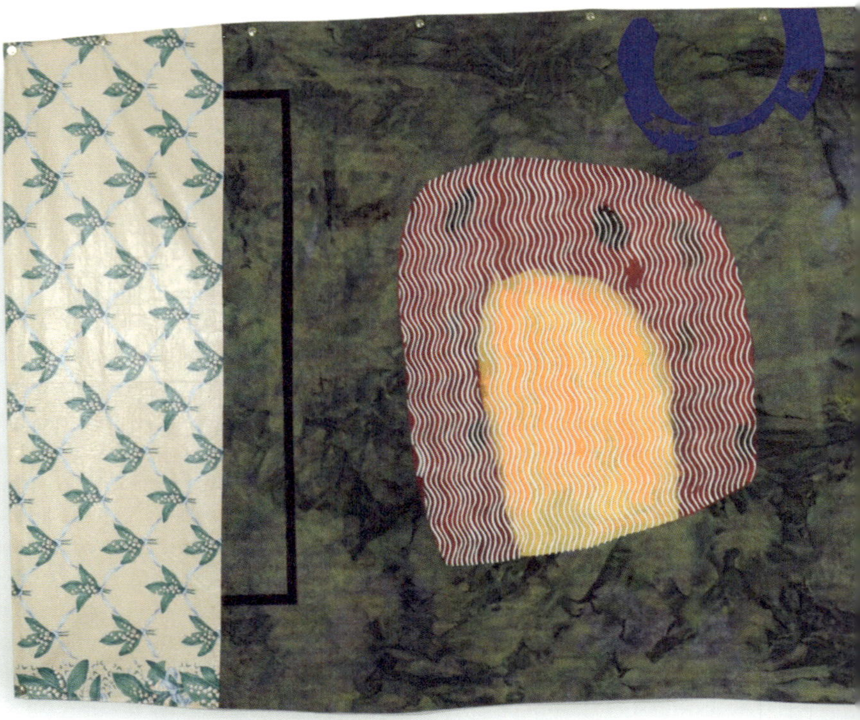

Colour is the main thing on first encountering his work. Aust has a startling and full-blooded sense of colour, which is built up in layers and is full of brilliance and contrast. Murky figured backgrounds are played off against blocks of clean, dazzling stripes, like psychedelic military ribbons. Compositions are abstract and roughly geometric, though sometimes there are figurative references – the stylised features of a face, a wheeled vehicle, a fork, a lemon with a blue label, a carburetor, pieces of writing we can't read. The colour is *textile* colour, dye and pigment. Dye is transparent and is soaked right into the fibres of the cloth, and has a very different quality from paint, which still rests on the surface, however thinly it is applied to canvas. Textile pigment is more like paint, and can be opaque if used thickly, and gives the singing richness that he needs to make colours float, visually, off the background.

The colour is silk-screen printed and painted. The rapidity and directness of the printing technique is appealing to Aust. Some screens are left open, that is they have no pattern fixed on the gauze, and are used

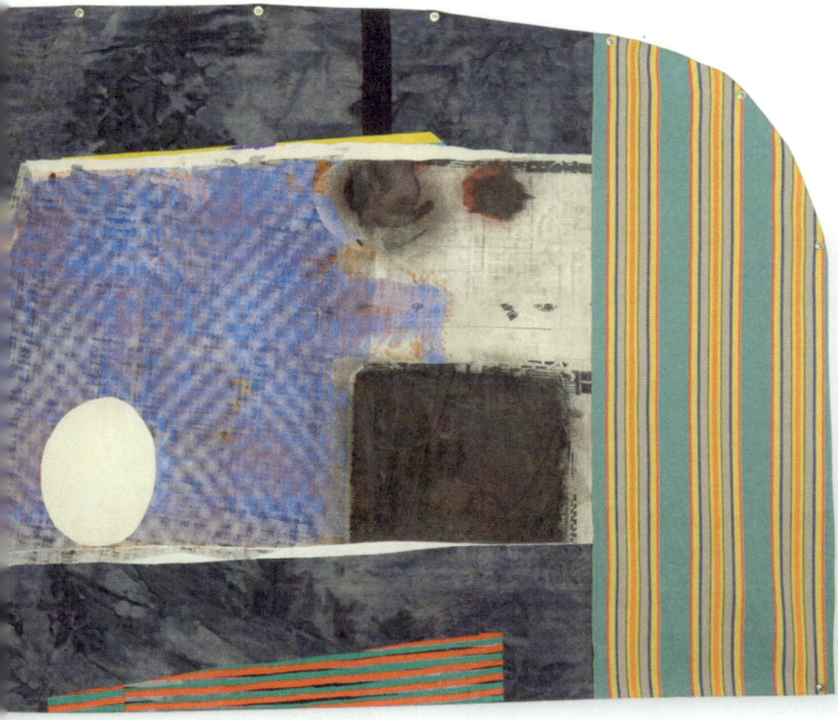

over a bold paper resist, or to make loose painterly stripes with mingling pigments. Old screens with rather conventional repeating textile patterns from student days are also incorporated, and bring depth to the gradual building up of layers. Discarded furnishing lengths may be the basis and the initial stimulus for a new piece of work, perhaps juxtaposing two very different pieces, and bringing them together through the overprinting. Stripes are often a feature of the bringing together. Pieces of existing fabric made by others are also used in recent works, like deckchair canvas or frumpy glazed chintz with climbing honeysuckle patterns, from the shops near his family home in rural Oxfordshire.

The piecing and layering, although the final surface is perfectly flat and all the sense of depth is illusory, contributes to the works having some of the qualities of collage. Collage puts discarded fragments into a new and justifying aesthetic context; it is built up from disconnected elements that make new sense in their visual relation to one another. The careful resonance of composing with disparate things, unexplained images, wild colours, is likewise the strongest impression of these powerful pieces of cloth. It is not surprising to learn that Aust finds and collects things, bits of interesting rubbish, old mechanisms, labels, fruit wrappings. His sketch books are of vital everyday use, and compile drawings and scraps and written messages. The flow of energy into the work is concentrated; he is a quiet and vehement worker.

Although it is not unknown for silk-screen printing to be a part of a painting, the second distinct way in which Aust's work defines itself as *not* painting is in the fact that the cloth, which may be canvas these days though he used to use lighter weight cotton, is not stretched tightly over a wooden frame to become a semi-solid object. We talk about hanging paintings, but we are really resting the stiff frame against the wall, suspending the frame and not the painting. Aust's pieces of cloth hang freely, so that a draught would ripple them, from a wooden rod slotted into the top, or from brass eyelet holes punched in along the upper edge. The flexibility of fabric is still apparent.

Large scale is not a problem for Aust, and for this exhibition he has made good use of the height of the space at Contemporary Applied Arts. For the first time the cloth is not always rectangular – some pieces are shaped into long tapering tongues or shield shapes. Some pieces are still on a domestic scale, but Aust is poised at the perfect moment for a really good commission for some splendid public space. An opportunity is presented here that should not be missed.

Previous spread: Rushton Aust, *Collected Elements*, 1989, photo: John McCarthy

The Manipulation of Skill
On the Outer Limits of Function

Essay, *Beyond the Dovetail, Craft, Skill and Imagination*, exhibition catalogue, Crafts Council, 19 September–10 November, 1991, pp.4–9. *Beyond the Dovetail* was a polemic exhibition about skill curated by Peter Dormer, the catalogue edited by Christopher Frayling. The last essay was Dormer's, aspiring 'to put art and craft and the whole business of 'self-expression' into perspective'.

In many people's minds there is a split between skill and ideas that is comparable to the split between craft and art. Furthermore, they think that skill belongs to craft and ideas belong to art. And tradition belongs to skill and craft, and innovation belongs to ideas and art. To sustain these notions you need to be thinking of skill as a manual thing, the gnarled and noble hand. But in reality the manual and the mental are seamlessly combined in the operation of skill, whether you are ploughing a field or painting the Sistine Chapel. The basic demand, of course, is excellence, doing it well. Thinking is a skill too that some people have more of than others. Seeing may also be a skill – certainly it can be developed and tuned up. Judging when to stop making something is one of the greatest skills the artist or craftsperson needs to possess. All kinds of awareness of life and society and appropriateness are part of the bag of skills that the artist needs, as well as the astute correlation of hand and eye.

Nobody, not even someone who retreats to idyllic isolation, can carry on a serious working and producing life in a vacuum. Acquiring the practical skills to achieve the chosen ends is usually fairly straightforward, though in the case of something like glass-blowing it will be long drawn out. But acquiring the sense of purpose, the discovery of what is viable and worth making, in the current and changing situation, is the hard part. In this pursuit the cerebral skills and the outward eye on the world, general awareness and nous, are the useful things to have. Some makers miss this point, get bogged down in practicalities, techniques and recipes, and seduced by what was traditionally useful. But what I would define as our main responsibility is the skilful achievement of relevance.

Obviously there was a time, and it is still this time in some cultures, when craft skills were essential to everything, to life going on at all. And art was entirely purposeful too, images were needed to demonstrate and illustrate beliefs. But in the industrialised, multi-nationalised and largely irreligious Western world, this clear context for art and craft has long gone. Of course there are craft skills in the building trades, in assembling bicycles, filling teeth. But the craft-made artifact, the independent handmade object, has become a self-conscious thing seeking to justify itself against the mass-produced, cheaper and more rational competition. I have no wish to argue any more about the distinctions between art and craft and where to draw the line, but I just know it is a continuum, unified by uselessness, or rather by a unitedly inessential existence outside the practical mainstream. Crafts are an extra. The motivation in making, and the expectations in consuming, the independent craft or art object are equivalent. Function does not differentiate them.

The question of relevance is important because it may undermine the practice of a familiar expertise. Picasso could draw a straight portrait perfectly well but for the large part of his enormous oeuvre he chose not to do so. I spent very many hours as a student learning to throw pots, I invested myself in the acquisition of that skill, and yet found it unsuitable for what I wanted to make. Throwing implies the production of a symmetrical round form, which did not seem to answer my desires for an improvisational mode of working. Throwing is generally thought to be more skilful than hand-building. The artist's path is habitually, in the modern Western world, a search for freshness, alternatives, new angles. The pace of life, technology and culture has shifted so fast in this century; there are so many links of reaction in the chain.

In previous centuries a high level of finish, smoothness, regularity and perfection was arduous to achieve and consequently high prestige was attached to it. Mechanical advances and mass-production processes in this century have turned the tables; streamlining is now commonplace. It is this progression that largely accounts for the oppositional craving for roughage and idiosyncrasy that is apparent among both the practitioners and the audience of craft and art. The switch from white to brown bread has its parallels in all levels of our culture. The ragged mark of the human hand/eye/mind is necessary and desirable both socially and artistically in this postmodern period. That is why artists and craftspeople sometimes choose to sidestep their skills and disrupt the polish. Smoothness suggests conformity and complacency, the hewn may be more apt for this moment than the honed.

There is perhaps another interesting parallel to compare with the sleek and the rough, and the functional and the useless, and that is the issue of representation and abstraction. A representational painting is a good manifestation of skill, because we know more clearly what the goals are. Does the painting look like the subject, revealed in the title? Verisimilitude is something you can tick off with satisfaction, and there can be further comfort in the choice of the subject matter itself. On a simple level, you can warm to a picture because the subject pleases you, an open landscape, a sturdy horse, a pretty woman, never mind the manner of its execution. The notion of a culturally acceptable subject is part of the study of developments in art history. Artists like Chaim Soutine, who went for ugly carcasses, stretch people beyond the conventions into looking at qualities of paint and modes of representation. But there will always be people who don't develop their skills in visual response, who only feel safe with representational art and functional craft. They feel they are being hoodwinked by abstraction and useless craftwork – there is always the threat of the emperor's new clothes. At another edge of the spectrum of the audience there are those for whom uselessness and abstraction are the ultimate virtues because of their aesthetic purity, their lack of compromise. It is just that the criteria for sifting the good from the bad in these areas are harder to pin down, and are more like opinions than rules.

The only representational work that I do is writing. I notice that finishing a piece of writing can give me an acute thrill quite unlike finishing making a pot. I think it is the sense of aiming for the target that is satisfying – capturing something, hopefully, the portrayal of a fellow artist, the expression in sharply approximate language of a sequence of ideas. Also, perhaps, I allow myself the thrill because it is not my real work. In my real pottery work the goals are unknown. I am not representing any known thing, loosely adhering to a pot category, but trying to make something out of nothing, to put an object into the world that looks sensible and wasn't there before. And finishing a pot is not very much of an ending, it is another stage in the continuing struggle to keep on the track of what is vivid and worth making, and to take another step.

I don't consider that I am using any fewer skills in the potting than in the writing. How different are the skills? The stages in the working process are the same. There is procrastination, a sense of empty and patheticness. The pressure of the deadline always motivates the ultimate start. Then there is exhilaration at being engaged, strengthening commitment and dedication to sorting out the knots. A sense of risk that is very pleasurable and anxiety about not overworking it, the avoidance of polish; leaving in time. I end up with a disinclination to change to another mode of work, the urge to stay doing whatever I have been doing.

These are the similarities of process. The materials are different. I think of words as an invisible material; manipulating punctuation is like focussing the attention on certain points in the painted surface of a pot. However, in potmaking a more manual and visual set of skills are in play: my experience of clay, the background expectations of what it will and won't tolerate, a sense of the right thickness, feeling when a joint is solid; my double vision for looking at a raw painted line that is sickly mauve and knowing it will be deepest blue after firing, and composing a balance of colours that is fictitious; spraying off-white glaze onto an off-white bumpy slip-covered surface, and seeing when it is just enough by the state of saturation (too much glaze leads to a fatal sheen and even bubbling). Most of these sensibilities are a personal kit of skills, useful to me but not in the same form useful to anyone else. That is the break with tradition. People develop new skills to achieve untraditional ends, and they aren't always of general and impartable use. I strongly believe that the traditional skills should be taught as a basis, but not as the whole curriculum. But we can't avoid the climate of appropriateness that moves on with time and changing purposes. Nostalgia is a dead end.

When the Impressionists started exhibiting they were thought to be atrociously unskilled, and John Ruskin thought John Constable was an incompetent painter. The shock of the new is a never-ending phenomenon. New work must always start by being judged on old criteria.

Sometimes in looking at craftwork now I have in mind the idea of 'good enough' making. Faced with the choice between a piece that is exquisitely well made and in a very well-trodden familiar form, and a piece that is awkwardly made but in a convincing and unexpected form, I would always go for the latter. There is always plenty of overcooked work around that has skill but no thinking; the virtuoso twiddles without the guts or sense of place.

The last convention about skill that I would like to question is the idea that skill and expression are somehow in opposition, that you have to have one or the other. Skill is orderly and controlled, and expression is free and exciting but it's going to be messy. I would say that a Sèvres porcelain classical figure from the 18th century is entirely expressive of the beliefs, tastes, aspirations and narrative interests of its consumers and makers. It is also a refined technical achievement, carefully modelled from historic references, moulded, cast and predetermined. In just such a way a Philip Eglin earthenware figure speaks of its time. It is constructed with great bravado and a knowledgeable looseness. The joints of the limbs say more about clay than flesh. The poses and the demeanour of the women are full of historical reverence, and yet he has painted all over them. Not just painted, he has slapped and sloshed fierce coloured metal oxide pigments over their bodies in great strokes and dribbles and scrawls of words. Why is this necessary, why has he messed them up? Unpainted they would seem like attempts at reproduction, too daunted by the past. As they are, they link the characteristic palette of ceramics, traditions of Staffordshire popular figures, with a homage to Lucas Cranach and the aggressive deconstructive dash of a modern urban upbringing. The control is there in the thinking and the making, but it does not confine the sense of exuberance. These are expressive works of admirable skill. They combine the comfort of the familiar with the sense of not going backwards.

Craft
Sustaining Alternatives

Introduction, Martina Margetts, *International Crafts*, Thames and Hudson, 1991, pp.5–9.
The publisher planned to produce a new version of this book every two years as the international craft world seemed to be so actively evolving at the time. In the event this was the only one.

The breadth and ambiguity of the craft field is what has always attracted me to it. You can be concerned with basic practicalities or with elusive ideas, feet on the ground or head in the clouds, or both. Work in the crafts today covers a very wide spectrum from the traditional to the invented, and from the functional to the abstract. All kinds of qualities can be manifested from the raggedly hewn to the meticulously detailed, from the brash to the restrained. It all depends on the object.

The crafts sit in the middle of art and design, but they are not a refuge or a backwater. The idea that the crafts are *safe*, a haven from the commercial guile of designed mass-production on the one hand and the provocative dangers of fine art on the other, is denied by the range of unforeseen and experimental work made by some of the artists shown in this book. The last 20 years have seen great developments in this middle field. Good craftwork can be exhilarating, tactile, reassuring, stunning, disconcerting – the whole gamut of feeling can be evoked. The response to a craft object can be physical, emotional, or intellectual. The narrative, the useful, and the purely formal all have a place in the crafts.

Objects can tell us a great deal about the people that made, used, displayed and owned them. Museums collect door handles as well as heroic paintings. (And museums now are buying contemporary craftwork.) New thinking in museum studies, and the development of writing of design and craft history, are making greater and deeper sense of the objects that have been gathered into museums over the centuries. In this enriched context the new craftwork has found an audience and a place.

But why do we still have the crafts? They are no longer essential to our existence in the modern world – there are other ways of doing things. The props of daily life are more quickly and cheaply made in factories. The crafts are needed and wanted for a complicated variety of reasons. These include nostalgia, aesthetic accessibility, notions of individuality and – what is more surprising – an ideology of opposition. In a succession of waves, the crafts have functioned as a small but serious crosscurrent against the drift of development in industrialised society. What might be called the self-conscious crafts, things that are made by hand, by choice, as a deliberate alternative to mass-production, are about a century old. The ideas of William Morris and John Ruskin are still a point of reference. While the Arts and

Crafts movement in Britain saw the crafts as a bastion against dehumanising industry, on the continent the instigators of the modern movement believed the opposite. They took great interest in the socialist aspects of Arts and Crafts theory, but they had a positive view of industry. They thought that by engaging with it, and harnessing craft practice to it, they could make things in mass-production which contained the values of beauty, utility, etc. and which really were available to everyone. These early design pioneers were not ostriches; they were open to technology. A new synthesis of art and design and craft, collaborating with industry, was seen to be the answer to social needs of the time. Artists, architects, sculptors and craftspeople of all kinds could work together. This was the spirit of the Bauhaus school in Germany (1919–33).

Bauhaus theory embraced craft as a very important part of the training of designers, but not as an end in itself. Craft was there to re-energise art and design, to put manual and material understanding back into an effete drawingboard approach. But modernist design, though it was rational, sensible, democratic and accessible, brought a uniformity and standardisation that was not ultimately what people wanted. (One of the ironies of modernism has been that the crafts were marginalised in an area where they could have made such a helpful contribution, in the humanising of the details of the built environment. In recent times this role is being recovered; both in building and in some areas of product design an input from the crafts is now more welcome.)

In the 1960s, I can remember Pete Seeger singing about houses that were 'Little boxes, all the same'. This conjures up the atmosphere of frustration with uniformity in which the crafts, like folksinging, had a place in reaffirming people's difference, their individuality, their do-it-yourself independence. People with PhDs became carpenters, grew onions, travelled vast distances, wore homemade clothes. *Making* things (perhaps badly) was revalidated. Making something yourself can be a gesture of protest in a technological world of increasing creative powerlessness and passivity. It is not possible to separate the roots of this amateur phenomenon distinctly from the craft revival that we are currently still experiencing, although we are now at a very different stage in its progress, with established professional practitioners leading the various fields.

I think it would be a surprise to the early modernists to learn of the survival of the craft approach. It does seem that the decades of impeccable, streamlined, regular manufactured objects have left people with a hunger for contradiction, for things that show signs of having been made by a human, with unrepeatable qualities. Made things communicate defiance of the machine, and express 'difference' clearly and instantly.

The philosophy and literature of this century often have been concerned with the idea of man as a separate being, an individual. People can express their sense of self through the things they use, own and wear, as well as by what they say and do. The choosing of something that is evidently not run-

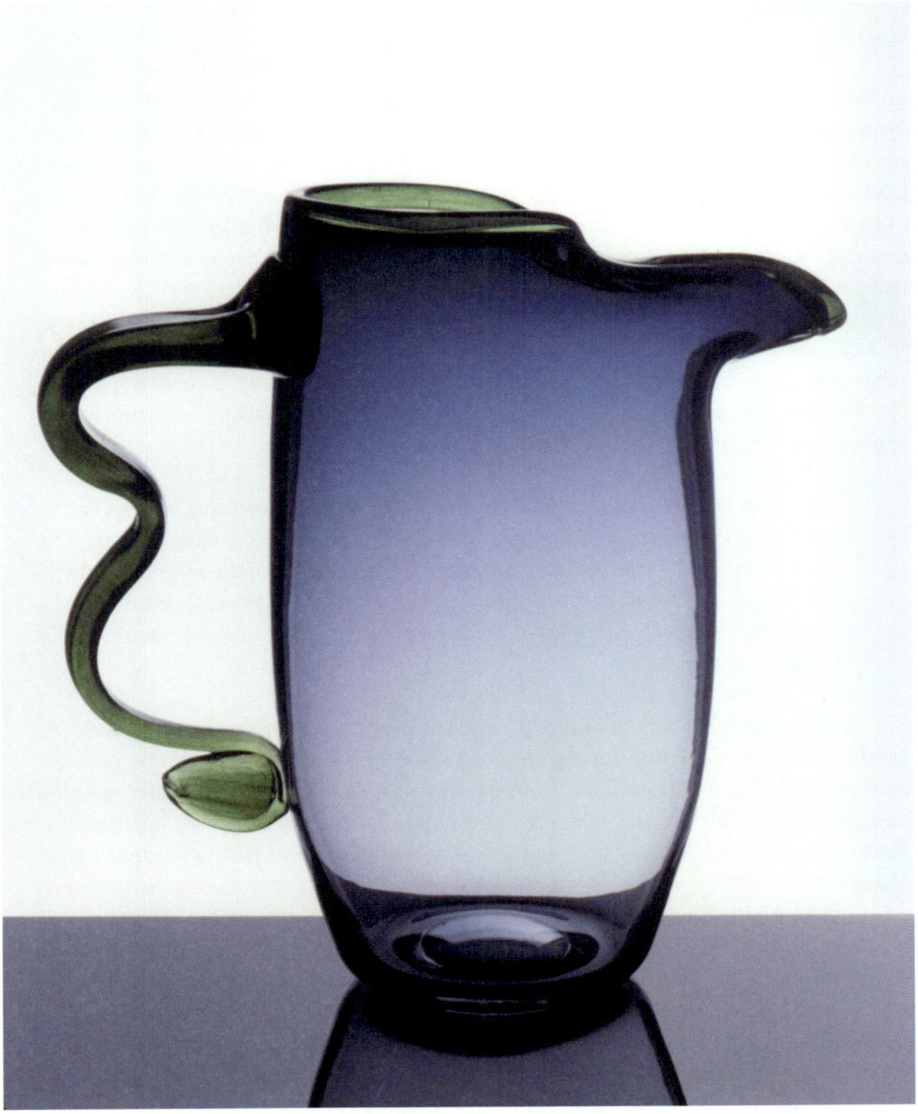

Christopher Williams, *Big Jug*, 1989, photo: David Cripps

of-the-mill can be self-revelatory in a satisfying way. This is why the one-off object has held its place in our desires.

Craftwork does nothing to threaten industry, but it does in a quiet way subvert the norms, in both the objects that it produces and in the peculiar kinds of living it provides. The idea of making things to sell and surviving in a hand-to-mouth fashion is one that has gained momentum in the last 30 years. Like many of the other arts practices, it is now an aspect of the 'alternative' culture. Craftspeople, in common with other artists and some of the self-employed, choose to work in a way that means they have maximum control over what they produce. They are stubborn, determined and independent, and usually put up with difficult working conditions and low and erratic pay to achieve this ideal mode of work. They need to feel convinced about what they make, or it wouldn't be worth it. Whether they live in a rural idyll or in the middle of a crowded terrace, the decision to be a maker is some sort of statement – an interruption of the mainstream.

> It is this that drives me to turn each pot into something improvised and different and to squander days, even weeks, on the making and painting of one vessel. I suspect that the making of art at all in this society has to be in defiance of economic pressures and psychic repressions; a kind of insistence on some measure of freedom and magic.[1]

But the craft world is not a random one of disconnected expressive spirits. Craftwork is inevitably linked to strong aesthetic traditions, and to proven techniques. There are times when reminders of past values are useful and times to push on and overturn the rules. I would not want to suggest that craft production has only opposed modernism and not brushed with it. Modernism, after all, is a principle and not a style. It is not just concerned with mass-production; it seeps into painting and novel writing as much as blocks of high-rise flats. The modern movement wanted to clothe the values of a new era in a different language, and who could complain about that?

The spirit of enquiry, without preconceptions, into new forms and relevant new materials has been very much part of recent crafts history. This has been particularly noticeable in jewelry, lighting and furniture. Many areas of the crafts have been questioning whether or not function is obligatory, and whether the *idea* of function is an interesting subject, as it is to the still-life painter of pots and pans. The catalogue to *The Maker's Eye* exhibition in 1982, for which a very mixed group of craftspeople chose objects that were important to them from the previous decade, is one that becomes increasingly interesting as time passes.[2] I wrote in it about 'two-faced' objects that were both functional and self-questioning, poised between real life and still-life. Having made my choices and written my statement, I realised that this was an area of concern at the time to a whole group of artists making objects across several different media. In a previous generation they might have been making sculpture; now they were keen to look closely into the characteristics of ordinary useable things – the chair, the jug, the box.

Besides looking around the house, the crafts have looked far afield for sources of interest and excitement too. They have inhaled the primitive and the exotic, which bring a powerful narrative of 'elsewhere', and the types of early modern art such as Cubism, whose exponents were so impressed with these strange forms. The last half of this complicated century has seen on many fronts a great reaching out to be surprised, refreshed and stimulated by unfamiliar non-Western traditions. Craft works from distant places, from other very different societies, have had great appeal to the jaded Western public. The development of a multi-cultural eye has broadened the range of what is made here, and what is wanted. The quest for new forms is not something that comes to an end.

The fascination for makers in coming across craftwork from far afield has partly to do with the way it is made – a desire to understand different kinds of skill. Skill is an issue at the moment in the crafts, the crafts having developed such new forms over the last 20 years. The generation that trained at art colleges in the early 1970s found their own paths with new approaches to techniques and unconventional materials, and a general quest

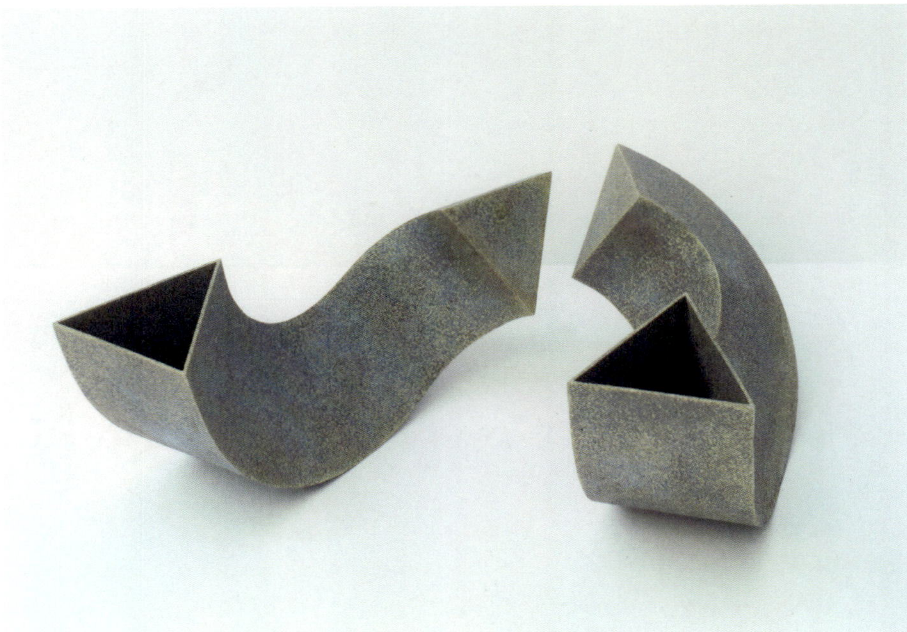

Robert Marsden, *Opposite Spouts*, 1986, photo: Robert Marsden

for colour in all sorts of substances. They usually had traditional skills behind them. The following generation is missing some of the basics.

In my experience of teaching graduates, fewer and fewer students of ceramics are able to throw, for instance, or understand much about glaze. The tendency in ceramics has been towards irregular and handbuilt forms and dry, unreflective painterly surfaces. Exciting new ground is gained, but there are potential losses in the breadth of the body of standard potters's knowledge. People became skilled in more personal and diverse ways, evolving specific means to suit a particular imagined form. There is great skill and ambition in some of the new ways of handbuilding, piecing together a thin skin of clay, keeping the plastic and immediate, unworked qualities. I know there are equivalent examples of innovative technique in other craft fields.

I am not convinced that we are facing a crisis in the disappearance of traditional skills. At present many of them are still in reach and I think that we should offer them in teaching while we can, where there is a sensible context and not just for the sake of preservation. The pursuit of personal expression will inevitably take up new threads of skill and drop some old ones. I believe that the critics who are mourning the diminution of skill forget that a culture has its own pace. At any one time, not everything is potentially interesting enough to raise the energy and conviction to get on and *do* it. With subject matter and with the necessary skills, some things are in the air and others aren't. To ignore this is to opt for dead work.

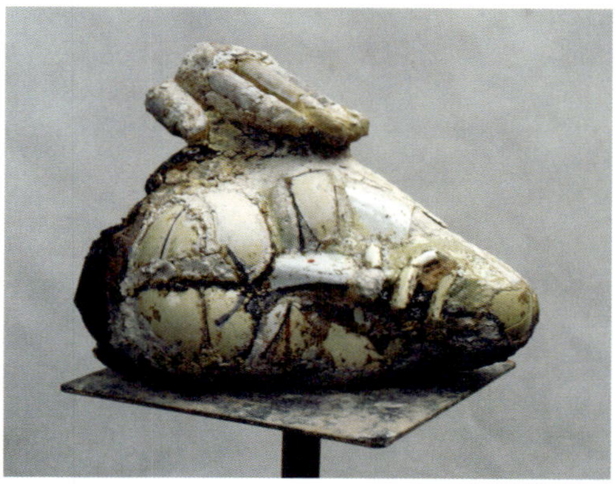

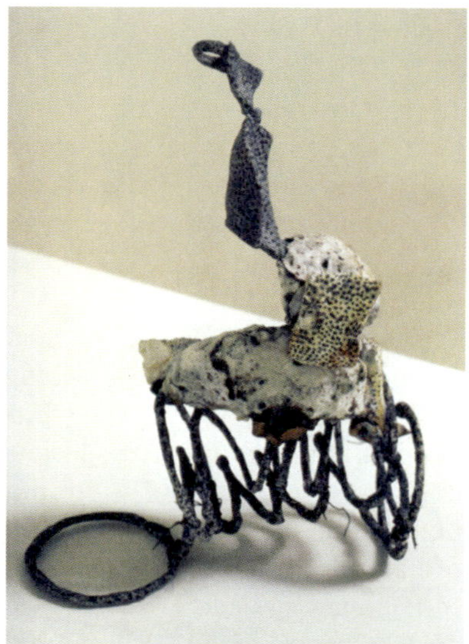

Left: Gertraud Möhwald, *Reclining Head*, 1990
Right: Gillian Lowndes, *Collage with Cup*, 1986, photo: Tim Hill

Certainly I know that I always have the same reaction of dismay when I see something that is made perfectly, a virtuoso triumph, but has no thinking behind it, no point to it, no relevance or life; where the use of the skill in itself has been a justification. There is plenty of that sort of slick and empty work about. It is one of the most disappointing cul-de-sacs of the craft world. Such work proliferates in a climate where great emphasis is placed on *how* things are done, often as a sort of entertainment. Popular interest in the crafts may well begin with the practicalities, watching demonstrations and so on. While this is not to be discouraged, it is a pity that so often people fail to get past an appreciation of skill into questions of context or meaning.

In contrast to the respect for 'polished' skill, sometimes we particularly value craftwork for its roughness and spontaneity. Ruskin was fully aware of this. He thought that liveliness and vigour and the positive mark of humanity were manifested in rough work. He cherished the unprecious handling of the carving in Gothic churches, the irregularities and the imperfections. The sense of the carvers having been happy in their work was part of the visual pleasure. This has echoes for us today: the direct gesture, collage, assembly, interest in used materials, evidence of making as a kind of decoration – all these have been seen in art and craft in modern times. They could all be described as kinds of roughness.

'Craft' means many different things to different ears. I must say that I do not find the word an easy one to use. Some people are put off by it altogether; it smacks to them of frumpiness and a retreat from the modern world. Paradoxically, that is exactly what others are looking for: comfort in the crafts. Writing in an exhibition leaflet in 1985 I tried to do without it.

> Craft is a means to an end and is not really anything in itself. It consists in doing something properly, and it is a basis of recognition of values and skills and methods and knowledge of materials. It has no real substance or meaning without one or other of these leanings: the design world and the art word have equal need of it.[3]

None of the terms decorative art, applied art, design art, craft – do quite the whole job of delineating the territory. Some craftwork, in furniture for instance, is indistinguishable in its aims from design but is made perhaps in smaller quantities and by slower means. Some craftwork blurs with fine art in its cerebral intentions, but may be made of materials unauthenticated by the conventions of fine art practice. A book like this may suggest that the crafts are a category with distinct edges, but this is not the case. It is quite fruitless to try and draw clear dividing lines between the three parts of the continuum, and it doesn't matter.

There is pleasure and freedom in the condition of being loosely defined. Ambiguity is the mother of invention. Makers have thrived on the variety of possibilities, the overlaps between disciplines, and the provisional

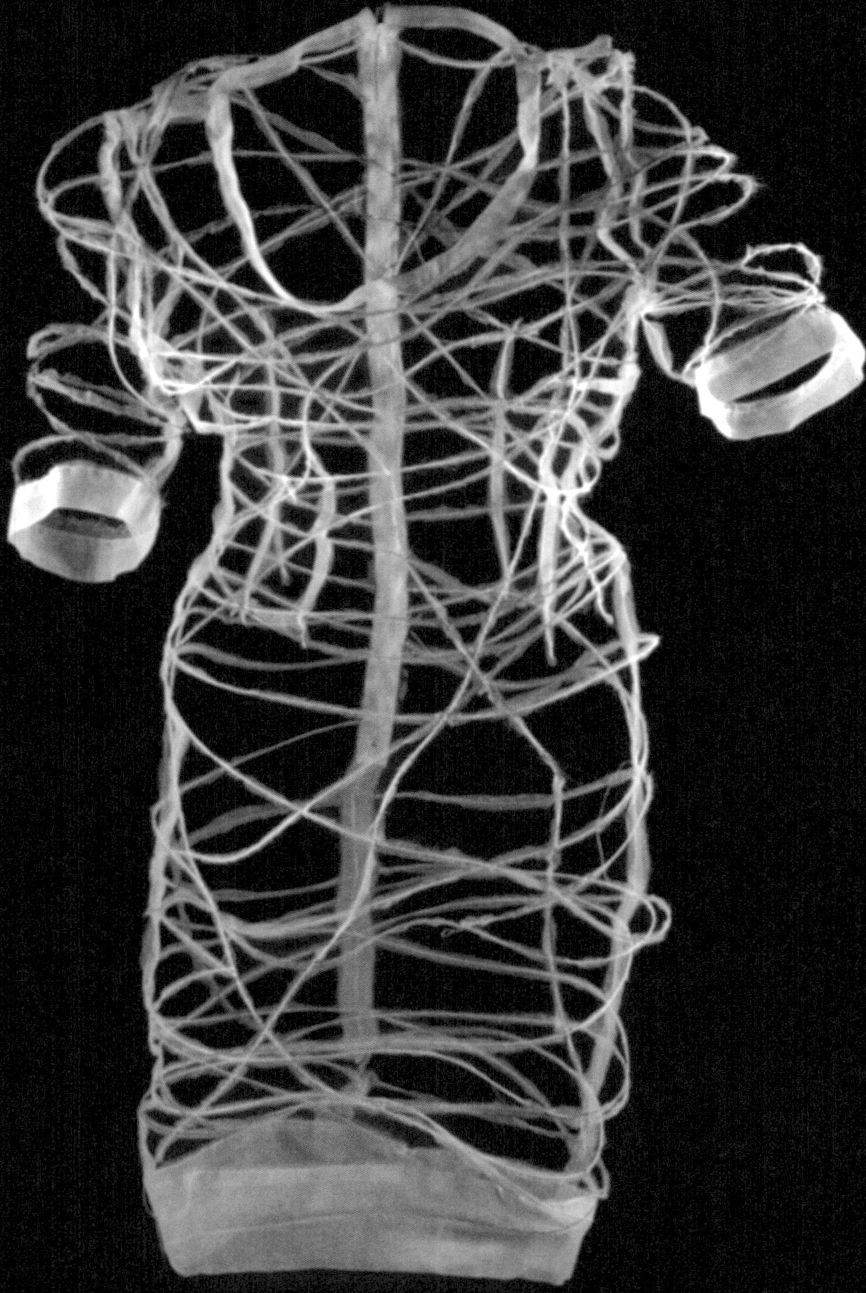

Caroline Broadhead, *Web,* 1990, photo: Graham Portlock

atmosphere. Some makers have stuck to a narrow path, others have crossed media, synthesised and accumulated. The conventions of the past have been of great interest in the search for meanings outside the functional. Figurative work, animal and human, is a current preoccupation among many younger artists. Perhaps the state of the world's ecology is the cause. It is also noticeable that artists are recycling pieces of wood, metal or cloth. The choice of already used materials can be metaphorical, or may express the conservational mood of the times. Work like this is triggered by the artist's attraction to the found object. It is a question of personality. Some people like to fill empty spaces, start from scratch, control everything others can only respond to a different kind of creative pressure and take their cue from something that is picked up, or something that happens – a clue towards subject matter. Some of the endless options are curtailed.

In the course of travelling to exhibit and talk in North America, Australia, Japan, Czechoslovakia and other parts of Europe, I have had the chance to see a great variety of practice in craftwork. The more I have seen, the less inclined I am to make a qualitative judgment. The differences, and the background reasons for those differences have amazed me. But I think that a common thread could be that many people choose to work in the crafts because close involvement with a material brings a set of limitations that are stimulating to work with. I would suggest that pleasure in limitations is a characteristic that distinguishes craft practice from that of fine art or design.

What I cherish in the crafts, besides this quality of blossoming through the constraints, is the celebration of the hybrid. Pieces of textile that are *like* painting but not confused with it, free-hanging, like tapestry. Jewelry that can easily be worn, but looks intact when it is by itself hung on the wall. The chairs or pots or sheet metal containers that tantalisingly echo the shapes of other ambiguous objects. Beautifully finished brooches made from tin cans; intriguing touches of the incongruous. Makers may need to ignore conventions to get closer to an accurate realisation of an idea or a feeling. They have been doing this for centuries – that is how a culture moves along. Like an amoeba unconsciously gathering up little gestures of advance.

To me the value and importance of the crafts exist in their refusal to be completely one thing or another. It may be middle-class and middle ground, but the crafts territory as it is now encourages some dazzling and subtle subversions of our expectations. This sort of work is worth doing and worth writing about.

1. Elizabeth Fritsch, *Pots About Music,* Leeds Art Galleries, 1978.
2. *Five Furniture Pieces,* London, 1985.

Scale and Meaning
Hopes for Public Art

This unpublished essay was written in 1992 at the end of a public art writing workshop at the Crafts Council, led by the architecture and design critic Deyan Sudjic, now Director of the Design Museum, London.

In using the word public we often manage to convey something inferior, substandard – the public bar, public housing, public baths – structures to accommodate the poor rather than simply available to everybody. In particular, the experience of living in Britain through the 1980s has reinforced the stigma, and established the curiosity of the word 'public', meaning with increasing frequency: 'private'. The Public School, of course, has always been there to confuse foreigners.

And so when it comes to a discussion of public art it is hard to escape the tainted idea of it being patronisingly imposed, good for you, and third-rate. It seems to be implied that this sort of art is presented to a completely different set of people than those who might choose to walk into a gallery or a museum, and that there are no overlaps. Art lovers are indoors exercising their discretion, while massive windswept constructions are planted in shopping precincts to divert the hoi polloi from excessive spending. It is like the gulf between a meal in a restaurant, carefully chosen from a printed menu, and school dinners that are plonked on the table in front of you. But, in practice – and the practice is on the increase despite the recession or perhaps incorporated in the recession – there is continuity between gallery art and public art, with regard to both the artists involved and some of the audience. Public art schemes can also be initiated and administrated by gallery or museum people. In practice, the two kinds of work are not so different.

In considering what public art might be, is it defined by who has picked up the bill, meaning publicly funded as opposed to privately owned? Or is it more significant that there are distinctions between outdoors and indoors, institutions and homes; works that are site-specific and those that are portable, permanent and ephemeral, or even big and small?

Bigness is a perceptible feature of the way in which artists have been thinking since the World War Two (certainly apparent in the dominant strains of American Abstract Expressionism). Big means confident and victorious. In the search for peaceful ways to be excited, and to stretch aesthetic boundaries, scale has been important in individually expressive modes; not as before when superhuman scale was reserved for expressions of commonly held beliefs, religious faith, height for holiness.

Big works are a challenge to the maker, a focus of intention for the postwar artist, and can generally only be accessible to people if they are out-of-doors. They are otherwise confined to an existence in a museum or a large bureaucratic building; they can't be lived with, since the homes of the art-buying classes get smaller and smaller. Intimacy is precluded. (Ownership is one aspect of intimacy). With increased scale, dwarfing the human frame, there is the chance of exhilaration as an alternative. For centuries we have registered the visual difference between the home and the cathedral (and private and public space). Scale and awe. The Richard Serra sculpture at Broadgate is awe-inspiring, much like a secular cathedral.

Public art represents an opportunity for art to engage in the real domain, to risk an open, broad audience reception, not to be ghettoised. It seems to me, and here I fall into the error of assuming that I know what is good for people, that at this late stage in our spending and consuming culture and society, it is still important even when it is contrived that such interaction occurs; between ordinary people and extraordinary objects; functionless objects that are Things in their own right, that can be seen but not bought, and change the look and feel of a place. A form of resistance.

Public art can be located in both rural and urban sites. For the artist the choice of competition is with nature or with architecture. Most artists seem to specialise, to prefer one or the other. Sculpture parks out in the wild are on the increase. The UK Forestry Commission has allowed sculptures to be made in several forests, of which Grizedale in the Lake District is probably the biggest. A number of trees felled by a big hurricane were made good with public art commissions. Jim Partridge, for instance, has made seats, paths, bridges and stepping-stones and shelters out of fallen trees in various wood and parks.

Richard Deacon is a sculptor who prefers the urban context, although he is planning to make a piece that will float on a river in Germany. He talks of the stimulus of his frequent antagonism to architecture. He makes objects not to complement it or to decorate it, but offering an alternative to it: the sculpture as another kind of form, unpredictable, throwing the raw in with the cooked. The particular site is an instigator of the idea. He has chosen areas of unexpected incompleteness on a few occasions, like bridges where the bridge has been removed and only the massive brick piers remain; sites where the landscape is unclear; conjunctions of disparate things, boundaries. In one commission for the town of Krefeld in Germany, he cycled around for several days and was allowed to choose any place he wanted.

Public art will only be as good as its administrators, however it is funded. Choosing appropriate artists, and getting them to work in sites that they have some feeling for, is essential but not easy. The 'Percent for Art' scheme as a blanket proposition is full of pitfalls, and threatens to engender an industry, spewing up excrescences for every 100th wall. On the whole the architects are still the enemy, and not usually the initiators of schemes.

Let us hope that with experience, local policy will broaden out in the use of this percentage to include temporary things – things that extend the visual experience of the site and are not only preoccupied with fixing things to it.

Urban living at the end of the 20th century is complicated and confusing. Our behaviour in, and understanding of, public and private space has been thrown about by the density and shifts of the population, the demise of shared beliefs, and the dominance of television as a main source of reality. You only have to watch people in cars in traffic jams to observe the behavioural confusion in the mingling of public and private territory. Art in the urban public space has a tough job communicating a universal meaning to a population that is increasingly tending to individual and separate cultural pleasure: the novel, the Walkman.

But the visual arts are physically evident, out there in front of us, to be seen to be believed. They can be taken in at a glance or pondered over, alone or shared. Public art, above all, is out in the open and inherently sociable. It can only do harm to the progress of alienation. Perhaps all art that aspires to the relation of meaning is public anyway.

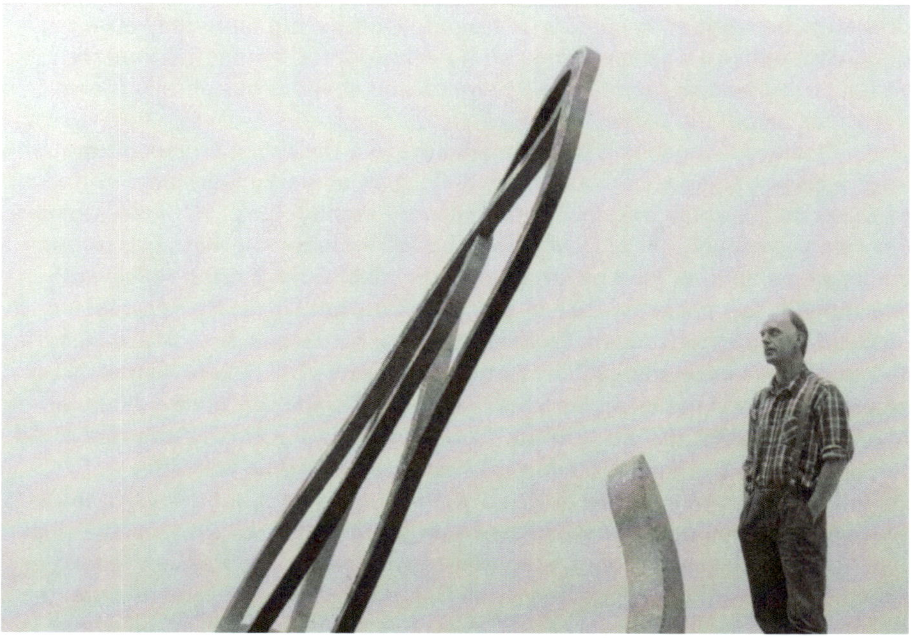

Richard Deacon with *The Bounds of Sense*, 1987, Bonnefanten Museum, Maastricht, photo: David Cripps

Thomas Eisl

Gallery leaflet, solo exhibition, Contemporary Applied Arts, London, 6 March–4 April 1992. Eisl is an improviser with found materials. After studying sculpture he made useable objects, lights and things that move. He now works on kinetic strategies for making music.

Thomas Eisl makes lights that sprawl across the ceiling with a delicate basketry of wires; lights that have to be pumped up from time to time to keep them upright, as inflated inner tubes support their structure; lights that are carried by toy tralns that follow you down a long dark corridor; lights that are a gathering of slender metal rods that sway and slide into various positions; lights that are a sheet of wired glass; desk lights that are so flat and thin that they are almost as unreal as a cardboard cut-out.

What these lights have in common is that the electric current is carried to the bulbs through the substance of the structure itself – some part of the object must be conductive, like copper or aluminium or steel. Eisl is against flex – it is crude and extraneous, a visual irrelevance. A transformer hidden somewhere in the base of the light or above the ceiling converts the normal supply into a low voltage. It is surprising how immaterially this electrical contact can be made: the tiny wires in Georgian wired glass, a narrow strip of aluminium foil, or the thinnest veneer of copper coating a sheet of fibreglass, can be enough. The light itself, the illumination, emerges from small, neat tubular bulbs, sometimes a series of bulbs in one structure. The light source is usually intimate in quality rather than dazzling, but Eisl recognises the range of necessity for light, and that brightness isn't always the aim.

Eisl is not the only person to make use of lowered voltage to clarify the structure of a light end elegantly do away with cables. But he has pursued and developed a whole spectrum of possibilities with this idea, and is also remarkable for achieving an unexpected synthesis of what is a fairly cool high-tech system of light emanation, with idiosyncratic and *made*-looking forms. They do not appear 'handmade' in an arty crafty or nostalgic way. Eisl's things are made beautifully and precisely, but it remains perfectly clear that someone has made them. These are not streamlined design solutions but personal choices and ad hoc decisions. Many of the pieces have been made to commission, and Eisl appreciates the particular demands – another input – brought by a specific situation. Adaptation and assembly, the collage and construction with reused and bought materials, are visually apparent. Signs of making can be seen in the beaten surface of aluminium, in the roughish finish of wood, the unconventional composition of shapes held by pegs and tension wires, in the bespoke quality of light bulb reflectors made of metal, infested with many little hand-drilled holes that let the light through. There is a polemic aspect to this evidently human fabrication. Eisl's work does connect with the strand of defiance that runs through the 20th-century history of applied arts,

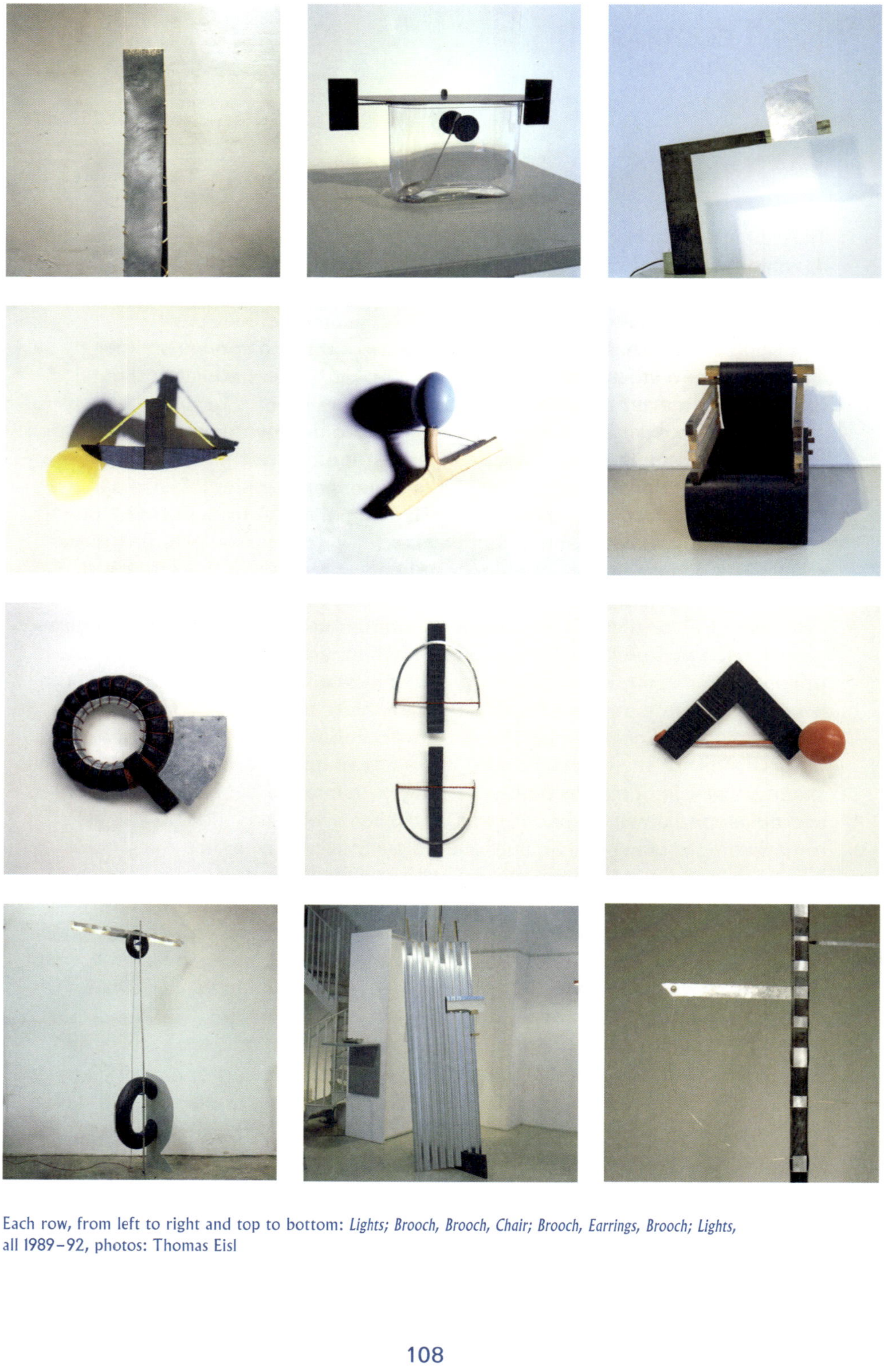

Each row, from left to right and top to bottom: *Lights; Brooch, Brooch, Chair; Brooch, Earrings, Brooch; Lights*, all 1989–92, photos: Thomas Eisl

of resistance against the capitalist over-produced lifestyle that we have arrived at, and the chain of commercialism in which product design is so entangled. The manipulative role of contemporary design – 'an attempt at *sophistication*, tempting us to feel good about ourselves in the face of ever-mounting evidence to the contrary'[1] – is one that Eisl objects to. He is neither an artist nor a designer, by self-definition, nor does he feel at all comfortable with the term 'craft'. Eisl's work is hard to locate, except in a hypothetical category that might combine all three, the whole spectrum of visual object production, from functional to conceptual, in an ideal world. His work belongs to the area in which making things makes sense; questioning the status quo, and not just putting up with the increasingly incomprehensible consumer/production cycle.

Need, logic and function are the roots of this making activity for Eisl, but the route is circuitous and the results end up more aesthetically challenging. Form is what matters, although function is the frame of reference that allows these things to exist at all. Easiness is to be avoided by the maker and the viewer. The bland, inert and stackable ethos of much designed mass-production is far from his intentions. The things Eisl makes, and they are not all lights but also furniture and jewellery, mirrors, pins and pencil boxes too, are difficult to take in entirely at a glance, and may be quite demanding to use. A more than ordinary engagement can occur between person and thing. Materials and mechanisms are juxtaposed with a subtlety and sense of contrast and detail that reward close viewing and using over a period of time. Some objects can grow significance.

Eisl uses materials not with a craftsmanlike commitment to a particular discipline or medium, but with an openness and confidence that allows ideas to develop. Ideas revolve around structures, but the feeling for particular materials and their properties is acute. Sometimes the aim is to use a material in a way that subverts expectations, to raise questions that may well be more interesting than answers. Wood and metal are often involved; the wood might be twigs or old planks or small pieces of carefully used hardwood; the metal may be shimmering reflectively or in a blackened and altered state. Rubber is a material that he is using currently, in flat sheets like the thick factory belt used to make a chair, or air-filled, plump and sensual as balloons in jewellery and inner tubes in lights and furniture. Rubber is quite a humorous material, and this is apt. There is a thread of quiet humour through all the serious intentions of his work. Most of the work is low-key in colour, being the intrinsic colours of the materials. Occasionally a spurt of primary red or yellow disconcerts the eye like a modernist joke.

Making for Eisl is both a habit and a philosophy, but it is carried on speculatively and paradoxically despite the knowledge that what the world needs is *not* more objects. With a twist of ambivalence and irony in his outlook, he is an exhaustive, unconventional, perfectionist, and imaginative maker.

1. Jon Wozencroft and Neville Brody, The Guardian, (2 December 1988).

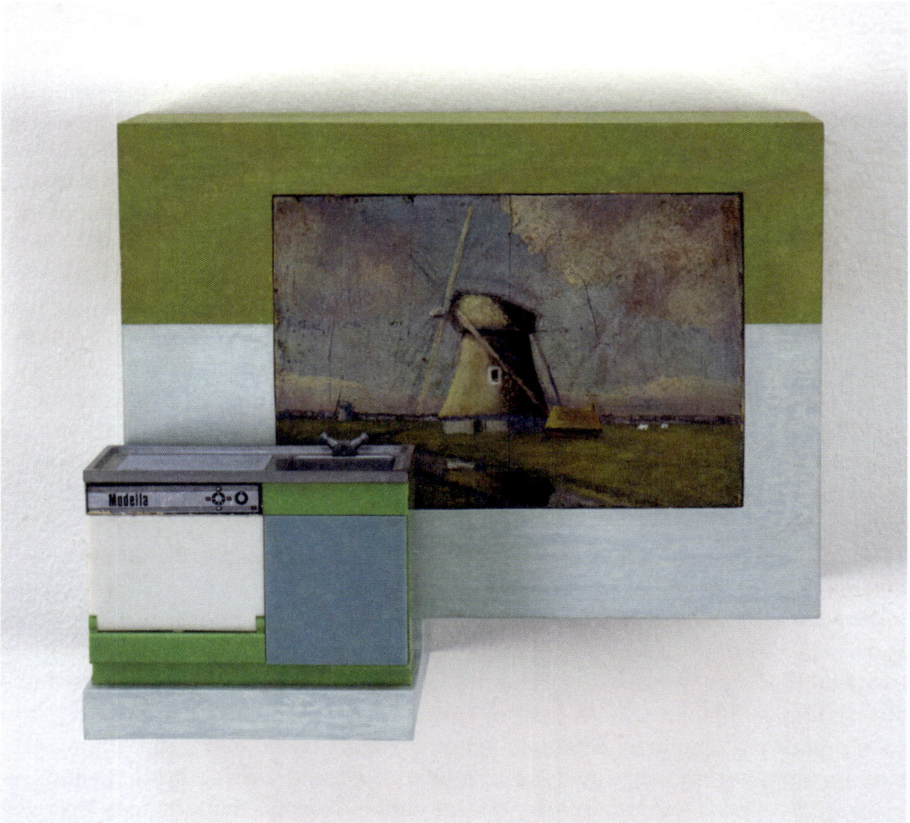

Tony Hayward, *Dutch Interior*, 1991, photo: James Newell

Sunlit Uplands
Tony Hayward

Catalogue essay, solo exhibition of Tony Hayward's work, Winchester Gallery, Winchester School of Art, 18 May–11 June 1993, pp.4–6. This exhibition of Hayward's small sculptures seemed to throw the domestic and the scenic against each other with gentle humour. His play with scale was made stranger by the jolt of recognising an air freshener, or an alpine souvenir, in the mix.

A stock list of possible titles pinned on the wall in Tony Hayward's studio gives an insight into the particular scope of his work. Phrases that jump off the tongue, such as *Worldly Good*, *Call of Nature*, *Kitchen Sink Drama*, *Land of Plenty, Amateur Ceramics*, these are well-absorbed sayings, as cosy and cryptic as headlines in the local paper, hints and clichés. They could even be the names of racehorses. Some of these titles have been used by now for earlier works, others await their object. The floor of the studio is piled up with cardboard boxes, carefully labelled and categorised, full of bric-a-brac. The gradual process that merges the ideas and found objects and the titles, which could be described as 'found phrases', into beautifully built and unpredictable structures, is broadly speaking one of collage.

The practice of collage has its roots in the two-dimensional, in the papiers collés of early Cubist painting, in the work of Georges Braque and Pablo Picasso. Braque described the pieces of fake woodgrained paper that he first applied to the surface of a drawing or a painting in 1912 as 'certainties'. Fixed points to flow around. Choosing is as much of an artistic decision as initiating is. An appreciation of the delicate balance between the ready-made and the invented, the cooked and the raw, which has been so influential in the development of art in this century, stems from here. Picasso's subsequent small reliefs and still-life constructions (most of which he kept in the studio) had a momentous and lasting impact. After nearly 50 years, André Breton recalled having seen them in 1913: 'Four of them were composed of an assemblage of materials of a residual nature such as slats, spools, discarded fragments of linoleum, lengths of string, all borrowed from everyday life.'[1]

The *ordinary* background of reuseable materials is significant. Artists now, and Hayward among them, still make creative use of a synthesis of plain facts and imagination, the found and the fabricated, refuse and origination, as a way of keying their art into life and vice versa. We usually expect sculpture these days to be enormous, hard, hungry for space and physically imposing. It makes its place in a museum or a windswept plaza, and requires attentive perambulation for a changing viewpoint.

But there is no walking around the work of Hayward; the journey of discovery can be made with the eyes. The sculptures are intimate in scale, domestic, though not always so in subject matter, and not entirely in the round. It takes time to absorb what they consist of. They are densely constructed, meticulously detailed, wall-hung, though sometimes lunging off it, visually, with deep complexities of form. It is tempting to try and describe a wall-based sculpture as a relief, but the jutting three-dimensional layers and architectural convolutions, the elaborate play with planes and viewpoints and perspectives, suggest a more energetic definition.

An earlier group of Hayward's sculptures that were quite widely seen in the mid-1980s were domestic both in scale and subject. Constructions included beached plastic from the jetsam line, crumpled metal, plastic cutlery and trays, doll furniture, pots and pans, the cruet, as well as simulated food and household appliances. They were made into still-life compositions of interiors that clearly offered some homage to the Cubists, but were idiosyncratic and fresh. A series of shoes/feet, where disparate items of worn plastic junk were united by colour into a subtle and curious state of harmony, are still vividly memorable.

Hayward has moved out of doors with the themes of his new works. Landscape is the main subject, and he is not depicting the wild Romantic sort of nature that you must discover by yourself, but the spectacular in nature whose value is confirmed by the existence of a coach trip, a postcard, a disc sequence on the Viewmaster, a few souvenirs. This is idealised landscape, exotic but available, within our ordinary reach, and thereby altered.

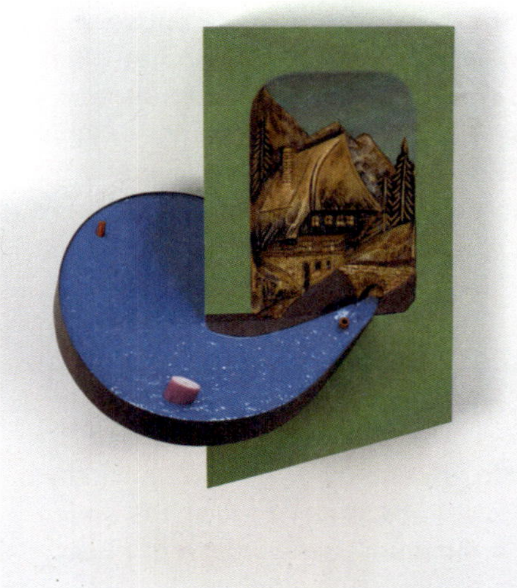

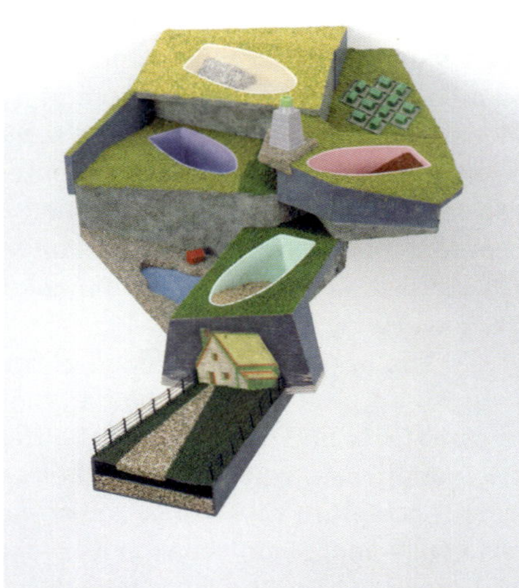

Left: Tony Hayward, *Gush*, 1992, photo: James Newell
Right: Tony Hayward, *Sunlit Uplands*, 1992, photo: James Newell

The wooden substructure, the built environment of these new pieces is increasingly inventive in form and has a stronger sculptural role to play. It is not finally perceived as wood on the whole, but clothed in a variety of perfect finishes that take the rough with the smooth: brilliant gloss paint for water, matt dry wall paint, selected grits, 'growmore' fertiliser which is like miniature pebbledash, model-maker's moss and lichen, wallpaper, stencilled patterns. The colour balance is remarkable, nostalgic and intense – the naff made serious and lovely. There are echoes of bonsai gardens and model railways. Small buildings establish a sense of scale, which is often contradicted by other features. Some striking objects are inlaid into the planes, the soles of plastic sandals, or plates or pools. These could be the reclaimed trophies of a holiday in the 1950s, but might as easily be part of a plastic airfreshener. A specific souvenir, an Alpine scene gouged in a wooden plate, and the anonymously familiar bathroom freshener, both have meaning as visual accents in a fabricated landscape; they represent a distant view, a foreground interest.

Transformations – these little shifts of perception, the ability to see something as something else – are important in Hayward's sculptures. It is this capacity that he so appreciates in children; the ease with which they approximate props into what they need them to be, in playing and making things. (He has poured his own energy into several residencies in London primary schools with great effect.) The adaptive instinct is present too in the way Third World toys and utensils are made, frequently from waste material. He has formed a collection of Indian objects in three visits to the subcontinent, not just for his own inspiration, but to show others and to be used in teaching.

Hayward works to include the everyday experience of life in what he makes, surprising as it may look, and to keep art off the pedestal. There is a warmth and tenderness, even, in the familiar strangeness of these constructions. Under awkward and debilitated circumstances, such as are common in the current world, fantasy is a necessity, as is humour. Art is perhaps an aesthetic and uplifting form of 'making do' – it can aim to foster and cajole the imaginative out of the banal, and for flagging spirits simulate 'a new world created from the mundane and ordinary at hand.'[2]

1. Quoted in Marilyn McCully, *A Picasso Anthology: Documents, Criticism, Reminiscences*, Thames and Hudson, 1981.
2. Tony Hayward, unpublished and undated notes.

Use, Beauty, Ugliness and Irony

Catalogue essay, *The Raw and the Cooked*, exhibition co-curated by Alison Britton and Martina Margetts for Museum of Modern Art Oxford, pp.9–12. The exhibition was on display at the Barbican, London from 8 July to 5 September 1993, and its international tour ended in 1996. A major event for ceramics, the exhibition included more than 30 artists of diverse kinds. Some of those exhibiting always worked with clay, others did so occasionally.

In borrowing the title *The Raw and the Cooked* from anthropology, there is an intention to recognise part of what is special about ceramics, and its surprisingly consistent place in our culture. Anthropology has made an immense contribution to the way we think about the world and our own society in this century, on an ordinary level. However this has been absorbed, through the National Geographic Magazine, the Sunday colour supplements, travel, television, looking at objects in museums, or the everyday experience of multi-cultural living, a comparative sense of our own cultural norms as against others that are so different has had to develop, and this has shifted Waspish parochial certainties. The work of anthropologists has revealed and defined the extent of difference, the subtlety and, perhaps too, the enviable clarity of other social structures. In response, Europeans have (at best) found in cultural comparison a broader base of respect for 'otherness' and an expanded, postmodern view of the world.

What I know about other cultures I have taken in as much from looking at objects, in museums or just being abroad, as from reading. 'Reading' an object, its use and its beauty, guessing at its significance or symbolic meaning, how it fits with life, its ingenuity with material and making, its economy or extravagance, has been a consistent part of art education in my experience. From secondary school onwards, an involvement with ceramics has entailed a dedicated 'looking out', with awe, at the widest possible range of objects from elsewhere. Ethnographic museums are a normal part of the curriculum in ceramics. On the other hand, pots, or shards, have a significant role to play in historical and anthropological studies of how other peoples have lived. Fired clay doesn't disappear; clay is basic stuff, universal, it is dug up almost everywhere, and almost every culture has a ceramic tradition, except where the earth is frozen. There is a communality of approach too: techniques have evolved with similarity in different places, or have been carried by emigrant craftsmen, or copied off imported goods. Ceramic objects are by and large internationally comprehensible, with the pot or container as the crux of understanding.

Arguably, we have Bernard Leach to thank for the survival of ceramics as a strand of late 20th-century culture. The practice of pottery as a self-conscious activity, not motivated by the need for utensils but by spiritual and aesthetic hope and expression, was confirmed by him with his concept of the 'Studio Potter'. It comes, too, under William Morris's umbrella of resistance

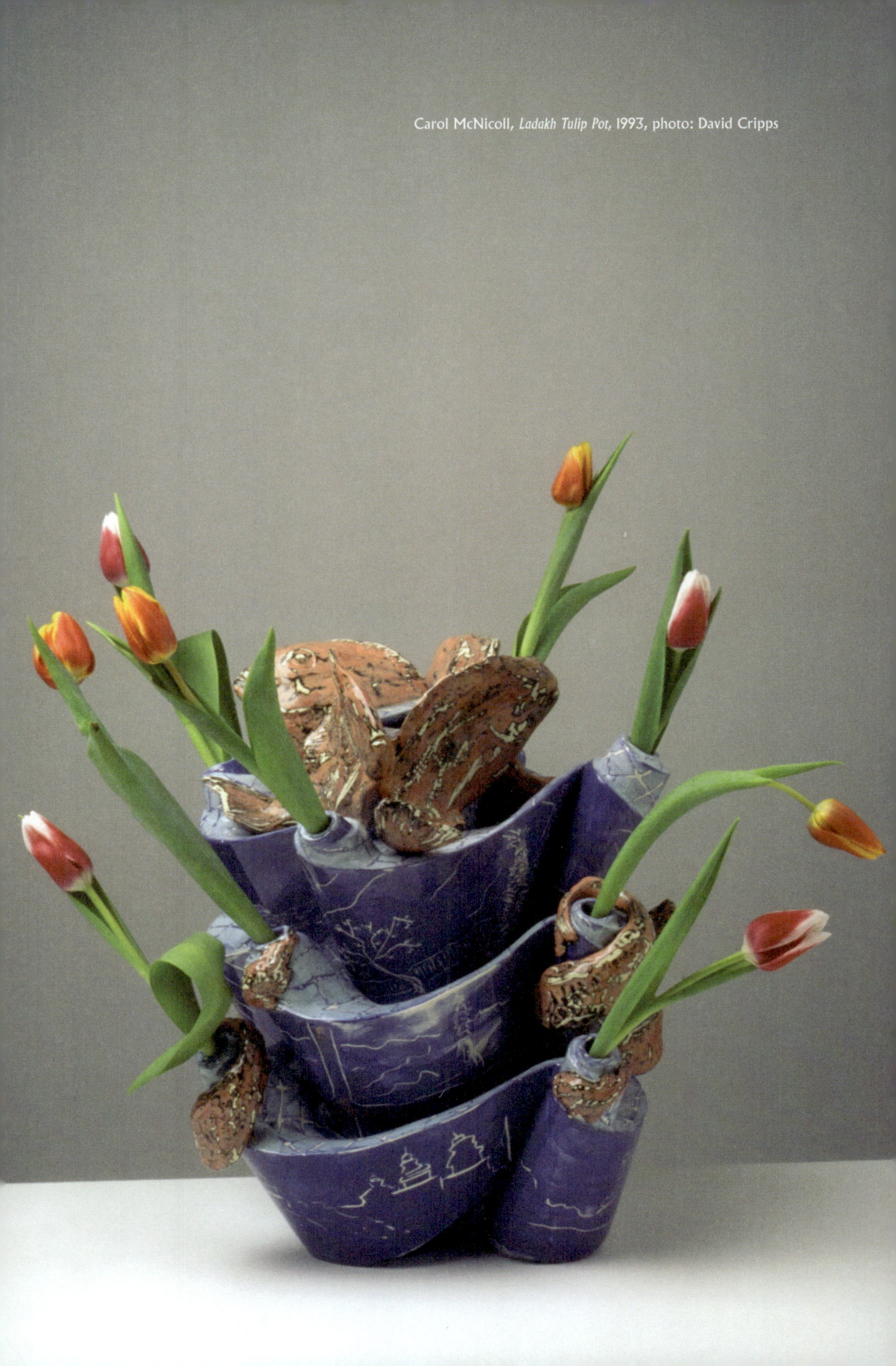

Carol McNicoll, *Ladakh Tulip Pot*, 1993, photo: David Cripps

to dehumanising industrialisation. Leach, on his return from the Far East with Shoji Hamada, set up a pottery in the west of England in 1920, and his subsequent fame and influence as a maker and a craft philosopher defined the territory that we still occupy, despite changes in the appearances of objects. It is striking that it was a cultural mix – medieval English with Japanese Mingei pottery traditions – that became so durably impressive in style. The Leach school looked with passionate admiration to the Far Eastern potters, not only for the aesthetics of the pots themselves but for what they perceived to be a more wholesome and spiritual approach to making, and to the relationship between man, art and nature. They had arrived early at a sense of European loss (the degeneration that comes with progress), and of shame at the poverty of their own production. Michael Cardew, the potter who worked for many years in West Africa, wrote of the impact of Leach's view, as if it were a David taking on the Goliath of Wedgwood; and of his own intense antipathy to the dead whiteness of industrial earthenware:

> Jean-Jacques Rousseau did not actually want to become a Noble Savage; nor Denis Diderot a Chinese, nor Montesquieu a Persian. They invoked those exotic and imaginary characters in order to question Western civilisation; not to destroy it but to fulfil it. ... We do not want to make Chinese, or Korean, or primitive pots. But we have seen clearly what they have, which our own, so badly lack, and having seen it we are not likely to lose sight of it again.[1]

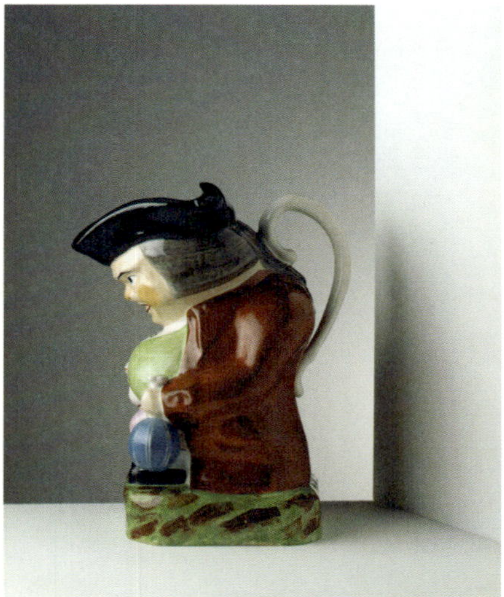

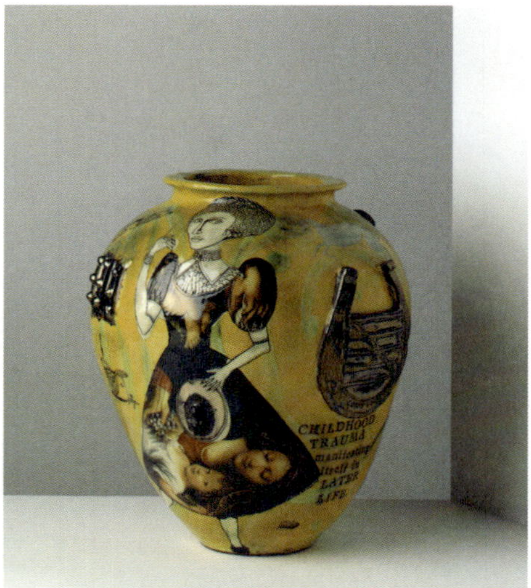

Left: Richard Slee, *Toby Jug*, 1992, photo: David Cripps
Right: Grayson Perry, *Childhood Trauma Manifesting Itself in Later Life*, 1992, photo: David Cripps

Whether or not they realise it, people who choose to work as artists in clay now are tapping into a 20th-century history of gentle or genteel resistance to some of the larger sweeps of modernisation, standardisation, overproduction, mechanisation, sanitisation, mass marketing, and other aspects of progress that threaten to crush the human spirit. This is our starting point for this exhibition. In anthropological terms the title *The Raw and the Cooked* alludes to the relationship between Nature and Culture. But here, having acknowledged a particular thread running between anthropology and the practice of ceramics, the title is more precisely a useful metaphor for art's – any kind of art's – urge to roughen, contrast and enrich the diet of sophisticated, smooth and increasingly passive modern life in the industrialised West. In addition, it can be read as a description of ceramic process; and we also perceive the exhibition as a synthesis, as a resolved combination of disparate ingredients, like a meal.

The ingredients of this meal are unusual in that pots and sculpture are not segregated, and neither constitute the main course. At the outset pots may be what is expected in a ceramic exhibition, while the sculptural work is less predictable – the cooked and the raw, perhaps, in terms of familiar visual experience in clay. The work was chosen out of personal interest, the combined vision of the selectors; the exhibition does not attempt to present a complete survey of the current state of ceramic art. The thematic groupings that the work, in a loose fashion, falls into, are ones that became apparent to us after we had roughed out a list of the artists we

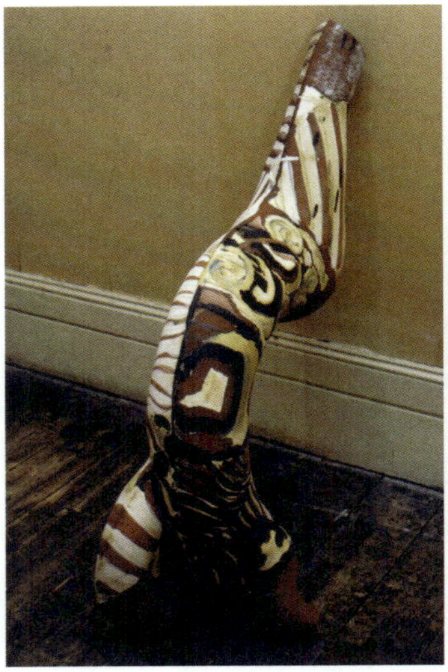

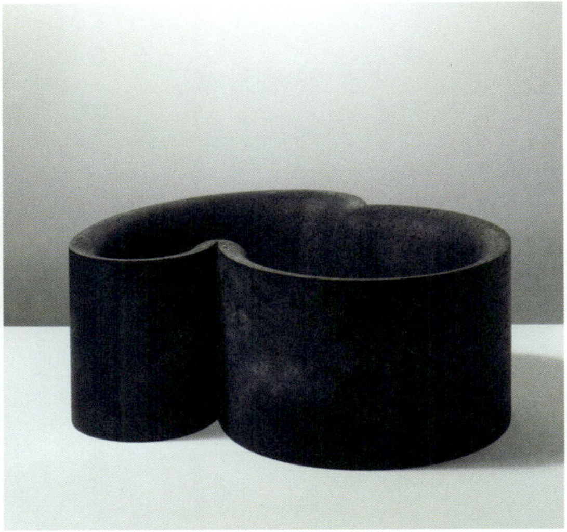

Left: Jacqui Poncelet, *Object 'Against the Wall'*, 1985, photo: Edward Woodman
Right: Martin Smith, *Substance and Shadow No IV*, 1993, photo: David Cripps

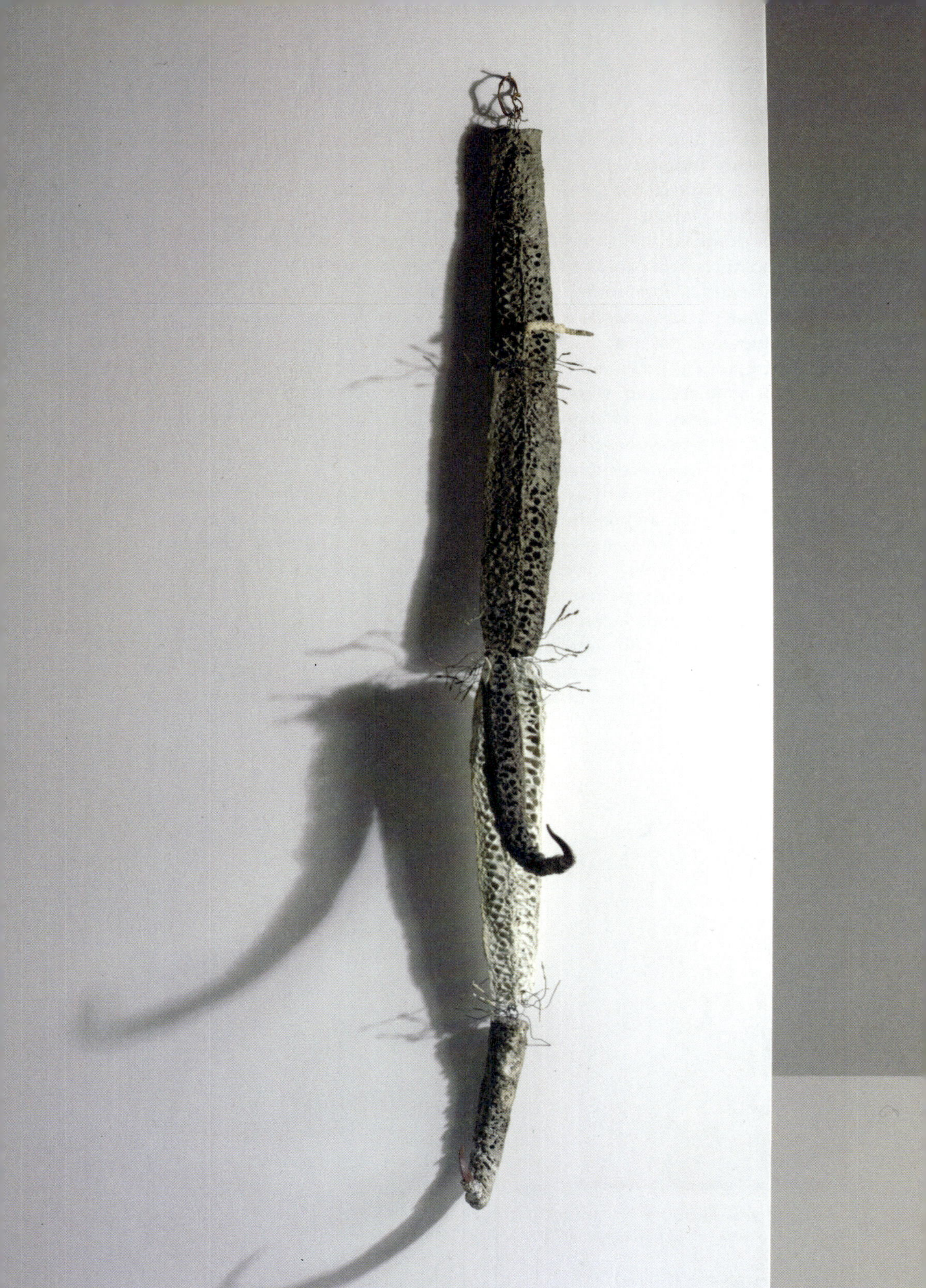

Gillian Lowndes, *Hook Figure*, 1991, photo: David Cripps

were committed to. Some work could be seen to belong to several groups, and sometimes the visual links that can be made between particular objects cut across categories, and these juxtapositions are just as interesting and important to us as any theme. An exhibition like this celebrates the value of mixture, drawing both on the diversity of cultural influences and on the mixing of supposedly pure categories: sculpture/pottery, representation/abstraction, aesthetic/useful, and so on.

The sense in mixing pots and sculpture, beyond their obviously shared use of space and material in this context, can be defined in several ways. The common ground is not just the substance of clay, but the common chemistry and technology that the practitioner has had to grasp with varying degrees of elaboration: ways of forming, glazing, firing, knowing as well as using the stuff. The vast spectrum of mundane to sublime ceramic production that is familiar to us – brick, urinal, teacup, urn, statue, altarpiece – has always seemed to me to be one of the reasons for working in the field. Such a varied traditional range can encourage a feeling of openness, of ambiguity and the hybrid, of intriguingly blurred categories. (The raw, the cooked, and the half-baked, perhaps....) Having one foot planted in utility, in the ordinary, can nourish the aesthetic. Work can come and go between these poles. Use and Beauty for Leach were supposed to be poised in equal parts; but clearly the balance can be shifted, and the meanings of both words seem now, after the developments of the last 20 years, a great deal more elastic and open to argument. The use-and-beauty measure can then be applied as purposefully to the art object as to the functional object. For Claude Lévi-Strauss, all social behaviour, like cooking and eating, however utilitarian, is always symbolic; in other words, it conveys meanings that go beyond its immediate function. In a related sense, utilitarian objects carry symbolic – and thus potentially aesthetic – values.

Is there still a problem with looking at a pot as a work of art, or a clay object as a sculpture, and is a plate hanging on the wall an aberration? This exhibition presumes not. There are more interesting dichotomies to consider, like representation and abstraction.

It is noticeable, broadly speaking, that the younger artists included in this exhibition are more interested in figurative representation – Philip Eglin, Susan Halls, Tracey Heyes, for instance. The middle-aged group are more clearly the children of modernism, concerned with formal abstraction, and some with the hollow container form. But to see the exhibition as split in this way is to oversimplify and diminish the subtlety of the whole range. The range extends to artists who usually work in other materials; or to those who have moved into or out of claywork quite recently. We also particularly wanted to show the work of several ceramic artists with a long-established independent stance: Gillian Lowndes, Paul Astbury, who couldn't be further from thoughts of pottery, however abstract, or Richard Slee, who felt in the early 1980s that abstraction was inappropriate to ceramics, and whose current work is an affectionate satire on suburban England and the Toby jug.

That something as concrete as a pot can be regarded as 'abstract' may seem problematic. The sort of pots that are part of this exhibition do not have utility uppermost in their offerings. They are operating like other abstract works of art in that they are aesthetic compositions of three-dimensional form (hollow in this case), colours, and surfaces. They make suggestions, references to other sorts of form, other objects perhaps, or attempt to symbolise states of feeling or ideas. They are carriers of meaning, open to interpretation by the beholder, of a subliminal kind. It could be said that although as pots they are objects, they also have 'the pot' as their subject matter, in a way that is both ironic and reflexive. It could even be said that although they function as abstract in the way I have described, they are also representations of pots. They portray ideas about pots in the past, ideas about use, and the relationships between people and everyday objects, the basic props of life (eating, drinking, washing, storing, watering, burying). All of these durable themes are made accessible in the choice of a hollow ceramic form. Containment, actual and metaphorical, is the key to it.

The formal and significant characteristics of pots have been written about at length in other places. To sum up: a form that is overtly hollow and frequently curvaceous, with a related interior and exterior appearance, can very easily seem to be a metaphor for the human body or self. More angular or geometric pots seem to relate to buildings, and perhaps to sleights of scale and to an architectural sense of space. See the work of Ken Eastman or Martin Smith. Combining these two references, body and building, the idea of the house as a metaphor for the self can also be perceived in pot forms. More loosely amalgamated, highly fused, and geological-looking pieces readily make suggestions of landscape, prehistory, and forces of nature. I am thinking here of the work of Lawson Oyekan, Ewen Henderson, and Sara Radstone.

We hope to show in this exhibition that work in clay is an open arena, and that people are making things currently in unforseeably exciting and varied forms. (There is a certain risk and pleasure in bringing them all into the same space.) Within this diversity some ceramic norms are challenged and others are confirmed.

One of the conventions of ceramics is that the clay is covered with a surface layer, usually of vitreous slip or glaze. This is to make it impervious. Certain clay objects, like bricks and flower pots, are meant to be porous, but in general, unglazed looks unfinished. High temperature firing of clay also vitrifies it, making it glass-like, but the glazing convention is so ancient that it has also become an avenue for decoration, or painting. Decoration, as 'applied' to pottery, was supposed to be subservient to the form (often, in industrial job-division, applied by women onto shapes made by men). Ceramic artists can choose to paint the surface of their objects now for different reasons and in different ways, but it has developed out of this practical requirement: the need for a waterproof skin, as well as the added

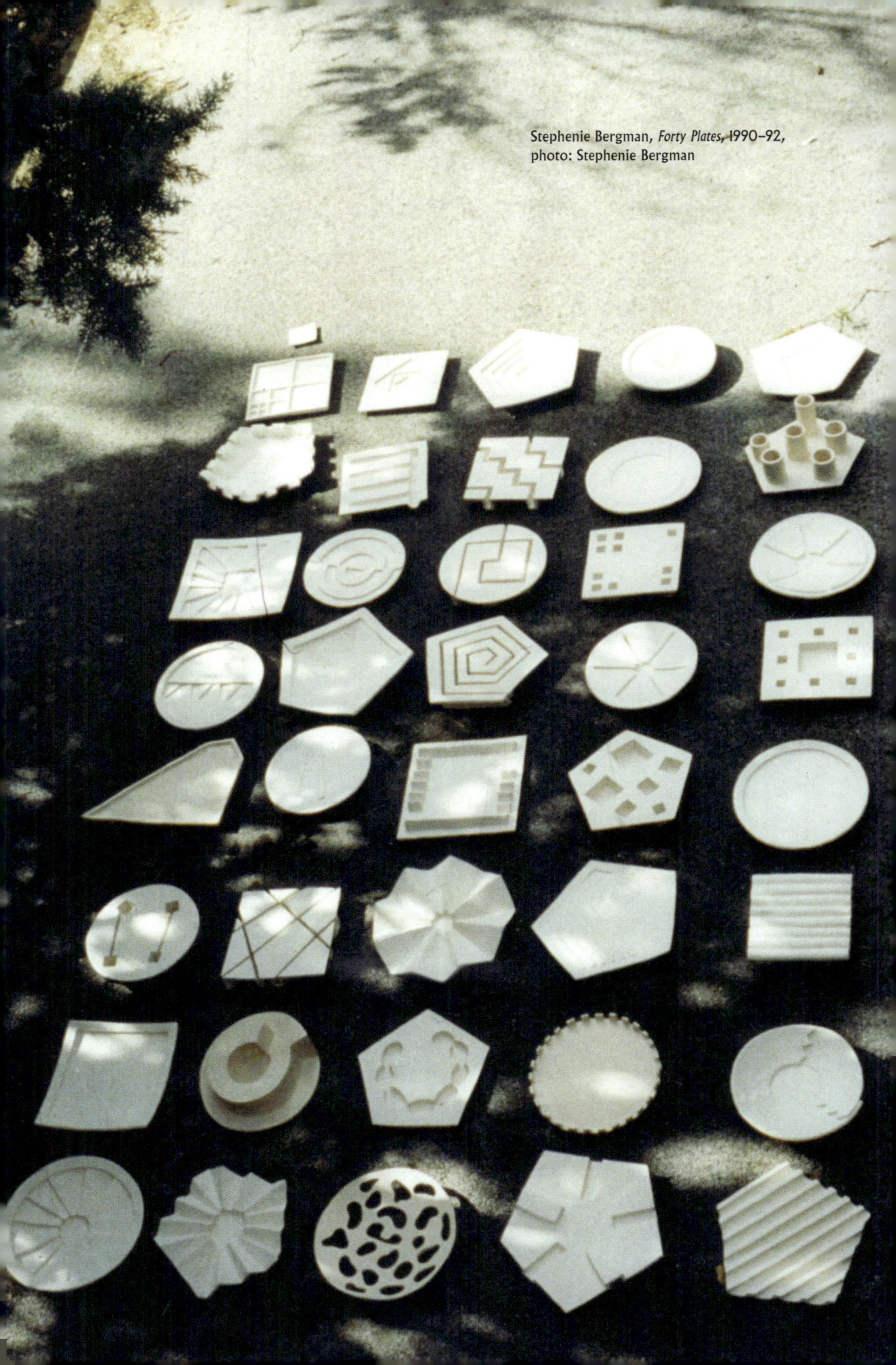

Stephenie Bergman, *Forty Plates*, 1990–92,
photo: Stephenie Bergman

value of ornament and colour. The separate concern for surface is something special to ceramic art, which in this way brings together sculpture and painting, as body and dress. In the way I make pots I have worked out a process where the painting and the form can develop in dialogue at the same time, without one dominating the other.

Plates and painting have a particular relationship too. The flatness of plates, their lower three-dimensional formal status, makes them potentially closer to paintings. They are objects in transition, poised between object and image. This is wryly commented on by Philip Eglin, combining an Edouard Manet painting and a willow pattern border. Karen Densham, too, has a gentle humour in her faint, careful horse drawings under bold splashes of glaze. The titles are potent and poetic, a racehorse's name with an optional innuendo. Stephenie Bergman's grand series of 40 plates is not at all concerned with painting and not much with 'ceramic quality'. Like a large number of pieces in this exhibition, her work is unglazed. This in itself works to confront ceramic norms. The Bergman piece is a structural surface in relief, raw and direct, a huge geometric drawing in pieces on a wall, playing with light and shadow. It is another manifestation of the irony that ceramics thrive on, glancing at function, picking up on a familiar acceptance of a basic form, and subversively aesthetic.

These subversive strands are pleasing and important to include because they suggest change and vitality. The untasteful ambiguity of Slee's oversized plants and Toby jugs, glossy and sleek; the wanton dribblings of pigment over the features of Eglin's ladies: any field that is founded on a single material and a few thousand years of craft technology is bound to have a certain orthodoxy that needs disruption as well as respect. This exhibition will, I hope, convey both upheaval and poise in its celebration of the long traditions of making objects in clay.

1. *The Maker's Eye* catalogue, The Crafts Council, London, 1981.

Opposite left: Angus Suttie, *Title Unknown*, 1992, photo: David Cripps
Opposite right: Angus Suttie, *Bony Restriction*, 1992, photo: David Cripps

Grateful Colours, Bright Looks

Catalogue essay, memorial exhibition, *Angus Suttie 1946–1993,* Contemporary Applied Arts, London, 30 September–5 November 1994, p.8. Angus Suttie had been at the core of 'New Ceramics', an exuberant, prolific, and experimental artist who died in his mid 40s. His memorial exhibition was a kind of retrospective but included his last, more sombre and horizontal pieces with chambers linking together, which I had not seen when I wrote this.

My title comes from a poem by Stevie Smith in her last book 'Scorpion'.[1] I think Angus Suttie would have liked it. It is about seeing what there is in life in spite of the drawbacks. Suttie's exuberant work is articulate both about the thrill of colour and the plastic freedom of clay. Working the stuff simply and softly, assembling prepared parts, an array of domes, blocks, cornets, rolls, cusps – pinched and slabbed – sometimes paired off for a sense of harmony amid the unpredictable, he built up forms of great innocence and complexity. However elaborate, the vitality of the whole united object was never undermined by the perception of its open-ended way of construction as a sort of three-dimensional collage; the gentle amalgamation of a troupe of elements without a particular end in view.

Colour was the making of them, loosely painted colours of all kinds: glaze, slip, enamel, gold sometimes. In the first works that I got to know in the early 1980s, a very untraditional zinging red was dominant. In later pieces, the junctions of the composite forms are emphasised. Chunks of the form are blended in, or made to stand out, with the use of different patterns and colour combinations; textures, dents and ridges, scratched and painted stripes and spots. Over the years the work became larger, more vitreous, less shiny, and quieter in colour. Suttie knew what he was doing, how to be organised and to keep essential spontaneity. He knew where precision was needed in the structure of living, and most importantly he knew how to play, in work.

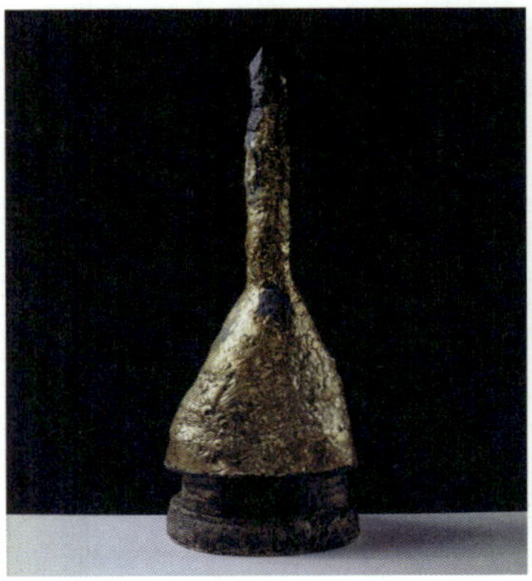

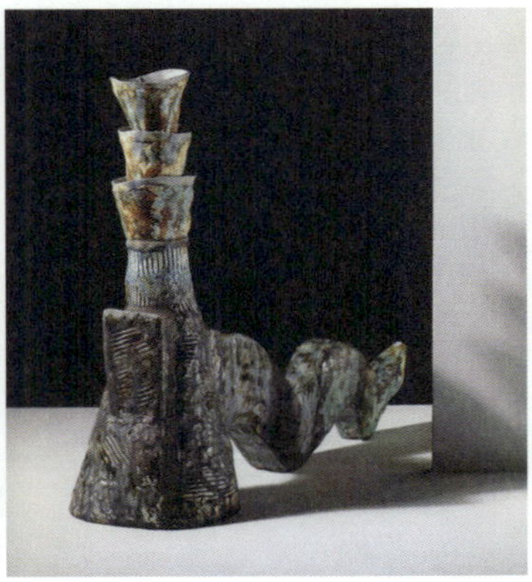

He didn't only make pots; he made rings and Christmas tree decorations and spoons on occasion too. He could state clearly, in an interview with a disguised version of himself in a Dutch catalogue from 1985,[2] that his work combined threads of folk art and surrealism, and that it aspired to be both *awkward and beautiful.* That could have been the motto of the whole group who had, at some stage, worked on 'the conditions of pottery' in the late 1970s and after – including Suttie, Jacqueline Poncelet, Richard Slee, Carol McNicoll, Henry Pim, Jill Crowley, Martin Smith, and myself.[3] In teaching and in writing and in the way he worked it was apparent how aware he was of the world outside, and of the importance of art and making within a deeply imperfect situation:

> In our pottery careers ... it is expected that our work should show a continuity from A to B, leading to C which evolves into D and so on. The changes should reveal a linear development and we must constantly renew our work and 'advance' stylistically. This progress is similar to capitalism's demands for new products and new markets .... I suggest that another way of understanding time and development would be to view the maker as the hub in the centre of lines radiating outwards. These 'spokes' are avenues of creativity which we may explore. The importance, however, is that 'forward' is not the only direction. By keeping the opportunity open of referring backwards (or sideways) in creative time, the idea of progress or perpetual revolution is not inexorable.[4]

Suttie was open to making all kinds of things. On leaving Camberwell College, he was known for wild shapes and brilliant colours, teapots with flailing limbs or like gilded bagpipes. There were cups from a Cubist still-life painting, and unuseable plates with vibrant wriggling surfaces of striped worms. Later pieces are mainly not about domestic pottery, but touch on the shared material underlying the poetic content of both contemporary and ancient pots, the body and the building. More idiosyncratically, Suttie adds glimpses of things like wheelbarrows, radiators, fountains, or sections of engine, as well. 'The government is stripping everything down to function, but life is richer than that. So I am looking at ritual things and in my work putting on things that have no relation to function.'[5] There is serious merriment in Suttie's work. It is wayward but to a clear purpose; cheerfully confronting a reality of dwindling positiveness that is not only personal, but universal.

1. Stevie Smith, *Scorpion and other poems*, Longman, 1972.
2. Aeschylus Orton and Angus Suttie, *British Ceramics*, exhibition catalogue, Het Kruithuis, 's Hertogenbosch, 1985.
3. John Houston, *The Abstract Vessel*, Bellew, 1991.
4. Angus Suttie, *Ceramics Review* 107, 1987.
5. *London/Amsterdam, New Art Objects*, exhibition catalogue, Crafts Council 1988

The Human Presence in Clay

Ceramic Review 156, November/December 1995, pp. 10–13. This essay was written on the invitation of East Midlands Arts. Lawson Oyekan was developing a new body of large work in a residency at Loughborough College of Art and Design, later shown in a solo exhibition at the City Gallery, Leicester, in 1995, with this text on the wall.

In the studio of Lawson Oyekan most of the pots are hidden. Huge, high-shouldered forms are shrouded in blue cloths. They crowd onto all the available surfaces, desks, plinths, on the kiln platform, into the fireplace, on the floor. Groups share a covering; the material is stretched across them masking their definition, clumping them into families. Pieces are veiled like this to give Oyekan a clear view, a mental space, in which to make the next one.

The studio itself is a large light brick-lined room painted white. It is part of a house, perhaps once the schoolkeeper's house, in the playground of a primary school in King's Cross, London. Oyekan is a resident artist in the school – he gets the use of the studio, which he completely renovated and set up, in exchange for some hours teaching every week. His own daughter will start going to the nursery in the autumn – a reflection of Oyekan's role as a well-settled and much appreciated occupant.

Above the cluttered surfaces, pot-encumbered, jostling with plants and files and cardboard boxes, a ghetto-blaster, chairs and buckets, serene expanses of white brick wall stretch up to the high ceiling of the room. Placed about the upper reaches of these walls are a number of isolated and beautiful things, some made and some from nature. The colour is attracting – the light gold of dried grass or straw, as a bunch of grain, or meshed into a pad like a sketchy nest; the darkness of a few wooden African masks; a piece of rusty metal like the blade of a plough; the silver of a line of dangling metal hooks; a brown brush made from a large fibrous plant. Seeing these things in their undisturbed clarity is like reading messages about the thematic material, both cultural and natural, out of which Oyekan makes his work.

And what does the work look like? It is challenging to the eye, and cannot be taken in quickly. There is awkwardness as well as comfort in his forms, and a forceful sense of energy, of life. 'Life' in a vessel form is what a potter always hopes to have achieved – that the form should imply its own growth and fullness, that its empty space is a potent one and not a slack pointless cavity.

Broadly speaking, the recent work consists of several groups of large and moderately large pots, some ovoid, full-bellied and closing in towards the top, others cylindrical like a pipe or an elongated jar. Some are in terracotta and some are in a rougher clay called crank. A few pieces are white porcelain. Most of the work is unglazed but does not have a uniform unfinished 'biscuit' look about it; slips of gently varying colours are part of the construction, and they define and enrich the surface. Glaze when it is used is often green, from a delicate tint to a heavy leaf colour. The glaze usually appears quite fluid and glassy.

Across all the work, the strongest impression is of the trail left by an energetic hand. The hand making a bold raw gesture, like the sweep of a brush or the slash of a knife, combined with the loving attentiveness of fingertips slowly pinching and piecing together.

These pots are built up from fragments. Sometimes the clay is rolled out and cut into roughly rectangular sheets like pages; for other pieces, round pads or patches are worked between the hands from a ball of clay. The pots are built up when the clay is still soft and plastic, and the joints strengthened with slip and a bristle brush. The structure, and the play of colour on the surface, are building up together. The clay walls are thin, risky, for the scale of the pieces. The material is being pushed to the limit of its tolerance, and timing is crucial.

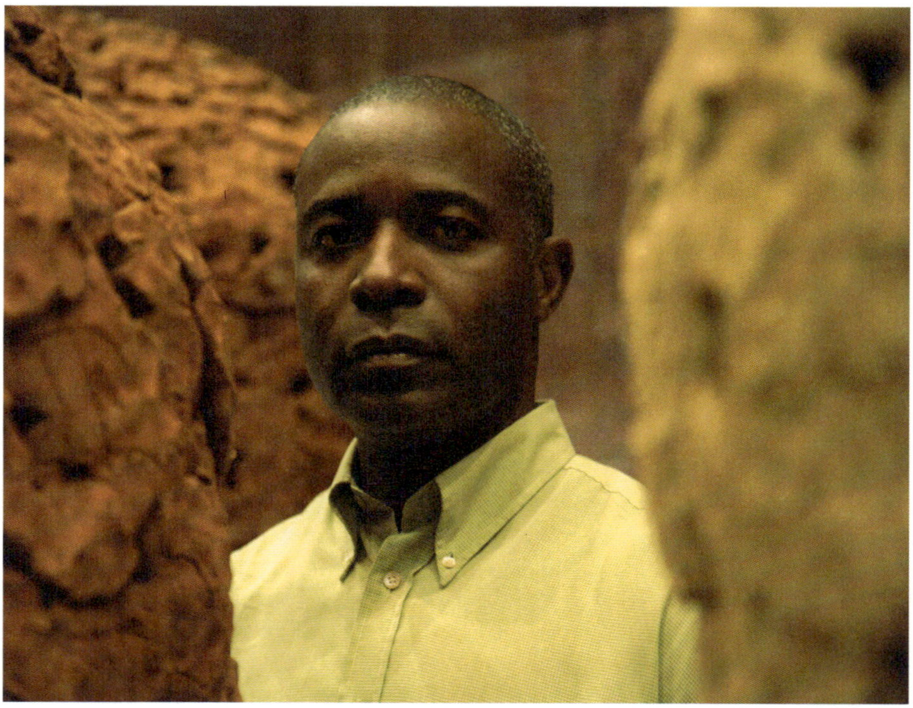

Lawson Oyekan, Portrait with Tall Pots, 2000s

The other striking thing for the observer, and it is a feature that flies in the face of our general expectations about pots, is that many of these pieces have pierced holes all over them. They are not watertight. The holes vary in size, some as small as a pinprick, while others carry the shape of a knife poked in and twisted, leaving a space like a winged insect. Combined with a gently domed organic form, thoughts of anthills or beehives come to mind. The pierced surface also lets light into the interior, there is no longer that strong contrast of light outside and dark inside that is held by solid pots. The pots, whether ovoid or cylindrical, have a convex base that curves up like the diaphragm in the chest.

This too is pierced and may be gashed in a fierce way. Most of the pots have a pair of larger holes near the top which are like eyes, perhaps partly veiled with strips of clay. The convex base, Oyekan says, is another reflection of the face. There is often roughly scratched writing on the surfaces, words in Yoruba, aggressive like graffiti.

It becomes clear, then, that these pots are human embodiments, of self or spirit or personality. They group like people, ranging in size; they observe; they are open to their environment. To some extent, pots throughout history and across many different cultures have shared this anthropomorphic sense, even in English we talk unselfconsciously about pots having lips and bellies and feet and shoulders. But the human presence in this new work of Oyekan's is more than the incidental language of pottery; it is vivid and motivational, part of the story that goes into the making of these pieces.

The work is still, to me, quite fresh and strange, though I have seen its various phases for a number of years. It brings into the field of ceramics in Britain a most welcome expression of otherness, outlandish news from elsewhere. The raw surfaces, slashing gaps, scrawled words, rough strokes of the brush – all are done with an evident assurance that arises out of different conventions, and is unfamiliar.

A Nigerian who was born in England, Oyekan spent most of his childhood in Africa and returned to Europe as a young man who wanted to see more of the world. Most of his study of art and ceramics has been in London, after spending some time in the sciences, chemistry in particular, in Nigeria. While at the Central School in London, Oyekan grew very interested in throwing, and he is now an excellent and unusual exponent of the wheel. In the 1970s, a number of potters felt the need to distance themselves quite consciously from the dominant Bernard Leach tradition. Most of the ideas that were hatched then by my colleagues and myself were in handbuilding, and in irregular, more sculptural, forms. It was as if, for a number of years, the wheel was out of bounds if you wanted to escape from the increasingly complacent norm of the Anglo-Oriental tradition. Now, I would suggest, sufficient objects of other sorts have been made for new approaches to throwing to be contemplated. And this, indeed, is what Oyekan has been achieving.

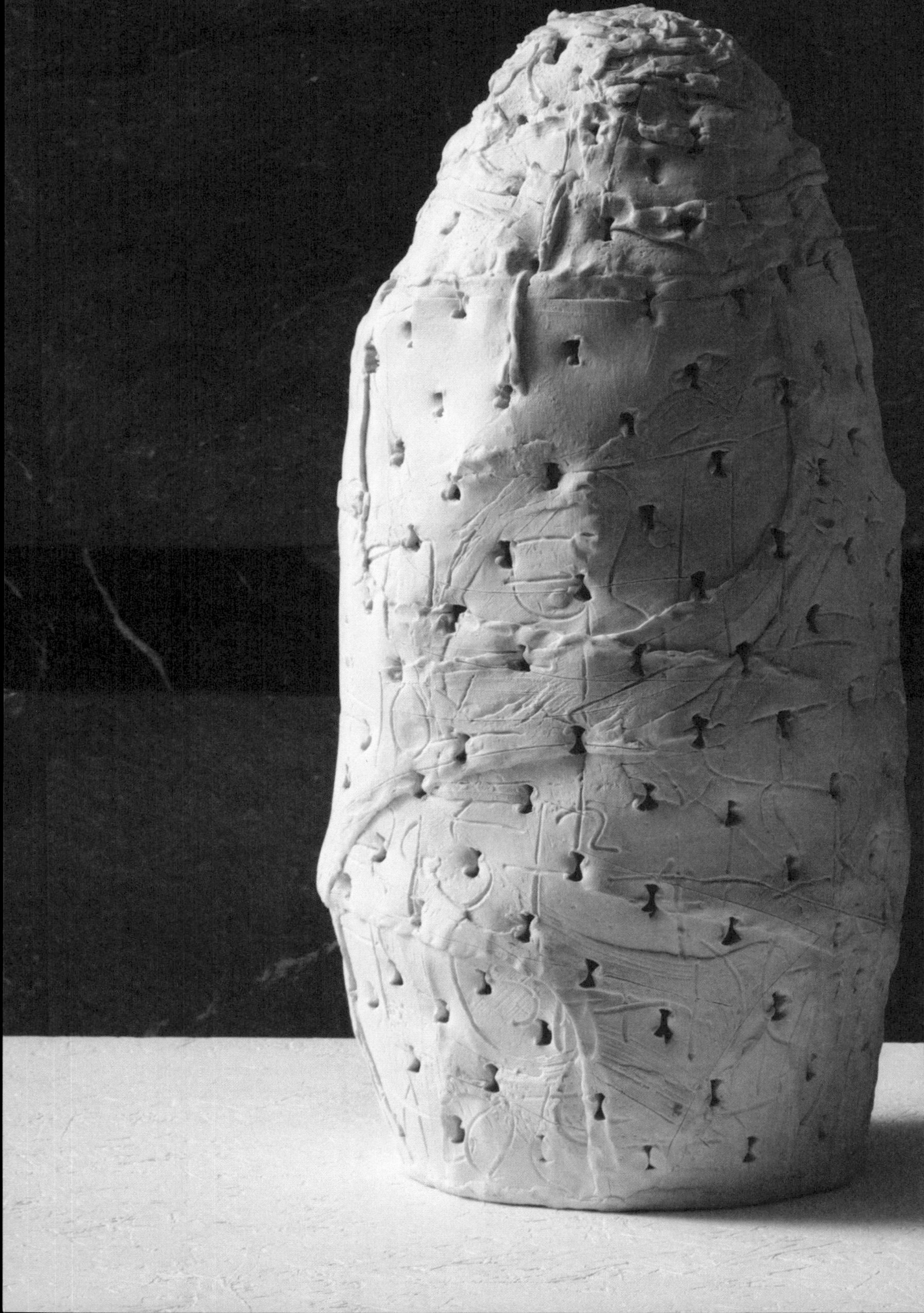

Lawson Oyekan, *Porcelain Pots, Global Working* series, 2012

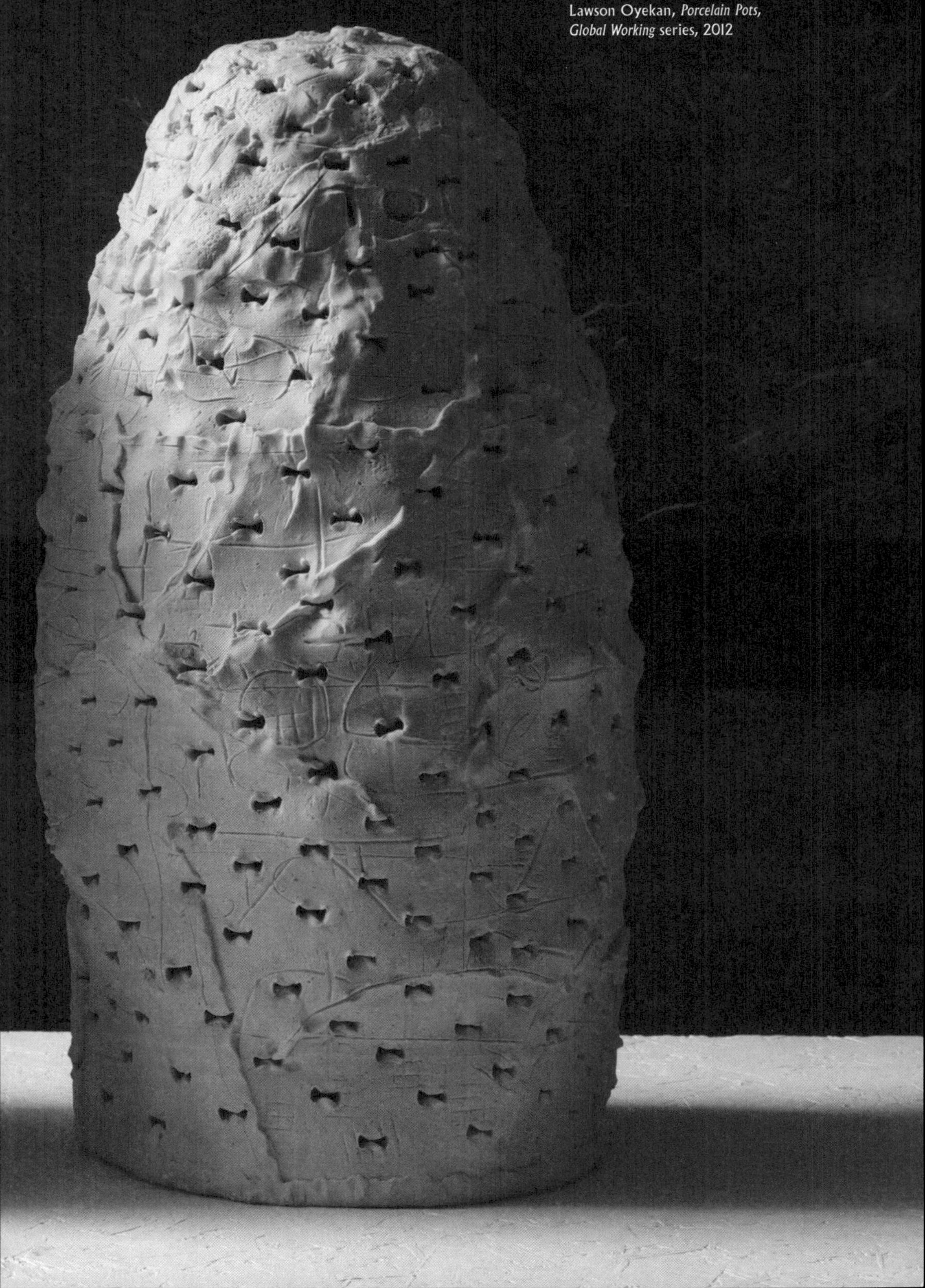

The last time Oyekan was able to concentrate an unbroken stretch of time on the development of a refined and idiosyncratic way of working with thrown porcelain was as an MA student at the Royal College of Art. He made a series of wide dish forms of extreme delicacy and daring. They incorporated ideas about movement and natural force in the controlled distortions of the circular form. They too had domed-up bases like a breathing diaphragm – here it was a structure essential to the survival of the thin walled piece, being able to give, and sink a little, in the stress of high firing.

It interests me a great deal to look at both kinds of work, the thrown and the built, in juxtaposition. I had the opportunity to put the two groups together in the exhibition *The Raw and the Cooked*, when it was shown at the Museum of Modern Art in Oxford. We had a 'family' of five large terracotta pots, raised on a high plinth, and beneath them, laid out quite formally before them, two of the very fine wide and shallow pierced porcelain pieces. One of these was green glazed and one plain vitreous white clay, both made at the Royal College of Art. I think it is the stretch of his thinking across the different forms and surfaces, rough or smooth, loose or controlled, pricked or gashed, his sensitivity to their different requirements to become themselves, that is exciting.

But handbuilding is better suited to the fragmented chunks of working time that Oyekan has now, in the general struggle with other sorts of work that keeps ends meeting. Most of the recent pieces have been handbuilt. With his current way of working, patching the clay together, he can arrive at forms of considerable size. His desire to work large has had to be fulfilled, over the years, in other people's kilns. For his latest series he had the opportunity to work in the pottery at Loughborough College of Art and Design, as an artist-in-residence. Dave Scott is in charge of the department there, and welcomed Oyekan into a working space in the third-year studios. He was provided with a student room to sleep in, free firings in the gigantic kiln, and some admirable flexibility from technicians who have stayed late when Oyekan has been working long hours. His presence, his way of working, his contact with students, was valued in the department. He worked there for two or three days a week over an initial session of five weeks before Christmas, which was then extended for another five weeks to develop what was clearly a very positive project. The only regret is that he could not carry on as long as the College hoped he would, because he could not afford to sustain such a commitment of time without other earnings. Scott, for his part, had become intrigued by Oyekan's ideas and his discourse on glaze, which is both scientific and metaphysical, and was sorry that there was not enough time to get one of the major pieces into a glaze kiln. What has been achieved in this relatively short and intense working period was ascertained in his exhibition at the City Art Gallery in Leicester. The gallery had suggested and arranged the residency to enable Oyekan to make the large pots he had in mind.

I have used the word 'outlandish' earlier in describing Oyekan's pots and I mean it as a compliment. I mean to convey my respect for the bridge he makes with another ceramic world. The smugness of a Western notion of supremacy in cultural matters has been weaker in the crafts than in many other areas. Craftspeople, for the last century at any rate, have known that they were in opposition to industry and needed to look out beyond Western confines for stimulus and a sense of meaning. Perhaps potters in particular have sustained a sense of awe at the pots from elsewhere, from South America, Africa, Islamic Spain, and the Far East.

But where do these pots of Oyekan's belong? How African can they be when he is almost entirely English-trained? Wanting to see him against an African background, I went with him to the Museum of Mankind where they are currently showing a remarkable exhibition curated by the ethnographer Nigel Barley. Straightaway it is apparent that there are links and resonances between this 1990s London potter, and the work surrounding us. There are pots with pierced holes in them, for practical or spiritual purposes; pots encrusted with little studs like insects; pots with faces. A number of storing jars and large bowls remind him of pots in his grandmother's house. Some of the texts up on the wall impress Oyekan with their resemblance to his own understanding of the significance of pots, which he has imbibed simply as part of his culture, without having learned it from any African potter. A quotation from the Museum of Mankind catalogue expresses beautifully the capacity of objects, ordinarily made by hand from clay, to channel thought and belief:

> Pots readily lend themselves to a language of inside/outside, container/contained. Often this may involve the creation of a humanoid image, although not necessarily so. Rather, it presupposes the body as a container of forces. The precise nature of this containing power of pots is unclear, it may be in the clay of the vessel or the cavity itself. In conscious and unconscious symbolism, however, thinking with pots is extremely common in Africa. In more general terminology, the potting process is a scenario that provides a concrete experience that can serve as a model for organising other experiences.[1]

Equal to that, Oyekan has made a body of work that is entirely of this moment, but that also brings us into closer connection with an old culture – arguably the richest culture for pottery – that retains a shared understanding of the meaning in objects.

1. Nigel Barley, *Smashing Pots, Feats of Clay from Africa*, British Museum Press, 1994.

Kerosene Lamps

Kerosene Lamps was a book in the series called *Indian Sandwich No. 2*, designed and published by Tony Hayward, printed in India in 1994. This brief text was as long as could be allowed to accompany a small concertina fold of nine images of lamps made from scrap metal and other found material. Hayward made annual visits to India and published several series of such books on different objects made by reusing leftover stuff.

Nine kerosene lamps, made of tin cans and glass bottles, by soldering, folding, fitting. The beauty of skill poised on the rawness of these materials. With guileless ingenuity forms are assembled for different needs – lamps to hang on the wall, tall table lamps stabilised with sand, lamps to carry.

One is recognisably a 'lantern', four panes of glass, a door, a handle on the roof over a ventilating cupola, like a paper ruff cut from a paint tin. The simplest is an upturned funnel of plain metal, with a looped handle, and the wick protruding from a fine green tube through a yellow disc with a few unreadable red words.

The randomness of the printed surfaces, the decorative side issue of their colour and their (former) content, does appeal. It is the aesthetic of 'making do', familiar in patchwork quilts and the like. 'Waste not, want not', they suggest from the other side of the world. These are objects of curious visual potency. Their ordinariness is their peculiarity – use and beauty are equated by a new route.

Kerosene Lamps, unknown makers in India, 1990s, photos: Graham Murrell

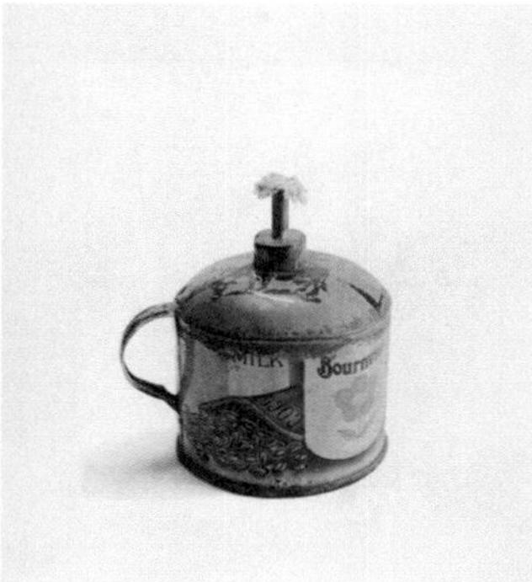
MILK
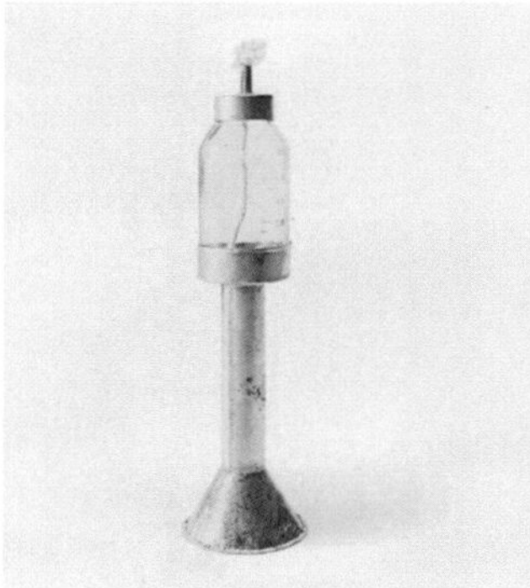
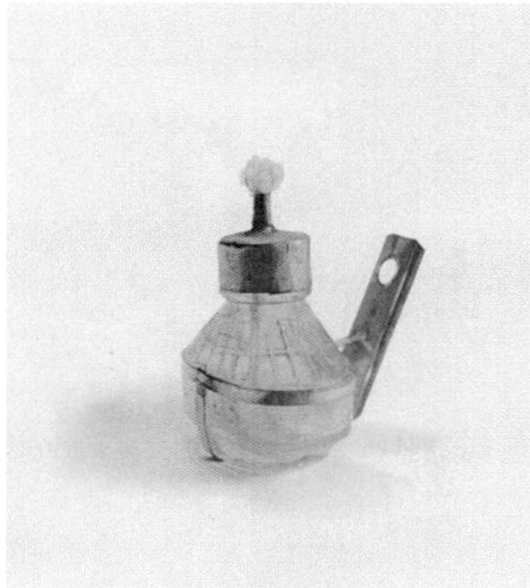
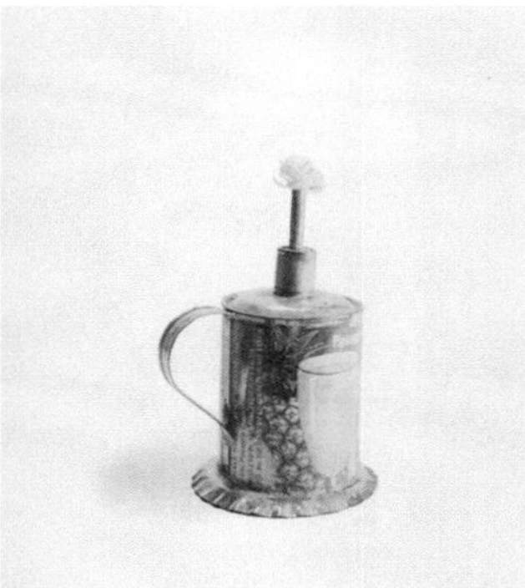
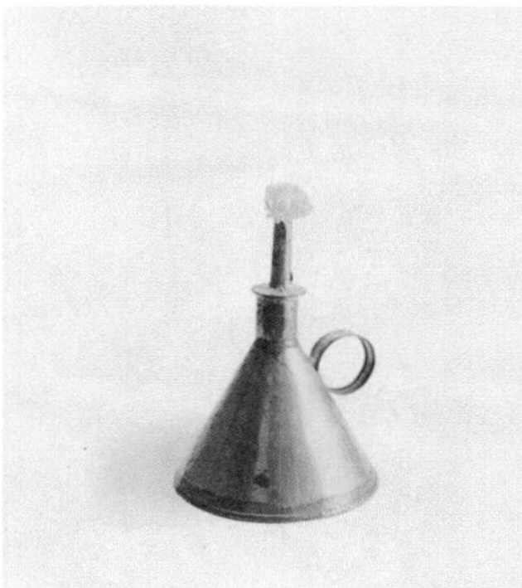
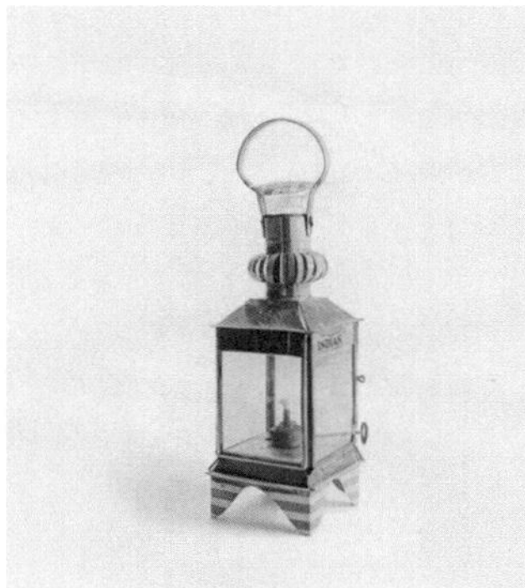
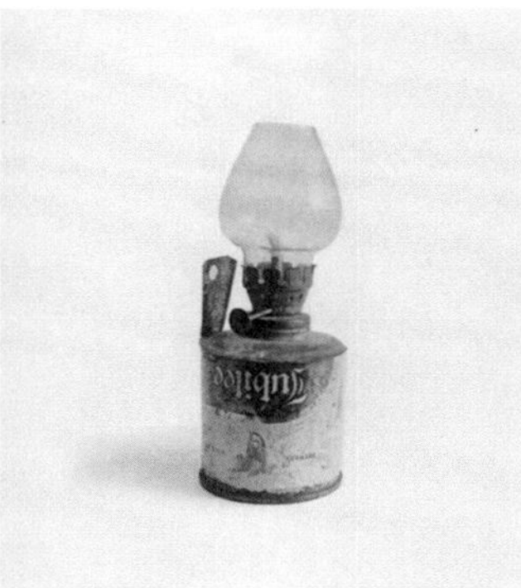
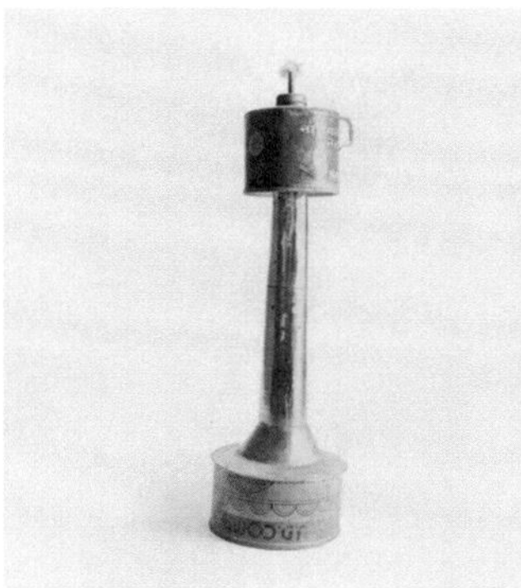
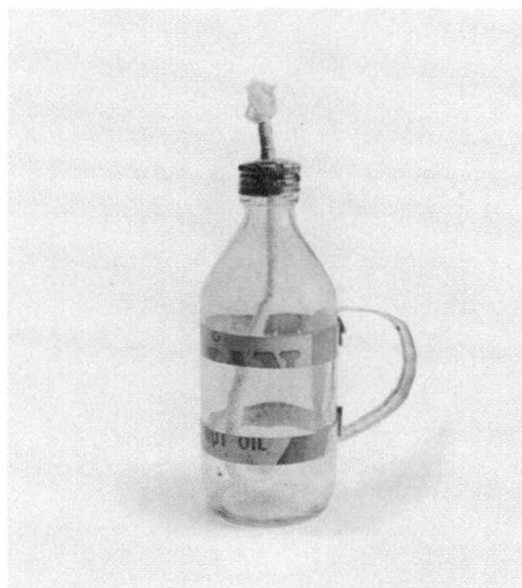
OIL

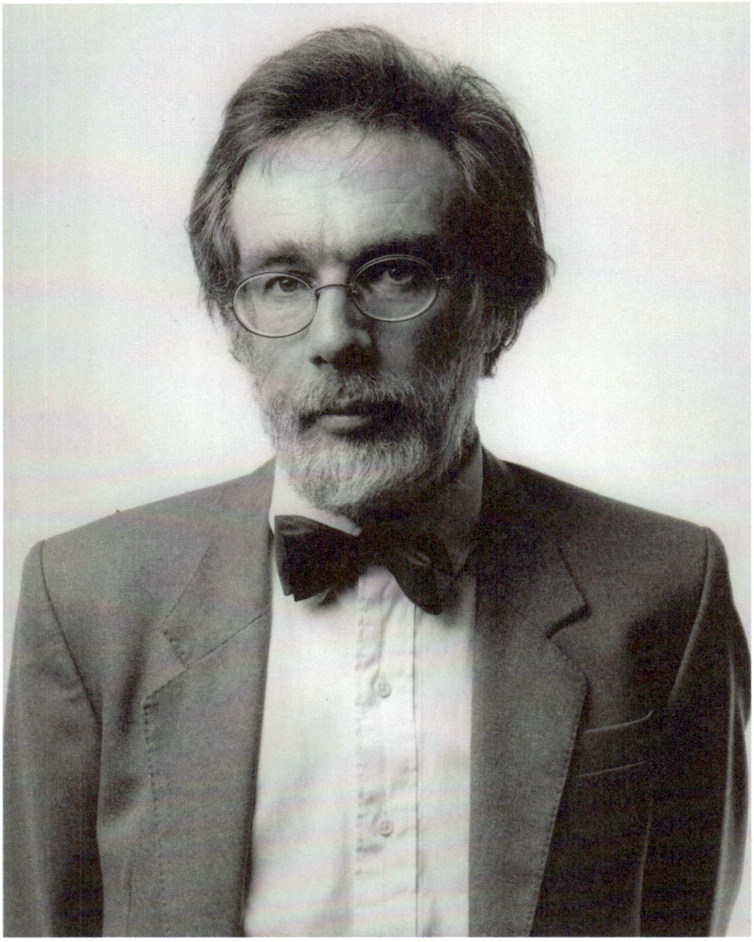

Portrait of Peter Dormer, 1990s, photo: Ed Barber

Peter Dormer Memorial Speech

Unpublished notes, 1997. I gave this speech at the reception following the first of the Peter Dormer Lectures, commemorating his work as a critic and writer, and still given annually at the Royal College of Art, London. Charles Jencks was the first lecturer in December 1997; Dormer had died the year before.

There are a number of people in this room who knew Peter better than I did, and what I have to say about him only describes a relatively small part of the work that he did. Peter worked with incredible energy and thorough concern and devotion, and his interests stretched over a number of areas, and more significantly his interests changed over the almost 20-year period of his highly productive time.

Perhaps one of the purposes of inviting me to contribute to this evening, when we are commemorating him, is because of my interaction with him, through my making, his writing, my writing, our both making exhibitions, reacting to each other via looking and uttering while he was working with the applied arts; and because my particular part of the craft world is quite close to the 'expressive' fence – what Peter called the noman's land between art and craft (and I might call the only satisfactory, if draughty, home). I am, if you like, one of the babies that could have been, may have been, thrown out with his changing bathwater.

To better explain what I mean by this, I want to look at a sequence of exhibitions that he made or commented on. Most of what Peter made was writing, masses of it. Eloquent, simple, often witty, usually thought-provoking. No gushing, no jargon. His writing, in books, catalogues, newspapers, and magazine articles really is a legacy, and is the way in which we will keep in touch with the ideas and arguments that he initiated, which roll on, and which he left with horrifying abruptness.

But his making of exhibitions was, to me, especially important. An exhibition is an experience, is ephemeral and visual. Sometimes, after it is over, that arrangement of objects in that particular space lives on in the catalogue – and Peter was responsible for some enduringly interesting catalogues – but they are not the same as the visual experience. Part of Peter's chosen job (and mine) was the attempt to share his ideas about objects, by showing them and relating them, creating a thread of an argument out of them, to a broadening audience. Translation from the visual world to the verbal one is necessarily imperfect but worth the effort. Some people have a stronger response with the eyes and others get more from the text, but the building of bridges between the two is some endeavour.

I first met Peter when I had just written my piece for *The Maker's Eye* catalogue for the Crafts Council exhibition of 1981, and his enthusiastic response and continuing encouragement to me as a maker starting to write, was important. I was even more pleased to be asked to write the introduction to his book *The New Ceramics* in 1986. Peter was very interested in ceramics but it did, in its contemporary manifestations, develop problems for him. He could see that the regurgitations of the Bernard Leach tradition could not be where youthful energy would direct itself, and in an exhibition like *Fast Forward* at the ICA, London, in 1985 he celebrated the alternatives.

But whereas furniture is always made for use, and jewellery, however daft it is, is only there to be worn, the field of ceramics encompasses a split from tableware to sculpture. And distinct, but not entirely unrelated, modes of working have emerged in studio ceramics that could, in Oliver Watson's terminology, be called 'expressive' or 'ethical'. As time passed, Peter became more interested in the ethical end, though not limited by Leach dogma, and increasingly anxious about the validity of the expressive end. The axis of his anxiety is the question of skill. Are we throwing it away?

So by 1991, when the Crafts Council reopened on its new site with Peter's exhibition *Beyond the Dovetail,* this was his subject. It was also the material for his PhD. Exceptionally for a critic and theorist, he had apprenticed himself to a calligrapher, a portrait terra cotta modeller, and I think a wood carver, to experience what he was researching. Unusually too, the exhibition included examples of craftwork that showed what was in Peter's terms error and misjudgment, pretention and sloppiness (I was never quite sure which section I was in) – and some people withdrew their exhibits in distress.

I knew which section I was in in the catalogue. Christopher Frayling, its editor, had asked me to contribute an alternative view, which I did in a piece called *The Manipulation of Skill on the Outer Limits of Function.* I never argued with Peter face to face, and I am sure he would have won if we had, but I did disagree with him in print. Peter had the last word in the catalogue (and went on to analyse the faults in my thinking in a two-page article in the *Art of the Maker* in 1994) and I want to read you one paragraph from his essay which I experience as being on the cusp between accuracy and significance, and deep irritation:

> I think handicraft is important: it can be an expression of human care, thought, service and creativity, but I believe it becomes all these grand things only through being channelled into specific goals, which have criteria that can be assessed publicly. At a time when fine art appears to be inward-looking and a matter of private concern to a relatively limited number of people, it seems all the more important to raise the handicraft banner as an accessible, understandable and wholly honest public art or design form.
>
> The very demonstration of craft skill is something that other people like to see; they can share in its triumph. The demonstration of skill, as much as imagination, is often evidence of the human mind at its best at work. The important characteristic of craftwork is that craft (and the designs that bind it together) has communal roots. It is a perversity to make of craft a private language. Function, skill and tradition are

> not reactionary ingredients, they provide the bridges of comprehension between a maker and his or her public. Traditionally, craft, and its peer activity, design, have looked outwards, not in.

He's right, and yet at the time it felt like the imposition of a National Curriculum for the Crafts. While I still object to this, I think now, on reflection, and working more as I do now in the education of ceramicists, that I was justly corrected. I had left a couple of bases uncovered in my arguments. I had for close to 20 years underplayed the importance of skills in my own background. At the time that I began to make and talk about work, I was emerging into a world where there was virtually no debate, only recipes, and all people wanted to ask at the end of a personally exhaustive, self-searching expositional talk, was whether my biscuit temperature was higher than my glaze. In this context I and my colleagues wanted to say 'that's BORING. We can take that for granted. We don't need to talk about that'. But perhaps we went on saying it for too long.

I want to conclude with a sense of gratitude to Peter for making the environment in which I work more difficult. His writing and the exhibitions he organised have made my world more stimulating, more contentious, with better channels for ideas to come to the surface and be challenged. He stopped the craft world from being so cosy and nice. If I were to find a metaphor for my rapport with Peter I would say that I was wet where he was dry; and if I could extend this image – think of an oyster – it is only the grit in the shell, needling the complacent self-expressive flesh, a job Peter did with gentlemanly precision and articulacy, that makes the pearl.

I think it is fair to say that there would be no cultural product without the phenomenon of the sturdy human ego, whether we're thinking of theatre or ceramics or anything else. But Peter, as a man, was exceptionally un-egotistic. He could not have been happy as an artist, which he found out early on after a painting degree in Bath. He found happiness and fulfillment as a scourge, one who could also be a gentle and considerate friend. He frequently punctured the vanity, posturing, vagueness and pomposity that invades art and craft practice, and he did it with courage and wit.

I want finally to recommend to any of you who might not have caught it at the time, my favourite piece of his writing. It is in an exhibition catalogue from 1986 called *Our Domestic Landscape*, published by Cornerhouse Gallery in Manchester. Peter's essay is entitled 'New Jerusalem and the Domestic Landscape'. It is a bit more personal than most of his writing and describes his growing up on a sparse council estate in Cambridge, glimpsing the 'other' world of ancient, beautiful Cambridge colleges, and the roots of his awareness of spaces: home, school, privacy, quality – and its absence – that led to his life's central concern for the interaction of people with things. He begins to address here ideas about class and taste in the art/craft/design world, and writes it clearly and simply, from the heart. Luckily, we can still hear his voice in his writing.

The Open-minded Eye

Crafts magazine 150, January/February 1998, pp.30–33 (an edited version of this article was reprinted in the Archive pages of *Crafts* magazine 233, November/December 2011). The London gallery Contemporary Applied Arts, after a couple of name changes, reached its 50th anniversary in 1998. While I was organising the exhibition *A View of Clay*, one of a series during that celebratory year surveying different media, *Crafts* magazine asked me to write about the exhibition-making process.

When Martina Margetts and I were working on the selection of *The Raw and the Cooked* exhibition at the Museum of Modern Art Oxford in 1993, at the outset we chose by eye and made up the story, the themes and the arguments afterwards. And in displaying the objects themselves on two occasions, both at the Barbican and at Museum of Modern Art Oxford, we were very aware that the visual juxtapositions of the work within the available space, arranged differently in the two venues, told different stories, led by the spaces and the architectural conditions. I hadn't expected to feel that the exhibition itself was plastic, that it could be moulded to a variety of meanings, transitory and distinct from what is remembered through the catalogue.

Things must come first. That is what it is about – the visual, how objects look and what it is they are saying; the particular impact on eye and mind of how an object makes sense, how it connects with other objects and suggests an idea, a past and a future, that is mainly indescribable in words.

In writing about other people's work, I am usually aware of my obligations as an 'insider', as someone who also makes, a fellow traveller rather than an official investigator. What difference my practical insights make to curation I am not so sure, but I suspect that the strength of feeling I have about certain pots and clay objects, which involves both the eye and the chest in the perception, comes out of a sympathetic inner sense of building form, and of originating. There is nothing casual in the process of choosing a thread through the huge array of ceramic work. It seems a wonderful opportunity, though one fraught with anxiety, to be given the chance by Contemporary Applied Arts (CAA) to be one of a sequence of guest curators in the celebration of its anniversary year – to be able to offer a view, a reading, of ceramics. In writing about it in advance, I am very aware that this is not the final story; I hesitate to pin down aspects that are still uncertain.

At the beginning of choosing an exhibition you look for key people whose work you trust, and whose creative past you believe in, because the actual works are still to be made. There is no way of predicting whether if the pieces that come into being will jointly make a coherent statement, or argue with each other. This is a considerable risk. It is not easy to surprise the audience, but this is what I would most like to achieve with this exhibition. I think that surprise is what keeps a culture alive.

I found it useful on this occasion, knowing that the gallery size at CAA implied a list of seven or eight artists, to opt for a kind of narrative, or diary, in my selection. My list is a thread that links back to the 1960s, of those who taught me and fellow students, people I have taught, and people who I've never worked with, but who reveal bits of the map by which I make sense of ceramic culture. All of them I admire for their understanding of clay. And, as a further excuse for this self-indulgent approach to curation, there is the coincidence of CAA's fiftieth birthday and my own. I now know that I am as old as an institution.

I first thought I wanted to be a potter when I was 12, and made quite a lot at school. An inspiring, energetic teacher made the difference, as usual – encouragement towards coil pots and murals was the start of it for me – who pinned up pictures of African hand-built pots. There was a wheel in the room but it was very stiff and difficult and not a lot of attention was paid to it.

Perhaps this early orientation accounts for the fact that I can't see the life in Bernard Leach pots – I am numb to them. As a motivating force they missed me completely, although I can admire the passion, the reaching out beyond Europe, and the rhetoric. I think I am both overexposed to the fervour of his following, and ignorant of the need for it. But the more overt symbolism of African ceramics has continued to be important and, with Cubism, which also looked to Africa, was the foundation of my understanding of the possible scope of ceramics.

When I was growing up I thought that Russell Square was the centre of London because my father worked at the Institute of Education and would leave me in the British Museum. William Newland was the potter at the Institute and I was able to work with him occasionally in the basement studio there. I encountered a different, more mysterious set of values about clay shapes and vitality and touch, and learned to hit my pots with a stick while coiling them. Through my first years in college I felt that he was keeping an eye on me. It has taken a long time to develop my own ideas about the values of ceramics, about what it means to connect to a long craft tradition and what the main point of it is now. This exhibition is an attempt to reveal my thoughts about what counts: the ordinariness and the peculiarity of clay form.

In the 1920s and 1930s there was a flurry of written commentary (by Herbert Read and others) about pots being the purest form of abstract expression, by which I think they meant that they recognised that a pot (a 'perfect' Greek or Chinese pot) could have an entirely satisfying aesthetic form and you didn't have to use it. I would contest that the pot, simply by being a pot, offers a function that is an equivalent for subject matter or representation, and is the opposite of abstraction. Can we have meaning in a pot or a ceramic form without either function or imagery? I would say yes, shape *can* be infinitely suggestive to the open-minded eye, and it is the undecided, ambiguous pieces that I particularly cherish. Duality as an undercurrent of interest in what I make, and in what I appreciate, became

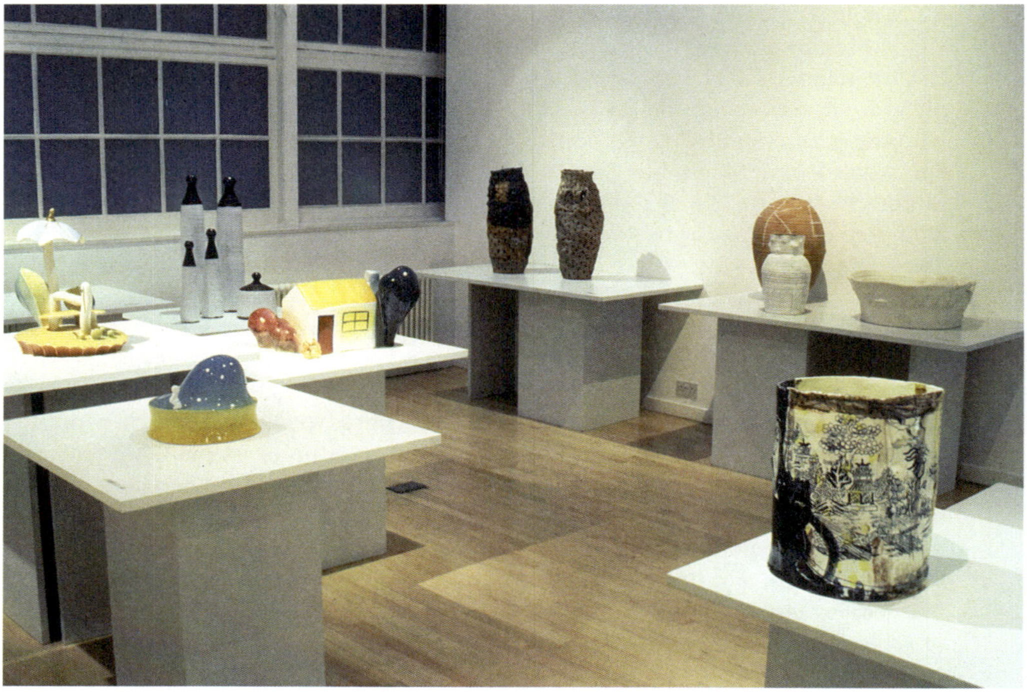

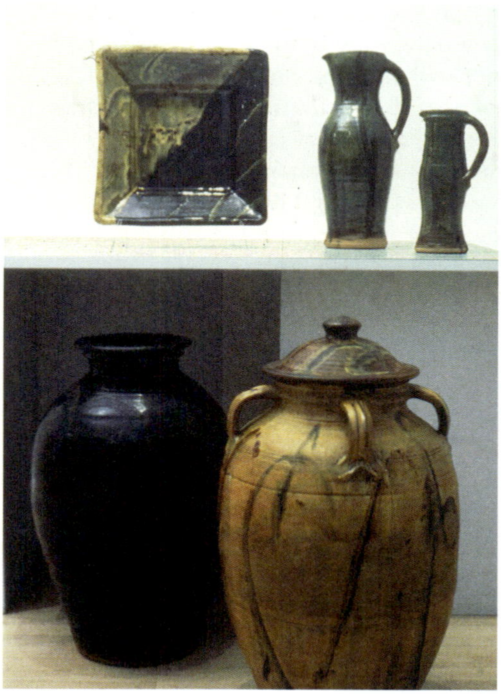

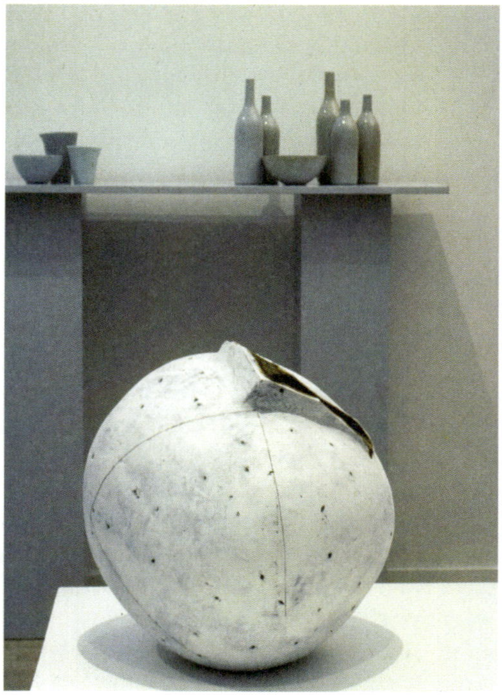

apparent for me when I wrote my section of *The Maker's Eye* catalogue in 1981 and referred to 'two-faced objects'. Ceramics is rich in these.

The Abstract Vessel was an exhibition curated by John Houston and Ralph Turner at Oriel in Cardiff in 1990, and Houston wrote the catalogue. It is an excellent, dense analysis of abstraction in pots and issues of modernist iconography, which needs regular re-reading. He reaches the conclusion with a recognition of the transforming value of witting or unwitting reference to the body in modern pots, which he calls 'the prime analogy of form to render feeling'. *The Abstract Vessel* included four of the same artists who are in my group: Richard Slee, Philip Eglin, Jacqueline Poncelet, and Gordon Baldwin. Not so surprising – their work is central to how ceramics has developed in the UK.

Not all the work in my show, *A View of Clay*, will be pots, though a sense of hollowness is a constant. In the seven years since Houston wrote that book, I have come to think that 'fiction' is perhaps a more interesting term for me in looking at some clay objects than 'abstraction'. The specific quality of fiction is that it is unreal – useable only in the space of imagination. 'Form and Fiction' satisfactorily twists the familiar modernist tenet 'Form and Function', and stretches the range of allusive, narrative, commentating possibilities that contemporary ceramic practice is tied up with, while not losing touch with ordinary prose.

To conclude with a few notes on the participants. I can't go into much detail, because every nuance is still up in the air. I know who to include, but don't yet know which things I can choose. As I described at the start, an articulate reading will not be clear until the chosen things are arranged in the space. I hope to surprise myself as well. So far all is plastic.

My selection starts with William Newland, who said of himself and his colleagues in the 1950s: 'It's not that we were anti-Leach, but there were other things to do...' I hope to include some early work of his as well as something recent. Baldwin, drawing on built form, Clive Bowen painting on thrown form – different strands of equal vigour. Gwyn Hanssen Pigott's thrown pots, now more of a crowd than a family group, multiplying and modulating elements of an extended still-life. Poncelet: some of the last ceramic pieces made as she began to compare her clay sculpture with forms in other materials. Slee with occupied ornamental landscapes, and Eglin's buckets rather than figures. My last choice is Lawson Oyekan, the youngest and furthest from home, who brings me back to the pictures of African pots on the school wall.

This represents the potential – now the challenge and responsibility is down to the artists.

Clockwise from top left: Views of exhibition with works by Richard Slee, William Newland, Lawson Oyekan, Philip Eglin; Clive Bowen, *Dish, Jugs, Jars*; Gwyn Hanssen Pigott, *Grand Still Life*; Gordon Baldwin, *White Vessel with Yellow Inside*, all photos: Graham Murrell

On the Edge of Possibility

Ceramic Review 174, November/December 1998, pp.15–17. This essay was a preview of a solo exhibition of Bodil Manz's porcelain pots at Galerie Besson, London, 21 October–20 November 1998.
The common ground between British and Scandinavian views of ceramics is still evident.

A fresh encounter with the pots of Bodil Manz is a visual shock. Coming upon them in a group exhibition among the lumpen and craggy forms of much fired clay, Manz's pieces are breathtakingly cool and sharp. Most of them are straight-sided porcelain cylinders of different sizes, coloured and patterned in a bold and brilliant way that involves both the surfaces of the walls, which are of unbelievable thinness. They are clothed with rectangles of clean flat colour – blue, black, red, yellow – or linear patterns playing fugues with the inside and outside walls. These walls are sheer in two senses – as in sheer cliff face, and letting the light through like sheer muslin. They are pots that go to a ceramic extreme. They have the weight of meringues. The delicacy of the cast shell, the straight lines of both the form and the drawing – in every aspect such qualities are very hard to achieve in this material. It means a passionate, obsessive perhaps even quest for an ideal, and an understanding of the material properties and the effects of heat that enable her to play right to the edge of possibility. The pigments, blocks and patterns, are mainly high-firing except for the red. They are printed and then applied by ceramic transfer. The colours are improved by several firings; they sink more beautifully into the body, but extra firings to high temperatures risk distortion. It is a knife-edge.

Do Manz's pots look particularly Danish? It seems to me that they do. I went to Denmark in the early 1970s, to visit Elizabeth Fritsch when she lived for a year in a visitor's flat inside the Bing & Grondhal factory in Copenhagen. It was unusual for a foreign potter to be installed there, but the project to bring artists into individual studios within the ceramics factory, give them materials, let them keep a portion of their work, exhibit and promote them as artists, and also hope that imaginative sparks might fly from them into mass production, was one of the special features of modernist Scandinavia. I found myself in the midst of this Nordic phenomenon, where the minds of art and industry could run together. The Danish factories of Bing & Grondahl and Royal Copenhagen, Gustavsberg in Sweden and Arabia in Finland all had such studios. The expectation of students taking up ceramics was that they could be both artist and designer, as many have successfully been. Both Helsinki and Copenhagen looked to me like Utopias of ceramic context when I was a student. (Overdeveloped notions of freedom that grew through the 1970s changed the perspective on art being owned by industry.)

Something I now realise I had found on my visit to the Bing & Grondahl studios was that the numerous little bowls, being used to mix pigments by the artists, were samples of an extensive tea service from 1955–57 designed by the remarkable Gertrud Vasegaard. Born in 1913, she is part of a third-generation of potters of the Hjorth family from Bornholm. She spent the years from 1945–59 in the studios at Bing & Grondahl. Her tea service, and also a design called 'Capella' made in 1975 for Royal Copenhagen, are in my view as good as anything ever done in tableware – both cool and warm, pure form with human touches. She has made many unique pieces too, such as low cylinders with linear patterns. Her exquisite sense of form, I believe, provides a background to the way Manz has developed her work.

Denmark has nurtured a lot of strong women potters. The cover of the Dutch museum Boijmans Van Beuningen catalogue of their Danish collection, made from 1970–95, is notable for the four 'key' illustrated potters all being women – Vasegaard, Gutte Eriksen, Alev Siesbye, and Manz.

Although not one of the artists in the factory's gilded cages, Manz has done design work for Bing & Grondahl during the 1980s and also earlier for Rorstrand in Sweden, where she went to work after the rigorous craft and design education under Richard Kjaergaard at the Kunstandvaerkerskolen in Copenhagen from 1961–65. It was a good decision because there she met her future husband and studio partner, the German-born Richard Manz. Setting out on a career in ceramics in the mid 1960s, breaking out of the modernist marriage of art with industry, they represent the approach of a subsequent generation. Bodil Manz has taken her strong Danish ceramic sensibility to other continents and experienced a wide variety of attitudes. She encountered both Bernard Leach and Peter Voulkos during the 1960s, and the Manzs studied and worked abroad, including Mexico and the United States.

Since 1967 they have shared a studio in North Seeland, and kept up their individual practice, making and designing, as well as jointly working on large commissions for monumental art in architecture. These have been realised in Denmark, Bahrain, and Switzerland.

The Manzs also helped form 'Keramiske Veje' (Ceramic Ways), a group of eight ceramic artists who came in 1983 to have regular exhibitions together. Bente Hansen and Sten Lykke Madsen are other internationally known members of the group, Madsen being the only one still to work in a 'studio-within-a-factory' context, now at Royal Copenhagen. All, I believe, studied at the Kunsthandvaerkerskolen, now called the Danish Design School.

Galerie Besson is one of the very few places in the UK where one can hope to see contemporary ceramics from other countries, and this has been a very significant aspect of the gallery's work. Besson has shown Danish work before – first in 1989 with a group of eight potters, distinct from 'Keramiske Veje' and more in the orientalist than in the European modernist tradition. Eriksen, born in 1918, is the highly venerated potter credited with forging the link between Danish pottery and Leach, as she worked at St Ives in the late 1940s. Besson held a solo exhibition of Eriksen's work in 1990.

Bodil Manz has shown at the gallery in 1995, but this is her first solo show in London. It includes new cylinders and recent pots that investigate other plain geometric forms. These are still sheer-walled, but may be angular oval forms, faceted, some with one half of the form slipped sideways. The show will add greatly to the gradual revelation of Danish ceramics and bring us a clearer cutting-edge view of its strength and vitality.

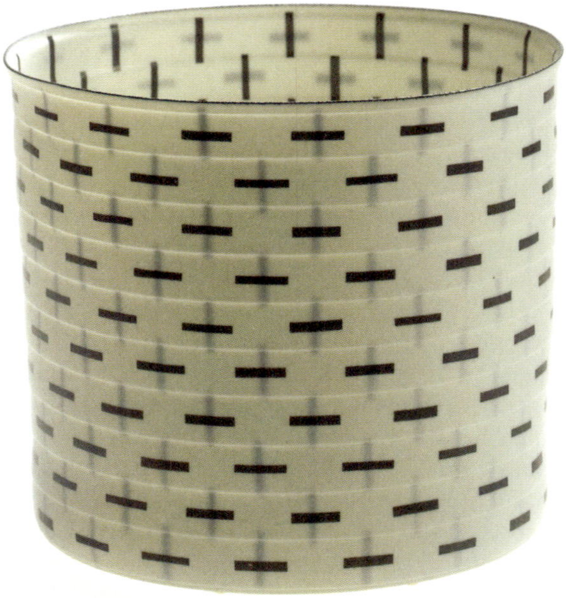

Bodil Manz, *Cross*, 2004, photo: Brahl Fotografi

Notes for the Write Stuff

Discussion notes for a forum of critics and writers at the Millenium Ceramic Conference convened by the distinguished curator, historian, gallerist and advocate for ceramics in America, Garth Clark. The conference ran for five days in Amsterdam in July 1999.

'Insider' and 'outsider' writing is one of the ways in which we could characterise the kinds of text, that concerns themselves with the crafts. Insider writing is what I would call most of what I have done in catalogues and exhibition leaflets. Even when writing about other people's work in other media, I have often approached it comparatively, as an equivalent maker with certain common insights as regards *doing*, and a sense of materials and aesthetic preoccupations that may be in the air at the time.

The categories into which we push works of art of various types are changing because of the way the makers choose to work. This interests me very much. From a more critical viewpoint I think it is important to try, through writing, to focus the reader on the actual qualities of made objects, their probable meanings, and their place in an increasingly manufactured and simulated environment. I want to write plainly without being dull, and without the use of jargon. Copy on the crafts is irritating if it has to keep referring the object in question to other art forms – often thought to be 'higher' art forms – to make it accessible to a general audience. I think that writing on the crafts, and ceramics in particular, has enough of a past now to feed its own commentary.

It is obvious from the working path I have chosen that I am comfortable with both the verbal and the visual. It is not so for everyone, I am aware, and many people think of Britain as a place that is culturally over-dominated by words at the expense of sights. Most people acknowledge that the translation from one to the other is difficult, approximate at best.

Using words to talk or write about something as different from text as art or craft must always I think be an attempt to go beyond the surface, or there isn't any point in it. With tact and precision we may be able to use language as a permeable membrane, letting things pass, letting a range of meanings and references through without fixing or changing the object.

Writing has on quite a few occasions improved and sharpened my thinking, clarified what I am doing, or shown me my working place in relation to others. I think it is not unusual for artists and craftspeople to use language to those ends, like a diary or a manifesto.

And then there is literature – poetry, fiction – words used more artfully to reveal ideas about the visual artifact. There are plenty of poems about paintings, there are even a few about pots that I can think of. Making a pot and writing a poem probably have something in common as processes. Prose and poetry, and the stretch between them, have been used as a metaphor for the differences between useful and contemplative pots.

Working Round

Gallery leaflet, solo exhibition of works by Maria van Kesteren, Barrett Marsden Gallery, London, 24 September–6 November 1999. Van Kesteren was for many years, as well as Holland's most celebrated woodturner, co-director of a pioneering gallery called Galerie Kapelhuis, Amersfoort, which closed in 1992. The exchange of ideas between British and Dutch artists and designers was a very positive aspect of the modernist/postmodern 1980s in particular.

My first impression of an object has to be surprising, consistent and refreshing, but above all convicing and inevitable. After all that, materials and techniques count for me.

Maria van Kesteren is both an artist and a designer in a way that seems enviably unfettered and effective in the Dutch context – a combined activity more valued, more fluid I think, there than here. For much of the 39 years that she has had her own studio, she has been making objects in turned wood, though she has also designed for other materials. She is, therefore, an artist/designer who is mainly engaged with a working practice placed paradoxically at the craftiest, hobbyist even, end of the applied arts spectrum.

A look through any woodturning magazine reveals a discussion of virtuoso techniques and incredible equipment more than any evaluation of objects. The things themselves frequently sentimentalise the substance of wood, playing to its quirks and seduced by its grain patterns and by craft difficulty. As van Kesteren says: 'The exterior features of the material (grain, capricious markings, knots, burls, holes) attract a lot of people, because it is tempting to think that a spectacular piece of wood needs hardly anything added. The reality is the contrary: the state of the surface distracts from the form'. She is an exception in the field of woodturning. She stands out because form is what matters to her, far more than tools or different trees. Van Kesteren is breathtakingly severe with her material – she is not swayed by the 'natural' qualities of wood, the charm of its irregularities, the tracks of its growth. An exhaustive exploration of the nuance and detail of hollow circular forms has engaged her for three decades. She has refined an acute understanding of curves and visual tension, the possible junctions of concentric shapes, the play of interior and exterior space. Vitality expressed in mass and absence, surface and depth, light and darkness, the visible and the touchable – this is what she pursues.

The process of woodturning is absolutely one of subtraction, the removal of surface to reach the desired form – there is no going back and rethinking, rebuilding as one might with clay. It is a surgical and decisive business. It has the advantage over a clay pot that the inner form need not echo the outside shape. (Firing clay requires even thickness.) Van Kesteren has made much of this possibility of the unexpected interior. The unlimited variations of the things she has made have been for the eye first, but also engaging to touch and sometimes offering a function as a box, bowl, or dish, though many have been entitled 'object'. Functional or not, the double venture of the box form holds a special place in her interests.

> Specially the box gives one freedom to express: to create a tension between open and closed, between in and out, between spontaneity and reserve, between openness and disguise.[1]

Van Kesteren usually chooses native woods, such as lime, elm, and sycamore, for the qualities of their workable substance and not their appearance. She wants a neutral kind of wood, and currently the final surface of the object is painted with several thin layers of acrylic. In the past she has used bleach or stain to take command of the woodiness. Colour is increasingly subtle and varied, mixed with great care, and a particular palette has emerged in her work across all media. Perhaps some of her discoveries of colour in glass or glaze have suggested a greater range of paint on wood.

This exhibition concentrates on the juxtaposition of two distinct groups of circular forms in wood. One series of flat weighty bowl and box forms is painted with a wood-like colour that has some of the sheen and tone of compressed facepowder. A second series of smaller more upright forms is painted a light off-cream. Both groups are tactile and mysterious, apparently simple, hiding their depths. There is also some of the design work in ceramic and glass to be seen to put the clear and subtle ideas of van Kesteren in a fuller context.

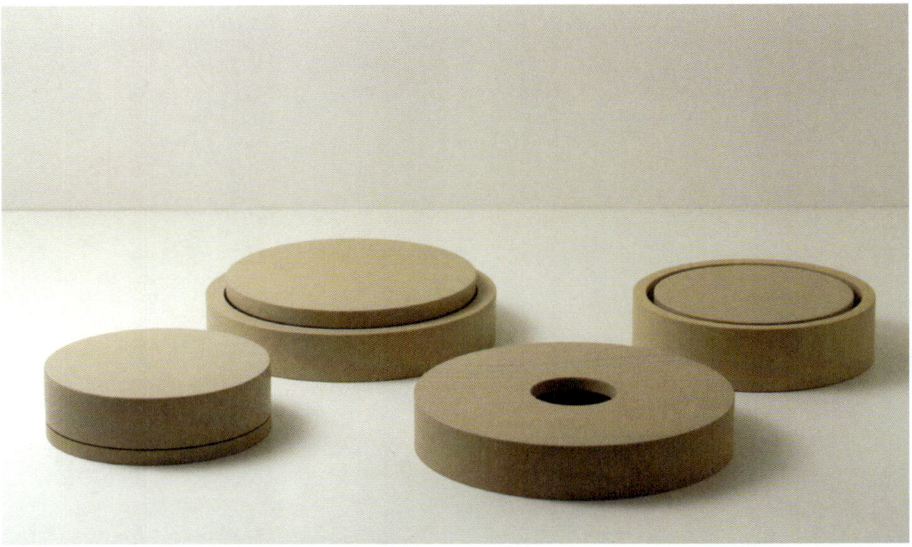

Maria van Kesteren, each entitled *Object, Elm*, 1999, photo: Philip Sayer, courtesy Marsden Woo Gallery

Born in 1933, van Kesteren trained in Utrecht in the late 1950s with the preeminent woodturner of the time, Henk van Trierum. She has run her own workshop in Hilversum since 1968, after being invited to set up a woodturning facility at the Kilkenny Design Workshop in Ireland. From 1968 until its closure in 1991, she was the assistant manager of Galerie Kapelhuis in Amersfoort. The most famous and long established applied art gallery in Holland, it was highly appreciated by a number of British artists for introducing a lot of their work, especially in ceramics, to a Dutch audience.

She had a retrospective exhibition, with an excellent catalogue, at the Stedelijk Museum in Amsterdam in 1995, which showed the whole span of her work. She has since 1983 designed glass for the Royal Leerdam factory, and is now working with a factory in Czechoslovakia. She has designed ceramics since 1987, vessels and funerary urns for factories such as Koninklijke Tichelaar Makkum. Some of her designs have brought wood and glass together, and she made a series of bracelets in wood shown at the radical jewellery 'Galerie Ra' in Amsterdam in 1986. When working with wood she is paring down, controlling every particle, feeling her way. She can also convey her ideas and exacting tastes to others to make glass and ceramics in production. The surface qualities of glaze, the pale colours and touchable forms, fit remarkably with the whole body of her work. Van Kesterens's sharp, decisive sensitivity is an essential part of her being both an artist and a designer – she finds what she wants.

1. All quotations are from notes for lectures given by Maria van Kesteren.

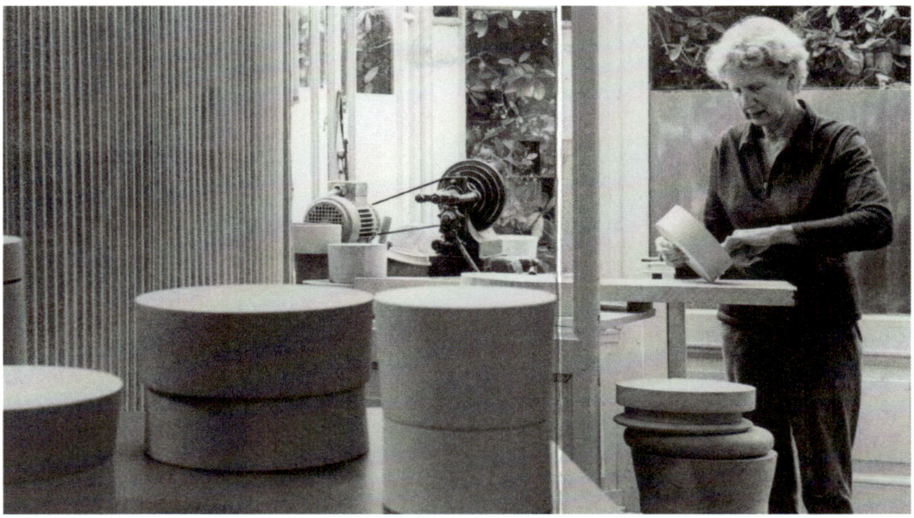

Maria van Kesteren in her studio, photo: Philip Sayer, courtesy Marsden Woo Gallery

Postscript
Skill and Anxiety

My writing in the 1990s found a firmer footing with a few good invitations. One was to write the introductory essay for Martina Margetts's book *International Crafts*.[1] I will return to the increasing tension about skill, a point raised in that essay, which during the 1980s I had been inclined to shrug off. Margetts and I also worked together to curate *The Raw and the Cooked: New Work in Clay in Britain*. Commissioned by Modern Art Oxford,[2] we had been asked to sum up the current state of things in clay.

The book reviewed in my first piece, for *RSA Journal*, gave me the historical knowledge that in industrial ceramics shape and surface had been gendered as work practices. For a week in the 1970s, as a Royal College of Art student, I had worked, or 'trained', with the underglaze paintresses at the Spode Factory in Stoke-on-Trent, so I had been in the midst of gender division in the workplace, but took it as unremarkable in 1971. Reading Cheryl Buckley brought a politicised meaning to that experience. Most of my thinking has developed from looking and doing, but can be underpinned, and often intensified, by reading.

In another ostensibly female domain, textiles, the visit to Rushton Aust's studio revealed a more postmodern complexity of fragments and layering. Aust put found fabrics with areas of printed/painted colour and pattern to make textile pieces that functioned as paintings. They communicated in a new language also seen in other media. Looking back through the 1980s clarified what the applied arts avant-garde had been doing across media. But an avant-garde necessarily comes to an end. Rosemary Hill noted the shift in emphasis for the Crafts Council by the mid-90s in *The Culture of Craft*:

> Popular interest and, it might appear, Crafts Council patronage, have moved towards the more decorative, workshop-based crafts, towards makers who see themselves more as small businesses than artists. Perhaps the focus has changed only because the crafts scene itself has been transformed. The avant-garde has passed, as it was bound to, and its place has been taken, at the more analytical end of writing about craft, by an interest in history.[3]

But the uncertain edges of postmodernity were still there in many things I was writing about in the 1990s. The 'New Ceramics' of Peter Dormer's 1986 book[4] was postmodern ceramics just as clearly as Memphis was postmodern furniture and product design. But in 1993 I wrote a doubtful note to myself while finishing an article for a German magazine about what New Ceramics meant in Britain:

> I have thought for a long while that 'New Ceramics', as it developed initially around us in the 1980s, was an artificial territory – entertainingly ambiguous and rich in first and second glances. But its borders are disconcertingly vague, it is perhaps a limbo, a place to stay in temporarily. The way out of it would seem to be towards 'real' sculpture or towards 'real' function.
>
> Many of my ceramicist friends have made one of these choices. But I am still on the fence, spinning out an old enjoyment of the hybrid.

Hybridity is a key postmodern word, in the arts and in social and cultural theory of the 1990s, and it is still apt. Two things are relevant in looking at work through this period. First the hybridity of craft blurring with the more defined disciplines of art and design. But the hybrid formal characteristics of patching, assembling, free-ranging quotation, historicity, and decorative mixture, within an object, are also pertinent.

Two of the texts in the 1990s relate to Dormer, the writer, curator and critic of craft and design, and he is the person at the centre of this reflection.[5] I much admire Dormer's straightforward way with words, the dogged arguments he makes against the tide of enthusiasm for the new, his wit and sarcasm. After curating a number of exhibitions with 'new wave' work, such as *Fast Forward* shown at the ICA, London, in 1985, Dormer lost his stomach for it and feared increasingly for the consequences of craft media detaching from traditional function and skill. Any hopes of overlapping craft and art, as he saw it, were doomed by the late 1980s. Perhaps you could say neither hybridity nor postmodernity really interested him. He couldn't look at the juggling games with form without unease, though he had liked decorative aspects of New Ceramics. Decoration could make an object domestic and unpretentious. The word *domestic* has grown in acceptability in the intervening years, in line with feminist and other critical thinking, but was a bit beyond the pale at the time. So it was bold to call an exhibition *Our Domestic Landscape* in 1986, as Peter did.

Who Dormer was is made clearer in his catalogue essay *The New Jerusalem*, as I said in my memorial speech at the first Dormer Lecture[6]. I value it because it is more personal. He uses his own history as symptomatic of what most concerns him about assumed values in design and architecture, the objects and surroundings of home, class and taste, elitism. Few in the craft world of that moment were so passionately connected to ideas about politics and social history to reflect on such things.

In my speech I said most of what I wanted to say about him, and I mention the disagreement we had in print, in the 1990 catalogue for *Beyond the Dovetail: Craft, Skill and Imagination*. Dormer's polemic exhibition targeted smugness in craft, its drift away from solid craftsmanship into 'artiness'. In his subsequent book, *The Art of the Maker*[7] he dissected my essay '*The Manipulation of Skill....*', dismissive of my view that skills are quite easily acquired when there is the motivation to make, and the idea that a sense of what is relevant is also a skill. He writes,

> Britton's thinking about skill has, I believe, been misled by the confusion, rampant in late 20th-century discussions about craft, between possessing a small number of techniques as distinct from having a complex body of craft knowledge.
>
> Simple techniques do not constitute a developed, articulated body of craft knowledge. A great many artists of the late 20th century, be they in applied or fine arts, confuse craft knowledge with the acquisition of a relatively straightforward fabrication technique.

I find his view of what craft should be, and that craftsmanship must be reinstated across the art/design spectrum, prescriptive and irritating. He wants the crafts to be a camp, a safe haven for honest values and accessibility. Skill should be measurable, matched against common understanding of traditional rules. This is asking a lot. I felt then that his eyes were stuck in an aesthetic of the middle ground, alienated by contemporary fine art, its severity and cold concepts, its de-skilled slide towards fabrication by others. He worked increasingly in his later years with design, a progressive and accountable phenomenon that might solve some of the problems of the world.[8]

So what do I think now about skill, function and ideas? I think that good ideas do appear out of the practice of making, out of manipulating materials and processes and tools, rather than imposing ideas on stuff. I think that if Dormer had got more manual skills under his belt he might have felt differently. Part of his PhD research was time spent in short craft apprenticeships that he apparently struggled with. This was despite, or perhaps because of, two years of art school early in his career.[9]

I can also see that I underrated the importance of my own skills, gained over seven years of higher art education. The provocation had been strong, though, in the early years of discourse about making, to shift the emphasis from 'how' to 'why'. The non-practical content of objects, especially ambiguous ones, needed to be articulated. In a talk given in 1994 called *Thoughts on Skill*[10] I said of my own learning:

> ... arriving at the Royal College of Art, my closest colleague there was Carol McNicoll. She came from a very woolly and expressive Fine Art course at Leeds where she had made films, collected garbage, thrown things together. She probably knew how to mix plaster when she started at college but that would be about all in terms of a traditional base of ceramic skills. I had been at the Central School where I knew

how to sprig and ground-lay, and I had a very sophisticated range of techniques, some industrial, some craft-based. When we arrived there, Carol got on with her work; I spent the first year thinking 'To what possible purpose can I put all this equipment that I have in me?' And it took me at least a year to feel that there was something, some meaning I could make out of my experience and my attributes, my carefully acquired set of possibilities.

I should have added how in 'getting on with her work', McNicoll quickly acquired the skills for bravado mould-making, model-making from a bunch of fresh daffodils, or combining casts from outmoded factory moulds to make a tea service with swallows flying through it for a famous fashion designer. Most of these capacities were learned in doing, driven by desiring the result.

Near the end of the decade, in 1999, Tanya Harrod published her large and remarkable book *The Crafts in Britain in the 20th Century.*[11] This put much of what I had experienced into the context of a whole century of off-beat practices. She, more than any writer I have come across, conveys the subtleties, complexities and tensions that seem always to have beset craft, with a grasp of detail and depth that make the book a work of social history and a critical framework as much as an exploration of what has been made.

Two essays concluding this section bring us back to the clear formal values of modernism in the work of the Danish potter Bodil Manz and the Dutch woodturner Maria van Kesteren, in exhibitions near the end of the decade. Both these women, as it happens, are also designers, and both have precise and definable skills that took a long time to acquire, and make their own way with them to great effect.

1. Martina Margetts, *International Crafts*, Thames and Hudson, 1990. Margetts was by this time a tutor in Critical and Historical Studies at the Royal College of Art.
2. *The Raw and the Cooked* opened in the Barbican and toured to Wales, France, Japan and Taiwan.
3. Rosemary Hill, 'Writing about the Studio Crafts', in *The Culture of Craft*, ed. Peter Dormer, Manchester University Press, 1997, p. 199.
4. Peter Dormer, *The New Ceramics*, Thames and Hudson, 1986, introduced by Alison Britton.
5. Dormer died of cancer in his forties in 1996. Martina Margetts, editing *Crafts*, brought Dormer into craft criticism as reviews editor from 1981 to 1983. He was previously a teacher, education officer, and local councillor. He worked entirely through writing art craft and design journalism, and curation, from this point on.
6. Held every winter at the Royal College of Art, '... the lecture's goal is to continue the debate about applied art and society to which Peter Dormer himself notably contributed' (Royal College of Art leaflet).
7. Peter Dormer, *The Art of the Maker: Skill and its Meaning in Art, Craft and Design*, Thames and Hudson, 1994. This book was the aftermath of his PhD at Royal College of Art, supervised by Christopher Frayling.
8. From 1987 to 1990, Dormer was a co-director, with John Thackara, of Design Analysis International, which organised design exhibitions and conferences worldwide.
9. Tanya Harrod writes of these years '... an experience that left him doubtful of the value of an institutionalised avant-garde. In particular artists' claims to a special level of risk-taking, experiment and innovation were seen by Dormer as "a self delusion that leaves most other professions (especially those who take real risks of life, death and possible penury) bemused".', Obituary, *The Independent*, 2 January 1997.
10. Talk given at a symposium on skill led by John Houston at the University of Westminster, 6 July 1994.
11. Tanya Harrod, *The Crafts in Britain in the 20th Century*, Yale University Press, 1999.

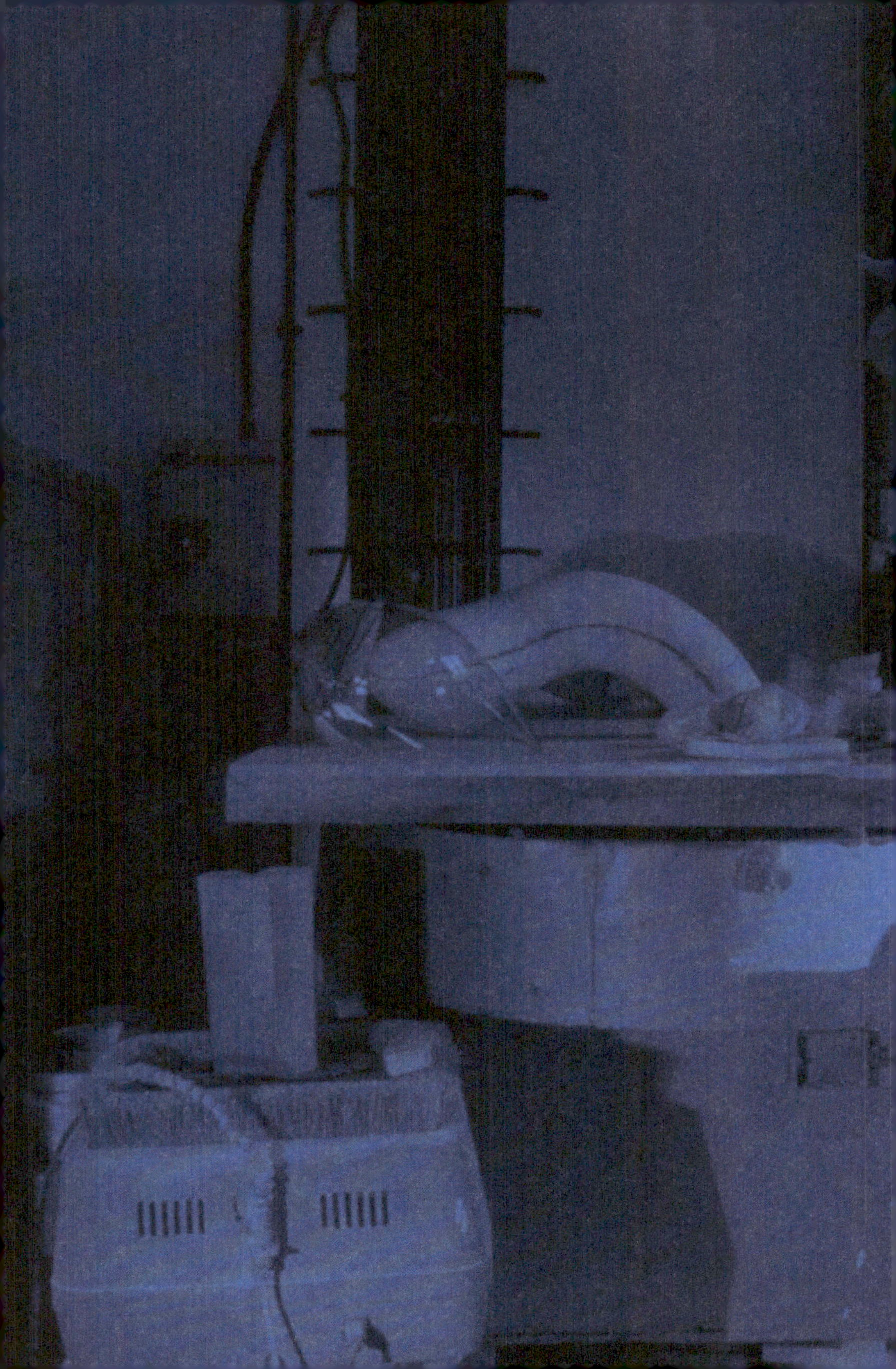

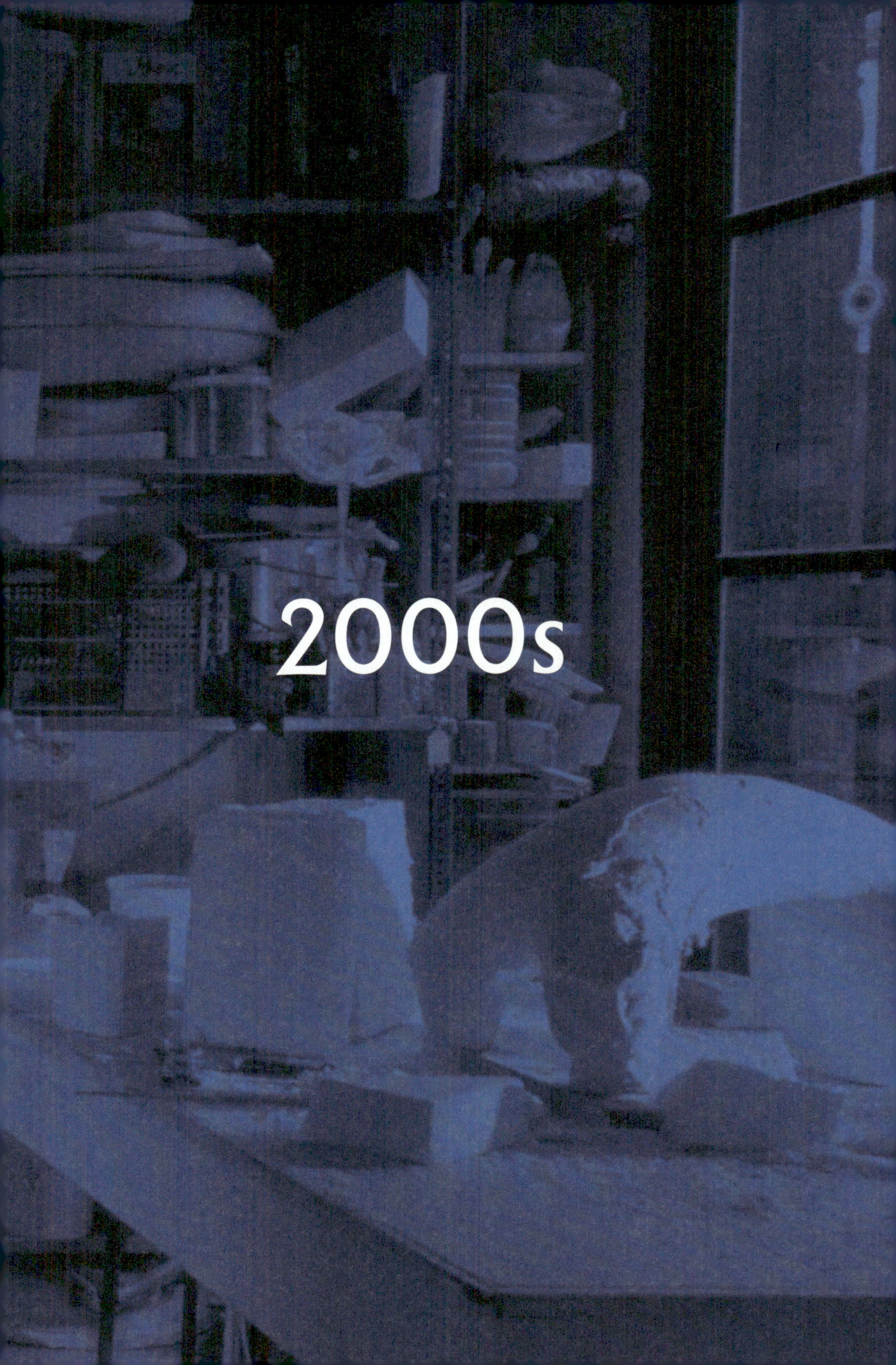

2000s

Clay, Fire and Body Performance

Ceramic Review 191, September/October 2001. Satoru Hoshino's reputation rests on his sculpture, in a genre of Japanese work in ceramics where clay is used on a huge scale to reflect the natural world. His performance was an experimental response to a dramatic climactic event, not a regular part of his practice. *Clay, Fire and Body* (V&A, 29 June 2001).

As part of the V&A's Japan 2001 programme, renowned ceramic sculptor Satoru Hoshino gave three presentations: a lecture, an installation *Rain in Ancient Woodland* (a large tree-like sculpture built from clumps of blackened clay) and, at the end of June, a performance entitled *Clay, Fire and Body.*

Five wood-burning braziers were placed on the central pathway of the V&A's Pirelli Garden. As evening fell, to the recorded sound of Monteverdi, a procession of ten naked figures, plastered with white slip, emerged from the far side of the courtyard. Their movements were measured and undemonstrative, slowly lining up in male/female pairs, first facing each other, and then back to back, over the braziers. The music was followed by the sound of waves breaking on a shingled beach. At times the sound changed to a menacing rumble, followed by silence. The figures froze at the silent moments, and then moved more freely before the repetitive tramp to and from the fires. The white slip, thick enough to clothe, began to crack in places after these wilder gestures. The sequence was sustained for almost an hour, when the sound of the sea eventually reverted to Monteverdi and the figures slipped away again.

Described as 'a haunting evocation of birth and death, and the creative and destructive potential of clay', the gravity of the slowly perambulating troupe of men and women, their hair clotted, their bodies shivering intensely on a very un-June like evening, was touchingly expressive of human endurance. Hoshino himself had a powerful and understated presence as if 'being' rather than 'doing' the performance. I believe the clay was meant to crack up more on their skin, to represent ageing.

But it is foreknowledge of Hoshino's own story that gave the performance depth. In 1986 a landslide destroyed his house, studio, a firing kiln, and almost his family, in a tide of mud. The nature of his work changed from that event, having felt clay as a destructive force.

Of slightly longer duration, two significant works of Hoshino, one from before the landslide and one after, are still to be seen until the end of August. A selection of the contemporary Japanese collection is on view in the Toshiba gallery, which includes some large-scale sculptural works, which rival much of what is upstairs in the ceramics collection for scale and modernity.

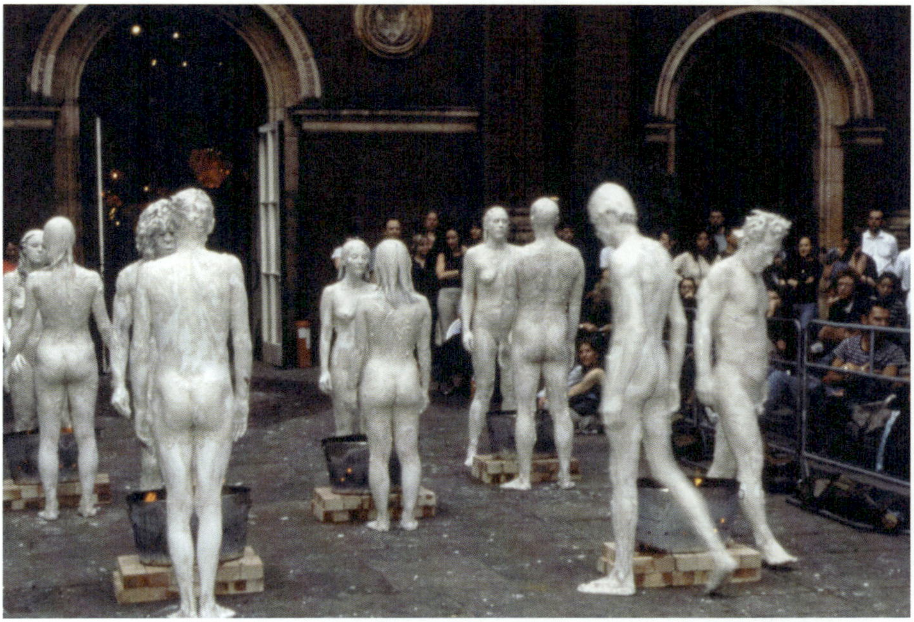

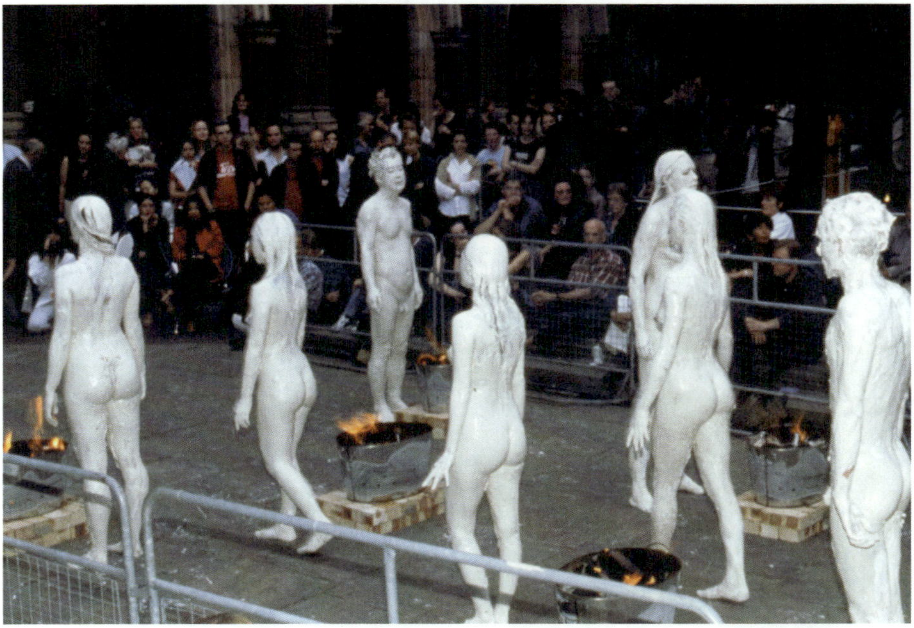

Satoru Hoshino performance, *Clay Fire and Body,* 2001, photo: Sara Hodget, courtesy V&A

Clay

Interview by Michael Rosen, *Stuff* series, produced by Louise Swan for Meridian Masterpiece, BBC Radio 4, December 2001. There were five programmes in this series, on wood, glass, stone, clay, and steel. For each conversation Rosen explored the studio of someone whose practice was centred on that material.

Michael Rosen: *Hello. Today I'm at the studio of someone who works with that most basic of materials, clay. This after all is a kind of earth, stuff we can walk on. For thousands of years, people have used clay to make the vessels we drink out of, and store food in. Today I'm with the artist Alison Britton who is internationally acclaimed for having radically changed the way clay can be used. I'm standing in what was once a butcher's shop, a kosher butcher's, actually, in North London, which now serves as Alison's studio. Round me there are pictures on the wall with large bulky forms on them and also some plastic bags which I'm guessing are full of clay, and Alison is at the moment working on something and handling the clay there and I'm wondering...*

> **Can I ask you what it is that you like about it? At this very moment you are using a brush to put some water on it but a lot of the time you are using your fingers. Is that something you like about it, the fact that you fiddle about with it, pushing and pressing it?**

Alison Britton: It's very good in many different states. Its plastic state is the most appealing I think, when it's just squidgy, and formless, really.

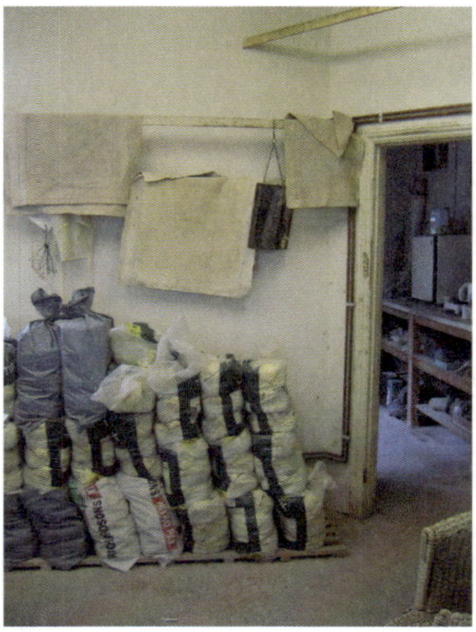

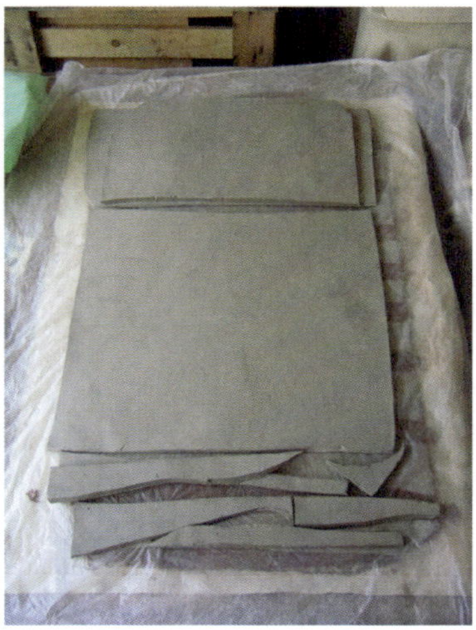

What actually is clay?

It's alumina and silica, chemically that's what it is. I mean it's mud, it's earth.

But it's not any kind of earth is it? I mean it's some kind of different earth, you've got to go and get it from somewhere special, haven't you?

Well, it would traditionally have been dug up. They would have found what is a nice sticky, plastic clay – it's laid down by rivers, it's silt. And thousands of years ago, people would have found places where it was good to use, for whatever characteristics they would judge it by, like plasticity, basically. It can be lots of different colours. If there's a lot of iron in the soil it will be red clay; if not, it's a sort of buffy colour. And then the purest form is the white kaolin clay. In China they found seams of beautiful white clay which became their porcelain, they would dig it up like that. We never had it in Europe; we had to manufacture it and we spent centuries trying to copy it. So it is a natural product that's dug up, but now many clays are synthetic, that is they are made from all the same materials that you would find in the naturally dug-up sort but they compose them together, they make sort of mixtures. I think this clay I am using is still naturally dug, it still comes out of the earth like this and it is just a buff clay. It's very very ordinary, people call it school clay, as it's used in schools a lot.

**So can we begin where it comes in to your studio?
Does it arrive in a big bag?**

It arrives on a truck, and a ton at a time. And if I'm lucky, I'm in when it arrives, and if I'm not it's left on the pavement and I have to unload it all myself into here. Bags have got smaller over the years; it used to be half hundredweight bags which were quite heavy and now it's half that much. The difficulty now is that it comes in bags that are light, degradable plastic – it's one of these ecology things – so I then have to re-bag it, otherwise the bags are going to disintegrate before I've used it all; it's going to dry out. So I've now re-bagged into nice strong bags that aren't going to rot away in the light. (*Crackling of opening a bag*) It's just called Buff Body and it's got a number, a code number so I know that I'm getting the same one every time.

We've basically got a mud brick, haven't we?

Yes, it's just a squidgy lump, quite nice and soft still.

**We're sticking our thumbs in it, can I stick my thumb in it?
Make a big imprint in it?**

Yes.

Now can you use that straight away?

Um, if I was throwing on the wheel, which I don't do, I would wedge this first, to make sure that there was no air bubbles in it.

What is wedge?

It's a kind of kneading, but when you're kneading bread you're getting air into it; when you're kneading clay you're getting air out of it instead.

Why would a potter working on the wheel need to get the air out of it?

If you're making fine-walled things, an air bubble in the clay is going to be a disruption, it's going to be a problem. Large air bubbles, when you're firing them, may explode, and may break the thing. Because I'm going to be using this clay to make sheets of clay in the first place, I'm thumping it with a rolling pin, I'm getting a big chunk and hitting it and hitting it and then rolling it, like pastry but much tougher. I'm going to be able to see any little air bubbles when I thump it, a little blister appears and then I prick it. And smooth it out, so I can get rid of them kind of locally like that. But if you were throwing something, say a large bowl, and getting to the very thin-walled stage with it, stretching it out, and some bubble appears, that's going to be a problem. I mean, people make a bit too much fuss about air in clay; it's really on the whole that things blow up in the kiln because they're too damp, and not because of little air bubbles.

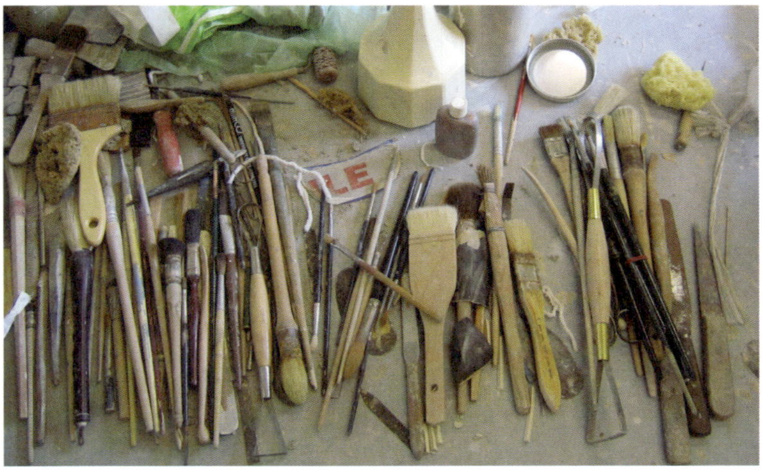

All images: Studio photos, tools, materials, etc., 2000s, photos: Alison Britton

So you're spreading some canvas over the bench, why do you do that?

I don't want the clay to stick onto the wood. And it means I can also flip it over.

Right. You've opened this bag to get a fair-sized brick out; I suppose you'd say it's about the size of two or three domestic bricks, house bricks.

Yes, well this whole bag is 12.5 kilograms and I'm going to take two thirds of it.

While you were talking there you took something that's rather like an old cheese cutter.

It is, very much, it's a piece of wire with two ends and it's the best way of cutting a big thick lump. So I'm not going to use this bit (*crackling plastic*).

It's straight, flat... it's like cake as well isn't it?

Yes.

Now what?

Now I'm going to hit it.

And that looks to me just like an ordinary rolling pin?

It's a nice one with no knobs; it's a straight rolling pin (*banging*).

So you're working to and fro across the slab to keep the thickness more or less the same as you whack it?

Yes, I want it to end up being an oblong rather than a funny shape.

Why's that?

It's just... professionalism... really. You know I just want something... it's like making a piece of material really.

I mean, tell me if I'm wrong, but this is quite an unusual thing to be doing with clay; most people working with clay, they either put it on a wheel, or they coil things, or they stick their thumbs in it, but you're flattening it into a sheet. Not many people do that?

It's one of the basic hand-building techniques. If you go back thousands of years it would have been – probably the first ways would have been coiling, coiling and pinching, just using the hand. And then to make a sheet of clay. I mean, there are prehistoric Chinese things made from slabs of clay.

So what would the ancient Chinese have built with slabs?

They would have sometimes made things to go in graves, replica houses, little buildings, that would be for housing the soul, in the afterlife.

How did you arrive at that point, did you start with coils and pinching and then move towards slab work?

It was one of the techniques I knew about, and I came back to it, as a student, because I knew I didn't really want to make symmetrical round things, so it's a way of freeing up the kinds of things you make. It just means that it's completely open-ended, you can make anything. Because thrown pottery made on the wheel was what everyone expected from ceramics … the emulation and adoration of Chinese forms, Chinese and Korean simple forms. By the time it got to the 1960s, there was a real need to do something else, to move away from that and have something that moved more towards sculpture, a sense that the forms could be anything. For many years I only used slabbing, so everything was quite angular, but I'm now much more mixing slabbing and coiling, because I want something that has a more varied plastic form. I mean clay is formless, clay coming out of the bag doesn't suggest anything in particular; it's just a lump. So really which process you choose to use next is a key to what you're going to be doing.

So you'll beat that down to what kind of thickness?

I'll soon start to roll it again; I've got to turn it over.

You're not a million miles from a pastry cook or a baker, are you at this moment?

No, not at all. It's a bit more resistant than pastry though.

Are you good at making pastry?

Yes! In fact I refuse to buy the kind of frozen pastry where it's already been rolled out for you. I won't have it. I want to do it. Now I'm turning it over, because what you do to one side you need to do to the other side, because there are various tensions you're putting into the surface, so it's good to treat both sides the same way.

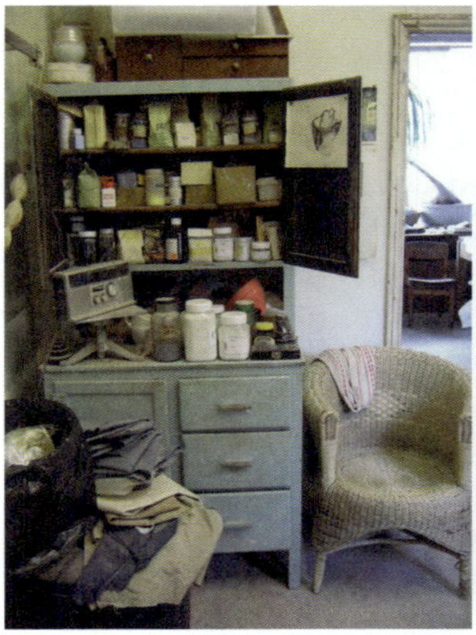

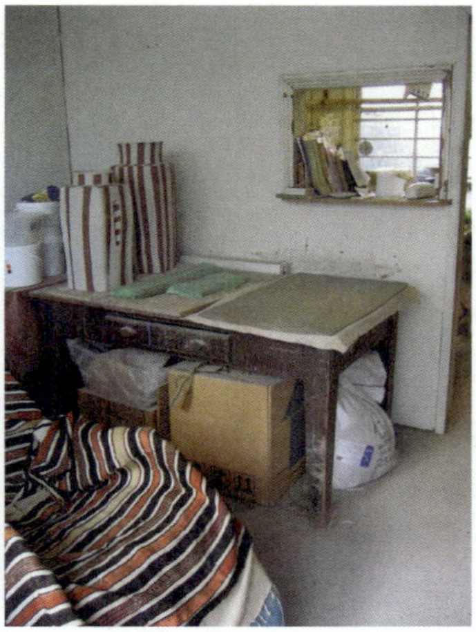

How do you mean tensions into the surface?

Um, because I'm thumping it, I'm condensing that top surface a bit, so I want that to happen on both sides so it's going to grow more evenly. I'm going to turn it over again.

It looks a bit like the side of a suitcase now.

One thing doing ceramics does for you is that you get a very good sense of the thickness of things. I think I can feel, between my finger and thumb, quite accurately, where something is thinner or thicker. Not just in clay, in anything; it's a sort of sensibility you develop. Now I'm going to roll, from the middle to the corners. I'll roll any way that will help it keep the particular shape.

So rolling on the diagonal at the moment...

And you have to keep freeing it from the canvas. I'm sort of bracing myself against the table; there's a nice bar under here that you can catch your foot under – it's a butcher's table.

I hate to be, um, mortal about this but isn't there going to be some point in your life when you're not going to be physically able to do this?

Probably, yeah.

I mean I think I'd be more out of breath than you are, at this point.

Ah, you probably wouldn't... but it's one of the nice things about when having a very cold studio, with no proper heating; to roll out clay is one of the things that warms you up. And I like the physicality of it.

You said earlier that the chunks of clay that are in the bags don't actually suggest any form to you, so at this stage when you are rolling and banging the material, are things coming to you now, or might you be having some sort of thought? I can see there are pictures around the walls, quite large bulky forms; there's a couple of big tree trunks there, and a couple gateposts, I say gateposts but they're big stone doorways really, a cattle trough I think over there. Do those suggest things to you, or does it also come from the material itself?

Um, those things are important – the sort of things I'm keen on at the time will be on the wall, then change... I'll put up other pictures, and other things that I already own will start to seem relevant. So that's one of the strands. The other... what comes from the clay itself is not really at this just-rolled stage; when I've painted the clay then it will be making more definite suggestions I think. I'll paint both sides of it before I use it.

Now, why would you do that?

Er... I would do that because... I think I described it before as making a piece of material, which is something that perhaps suggests tailoring, or like making the fabric before cutting into something. It's a kind of way of *possessing* it; I'm making it more mine by painting on it.

Now that's quite unusual, isn't it? I mean, traditionally the idea of a potter is that someone will make something quite raw, perhaps on a wheel, and then glaze it, paint it, finish it, as part of the last process, but you're sort of intervening much earlier in the process, aren't you?

Yes, that's something I developed quite early on, and it worked.

What's that (*looking at a tool*)?

This, I think, is something to do with cake decorating. It's a little plastic scraper that's nearly worn out, but I can't find another one that's so good, so I'm sticking it together with tape, and I'm just going to check for bubbles – I'm going to scrape it all over the surface (*scraping, smoothing sounds*).

Why are you doing that?

I'm partly tautening the surface, I'm getting it nice and smooth, and looking for bubbles by pressing down... there's one... you see?

Oh, right, so what will you do about that?

Just looking for something sharp, and I'll stab it.

Stab the bubble?

I'm going to stab it in one direction and then smooth it the other way.

I don't see them at all, you just suddenly spot them and dive in with that little spikey thing...

Well, partly I'm feeling them, it's like a little bump you go over.

So what happens next?

I'm going to paint slip over the surface.

What's slip?

Slip is the same clay that I'm using here, mixed with water, and a colour put into it, which is a colour made from metal oxides.

Why can't you just paint straight onto it; why do you have to make this other clayish substance?

It needs to *fit* onto the body. It's going to go through drying, and firing, it shrinks a lot, it needs to be the same substance like this. So the closer it is, the better it will survive. When I'm using a white slip, I make a mixture of 60% of this clay and 40% of kaolin, straight china clay. If it was *just* china clay it would fall off again because the shrinkage would be different.

So you are going now to a whole set of bowls that you've got waiting over there. What are they?

These are all different colours, mixed up. I'm making it from dried pieces of clay, so when I've finished making a pot there's always a few scrappy little shardy extra bits; I save them in plastic bags over there, and then I can weigh them out for my ingredients for the slip. I'm putting perhaps a kilo of dried bits in here, plus between 10 and 15% of pigment, which is a powder I buy separately and then weigh out and add, and then water, obviously. The dry clay and the water sit in the bowl until they've sogged right down again; dry clay and water, it almost explodes and breaks into little bits. It's not dissolving, because it's going to end up as a suspension not a solution.

So each individual grain doesn't absorb the water, the water is between the grains.

Yes. And I need to find a stirring thing – that'll do. These colours, I've got about ten mixed up, a beautiful pistachio whitey green, the buff, I've got yellow, pink, three kinds of blue, this one I'm stirring up now is light grey. So it's the same clay I'm using, plus 15% of pale grey stain. And because my clay is not white, when it's fired it's going to be a warm buffy colour; all my colours will be muted, which is what I want. I don't want them to be brilliant, pristine, like printed colours, I want them to be softened down from that.

Why's that? Why do you like those?

It's just taste...

English colours you could almost say... as opposed to the bright colours, say of the Muslim world, the bright iridescent blues and so on – are you not attracted to those?

You can have very bright blues. Ceramics does blue wonderfully, because of cobalt oxide. It doesn't do red wonderfully; it's very difficult to get a bright red. And I think, from my love of the great long tradition of ceramics, I'm very attuned to the palette of ceramics; I love it's limitations. I mean, manganese oxide will give you a kind of dirty purple, it won't give you a bright purple – I like working with that limitation really.

So what have we got now... you've been stirring.

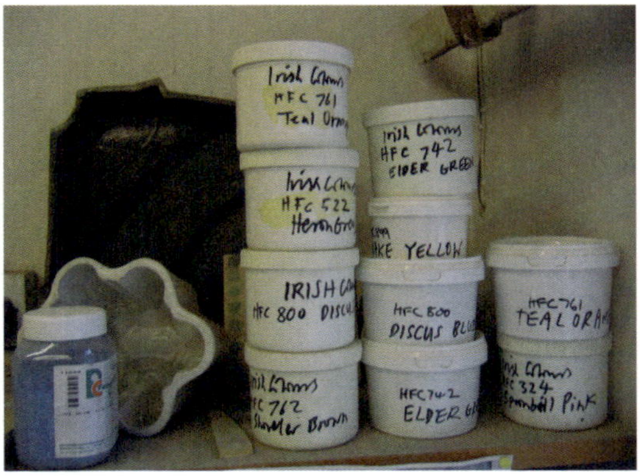

Because it's a suspension, when I leave it alone for a few days, the water comes to the top and the heavy particles sink down, so I've stirred the water back in again so that I can – so it's kind of like custard now, isn't it? I can brush it on.

And have there been times in the history of pottery when you can actually draw with it, do a figure out of the slip?

Yes, that of course is what the Greeks did – there was an incredible painting tradition on Greek pottery. They were using red clay, and the slip they were using was red too, but the way they fired it, the very fine-particled red clay went black, so you could get this wonderful black pattern on a red background.

So that's the traditional Greek vase that we see in museums, that's made with a form of slip?

Yes. There's no glaze on it at all, it's burnished slip.

So you've got a bucket full of the red slip, that's going to give you a different texture?

It's going to give me a different colour, not a different texture (*mixing the slip in the bucket with her arm*). It's all really messy, people who don't like messy things don't do this. I like mess. Now this is the right consistency; I'm going to slosh it on here. It's a nice wide brush. I always seem to do a slightly diagonal kind of mark, out of habit (*wet slapping sounds*). Now I'm getting it fairly thick. I'm also going to make some marks on it now. I've got this pale grey all over it. And then I'm going to trail a few brown lines over it.

What's that?

This is a brown slip – it's made from just red clay, by itself, with water.
And this is a little slip trailer.

It looks like a little medicine dispenser.

Yes, this is an especially small one, the normal ones are these black rubbery bulbs, with a bigger nozzle. I just want if possible some very thin lines, that's why I'm using this little skinny one. I'm going to put a few stripes across it, they're going to be nice and thin, the faster you move the thinner they'll be, so I'm just going to zip across it (*squirting sounds*).

So we've got a set of lines, some very thin and straight, some a bit dribbly, like a few dotted lines, all over it... um, now what?

Now it's got to dry out, not completely but so it's dry enough to hold it's shape when I cut a piece off and stand it up.

Now you're not going to cook the clay before you do anything else yet, are you?

No, I'm going to build with it once it's gone a bit harder, which in winter means leaving it uncovered overnight, and then it'll be nice tomorrow morning.

So we can jump ahead a bit in the process to the point where we came in, because at that point you had a, well I'll describe it as a vessel, that you were scoring, and building coils around the top of it – so were you at the next stage, at that point?

I was at the stage when the clay has gone to leather hardness, yes, where I can do anything with it, really. What I've got here are two parts that will eventually be part of the same thing. This is going to be two square-ish things that will be joined together eventually. What's different about this one is that I've made a double wall. I've made as it were the inside pot, and then I've turned it upside down and put this outer wall all the way round, and the reason for doing that is that I want it to seem really massive and heavy (actually it *is* going to be quite massive and heavy...), and I've got little joining wedges in there that hold the two walls apart, all the way round and on the bottom. I've never done this before, a double wall.

So these are quite rectangular. I can imagine people listening, you know, who've been working with pottery, and what's immediately coming to mind are round-y things, vessel-y things, jug-y things... But what we have here is quite rectangular. I'm reminded a bit of the pots we have in the garden that we grow shrubs out of, and you've got, basically, one sitting right inside another.

Yes. And there are some funny details, on the inside form; it's not simply a square, is it, I've put these strips in the corners so it's a kind of broken square, which is a softening kind of thing... Although you could use clay in a very angular way, I think it somehow undoes it's clayness. I think you want some knocking off of that very sharp corner. So I will always, you know, at the scraping stage, be softening the edges, just a bit, or bashing them in a bit. Otherwise you might as well be using wood. For me it's fascinatingly much easier to work with than using wood, because it is endlessly giving, you know, even when it's nearly hard you can push it a bit, you can get a bit of a curve. All my lines here have a slight curve in them, don't they, and that's my language, not to have it really rigid.

**At what stage have you got to cook the piece?
Is it after you've glazed or before you glaze?**

I'm going to cook it twice. The first firing – which is called the biscuit firing– is at the point where it stops being clay, and I would not be able to reclaim it. If I broke it, it would still be pottery. And then, after it's been biscuit-fired I will paint – these slips are opaque colours – and after that I will paint with just the pigments, and probably not much. Probably just a few lines, you know, sort of tying the thing together. And then I'll glaze it, and the second firing is what completes it, because it fuses the glaze onto the body. And the glaze is just a surface, it's a transparent but slightly matt surface, which makes the colours look much better – it enriches the colours.

So lets go and look at a finished pot. We've got two hollow shapes, one square and angular like, and one more round-y, and they're joined together by a bridge, and the glaze is buff, brown and black,

The glaze itself is just transparent, so all the colour you see here is underneath the glaze, it's the slip. In fact all the colour here is slip, there's no extra painting with pigment. So there you can see what were red clay lines, and they're quite deeply buried by now, they're underneath two or three layers of cream.

So we've ended up with something where you've made the clay do very different things. So the round one, though not symmetrical, is perhaps similar to a bowl or a vase, and the more columnar angular one is almost like a pillar and you've got a piece of asymmetrical fluting up the side.

And the attempt here was the bringing together of difference.

Thinking of some of the other materials that we're also looking at, convention has it that glass is very beautiful, and there's something special about stone, it's got a particular finished quality when sculptors work with it... I mean in a way, as we've said before, this stuff is earth, it is mud, and traditionally people think of that as quite ugly, don't they... Do you ever think of it in that way?

Um, I can see that mud has its connotations with dirt... and I like all that, I like that it contributes an undertone, an undercurrent of 'not beautiful' and then that makes the challenge: that you make something beautiful out of it. It's very *ordinary,* and that I really appreciate. I like the fact that it's not an expensive material, it's very easy to get hold of, with lots of different variations to it. One of the words I use about clay is that it's 'kind', it's a giving material and it lets you do so many things with it; it's so adaptable in its different phases of wetness and dryness, that it's just 'generous' somehow...

Lucie Rie
Urban Idyll/Ideal

Essay, *The Life and Work of Lucie Rie 1902–1995*, ed. Emmanuel Cooper, Ceramic Review Publications, 2002. Published for the centenary of the birth of the potter Dame Lucie Rie. Eight essays in the book approached different aspects of her life and work – one discussed her famous technical notebooks, and there were many pictures of her pots as well as photo sequences of her at work.

Lucie Rie is vividly recognisable through the great array of her pots with their clearly defined language of shape. She investigated a number of formal types, and had a rich and broad understanding of glazes, which astonishingly were applied to raw pots, and fired only once. Clearly she loved contrast, and used very varied textures and colours. She made series of pots that reveal the labour in gradually perfecting an abstract form, nuance after nuance: the search for resolution. Her pots are a poised combination of daring and restraint.

There has never been a time through the decades in which I have been a potter when the work of Rie and Hans Coper did not seem to matter, or even temporarily disappeared from view. During the 1970s they seemed so significant that they were perceived by many to have forged the only alternative strand in Britain to the Bernard Leach tradition, which now seems to have been an oversimplification (see Tanya Harrod's writing on the 1950s). But they were also seen as 'parents' of the kinds of ceramics that developed next, partly through their teaching roles at Camberwell and the Royal College of Art, London.

Since they have both died, leaving the prolific evidence of their lives's achievement very much with us, it has been interesting to re-evaluate the things that connect Coper and Rie and the place they occupy. The exhibition *Potters in Parallel*, curated by Margot Coatts at the Barbican Art Gallery in 1997, was excellent for this, coinciding as it did with *Modern Art in Britain 1910–1914*. This adjacent exhibition looked at the development of modernism in that formative decade, and the responses of British artists to painting and sculpture brought from the 'continent' in a number of exhibitions, such as Roger Fry's *Manet and the Post Impressionists* exhibition in London in 1910. As the ever more industrialised century proceeded, it also became important to look at studio pottery in the context of painting and sculpture (as well as design and the interior) or there might not be enough reasons to go on making it.

In *Potters in Parallel*, groups of both Rie's and Coper's pots were laid out in two parallel lines of glass cases. Pots were defined as different formal types in the catalogue[1]. Besides tableware (some of which they jointly produced during the 1950s when they shared a studio), Rie's forms include bowls, vases, beakers, bottles, rugged pots, bottle vases, and cylinders. Perhaps she is most

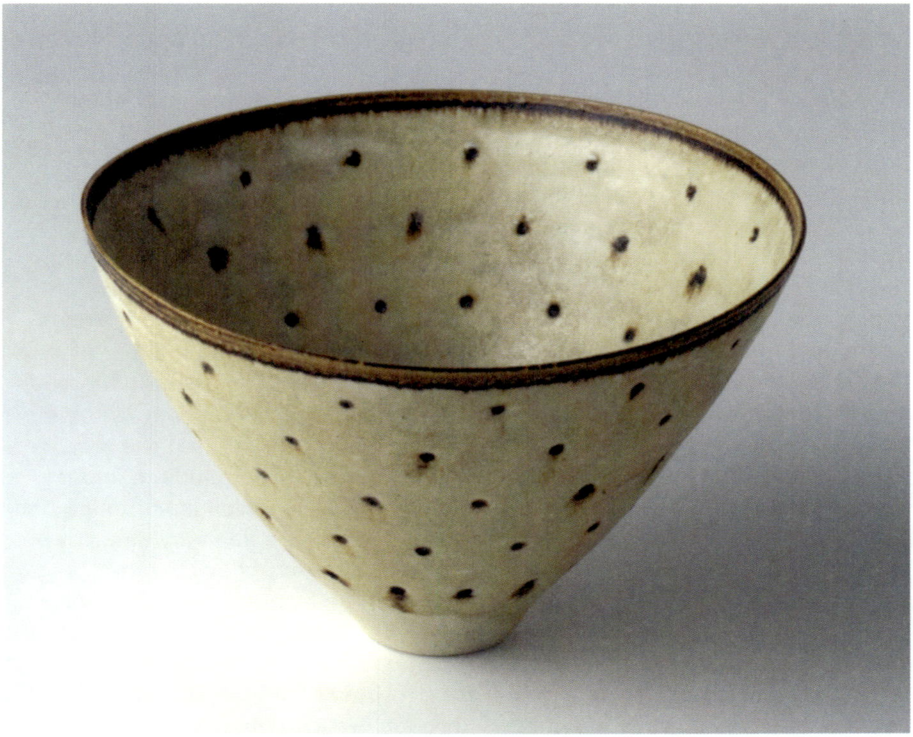

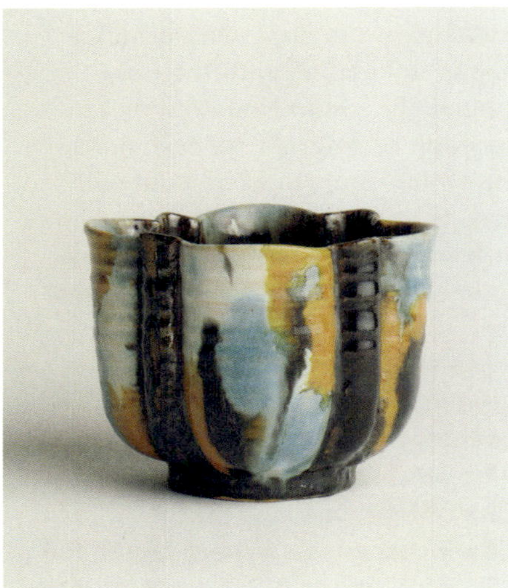

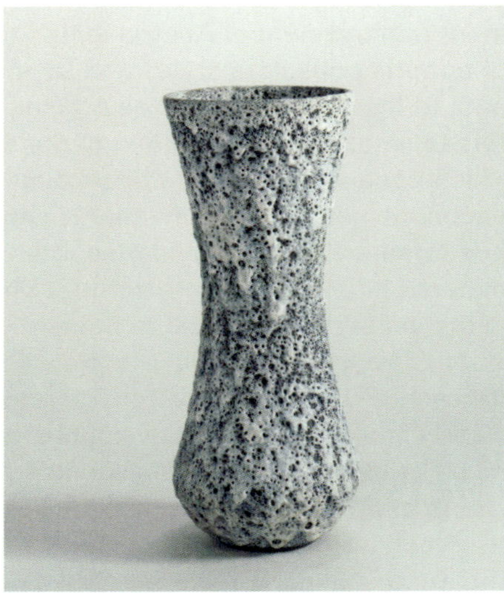

Clockwise from top: *Porcelain bowl*, 1956; *Bottle, pitted glaze*, 1980; *Earthenware Bowl*, 1926
All works by Lucie Rie, photos: David Cripps

highly regarded for the bottle-vase forms, where a more curvaceous body tapers into an elongated neck, and the top edge stretches into a funnel shape that is wider than the base. They are sinuous, delicate, risky to make; though open bowls are probably the form she most continually researched, some memorably with fine sgraffito markings like ancient images of basketwork. A lot of her bowls carry astonishing colour blends that are surprising for pottery – pink, green, gold – that sound overpowering but are in balance.

For many years my favourite piece was an unspectacular one. Made in 1956, it is a small pale fine flared bowl, only 14 cm across at the brown rim. This edge suggests to me the metal edges on Chinese Ding ware, which is also creamy white. But the bowl is pocked with translucent brown spots, just iron and glaze. The elegance of the shape and the humour of the freckles are perfectly connected. It is, as she was, severe, elegant, and warm. Recently, though, I have found that I am more drawn towards some larger craggy pots, bulbous or cylindrical, or beaker forms, that are simpler and stronger, that I did not 'see' so forcefully before. Their sudden impact relates presumably to some changes in my own work, which is softening and simplifying. Rie worked for so many decades and made so many kinds of pot, we can grow old getting to know the different phases of her search.

Where does the work come from? From the first it looked European, somehow clean, sophisticated, urbane. Her Viennese bourgeois background was one she had to leave abruptly in 1938, but she had already absorbed the cultural frame of Otto Wagner, Josef Hoffmann and the modern movement at the start of the century through her art school education at the Kunstgewerbeschule from 1922–26. As Hoffmann recalled in 1930, the modern movement in Austria aimed to 'break with the prevailing practice of adopting obsolete styles and to endeavour, in keeping with the new age, to find new forms for all articles of necessity'. John Houston quotes this to establish Rie's context in the monograph he edited:[2] he continues, 'this intention had a vital ethical dimension which could only be built with uncontaminated material – that is why there is still such power in the archaic and primitive and vernacular sources that have been brought back as raw material into 20th-century culture. The sources are wonderful; the wonder is the quality of our belief in them.'

This kind of trawling for new life, fresh stimuli and 'an area of excellence' from far afield, characterises the modernist project and has clearly had an effect on developments in ceramics in the 20th century as much as on architecture, design and the fine arts. Leach was doing it just as Coper and Rie were – the intrigue lies in the differences in what they chose to investigate and what they made out of their responses. Where Leach found the Sung 'standard' unsurpassable, as well as looking to Korean pottery, English medieval pots and vernacular slipware; Rie and Coper (and others) found more to excite them in ancient Mediterranean art – Roman, Mycenaean, and Cycladic.

Recently I had the chance to handle two red-ware cups and saucers at the V&A, one roughly made by Leach in the early 1920s, with slip decoration and shiny earthenware glaze. The other was from a Rie tea set made in Vienna in 1936 – shallow, sharply horizontal, with a fine burnished unglazed surface. The contrast in the feel of them was remarkable – they were illustrations of Town and Country, like the pairs of cartoons they used to have in Punch.

Rie, coming from Vienna, staying in London though her husband went to America, was so evidently an urban person, settling in a small mews studio and flat in the centre of town, getting her specially designed modern furniture sent over and reinstalled, and never moving away. Her engagement with the prevailing English concerns in pottery was complicated, though she tried to fit in, and Leach and colleagues tried to welcome and advise her. Both Coper and Rie were present at the famous Dartington conference which lasted for ten days in 1952, where Soetsu Yanagi, Shoji Hamada, Leach and Michael Cardew were key speakers. Harrod quotes an interesting review of the exhibition which accompanied the conference written by Robert Melville in *The Architectural Review.*[3] He implies that the craft world as it appeared to many in these postwar years was quaint and detached, and did not convince a non-believer:

> The general effect is of an ethnographic exhibit of the remains of a lost civilisation, of a village and town community of highly aesthetic peasants. Only the stoneware of Hans Coper and the porcelain of Lucie Rie remain outside the prevailing atmosphere of rural quietism. They alone make the point that the whole exhibition was presumably intended to make. They show that the artist craftsman is not necessarily an anachronism in our time, that it is not impossible for him or her to be, so to speak, with us.

My main purpose in this essay is to suggest that the particular value of Rie's work is in confronting the limitations of studio pottery being seen largely in a pastoral vacuum. The main thrust of the discussion at Dartington proposed the crafts as salvation and escapism, ignoring the products of industry, modern architecture, metropolitan sophistication, and cultural breadth. If work is to be about form, as I believe Rie's was (more than about a narrative of otherness, or props for the rural idyll) then industrial things, handmade things, and other art objects can be fruitfully juxtaposed – can communicate and can all be inspirational.

A showcase of 'British' work placed as background to the Martin Smith retrospective of 1996, at the museum Boijmans van Beuningen in Rotterdam, contained an interesting mixture of industrial and studio pots. There was an early 18th-century Elers brothers red stoneware engine-turned teapot with a silver chain, a Wedgwood black basalt sugar bowl, two 1980s pieces of Smith's, and a Michael Rowe tinned vessel. One of the two Coper pots was a black spade form – a type which first appeared at a Boijmans exhibition in

1967 shared with Rie. I found then, as ever, that to see Coper and Rie in this remarkable museum where the applied arts have been taken so seriously for so long, and in the Dutch urban context, is an extension and a deepening of my understanding of their pots.

Holland provided a conceptual home for their work – a place to show in 'modern' cosmopolitan Europe that was not Austria or Germany, which they wished to avoid for a long period after the War. Both the Stedelijk Museum in Amsterdam and the Boijmans in Rotterdam were early in appreciating Coper and Rie, and invited them for dual exhibitions in 1953 and 1967, respectively. I think the sustaining chain of connections achieved through the movement of artists and the transporting of works between Britain and 'Europe proper' has greatly enriched our reading of modern ceramics, and its various roots. The Elers brothers, after all, came to Stoke-on-Trent from Holland, and found the right sort of red clay in Bradwell Wood in the 1690s.

In writing about Rie from a 'continental' perspective in Houston's book, Dorris Kuyken-Schneider of the Boijmans comments on the apparent caution in early reactions to Rie's pots: '... but the British, more inclined towards Bernard Leach than towards William Staite Murray, listening more to the rustic song than to the urban harmonies, at first did not respond to her work. It was only after 1945, with the assistance of Hans Coper, that she could start up her workshop properly. Stimulated by Coper's keen perception and appreciation of her intentions, she went her own way...'[4]

Kuyken-Schneider also points out that studio potters did already have an established artistic status in France, Germany, Scandinavia and the Netherlands by 1930. If such status came later in Britain, it was because we were confused by the rustic heritage and the threads of nostalgia which still beleaguer us in ideas of craft. The Leach phenomenon, for all its strengths, can be said with hindsight to have been a big red herring. Too much solace is stultifying. A part of the audience has been perpetually lulled into expecting nothing more from ceramics than utility, harmony with nature, and the rural image – only a small strand of contemporary reality. The tenacity of this myth makes Rie more precious – where would we be without her foreign input?

The names of Coper and Rie go together as trippingly off the tongue as Morecambe and Wise. But we need to ask what meaning there is in always lumping them together. Obviously the personal bond between them was of great and enduring significance – the small London workshop shared for 12 years, the button-making business, the joint production of tableware, the continuous friendship. When they went on to develop distinct languages of pot making, they still had in common an exactitude and an equal force. Both were refugees, cultured and urban. Both Rie and Coper made forms that stretched the conventions of British studio pottery, and came to express a perfect distillation of the 1950s and the 1960s (though much of their most admired work was made later).

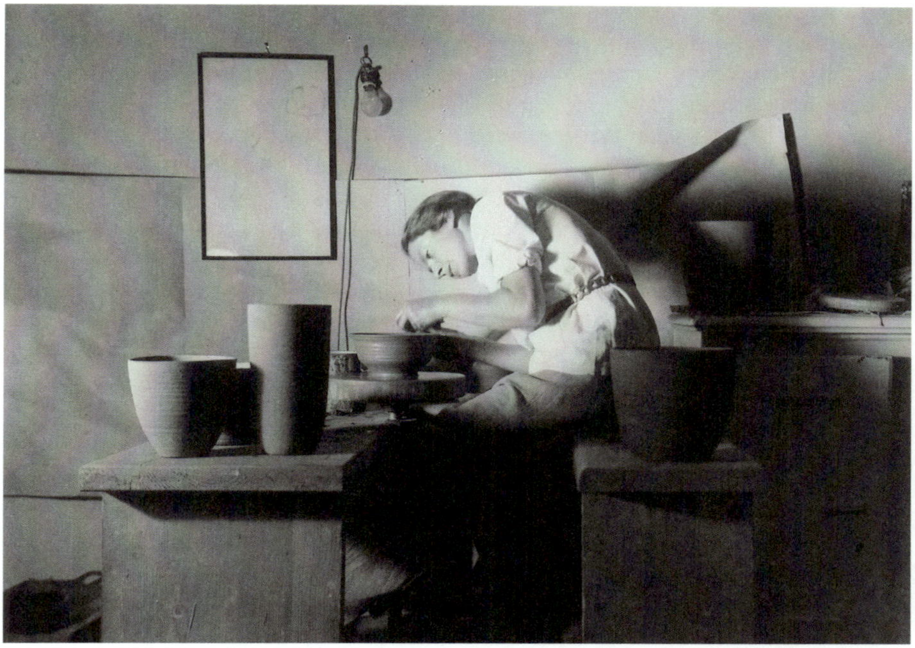

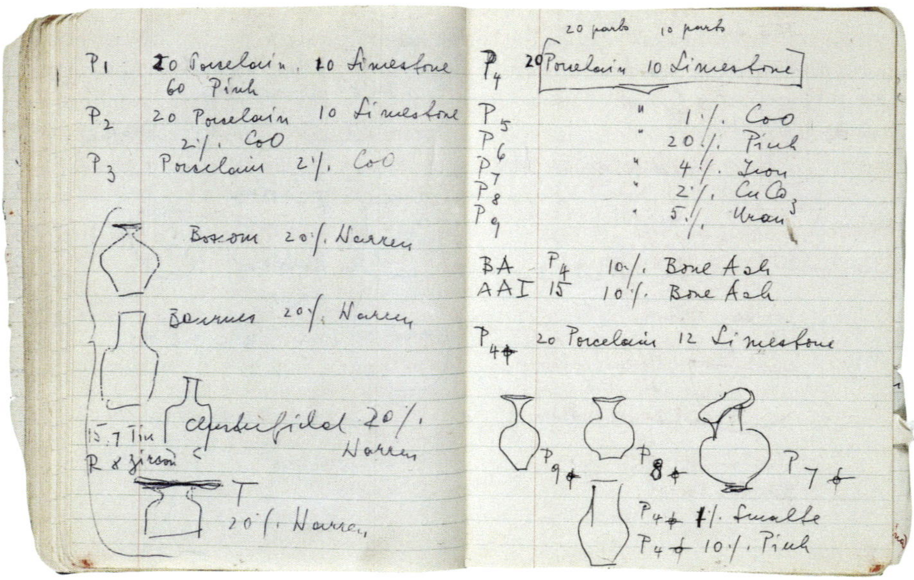

Top: Lucie Rie working at the wheel in her studio in Vienna, c.1930
Bottom: Lucie Rie, pages from glaze notebook, photo: David Cripps

As in early reviews of their work in joint exhibitions, it is tempting to remark that their pieces have distinctively masculine (Coper) and feminine (Rie) characteristics. In the imaginary spectrum from useful to aesthetic, the work of both sits somewhere on the arty side of the middle. But Coper seems to be more interested in three-dimensional shape and hardly at all in colour: juxtapositions of thrown and altered forms, light and shade, and the roving viewpoint that a non-regular sculptural form invites. Whereas Rie keeps the all-round symmetry, the wheel-made form not cut and reassembled; she explores the minute variations of 'basic' pot shapes, making great play with the surface.

As a person I knew Coper better, having been taught by him in the early 1970s at the Royal College of Art. But to get to know Coper meant to come closer also to Rie. I think of her as an ideal version of the potter's life, satisfying, positive and rigorous. To visit her was always uplifting – the concentrated atmosphere both in her small studio and in the signs of a quiet domestic life above it in her flat; cake and conversation. Her regard for Coper was often touched upon – if you admired a pot of hers, she would tell you how much more of an artist Hans had been. His pots surrounded her, many with flowers in them.

Coper only published one piece of writing, a catalogue statement for the V&A exhibition in 1969 which is still so much quoted, about the compelling dilemma of pots without function and the phantom pitch of a demented piano tuner. I and many other potters could probably recite it by heart. Rie declined to write any commentary, saying 'I just make pots'. Satisfaction came more readily, perhaps, to her – could this have been because she did not question the usefulness of what she made? Both Coper and Rie had a wry, sardonic way of talking that was redolent of their cosmopolitan culture and extremely attractive. They sustained each other, and were a partnership in mind long after they ceased to share a studio, and I suppose, still, for her, in the many years that she outlived him. They were coworkers, quite distinct from a couple. They were intense, exotic, creative, generous – a wedge of inspiration – and we are lucky to have had them in our midst.

1. *Lucie Rie and Hans Coper – Potters in Parallel*, ed. Margot Coatts, Herbert Press in association with Barbican Art Gallery, 1997.
2. *Lucie Rie*, ed. John Houston, with photographs by David Cripps, Crafts Council, 1981, p.21.
3. Tanya Harrod, *The Crafts in Britain in the 20th century*, Yale University Press, 1999, p.222.
4. Lucie Rie, ed. Houston, op cit, p.25.

Souvenirs from the World of Art

Ceramic Review 199, January/February 2003. Review of Carole Windham's solo exhibition of ceramic sculpture at No.1 Audrey Street, London, 18–22 October 2002. In the history of ceramics a lot of clay has been used to make figures and figurines – it is a versatile modelling material. Quite a lot of these have had satiric intentions, especially in the 18th and 19th centuries, and Windham follows this pursuit of visual wit.

There is probably not enough satire in the ceramic world these days, though the versatile plasticity of clay allows any amount of pastiche and mimicry which could have a lampooning intent. Ceramics through history has had a jovial side. We have Steve Dixon though, Richard Slee, and Grayson Perry, who are all engaged with a satiric slant, as well as other kinds of humour and caricature, irony and layered allusions to art, society and politics.

But Carole Windham seems rather to tackle her parodic subjects head on, or full-frontally. A skilful and overt kind of modelling plainly reveals her targets' foibles. She does not hint, she states. She has worked with clay for a long time now, and could build anything. In the past few years, her ability to simulate with surface painting, which she builds up in layers over a number of firings, has greatly developed.

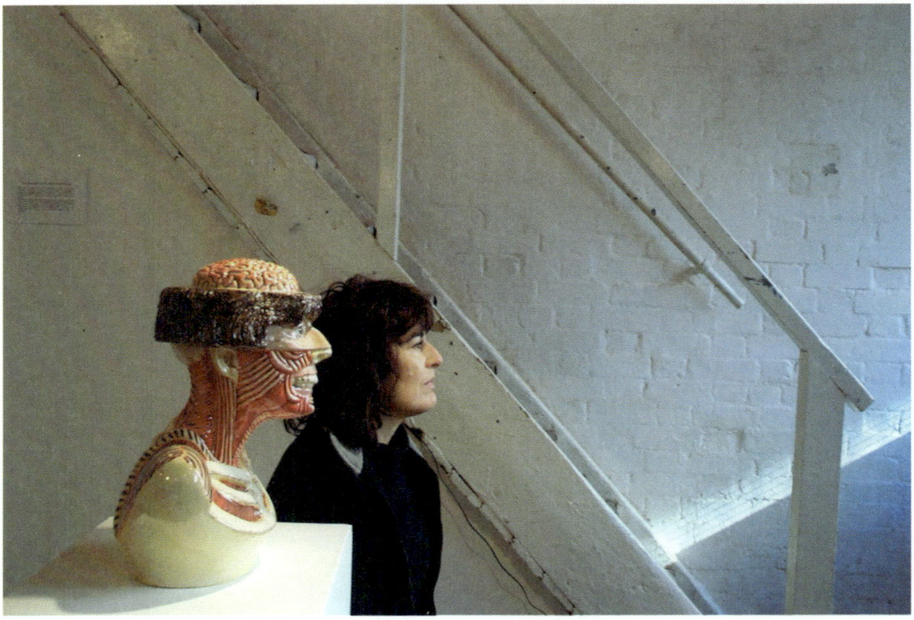

Carole Windham and *Only Flesh and Blood*, 2002, photo: Geoffrey Windham

An early enthusiasm for pop art and a passion for Robert Arneson, whom she interviewed in the 1970s during a long trip to the US, set the conceptual background for Windham's late immersion in the MA course at the Royal College of Art, which she completed in 2000. She boldly established a wonderful body of work while studying there, which defined her as a comic commentator artist, playing with the conventions of the bust, the flatback, and the figurine; taking inspiration from ceramic artefacts (Mimbres shards, Wedgwood cherubs, china dogs), and finally scrutinising the contemporary art world through the clay ornament.

In this, the first solo exhibition to take place at No. 1 Audrey Street, Windham showed seven substantial pieces of new work. The sculptures incorporate humorous ideas about Damien Hirst, Gilbert and George, Francis Bacon and Tracy Emin, as well as self-portraiture, statuary, Staffordshire, and play with two- and three-dimensional representation. Is it just poking fun, or is it homage? I am sure there is tenderness in her painted references to Bacon's triptych *In memory of George Dyer 1971*, which appear in the split bust *Occupying the space...* She says she admires her chosen artists for their willingness to reveal themselves and the risks they take: 'Without this kind of courage, skill and technique are empty gestures, no matter how clever. My aim is to respectfully parody their work and also expose myself.'

With splendid topicality, in the most 'exposed' and recent piece, Carole has turned from modern art to the new phenomenon of the anatomist/sensationalist Gunther von Hagens (inventor of the plastinated corpses exhibited as *Body Worlds*). A self-portrait bust of desperate and comic gruesomeness has Windham's eyes and fringe peering bravely beyond her scalp, blood vessels, muscles and bones, exquisitely depicted in enamel painting over slip, underglaze pigment and shiny glaze. A ceramic triumph of scathing wit and craft.

The Persistence of Craft

Ceramic Review 201, May/June 2003. *The Persistence of Craft,* ed. Paul Greenhalgh, A&C Black, 2003. Greenhalgh has had a prolific career curating, writing, and lecturing in museums and in education here and in North America. He is now the Director of the Sainsbury Centre for Visual Arts at the University of East Anglia.

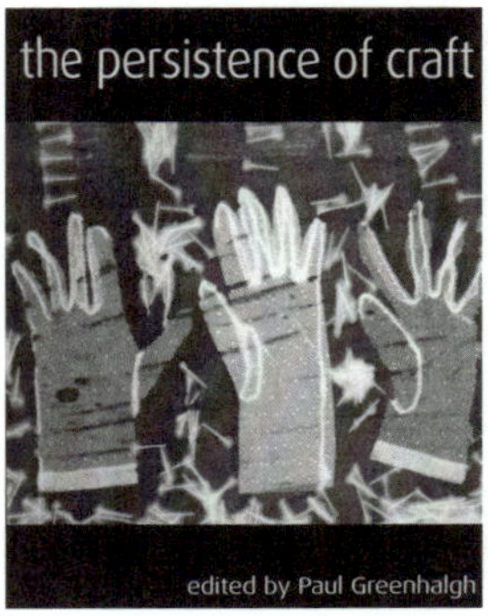

It is always a pleasure to read Paul Greenhalgh. He is witty, daring, fluent, fast, and posits theoretical connections that are just outside what we knew. In this book he writes the introduction, the first chapter on 'The Genre', where he explores a division at the heart of the visual arts between positivist and ironic practice, and the conclusion, where he glides through a fashionably scientific comparison with complexity theory. In all of these his skating and fireworks style is in full force.

Importantly, in this book the coexistence of international perspectives is taken seriously, and there is great diversity – of theme, quality, and approach – in the other 15 essays, which include authors from Canada, Australia, Norway, Japan and America, though half are from the UK. They are more like essays than chapters, without discernible meaning in their sequence. Only Karen Livingstone, a former colleague of Greenhalgh's at the V&A, had the chance to cross-reference her piece with other essays.

Some of the essays are excellent and precisely illustrated – Simon Fraser on the avant-garde in jewellery; Yoko Imai on the transformation of textiles in Japan; Gareth Williams on furniture and appropriated materials; Edmund de Waal on ethnicity; and Linda Sandino on jewellery and the body.

However, some essays are frustratingly illustrated – pictures are sprinkled into Greenhalgh's texts with no context, and Kaneko Kenji of the National Museum of Modern Art in Tokyo makes reference to numerous key practitioners in the early development of modern ceramics in Japan that we are not shown. Moreover, he bases much of his argument on a misreading of a quote from me.

This book has been a long time in the making and the bulk of these essays were completed in 1999. It is a pity that so few of the pictures are from this millennium. Moreover, we are not always given enough details on picture captions – size matters.

Size also matters a great deal to Albert Paley, the American metalsmith whose essay is an 'architectural dialogue' with site-specific metalwork; only it is really a monologue on personal achievement and bigness. America comes out badly – the Ronald Kuchta piece on ceramic sculpture does not have its finger on any current pulse, and while the essay on furniture by Joellen Secondo is much more interesting, it includes only a couple of American designers.

Some writers have evidently been asked to survey their national scene, which offers glimpses of the unfamiliar but is less exciting to read. The anthropologist Carole E. Mayer writes interestingly about 'first' and 'second' nation artists in Canada. But why pick Norway, Japan, and Australia for the surveys, one might ask; what about Korea or Holland or Estonia?

'The idea of orchestration is key', Greenhalgh tells us in his conclusion; but orchestration is exactly what this book lacks. It is as if the conductor went home after an impressive overture, and the orchestra – which features some terrific soloists – played on as best it could.

Doffy's Questionnaire

Unpublished correspondence with a mature student at Havering College, March 2004. The student had to write an essay about an artist. Many students over the years have sent me questionnaires – it is one of the triggers for writing when art students in contextual studies courses are asked to find out about an artist. This one was direct, not boring, and enjoyable to answer.

When did you have your first exhibition, and do you still have the same feelings about showing your work now as you did at the beginning?

In 1976 I had a small solo exhibition at a gallery in Barnes with hessian on the walls called Amalgam. All my work then was covered in images, and I showed a combination of big tile-like pictures and a group of jugs. I was very excited to be exhibiting; had got out of doing tile commissions and into making objects, and was therefore exhibitable for the first time. There was a heat wave still in September and I was about to go and drive across Canada in a pickup truck. I was wearing a red pleated skirt at the opening, I was 28. Now when I have a show, it is of course still exciting, but more loaded. Something is expected of me that wasn't at the beginning. I also care more and notice more these days how the work has been displayed. But I have always liked showing people my work – it is the point of it all really, I'm not shy about it. (Not shy but still nervous in a good/bad anticipation way.) There must I think be a 'showing off' streak in most artists; it's like doing fancy dives in a swimming pool or reading a poem at a funeral.

Did your education at school help you to become a ceramic artist, and if so, how?

Yes. I went to an academic girls school but one that had a fantastic separate building called the Art Block on the other side of a pond. I did some pottery from the age of 11 and as a sixth-form girl helped my pottery teacher put up a big clay mural done by many children at the school, and then a commission of hers at Leeds and Bradford Airport. (I had also met the potter William Newland through my father, because they both were involved in teacher training at the University of London, and I worked with him very occasionally as a teenager in the pottery in the basement of Senate House in Russell Square.) So I knew that some people did ceramics for a living, though the people I first met seemed to do it along with teaching, as I have also.

Do you make sure that you spend a certain, fixed amount of time each day/week working in your studio?

I work there as much as I can. Some weeks I am at the Royal College of Art a lot, such as now, when we are choosing next year's students. I get to the studio a bit less than I would like to in term time, and then it is the main thing I do with my time during the holidays. But there have always been different things pulling me in different directions – things to be written, things to go and look at, things to do with my two daughters, other people I need to talk to and see. If I'm not in the studio for a whole week I feel funny and detached from myself, and it's always good to go there again, though there's nothing special about it as a place. It is another kind of home. There's a sense in which the Barrett Marsden Gallery is yet another kind of home in my work life.

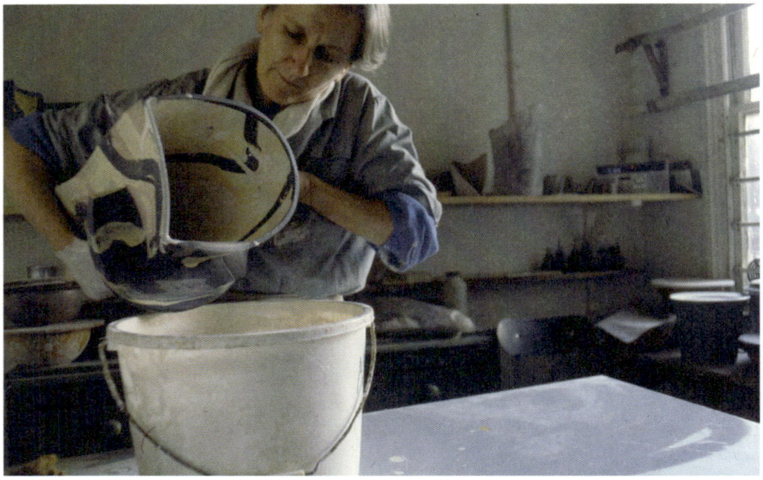

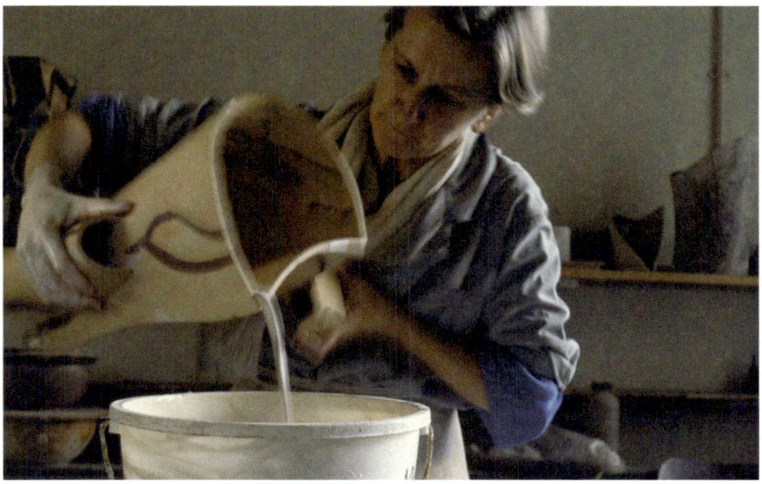

Alison Britton glazing pots, 1998, photos: Andrew Greaves

What are your biggest technical challenges?

The glaze can misbehave, if too thin or too thick or cooled too quickly. I am about to find out more about other kinds of glaze and temperature ranges, experiment a bit with the surfaces. I don't think my biggest challenges are technical. I worry more about making something new and surprising, and keeping it 'alive' aesthetically. I have started to work bigger though with a new kiln, and am changing a few things like clay thickness because of that, so pieces are heavier as I get older and weaker. Glazing large pieces nowadays I have someone else there to help lift and shake the piece when I pour the glaze on the inside. I have had inflamed tendons in my elbows a couple of times recently, which take a long time to get better.

I am a bit disabled, and some of your works have nobbles or handles on them, is this so that they are easy to pick up?

To begin with it wasn't – I wanted the odd look of them. But with the handles and the depressions, as opposed to the nobbles, I think they add a sort of invitation which I like. The handles have an aspect of being like limbs sometimes too, and contribute to the anthropomorphic thing that appears with an awful lot of pots from all times. But as pieces have got bigger, it has also been important in not dropping them when they're slippery being glazed.

When working, do you hide away on your own?

My studio is an old butcher's shop in Stamford Hill, London. It has four rooms of different sizes, a yard and a garage. The first room fronting on the street is the biggest and I don't work in it. I leave sheets of clay drying in it, pots to be looked at to decide how to paint them etc. I also fall asleep occasionally in the front room in a reclining chair that was my mother's. The second room further from the street is where I work – perhaps that is a bit like hiding away on my own. Then there is a small room with a bench, sink, kettle and a fridge in it with a door to the yard and the loo. The back room has two kilns and a spray booth. A friend paints and makes jewellery in the garage – we overlap for some hours on the days when I'm there – he starts and finishes earlier than me. We usually have a cup of tea and talk, maybe about work, most working days. I'm often there at the weekends when he is not. It's important that we work out of sight from each other.

Do you like people in and out?

If I know them well it's OK. Having visitors is also fine, when I have enough time to myself like in the holidays. But the studio needs to be a peaceful place with few interruptions. I'm never lonely there – partly because of the radio and the telephone.

Do you have music on?

I mostly listen to Radio 4, and switch to music sometimes if there's a repeat of a programme or I'm just bored with it.

Do you have the TV on?

No, that would be ghastly. I hardly ever watch TV at home either; maybe two or three programmes a week.

Do you do commissions, and if so, do you enjoy them?

Not really. If someone I know says they'd like a pleated piece, for instance, I'll try and make them one but it's not very specific and never pre-designed.

If a piece of work goes wrong how do you react?

If its shape is bad – at the clay stage – I keep hacking away at it or rebuilding bits of it until I like it better. If the colours seem wrong after biscuit firing, I use underglaze pigments as washes or as stronger painted marks to alter the balance. If it's horrible after glaze firing, I'll try painting it again with underglaze pigments mixed with medium, then spray a little more glaze on it and refire it. If it's still horrible, I might take it to a friend to sandblast the surface off then paint and glaze again. Maybe four or five times in 30 years I've smashed a piece up. There are a few pieces out in the world that I wish I had smashed up.

How do you want people to respond to your work?

I want them to look at it hard, from all round, and be engaged/amused/elated/surprised. I would be pleased if they touched it and wanted to pick it up. I would be pleased if they compared one piece with others in the group, say in an exhibition, and if it made them ask questions.

Do you ever get so fed up when your work is going wrong that you want to give it up?

If you mean that one particular piece – then not – I keep trying to make it work. If you mean give up making pots altogether and do something else – then not either – it seems too late in the day to become something else! But if nobody wants to show them or buy them for a long while then that will make a difference – I am making them to be out in the world and not sitting around in my studio. There are lots of ways I would try to adapt though, and make new sorts of things with the skills and ideas I have, and maybe write more and pot less when I get vold and feeble.

Steven Newell

Gallery leaflet, solo exhibition of blown glass by Steven Newell, Barrett Marsden Gallery, London, 30 April–12 June 2004. Glass, like clay, has an enduring relationship with the container form, inside and outside. I chose to include this text because narrative on the surface, not unusual in the history of vessels, is more complex and subtle with transparency and seeing double.

Steven Newell does various kinds of work – glass you can eat off in distinguished restaurants, and flat glass for architecture. He also makes glass for a closer sort of scrutiny, large plates and bowls that are narrative and pictorial, where you can ponder over their layers of meaning, delicately detaching the elements of universal myth from the suggestions of personal record. It is these more complex objects that make exhibitions. The pieces in this exhibition are all expressive of a single theme, *The Iliad,* Homer's epic poem about the Trojan War and 'the universal fate of mortals in the divine scheme'[1].

Layers of meaning are perfectly conveyed in glass because it's transparent. Subtleties of content are possible especially with the bowl form, where the outer and inner surfaces are both workable, and simultaneously visible. There can be two stories at play, interwoven, inter-textual, indivisible.

There is a looser sense of fluidity in the forms of Newell's bowls in the past few years – they are occupying space with more élan. This is achieved by reheating them in a kiln after the drawing has been sandblasted through the encasing coloured glass. They are then picked up on a punty[2] – a hazardous moment – and put back in the furnace a few times. Rotation in the fire and forming with metal tools stretches and softens the bowl. Even better, the drawing itself makes a difference to the shape; where more glass has been cut away, the wall of the bowl is more responsive to heat and distortion. Form and image have become closely enmeshed.

The scale of these objects is domestic, possess-able; they are objects to be lived with and not just seen in a gallery. His use of colour in this series is powerfully suggestive and predominantly dark. Olives, blues, brown with yellow, a dark colour that reduces to a metallic black, a Poseidon green. Some bowls have images in silver leaf on the outside surface, which look yellow on the inside, absorbed into the glass.

Frequently these outside images are of fighting – two faces at loggerheads making an embattled context for the larger event inside the piece. An exceptional bowl is delicately pink, with beautiful Helen, a main protagonist in *The Iliad,* being assured (falsely) by the gods that the Trojans and the Achaeans have stopped warring and everything will be all right. Another key event in the whole catastrophe is portrayed in a golden yellow bowl, Patroclus in Achilleus's armour, his all-signifying shield in thick silver foil on the outer surface of the glass. Seeing *through* the whole object,

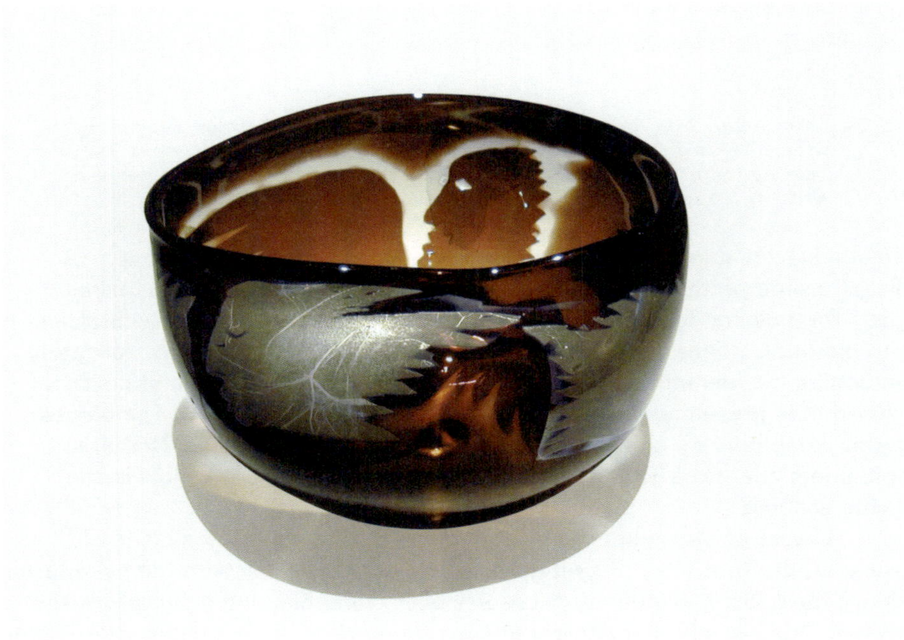

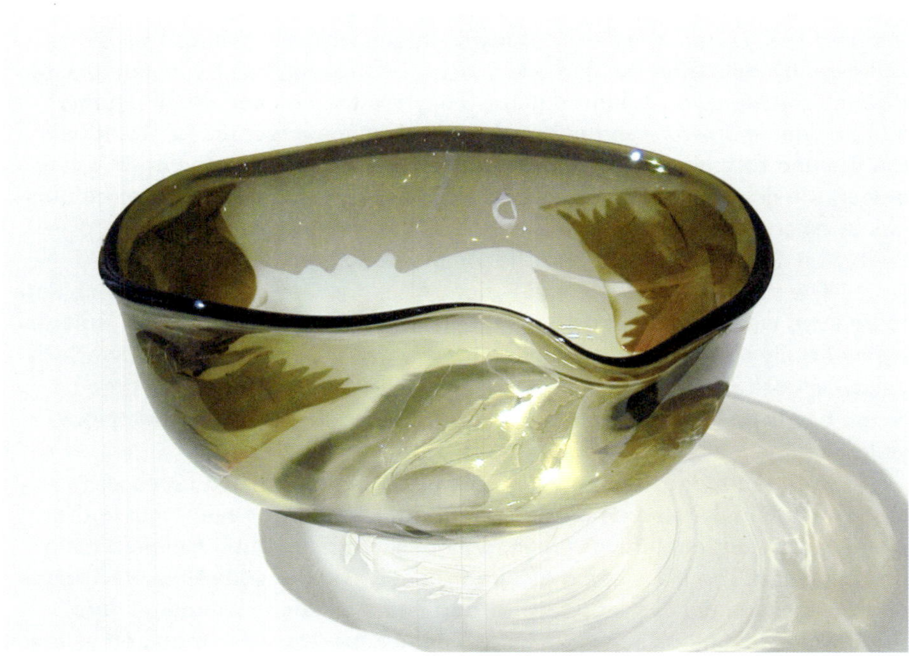

Top: Steven Newell, *Death Unfolded and the Spirit Flitted his Body*, 2004
Bottom: Steven Newell, *The So Weary Eyed Son of Kronos*, 2004

we get the interaction of story and context, event and background, before and after, action and reflection, as mingled narratives peculiar to this transparent medium.

Steven Newell's plates function more as paintings, seen in one eyeful against a wall, graphic and sharp. The plates are more pristine than the bowls – blown and then drawn on, not subjected to reheating. One plate though has been slumped into a shallow dish form and is raised on a blown foot. The cut edges of its image are slightly softened by the return to the kiln.

There are fewer plates than bowls in the current exhibition, but one (which fleetingly refers to his five daughters) in a deep combination of blues, has in it the five goddesses Iris, Hera, Thetis, Athene, and Aphrodite. At other times when Zeus, the big boss, is portrayed, some autobiographical wishful thinking is presumably involved. Newell's drawings of humans, usually mythic ones, have developed certain characteristics over the years, in the way they fill the curvaceous form, for instance, billowing into pointy feet – because it's glass, he says, a floating world. The stories fit loosely in the form, suspended in glass. They are readable in different ways; transparency is key.

'What's new?' is an American greeting that doesn't hold much appeal for the Europeanised American that Newell is now. 'What's so interesting about new...' he might say; it's a fashion question not an art question. Continuities of meaning are much more important to him, which explains why archetypal content, human interaction, or at times a kind of diary, the play of image over three-dimensional form, is still the path he treads. His work evolves rather than changing, and he is not afraid to hoe in the same row. Repetition seemingly adds to the beauty of the elaborately structured text of *The Iliad*, as in the echoing phrases when a hero is killed in battle 'and his armour clattered about him'.

Common currency, shared understanding: how elusive they become in our much-travelled and increasingly complex social world. There was, after all, a time when porcelain figurines were not just amassed in glass cases but had jobs to perform at banquets, enacting scenes from classical stories that all the diners knew and could interpret as theatre, in a changing entertainment between courses.

Story in artworks has not been much in focus in the last decades but Newell cannot do without narrative and figuration – they invest more in an object he says, and are extra-verbal. It pleases him to think that a resurrected ancient Greek potter could comprehend the meaning of his bowls.

But what makes myth an important kind of fictional material to reinterpret? Newell suggests that we need mythology to make sense of the world – that these are the *real* stories, essences, the core of how we think. Before he came to England he was interested in the stories of Black Elk and Carlos Castaneda, the mythology of native Americans. Drawn to Europe as a student, and having lived here now for over 30 years, he looks back on the

American stories as much more abstract, with man pitted against natural disasters. We come back to the Greeks, he thinks, because of the emphasis in these epic poems on humans – they are close to us. Human responsibility, emotion, culpability, and the severe constraints on mortal power and control are the themes of Homer's works composed in the 8th century BC, in the Bronze Age (whose real events took place 500 years before, and were described and passed down via oral tradition in performance) and are part of a cultural continuity that has threaded through Europe for millennia.

Homer's *The Iliad* is a great and tragic story, extraordinary for its time and resonant for ours. The first extended battle between East and West to be defined in literature, it is an apposite frame of reference for an artist working now. *The Iliad* is not about war or heroism as much as it is about human suffering and death: 'young men, for all their god-like greatness, die; old men, women and children suffer and grieve; the gods, exempt from pain, look on...'[3]

The comfortless fact of the gods's overall control, constant interference, and callous detachment, gives pause for thought – it is useful perhaps in these times to compare the predicament of humans entangled with such gods, that nobody now is left believing in.

Newell's current involvement with this powerful theme makes sense, and the pieces in this exhibition are clearly carriers of meaning.

1. Homer, *The Iliad*, trans. and ed. Martin Hammond, Penguin Classics, 1987, p. xvii.
2. Steel pole used to hold a piece of hot glass in the furnace, rotated to keep it in place.
3. *The Iliad*, p. xvii.

Takeshi Yasuda
On Celadon

Ceramic Review 213, May/June 2005. Review of an exhibition of work by Takeshi Yasuda, the Crafts Study Centre, The Surrey Institute of Art and Design, 11 January–25 March 2011. Takeshi Yasuda arrived in Britain in 1973 and his work here, moving away from a traditional training in Mashiko pottery, has brought change to ideas about throwing. His influence is profound; that he is Japanese rather than inspired by Bernard Leach and Shoji Hamada's Japan, is important in the British studio pottery context.

Takeshi Yasuda's enquiring mind, looking into process, handling, material and potent forms for pots, has taken him through some dramatically different stages in the last few decades. Soft green ash-glazed stonewares, brilliant dribbling evocations of Tang Sansai wares made in his first encounter with an electric kiln, creamwares using earthenware temperatures but porcelain clay. More recently he has made pieces in oxidised porcelain, such as tall elongated vases that are thrown upwards to the point of collapse because the clay is so far stretched, and then hung upside down to dry, to revive them, let them fall back into a viable container shape through gravity.

In 2004, he made his first trip to China, investigating, teaching, becoming fascinated, revelling in the food, and establishing connections with a studio where foreign potters can be resident artists. He is about to return there for a more extended stay. In some Chinese historic collections he saw extremely thick lush glazes on reduced porcelains, celadons, that category of refinement and ceramic prestige that we have so desired in the West. These sights have inspired some new possibilities for his work.

On Celadon is a good title for this show, suggesting Yasuda is thinking about it rather than joining the converted, making an exploration around the subject. What he has made is perhaps an essay on celadon rather than a tract. The exhibition consists of about 60 pieces with a strong visual coherence running through the whole group. These are ordinary kinds of object – cups, mugs, teapots, plates, bowls short and tall, and two sizes of vase. The scale varies from the espresso cup, a small footed goblet form, to the great platter shaped like a beached sea creature or a ripe brie. Some pieces are to use everyday – there are quintessential round white teapots, elegant mugs with a simple coil handle – whereas other bowls and vases simply invite gaze and touch.

A sense of a lively but thorough kind of research into formal permutations, body and glaze combinations, and decorative devices that express making, pervades this work and connects the different formal types in subtle ways. Playing with gravity, on and off the wheel, has been a preoccupation. The new forms seem to express both fall and flow, with lapping skirts surrounding the bases of pieces such as the platters or tall bowls. Clay has been pushed around – tall bowls are oval, platters softly squared.

Fingerprints and spikes on edges reveal the slippery motions of joining, and rapidly leaving, parts of the very plastic form.

Finding new ways to make objects is one of Yasuda's admirable strengths; understanding his materials is another, adapting and testing body and glaze until his pots come to life. His glazes here are fat and sleek and range from a cool glassy Yingquing glaze, to others matt like silk and lard and polished stone. Whites range to pale blue and turquoise, classic celadon green, and a custard yellow. Some of the clay is dark reduced red, under a pale blue or amber glaze. Glaze is allowed to drip fattily off sharp angles in the forms.

The vases are real innovations in the canon of Yasuda shapes. They have a stalk and a full body, two pieces joined while wet in a loose and unlaboured way, and a fat oval lip with a pattern of grooves, made upside down and cut off the bat with a twisted wire.

A sense of touch is present in the form of every piece, embodying the wet-become-dry visual qualities that are special to clay – the dimples and distortions that exemplify the grace and speed of the potter's hand. This is not a show to miss.

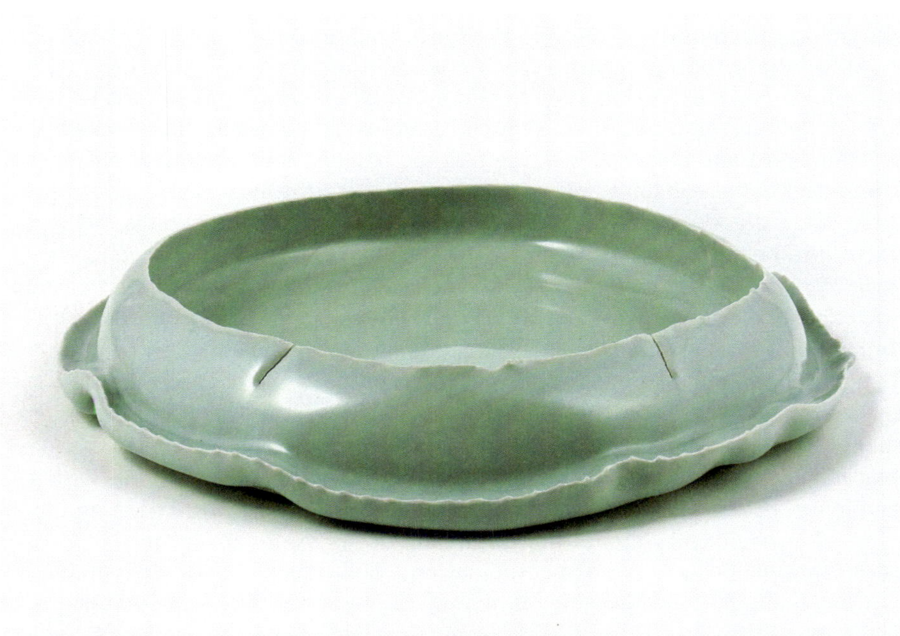

Above: Takeshi Yasuda, *Celadon Platter,* 2003, photo: David Westwood
Right: Takeshi Yasuda, *Celadon Vase with Ice Crackle Glaze,* 2003, photo: David Westwood

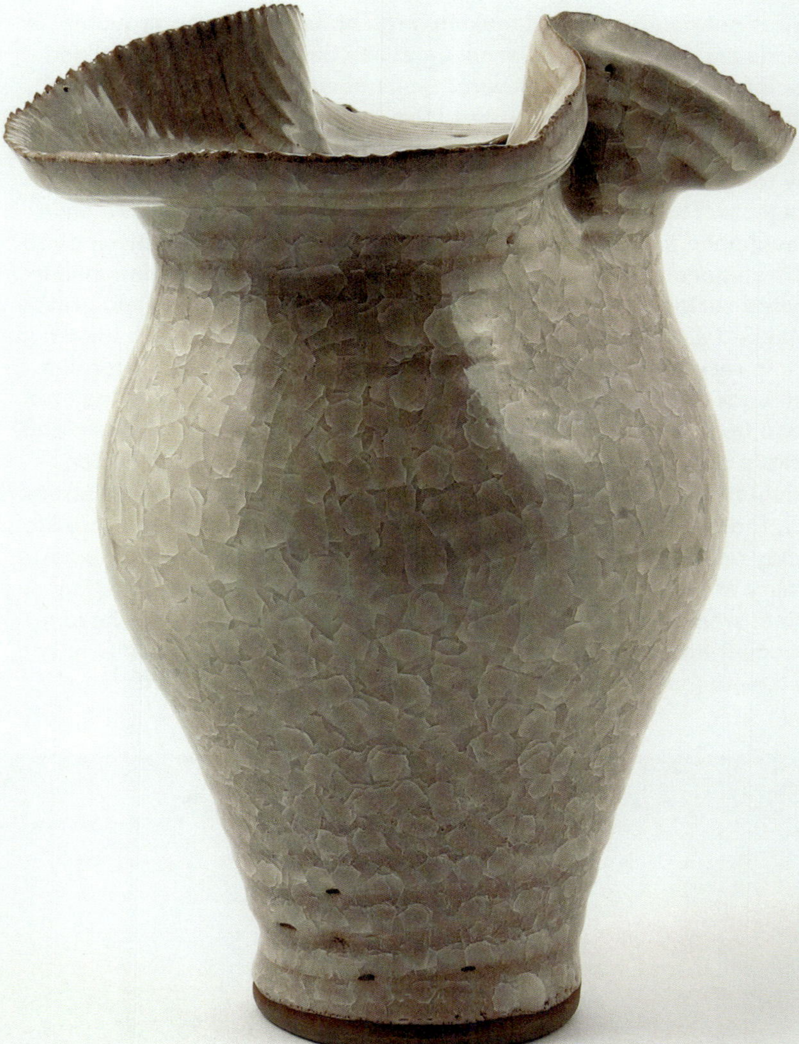

Philip Eglin

Gallery leaflet, solo exhibition of ceramic works by Philip Eglin, Barrett Marsden Gallery, London, 16 June–29 July 2006. Philip Eglin has a huge vocabulary of skills, a spirited understanding of clay, and a humorous outlook. He takes risks with scale and layers of imagery that could make the work look casual and slapped together, but doesn't.

Philip Eglin is not cautious about making large statements, and arguably his bigger pieces are the most wonderful. Eglin has developed his formal and decorative language by making several types of work – and all are hand-built. He has worked with undecorated form, as figures, and also latterly small jugs in series. Such pieces, modest in scale, have become increasingly defined by the pattern of relief textures and details borrowed from other kinds of objects. These plain glazed pieces are sometimes white porcelain, or buff clay dipped in the muted honey brown, ochre, green and black glaze palette of traditional earthenware. He has explored the busier relationship of the painted surface on elaborate form, with the brush strokes and graffiti slogans slapped and dripped across the figure, that first made him known in the 1980s. In recent years he has frequently chosen a very simple form, a cylindrical 'bucket', that can be loaded with printed, scratched, and painted imagery and text on the surface, referencing a great variety of things – and these buckets can be huge, almost a metre high. The iconography often includes quotes from newspapers, preoccupations of his children, celebrity, mundanity, football, Jesus, the humorous predicament of contemporary life, the everyday and the sublime crashed together; but it would be fair to say of the totality of his work that women and art have both been a constant source. Most women have been naked and many have referred to the long-limbed innocent-looking women in 16th-century paintings by Lucas Cranach, but a few have been clothed and these ones have a religious bent.

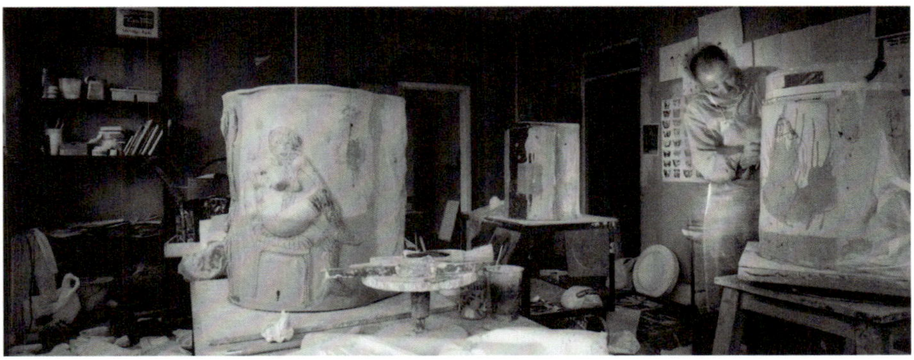

Philip Eglin in his studio, 2000s, photo: Philip Sayer, courtesy Marsden Woo Gallery

The big Madonnas that Eglin began to make in the late 1990s brought his work to an imposingly larger scale and powerful imagery, and they are among the works in clay that have most enlivened the field here in the UK in the last ten years. Echoing European Gothic sculptures in wood, Eglin's large polychromatic earthenware Madonnas, of which ten or so were made (regrettably, none presently in British museum collections) mimicked the architectural ambiguities of their inspiration, part woman/part building, column and niche. Viewed from the front, the child sat stolidly on the Virgin's knee, both enfolded in rippling painted garments that implied the sculpture-in-architecture attributes of load-bearing structure. The back view was emphatically that, the back, indented and awkward, the part the public doesn't normally see that offered a visual disjunction, and his decoration of the surface added layers of provocative imagery in the recess. A reminder, perhaps, of the iconoclast wrenching the figure out of the building.

The freedom and ease in the way potters have sometimes painted the undersides of plates – hispano-moresque platters come to mind – has always been a joy to this viewer, and the backs of Eglin's Madonnas brought the same kind of frisson. The massive forms provided liberating stretches of surface for Eglin to make his secular marks on, churning up the familiar with heartening brio.

Irreverence is a great characteristic and it is one that Eglin manipulates well; it is cheek contained and upheld by the beautifully realised construction of his forms.

One of the larger pieces in the current exhibition is a bucket with a triptych of figures painted on its outer wall; the last Pope, Wayne Rooney, and Jesus all in typical, significant, and related poses. They are combined because of a recent survey of children under ten in Britain who were asked to name the most famous people they knew. After God, Wayne Rooney, Jesus, and David Beckham came top in that order. As might be expected, layers of other contradictory messages and signs, print, transferred drawings, big brushmarks, and suggestions of relief overlay the essential trio to enrich the graphic confusion and engage our attention. The piece is entitled *Let Us Play*.

Besides the bucket, this exhibition brings together two other types of Eglin's current work. There are five sets of six small jugs, specifically grouped and modulating closely toned plain colours and rhythmic variations of ribbed textures and skinny handles. These are shown on wall shelves and can be read like sentences, and in the viewer's awareness of the repeating jug features: lip, neck, shoulder, belly, foot, etc. – probably sentences about the pot as a metaphor for human form.

The rest of the room is filled with figures, two large and five smaller ones, and we are back to nakedness, but with complex decorated surfaces. The women sit, stand, recline, and crawl. They are clothed in painted marks, relief textures, scribbles, inlaid drawings and printed lines; and little

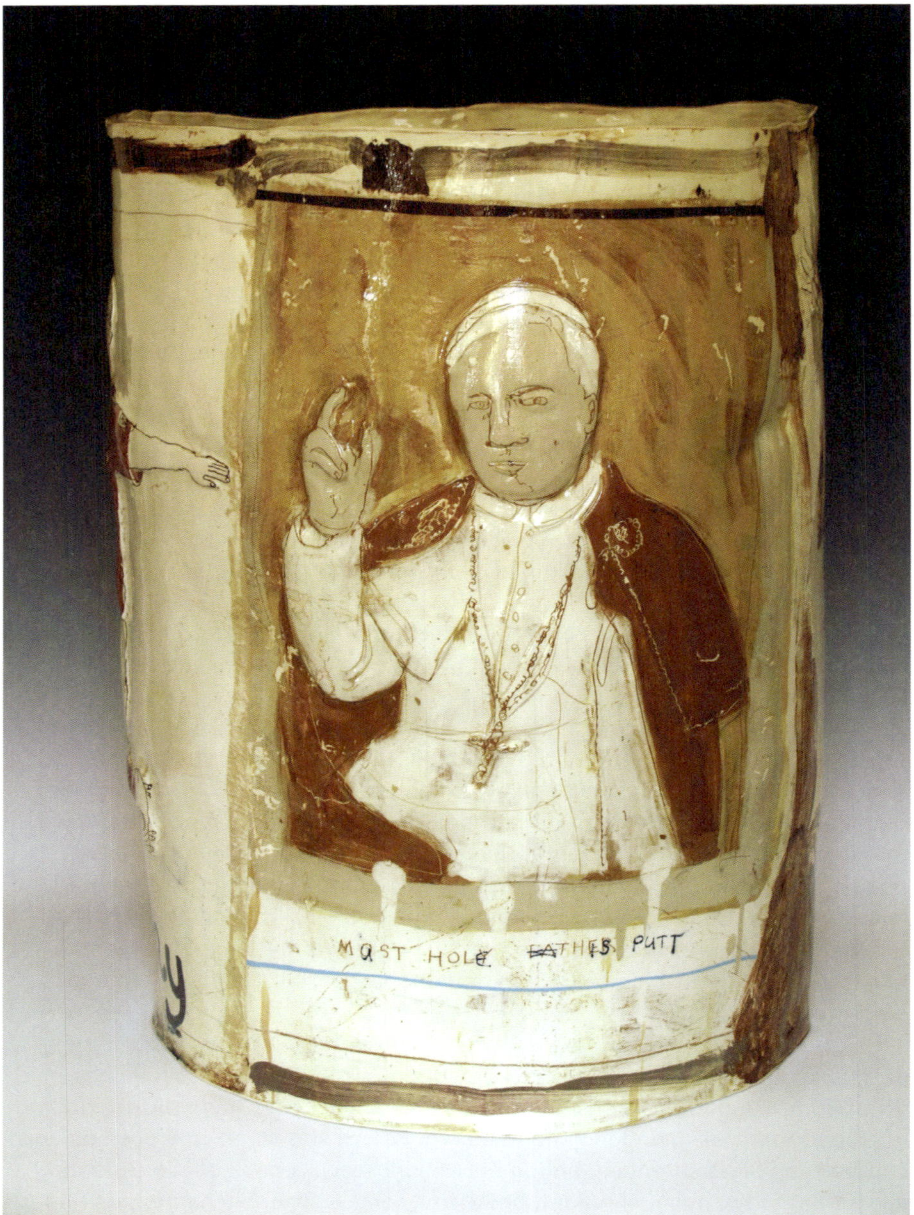

Philip Eglin, *Let Us Play,* 2006, photo: Philip Eglin

conventional Stoke-on-Trent flowers ornament some of the blocks they are supported on. The women are not smooth and ideal bodies. They have a slightly crumpled but calm air, of accommodating the reality they find themselves in, and real flesh sags a bit. They have a potent presence as female images; as clay objects they intrigue on another level at the same time, in the layered complications of their skilful composition. Eglin builds them up from the bottom, supported by the block they rest on which is made first, with soft clay slabs held until firm by inflated balloons. 'As much as possible I want to leave the uniqueness of the surface quality obtained through pressing clay onto plaster untouched', he says, and this is the first time that the imprints of plastic packaging, his vocabulary of the blobs and corrugations from the vacuum presses of the manufactured consumed world, have also been used in the large scale figures. He now wants to model as little as possible – toes and fingers, even eyes and noses, begin with an impression on a piece of soft clay from plaster casts of packaging when a suitable niche can be found.

A transformation of dross, of the chaotic overpacked consumer culture we navigate day by day, is attempted in this urge to recycle both stuff and meanings. Eglin's great achievement is to make *wholes*, poised and affecting images that are not bitty or derivative or fanatically 'crafted', out of three kinds of complexity. Over the years he has been working, complexity has deepened. First he invented a way of building with a slab of clay on which he had picked up a fine line drawing in a dark coloured slip. The drawing was made by scratching on a plaster bat and filling the lines with slip that was then scraped back. This need for integral ornament was later incorporated into building up a figure (knowing about the support systems of the Staffordshire figurine and how men on horseback lean against tree stumps) from many different pieces of clay. More recently, the flat slabs of clay have been processed further by pressing them into plaster moulds of detritus from the modern world. (The reason that plastic bottles are so enchantingly corrugated is for added strength in a thin plastic wall.)

Through these discoveries and the evolution of his making language, both the form and the surface have referenced more and more aspects of painting, news, junk, newness and oldness, the personal and the political, high and low culture. Bravado and irreverence is the key to it, iconoclasm and the building of new icons. 'It's about the material…' he says; but it's about us too.

If Only...

Ceramic Review 223, January/February 2007. This was the start of a magazine series in which potters reflected on things they wished they had known when starting out. I thought it needed to be approached buoyantly; not as a dreary list of complaints.

The way I make pots is very open-ended so I can change and visualise and think through them as I go, reacting to what there is, with an idea rather than a plan beforehand. I wouldn't have known as a student in the 1960s at the Central School of Art and Design in London that hand-building was going to be my thing; we learned everything, and I enjoyed pretty much all of it except the glaze chemistry day, which was taught by a man who hardly used glaze himself and taught us as if he were undergoing some sort of penance, which he probably was. Things were not much better at the Royal College of Art in the early 1970s, where glaze chemistry was taught by an elderly exile from a Stoke factory who was more interested in chihuahuas, which he bred. He liked you to learn by not giving you all the information the first time round, and looking superior when it went wrong. I probably wish I'd known that glaze could be a delight, and hopefully I am now going to find out.

I never felt supremely confident about throwing, though I was proud of being able to do it; and tea sets, which everyone had to make, with six cups the same size, impressed my relatives. I wish I'd understood more about the scope of 'thrown and altered' pots (not a term then used), cutting the wall from the base and fooling around with the sleeve of clay, resettling it on a new base, abandoning symmetry. I fell in love with the Walter Keeler ovalled jugs and teapots when he first made them in the 1980s. I've always had a thing about the oval, and like circles more when they are distorted. *Almost* perfection is more interesting to me; I avoid absolutes and strivings for exactness through all aspects of life. So I wish I'd known about squashed circles – I envy the speed of throwing, the lyricism of touch linked with machine tool.

I wish I'd known that skills really matter; I rather took them for granted because of the emphasis on them in the way I had been taught, and in my teaching over the past decades I have seen them slipping away from the norms of people's lives.

I wish I'd known how difficult it is to be part of a large interview panel and arrive at the right decision in appointing someone to lead an organisation – I've twice been on a panel that made the wrong choice that made things worse for years.

I wish I'd known that things don't stay fixed – since the time in the 1960s when almost all schools had installed kilns, for instance, and clay was going to be a material that everyone got to know, and children would all do three-dimensional work in art as well as drawing and painting.

And broadsheet newspapers reviewed ceramics exhibitions, mine included, on an occasional basis in the 1970s and early 1980s, suggesting that ceramics was from then on going to be taken seriously in a general way. New Ceramics was a buoyant phenomenon in the 1980s, and I felt I was part of a group. This of course has not lasted, and other more independent connections have been needed. Perhaps if I had known this I would have relished the sense of context more at the time.

I wish I'd known that procrastination is part of my creative process, so I wouldn't have wasted so much time on self-reproach and guilt. I wish I'd also known how to be less edgy early on in my working life and arrived earlier at savouring uncertainty – the pleasurable and purposeful state of 'not knowing' is something that grows stronger for artists, and needs sometimes to be defended, and is perhaps one of the few perks of getting older.

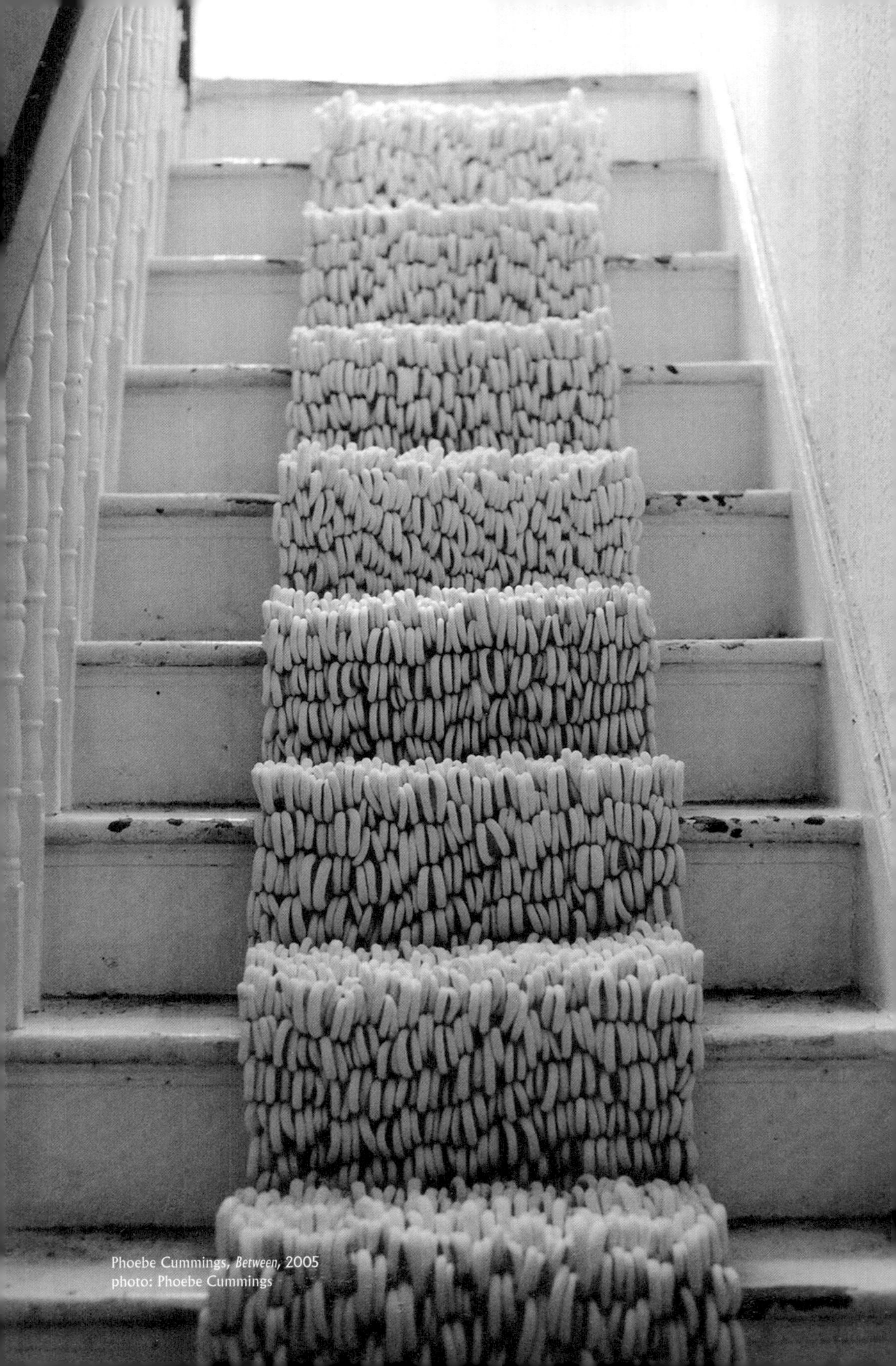

Phoebe Cummings, *Between*, 2005
photo: Phoebe Cummings

Breaking the Mould
New Approaches to Ceramics

Book review in the online journal *Interpreting Ceramics*, January 2008. Robert Barnard, Natasha Daintry and Clare Twomey, *Breaking the Mould: New Approaches to Ceramics*, Black Dog Publishing, 2007. Books that catalogue innovation are important, but difficult to achieve beyond the pictures. In assembling a cluster of self-written submissions from artists and designers with new approaches, background knowledge and editorial clarity is needed.

I have seen this book on a number of student desks and as an immediately attractive book it seems it will be very popular with a young, fresh audience. Its strengths are particularly graphic ones – the section title pages are witty and arresting, with well-chosen images and coloured grounds, such as Robert Dawson's beautiful tile panel for the final chapter on page 182. Sixty or so contemporary ceramic artists and designers have contributed. Some are a lot more contemporary than others; some are famous and some are barely out of college. The quality ranges a great deal, and this shows evidence of the need for a firmer editorial hand. A stronger, better informed selection of work would give this book some of the conviction it lacks.

The work is divided into seven categories with slightly clichéd titles such as *Earthly Inspirations* and *Surface Pleasures* to cover pots, playing around with pots, figurative, nature-inspired work, sculpture, installation and decoration. Meaningless conjunctions, such as coming upon Jane Hamlyn and Grayson Perry on adjacent pages in the Vessel section, when their intentions could not be more different, are opportunities sadly missed for rational interpretation of the field. Some better categories could be imagined – what about *Satire* for instance, which could bring together Richard Slee, Stephen Dixon, Carol McNicoll, and Perry, to name a few? The issue of what design is in contemporary ceramics is also not addressed at all, and various designers's contributions are scattered through other sections. No conclusions are drawn from the international mix either, and what it signifies. The book will thrive on the power of some of its pictures – Phoebe Cummings' staircase, Kjell Rylander's hybrid forms, Clare Twomey's bluebirds infesting the ochre coloured Sculpture Court at the V&A, Keith Harrison's Last Supper firing spectacle; another photo from the same evening event *Clay Rocks* held in that museum (and unmentioned in the captions). Dawson's tile patterns drifting in and out of focus, and Linda Sormin's gutsy chaotic sprawl of raw and fired clay filling space, are also a visual delight. Many casual seekers for the current cutting edge in contemporary ceramics will be happy just to look at the pictures – but 'new approaches to ceramics' need to be described as well as shown.

What the text does give us is a vague and upbeat introduction, followed by three essays and their accompanying illustrations. The smaller significant details of captions with dates, size, country of origin, these categories and specifics for those who know more and want to enquire more deeply, are erratically provided.

The essays, all by makers, seek to carve up the territory in different and interesting ways, but this book is on the whole less satisfying to read than to look at.

The essays begin well. Natasha Daintry's *The Essential Vessel* explores the pot and containment through its two opposing sections on formlessness and form, and is written with grace and style, a sort of elegant passion for the quotations she includes as well as her arguments, and the illustrations are well chosen, striking, and specific to her text.

Robert Barnard was a strange choice for the second essay *The Idea of the New*, when newness is really something he sees dangers in. His account of the development of postwar ceramics, a useful framework for a book such as this, is rooted in the wistful thinking of the 1970s, and in an American experience which was different from Europe's in several significant ways. Artists at the cutting edge in the formative New Ceramics period of the 1970s and 1980s never ditched the pot form in much of Europe, the UK, Scandinavia and Holland for instance, to the extent that American artists did, where sculpture denoted ceramic modernity. The book has an international scope which is vague and unexplored but is otherwise predominantly European.

Regarding the development of the debate about ceramics's aspirations as art almost half a century ago, I was irritated by Barnard not telling us what *kind* of work Rose Slivka is writing about in her famous essay from 1961, 'Craft Horizons', about about clay and painting, that ruffled so many feathers – it was Peter Voulkos and his colleagues that had moved her to write it, and as we have already seen a picture of him in Daintry's essay on page 7, to omit this seems to erode meaning. Was he afraid of causing offence?

Barnard's essay has an interesting three-part structure in which he is critical of both the status-seeking arty ceramicists whose endless search for novelty is specious, and the die-hard orientalists tied at all costs to the functional pot and Japanese traditions in an American landscape. He argues instead for work to show a deep comprehension of ceramic language, with reference to Philip Rawson's definition of this in his book *Ceramics.* This makes a good point – vitality is always what matters.

> Rawson's idea of a ceramic language gives us a way out of the dead-end approaches that modern ceramic art has clung to over the past 50 years. It does not pit the past against the future, the useful against the purely artistic and puts the technical aspects of ceramics into their proper perspective.

It is not clear however what kind of ceramics Barnard does regard as 'complete', though it seems that timeless, poetic, and classic qualities are ones he endorses. The illustrations to his essay are less clearly attached to the writing, apart from a reference to Bernard Leach's Standard Ware and a pot by Kazuo Yagi.

While Barnard writes well, his slightly injured tone is reminiscent of the 1970s, and I think the arguments have shifted. Culminating in quotes from British writers Rawson (*Ceramics*,1971) and Virginia Woolf (died 1941) seems not to be nearly *new* enough for a book of this title.

Clare Twomey's essay *Contemporary Clay* is divided into five sections on objects, hybrids, sculpture, the gallery as context and site, and lastly tackles the important and relatively new territory of ceramic objects as *installation*, rather than discrete objects which could be shown anywhere. The installation field is where her own work resides with great aplomb.

The different sections of her essay have potential overlaps and are not quite convincing – surely all of this can be called sculpture? She writes with a rambling and uncertain style, sometimes with the breathless enthusiasm of a press release, especially in her awkward introductory paragraphs which would have been the chance to pull it all together. The illustrations, though, are well placed, and all referred to in her text, even if some captions leave you hungry.

The categorisation of new work is an area for fresh interpretation, and some imprecision and confusion is likely. How are we to discern the difference when McNicoll puts her pieces on old furniture in a historic exhibition hall in Norway, which in my view, and I believe McNicoll's, does not make it *site-specific*? And don't all exhibitions make use of the verb *to install*? Confusing too when Edmund de Waal, who is a key figure in the site-specific approach, and has for years been carefully placing porcelain pots in different buildings, is described but not illustrated. The Belgian Piet Stockmans, who has made installations in clay since the 1980s if not before, appears in Twomey's *Gallery as Context* section as part of a new wave because they were not shown here until 1999.

But when we get to page 133 of the artists's sections and see Twomey's bluebirds installation for the V&A *Trophy* in full performative action with some blurred outlines of people on the move and children wriggling on the floor, more is made clear of these nuanced distinctions between site-specific and installation works.

This book has valid ambitions – there are new things to be revealed and written about. Stronger overall editing with a real understanding of the contemporary clay scene and its recent past, and a better budget for commissioning essays, could have made this an important book.

Betty Woodman
Trois Grandes Dames III

Ceramic Review 233, 2008. Review of solo exhibition *Betty Woodman: Trois Grandes Dames III*, Galerie Besson, London, 11 June–10 July 2008. Betty Woodman's work is international in its context and flamboyant in its manifestation. Not many artists who start out repetition-throwing tableware arrive at such brio and spatial command.

In this, the final stage of Galerie Besson's celebration of great women potters, Betty Woodman is showing ten colourful, casual, vibrant works, mostly made in the last decade, but backed up by a couple of pieces from the 1980s. All this work was made in Italy; Woodman – one of the most eminent and spectacular American ceramic artists – is a woman with two studios, one in New York and the other in Tuscany.

I used to be able to tell which pieces were made where – the Italian ones having a slight reduction quality of soft lustrous greens and milky browns, like the *Vase Diptych* from 1982 exhibited here. The American ones used to be jazzier in colour, but now her brilliant painterly flow seems to have gone international. The newer works, such as the large wall piece *Palazzo Massimo* made especially for the Besson space, are vivid and extraordinary.

Woodman's work stretched beyond the discrete three-dimensional vessel object long ago – walls are included, images are fragmented into energetic parts like painted gestures, cylindrical thrown forms 'wear' flat picture planes of clay slabs like sections of a painting. Many pots are paired, sharing an image, one wearing an orange apron, the other a theatrical finale of small pot characters on a stepped stage with flat cutout clay scenery. *Palazzo Massimo* is built of many elements: a painted canvas backdrop; a small wooden shelf carrying an unglazed vase; a few flat images of vases and rococo squirls and leaf forms, all brightly glazed and the colour heightened, taken up another dazzling notch in the spectrum with dashes of lacquer and paint. The end wall of the gallery was like an exuberant hedonist altar, flanked in both alcoves by a tall painted vase that flowed into fragments of wall decoration.

Woodman's unflagging pursuit of new directions for the clay object/image seen here reinforces the fact that it is crazy that her work has not had a major exhibition in the UK. This show is like an aperitif; and I think slightly odd as a group of works for including the 1980s pieces, when her current focus is so clearly on the magical shift from three to two dimensions, disconnection and connection, all starting from the wheel (every flat slab has been thrown too) and the delighted paintbrush.

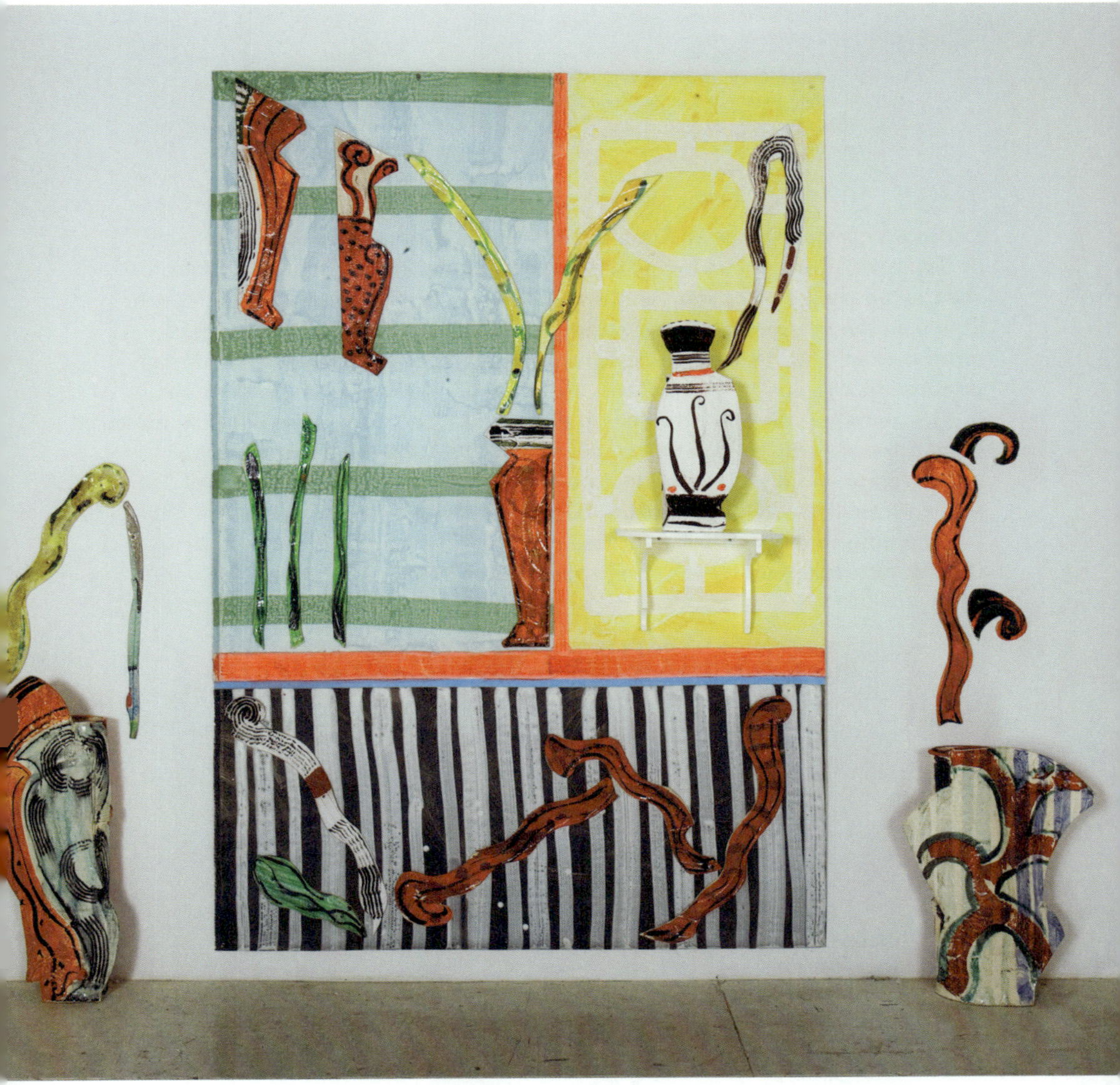

Betty Woodman, *Palazzo Massimo, Orange Profile* (left), *Red Swirl* (right), 2007

The Fiction of Form

The Journal of Modern Craft, Vol.2, No.1, March 2009 (reprinted by permission of Berg Publishers, an imprint of Bloomsbury Publishing Plc). This essay, one of the 'Statement of Practice' series, was paired with the text of a talk given at the Royal Society of Art in 1975 by Professor David Queensberry, entitled 'The Designer, the Craftsman and the Manufacturer'. He had led the Ceramics department at Royal College of Art when I was a student there, and had built up a real creative environment.

1970

I brought my protractor and compasses to the exam at the Royal College of Art in 1970, prepared by my Diploma teachers at the Central School for the design project that the exam was known to be – quite an ordeal for me. This was the first year, however, that the sculptor Eduardo Paolozzi had set the exams, and cheerful exuberance was expected, covering sheets of paper with imagined masks. Carol McNicoll walked out halfway through, but I was happy. At the interview, the large body of men, seven I think, asked each other if I wouldn't be better off applying to textiles after they saw my etchings and my pattern-filled portfolio. But I was offered a place, and so was McNicoll, and looking back I wonder if some of them thought I was a potential convert for surface decoration in the ceramic industry (a job often taken up by textiles graduates).

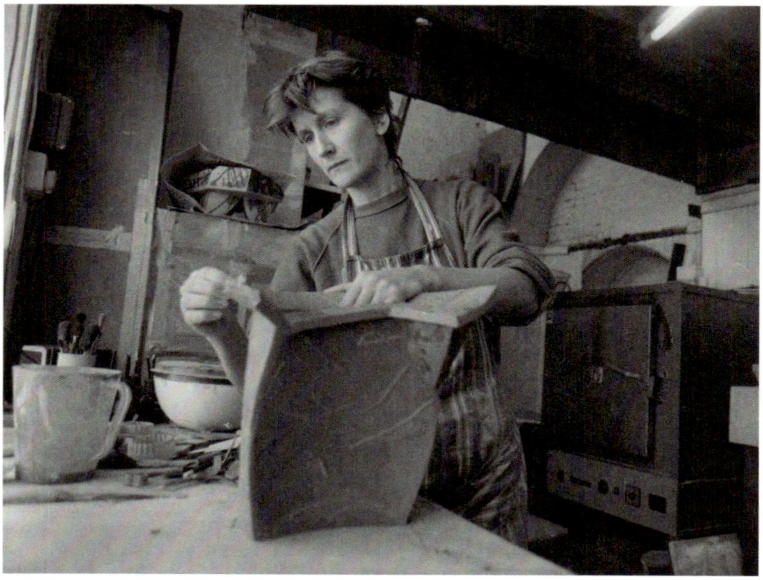

Portrait of Alison Britton in Kings Cross studio, 1983, photo: Garry Weaser, courtesy *The Guardian*

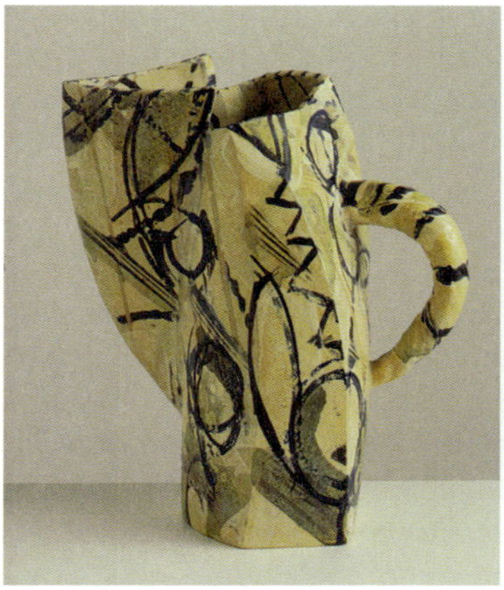 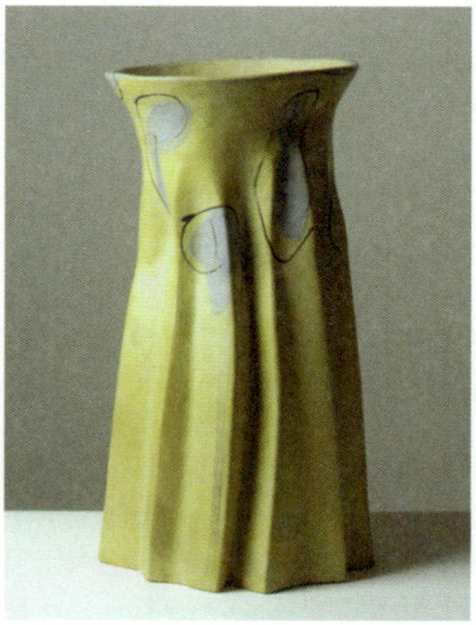

Left: Alison Britton, *Jug*, 1986, photo: David Cripps
Right: Alison Britton, *Pleated Yellow Pot*, 2000, photo: Philip Sayer

In the mid-1960s, Professor David Queensberry had brought the strong personalities of the potter Hans Coper (from 1966) and Paolozzi (from 1969) into his department to expand the teaching on his course. From the top, a certain zeal for recruiting designers for the ceramic industry was always a slight undercurrent of the department experience, but it made no sense to me. After a strange start (lots of photography of architectural ornament and hours printing in the darkroom), I gravitated more and more towards Coper for the most responsive tutorial discussions, objects and feeling. By halfway through the course I had decided that he was my personal tutor, and that seemed to work, although I was painting on tiles more than making pots.

In the year before my arrival at the Royal College of Art, Coper had shared an exhibition at the V&A with the modernist textile artist Peter Collingwood. The only known publication of an 'artist's statement' was wrung from Coper for the catalogue, and has been much quoted:

> Practising a craft with ambiguous reference to purpose and function one has occasion to face absurdity. More than anything, somewhat like a demented piano-tuner, one is trying to approximate a phantom pitch. One is apt to take refuge in pseudo-principles which crumble. Still, the routine of work remains. One deals with facts.

The concentrated enquiry in these sentences was alluring to many of us as students, as was the focus on ambiguity, the intrigue of the *phantom pitch*, which proposed that ideas could be pursued with uncertainty, within craft. Coper outlines an ambivalent connection with function and content. The words 'absurd' and 'economy' are repeated through the whole text, revealing an austere and understated existential pull.

Turmoil was in the air in those years for postwar babies becoming adults; politics, the student union 'sit-in', reading *The Female Eunuch*, developing a 'whim of iron'.[1] We were, it seems to me now, growing the strong capacity for *not knowing our place,* both as artists in the craft world and as women in the art world.

1990

In 1990, Tanya Harrod curated a retrospective of 70 of my pots for the Aberystwyth Arts Centre, which toured museums in the UK and ended in the museum Boijmans van Beuningen in Rotterdam. By this time I was 42, I was a single parent with two daughters, I had made a working system that included some teaching and some writing, and occasionally curating. I had worked in three studios – sharing first with McNicoll and later with Jacqueline Poncelet, both fellow students and continuing friends from the Royal College of Art. By 1986 I was in my current studio which is an old butchers shop in Stamford Hill, London. I had got away from the tile commissions, and had been exhibiting pots since 1976. It was a sociable time – there had been a lot going on with the emergent Crafts Advisory Committee (later the Crafts Council) and the British Council, both energetically commissioning exhibitions of new craft work here and abroad. Museums were purchasing the contemporary and there was lots of attention for a group of artists that included my Royal College of Art generation and others more established. In his book from 1986, Peter Dormer designated us the New Ceramics. The Crafts Council shop at the V&A was run by Tatjana Marsden and was the best place to see rapidly changing small exhibitions of new work in the 1980s. It was an expansive period and we were a lucky generation.

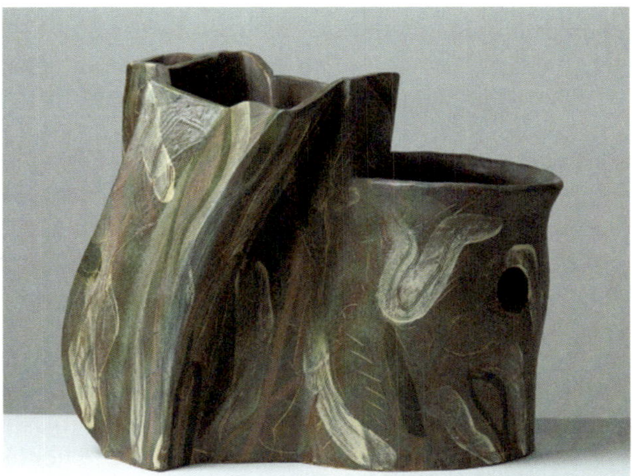

Alison Britton, *Double Green Pot,* 1995, photo: David Cripps

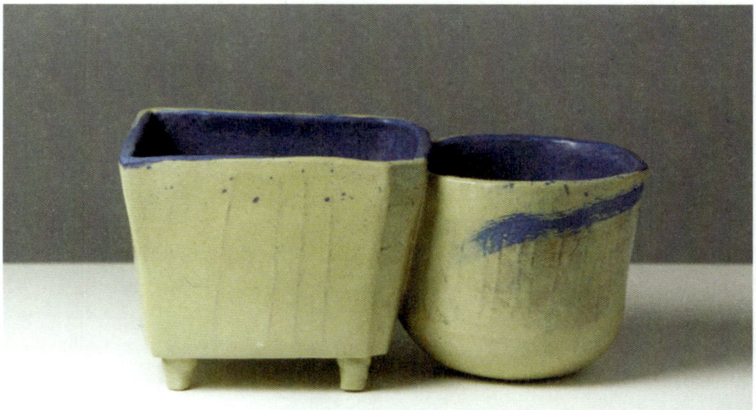

Alison Britton, *Trough*, 2001, photo: Philip Sayer, courtesy Marsden Woo Gallery

A number of things had become norms in my way of making. I rolled out sheets of clay and painted them with slip on both sides in a relaxed way before cutting them up to make half-planned forms, a kind of equivalent to tailoring, without the crispness of intention or pattern-cutting. Pots were painted therefore two or three times; first with slip, which is opaque and can be stained any colour, and then with underglaze pigments, also derived from metal oxides, stronger and not opaque. I painted them when flat, when built, and then after they were biscuit-fired. It was like negotiating both body and dress, with the dressmaking the most of the body, and the final painting being the point where resolution was attempted. I worked with stoneware clay but made earthenware objects, out of obstinacy (earthenware was seen as inferior by the dominant preceding potting generation) and a desire for warmer colours. All the surface events on my pots were under the glaze; the glaze was just a clear matt surface that pulled it all together and enriched the colours.

'All art is a synthesis of improvisation and order', says the film director Mike Leigh, who is famous for starting without a script. The system I described above was my order. The rest is improvised, changing a little from piece to piece. I had gone through a series of formal and thematic preoccupations that were visible in the pots. I made many jugs; I drew narratives across their surfaces; I compared imagery and pattern as signs of nature and civilisation; I used fish and tulips as male and female symbols. Moving past the anthropomorphic jug, I made more box-like forms that often turned out to be torsos, and the brush marks on the surface got rougher and more vague and abstract. The forms leant and lurched, or were made of stacked parts, or awkwardly conjoined chambers, sometimes in pairs or groups of associated pieces.

I had finished with drawing pictures on the pot walls after my Crafts Council solo exhibition in 1979, but certain forms – jug, square dish, double pot – have circled and re-entered my imagination, time and again, lightly disguised to move things on.

In the monograph Harrod wrote for the 1990 exhibition, I still enjoy the gift of this quotation from the psychoanalyst Marion Milner's book *On Not Being Able to Paint* from 1950 (published under the name Joanna Field):

> I woke one morning and saw two jugs on the table; without any mental struggle I saw the edges in relation to each other, and how gaily they almost seemed to ripple now they were freed from this grimy practical business of enclosing an object and keeping it in its place.

Here Milner is writing about perception and representation, about suddenly seeing form; an artist taking charge of a sight in the world and feeling moved, through the eyes, enough to paint it; about the process of catching an image out of reality, and making an imaginative construct that stands for the real thing. I can feel all that – have felt it as a painter and a photographer stimulated by what I see. But I feel something three-dimensional too, shapes in the chest. I don't know what jugs Milner was looking at, but I can visualise *my* two jugs on a table, a double image, compare and contrast, a slice of life and still-life at once (which is what I wrote about in *The Maker's Eye* catalogue for the Crafts Council in 1981, the first bit of writing that pushed my thinking somewhere it hadn't been). These words of Milner's are like a small manifesto for me. It's about not being kept, neither me nor the pots, in our place. My pots, too, ask to be freed from any grimy practical business, although I am stuck with the container form – I need to make open objects, not closed ones.

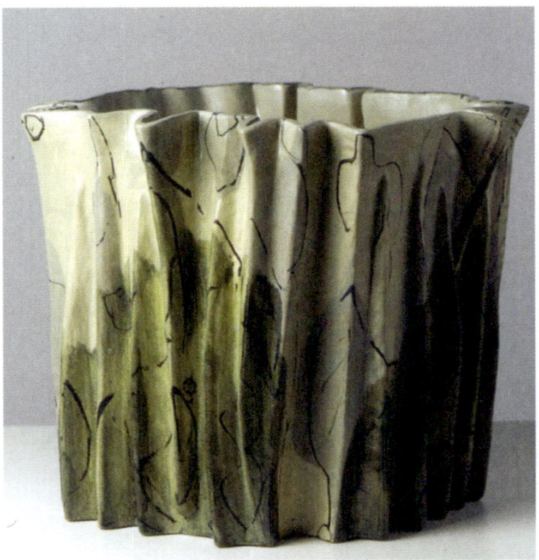
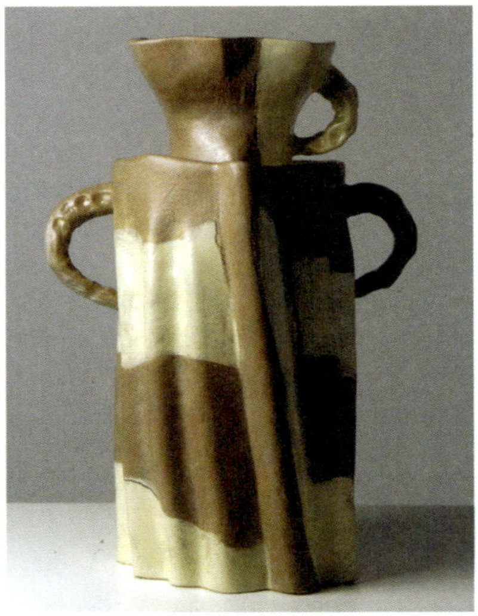

Alison Britton, *Scrawl*, 2003 (left); *Sprite*, 2003 (right), photo: Philip Sayer, courtesy Marsden Woo Gallery

There are so many layers and possibilities to allude to: bodies, buildings, ordinary domestic stuff, inner worlds, etc.

Curiously, I already knew about Milner. I had tiled her fireplace when I was a student at Royal College of Art. She was a friend of my aunt.

1990 was a good point to wind up a review of my sheerest work, all planes and angles fused together, lots of flat surfaces, a few curves. Pots like these were photogenic, easy to focus on. Pots made after the retrospective gradually included softer, coiled and modelled aspects as well as slabs. They became more fully three-dimensional, more plastic, less haphazard (and harder to photograph).

In 1995, I called an exhibition in Germany *Form and Fiction.* Detached from their normal partners, *function* and *fact*, that pairing of words is still a useful prod to my thinking because fiction is as important as food. Pairs are significant too: the *double* as an essential form, probably conflicted but nonetheless attached. In an exhibition leaflet for a small show in Wales in 1996, Bryan Illsley, my studio-sharer, wrote that my pots conveyed 'provisional accommodation, power sharing, partial peace... Disjunction is her forte, disparity her game.' The lashing together of parts, the awkward marriage of shapes, is a pot type I revisit, as in 1995 with *Double Green Pot*, where there were hints of figuration again; I thought of it as a forest.

Since 2000, I have tried to be less boring with titles, to use words more suggestively without going over the top poetically – *Borderland Pot*, *Hybrid*, *Overlap*, *Shelter* and *Prospect*, *Side Issue*, *Bearer*, *Dry Space*, *Tank*, *Undergrowth*.

I have since recycled some of these words as stencils layered into the surface painting of later pots. The small double piece that wasn't ready for an exhibition in Paris in 2001 that opened on 9/11 was called *Trough*. With this piece my interest in *flow* as a subject began. In life, swimming is my dream medium. I can't ignore water and in Venice I have trouble staying on the pavement. Flow is a connecter of parts, whatever they are; and in the collection of the Institut du Monde Arabe, a frequent stopping place for me in Paris, I had seen a North African ceremonial sink-like object made of stone, a stepped form where water could run from chamber to chamber.

2008

Pots for a show at Barrett Marsden Gallery in 2003 (the Marsden part is the same Tatjana from the V&A shop in the 1980s) explored an unexpected interest for me in some aspects of classicism – despite the fact that to me it has always seemed a very masculine phenomenon. I used the acanthus leaf, for instance, as both a relief and a painted image, which has been used so diversely in successive cultures and is still to be found everywhere in architectural ornament. I made a group of single forms (except one double piece) which were of two kinds, square open pieces like the capital, as in the piece called *Scrawl*, and tall fluted cylindrical pots like the column, as in *Sprite*; heads and bodies, males and females, houses and treetrunks. After that, I started to work with the pipe form as an animating attachment – a male image, you might say, but also a continuation of ideas about flow.

The constants in my life and practice are important. There are stable practical things I can take for granted, so the work is able to freewheel a little all the time. I can doodle around the consistency. I have taught part-time at the Royal College of Art for ages and love the ongoing connections with new ideas and people at the start of their careers. Tatjana Marsden has been my main agent/confidante/dealer since the 1980s in four different locations; I have lived in the same house for more than 30 years and in the same studio for more than 20. And I still make pots. The pleasure in doing so has a lot to do with accepting the balance of what you can control and what you can't, and in letting the strength of clay's material qualities be evident. In the last couple of years my weariness with spraying the outsides of my pots with glaze has been suggesting change. It is a boring way to make a surface and implies that uniformity is desirable. I now want to use glaze in a fleshier way, to include colour in it, to immerse in it, to pour it, slosh it on. I need to leave more unpainted space for lapping and flowing, and there is more risk and uncertainty for things going into the kiln. This led me at first to make smaller pieces that I could handle easily over a dustbin of wet glaze. I am trying not to be thrown by the plethora of new possibilities; to be both aloof to, and engaged with, the danger of glaze dominating form.

In 2006, I made two trips to Istanbul in spring and autumn. I had to go and see this city full of chaotic complexity and overlap after reading Orhan Pamuk's novel *My Name is Red*, which is concerned, among many things, with the relationship between words and pictures, and old and new influences. It is also a thriller and a love story. Both in narrative and content it depicts many viewpoints – even the horse in a painting writes a chapter, as does the colour red.

As I make pots now I am interested in seeing how fiction might alter form. Some of the qualities I'm pursuing have been affected by things seen there, mostly non-ceramic things though glaze and colour is vibrantly everywhere on the tiled surfaces of buildings. In Istanbul walking, looking, photographing, and reading, the place is stuffed with sensory depth and disorder. I loved the ubiquity of the colour turquoise, even on the tram hand-rails – just right, not cloying or sweet. There is water everywhere in the views.

In current forms, I continue working with the pipe as a daft attachment, and with cylinders and squares, columns and boxes. In a piece like *Sluice*, made in 2007, I am still taken with the collision of architectural and domestic forms and the underlying body, the human scale of pots, holdability, disjunction and flow. An unfinishing journey.

1. On the new tendencies of his students that Queensberry called a 'para-art activity... It is, as somebody put it, working with a whim of iron. It is a fine art approach to subjects that have been, from an historical point of view, related to products.'

Three by One

Exhibition catalogue, eds. Alison Britton and Simon Olding, Crafts Council/Crafts Study Centre, 2009. Introductory catalogue essay for an exhibition of my selection from three public craft collections, Crafts Study Centre, UCA Farnham, 13 January–19 December 2009. Curating objects that were already part of three different collections, not newly made, was an opportunity to think about history in a very tangible sense. I also found that I was describing the organising process, in its indirectness, in a way that resonates with how I approach other things like teaching or making pots.

The nub of this project is the bringing together of objects from three different public collections of craft, seen through one pair of eyes. The exhibition is a synthesis, a visual exploration of mixture, as well as a view of history and fabrication. Each collection has developed in its own way; objects have been acquired for exhibitions, through committees, bought, donated: sedimentary layers of taste and decisions. This book echoes the exploration of synthesis with essays from five authors, voiced from each collection and from museological and critical contexts in the wider frame. For this reason the composite photographs of several objects, combining the collections, are true illustrations of the exhibition's aims; and the different calligraphic titles of essays reveal the notion of bringing a range of opinions together, and emphasise that books are also made things.

Picking my way through hundreds of objects in the online archives of the British Council, the Crafts Council and the Crafts Study Centre last summer, I felt at first a sense of the absurdity of the task. Myriad paths could be plotted through them, thousands of permutations – what was I to aim for? I had been given the wonderful brief of following my own judgement, not the obligation to assess and analyse the underlying strengths of each collection. Shelving an anxiety that my personal taste is of no general interest, I plunged into the great pool of possibilities. I wanted to arrive at visual coherence in an unobvious way, hoped to surprise myself as well as the audience, and to juxtapose differences and connections to illuminating effect. Making is intrinsic in the language of all these objects; my task was to respond to the stuff and skill and bravado of them and then to make a whole out of their random parts. To find a sense of a realisable order, something of subtlety and clarity to show.

Common to my working process across all fields – in making a pot, planning a lecture, writing a text, curating a show – is my need for a casual beginning. It is the opposite of a strategy. I want to *not know* about it, to suspend forethought and conviction. Browsing with apparent idleness, like window shopping, sidling up to the ideas, keeping it open-ended; once a fresh thought, a point of entry, has been sensed, then it is much simpler to build the substance of the project and bring it to completion. Not unlike the animal in Ernst Gombrich's introduction to *The Sense of Order*, who 'must

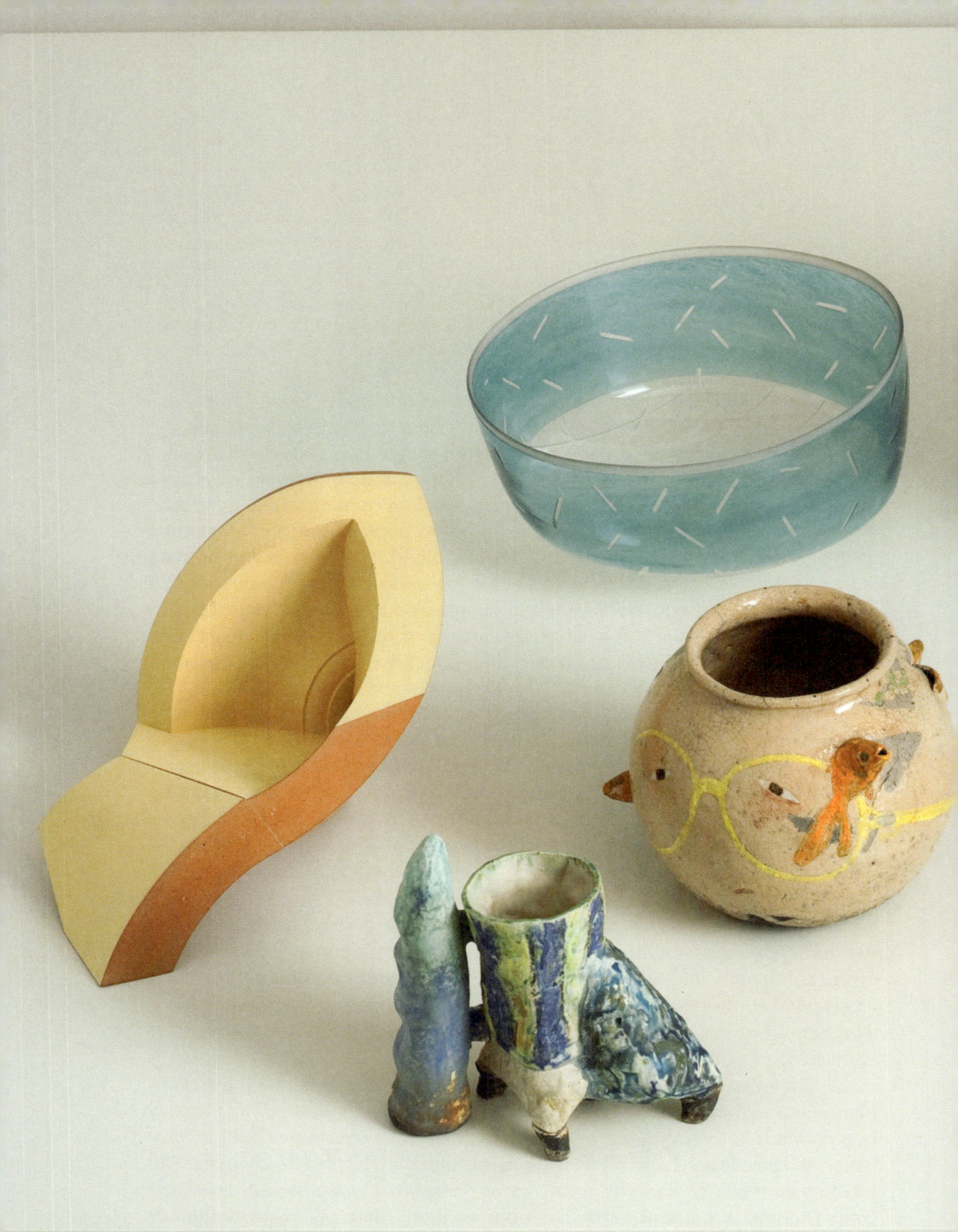

From left to right: Martin Smith, 1982; Angus Suttie, 1991; Christopher Williams, 1984; Jill Crowley, 1995; Michael Rowe, 1985; Jacqui Poncelet, 1980; all from Crafts Council Collection; and Chinese teapot, 20th c. from Bernard Leach Source Collection, Crafts Study Centre, photo: Edward Park

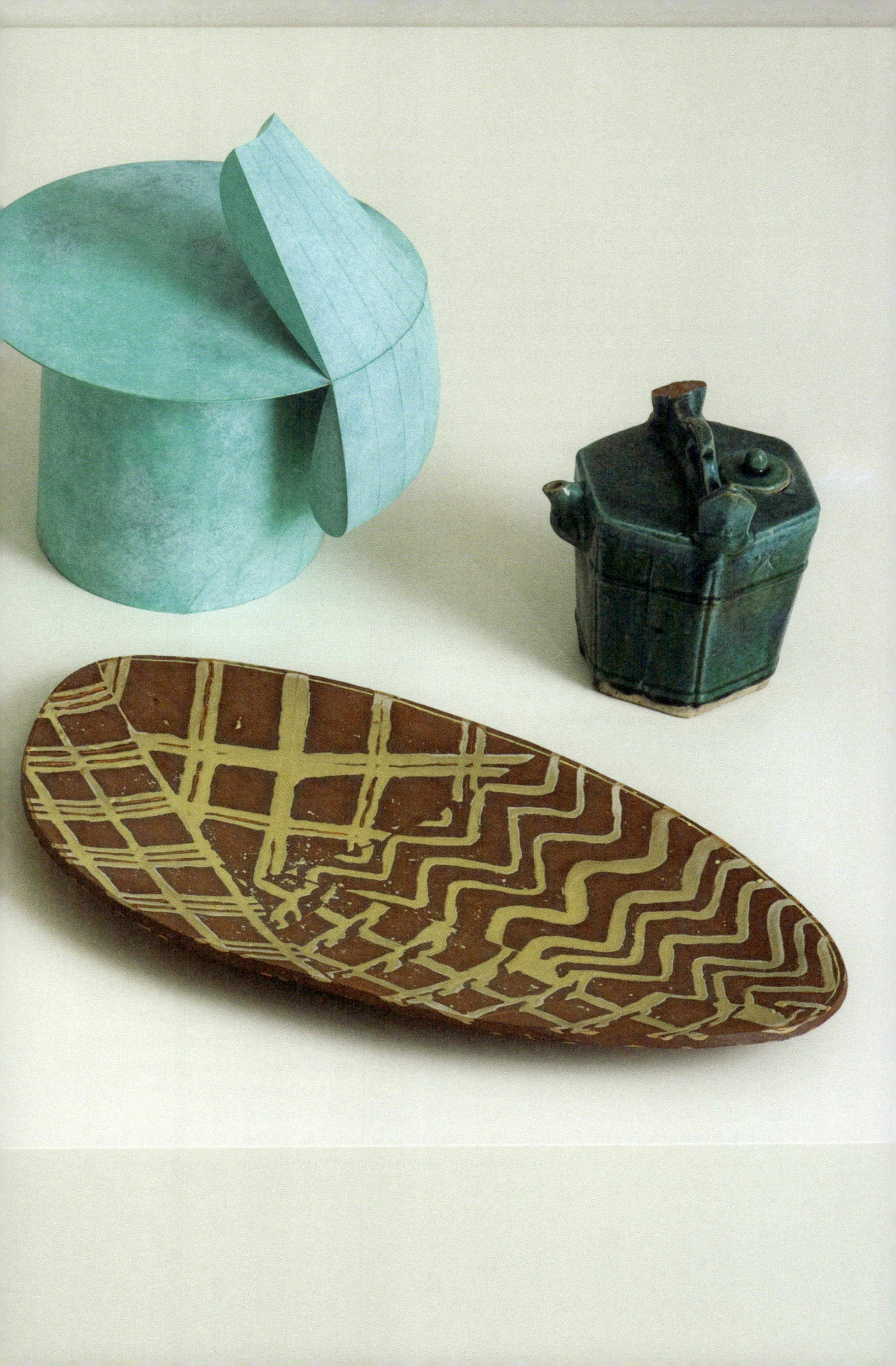

seek its goal in a complex and flexible way'.[1] And order, a discernible pattern or an evident thread, is what is wanted in the end for every pot, essay, lecture or exhibition made. The limbo phase at the start of an act of making is a slide into a kind of mental wilderness, perhaps to see cleanly what the point is, from a new angle. Making meaning is the real point, optimistically, in the manipulation of ideas, writing, or things.

I started to make a shortlist from each website, with the background idea of building a personal object language. There were some constraints. I found that some objects I would have chosen were already out on loan. And that in the case of some favourite artists, the particular pieces I could choose from were not what I wanted. How could I make meaning out of the whole exhibition if each selected object did not mean something to me? Many pieces I already knew, which helped in the early stages. Unknown ones I checked out in other ways, in books and catalogues, artists' websites. A few I have borrowed before, for a British Council exhibition, for instance, that I curated in the former Czechoslovakia in the 1980s. A few things in the Crafts Council Collection I had helped to purchase as a committee member many years ago. Long lists had to become shorter lists – I was aiming to end up with about 30 objects from each collection. The confidence to pare down my selection was based mainly on gut reaction and decades of the visual appraisal of solid things. I knew there would be a good range of pots in the synthesis, because it is my home ground, but I also knew that comparing materials, craft disciplines, and types of work is the focus of interest in a show like this. In pursuing my own pot-making work in the studio, many useful historical sources for me are not ceramic. I am intrigued by the translation between materials, and respond to the decorative and formal conventions that distinguish clay and stone, clay and metal, or glass, or textile.

The online trawl was followed by visits to see the actual objects and face the real decision-making. The Crafts Council selection was the first to be firmed up, which gave me a core group of major 1980s New Ceramics pieces as well as contemporary metal and glass and the most recent jewellery and textiles. The great range of scale in my selection was suddenly apparent, from the long horizontal Ruston Aust textile hanging to the Hans Stofer ring with a glass bottle end in it. The Crafts Study Centre Collection was less familiar to me, and I took the chance to explore in particular the wonderful hoard of early printed textiles, such as Enid Marx and Barron and Larcher, and works on paper. At the British Council, I found objects I wanted at both the domestic end of the spectrum and the large and spectacular. All these chosen objects communicate to me, the vitality or imaginative life in an object is its most important quality and works differently for two- and three-dimensional things. The sense of touch is another part of the aesthetic experience that makes us perceive and connect with three-dimensional things. The subsequent task is to make things speak to each other. Like words in a sentence, it is the relationships between objects that make them mean more to the eye.

I have collected postcards of art objects since I was a child; I was first exposed to museum-going because my father worked very near the British Museum and my sister and I used to be left to wander in there from an early age. With a pile of diverse cards, I started a brown envelope filing system, labelled with what I thought at the age of nine were sensible categories. Before I knew much art history, or even geography, which envelope to put things in was an issue; and I struggled with cards that could belong in more than one envelope. That hasn't changed – in fact there is always a choice of envelopes to file objects into. The process of categorisation and the emergence of exhibition themes from a loose beginning, the cluster of objects one has responded to, is, as for Gombrich's wild animal, another goal to be sought in a complex and flexible way.

I like the image of treading water for the inchoate stage of an artefact, such as an exhibition of 100 things, that will have to be decided on and be put into a defined space. Imagine all the shortlisted things in a watery medium, so that things can flow in many directions at first, a pool of possibilities. As you run your mind over images of the chosen, shoals form, correspondences, maybe in more than one direction. Some of these are a surprise to the curator.

The shoals I began to discern within the mass in the categorisation process included alphabets, yellow things, plates, bobbles, little touches of gold, very old things, hints of the body, reflective surfaces, basic colours from metals like iron and copper, and everyday history in cups and saucers and tube signs. Certain times seemed to stand out, such as the 1930s and the 1970s and 1980s, periods with stresses which have perhaps spurred change and creativity.

To sum up the contents of the show, it is emphatically an exhibition of craft objects but it touches the sides of fine art and design, as you might expect. The very big jug made by Bruce McLean in 1987 belongs arguably alongside the rest of his work in fine art and performance, and the small jug with a sepia print of garden tools by Eric Ravilious, manufactured by Wedgwood in 1939, is a design on a factory shape. The decorative fluency of the print is close in spirit to the hand-painting on the blue and white tile of an 18th-century gentleman walking downstairs, attributed to Ravilious in the 1930s. Other pieces I have chosen hover on the borders of production on one side and sculpture or painting on the other, and, as ever, a definition of the craft boundary as permeable is preferable.

A great reward in working on this exhibition has been the chance to engage with historic objects. I had not expected to find and draw on the collections of inspirational objects owned by the craft pioneers Ethel Mairet and Bernard Leach. These two so clearly demonstrate the modernist urge to seek out new sources, roots and essences, across the world, to invigorate a revision of thinking about the handmade and its place in an industrialised society. The 13th- or 14th-century *Pot with pricked strap handle* from Leach's collection is a sober greyish piece with a wild splash of green glaze on it, and is the oldest in the exhibition. A group of braids from the former Yugoslavia and India from Mairet's own collection vividly represent artists's need to widely research and learn from folk traditions. This need was fresh and acute in the formative modernist period, and matters still. A need for historical sympathy, an impassioned connection with how things looked in the past, is inherent in the production of all art that is able to avoid arrogance. What we get, as artists in an engagement with historic objects, are sounding boards, measuring sticks, echo chambers; referential reflections of other systems of meaning from other times in other places. Craft moves forward through its uses of history, looking and comparing, in pursuit of a skilful contemporary relevance.

The exhibition began to set when the objects were installed. Placing the stuff is another part of making its meaning; ideas were defined by filtering it piece by piece into the gallery space. The fit of forms in space is the underlying thing, how we meet the ideas and the aesthetic proposal. In the process, there are more facts to respond to, the exact dimensions and types of case, the overall context of plain wooden surfaces and glass shelves, and the relatively large number of objects to locate. I mentally tried out groups beforehand, that considered the type of objects but also their size and colour.

The fixed furniture in the gallery was a boon, not a constraint. It also helped to complete the selection; the way one sees things inside the sequence

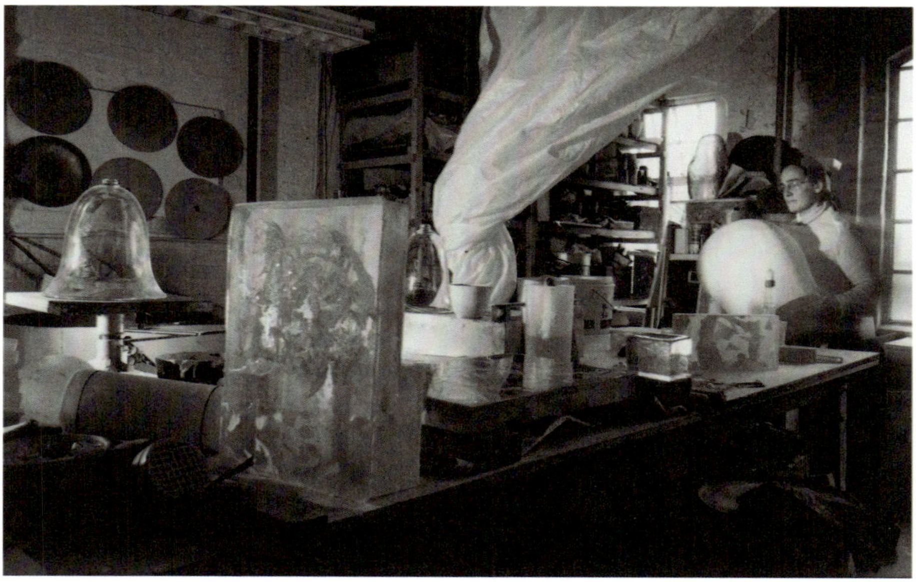

Emma Woffenden in her studio, 2004, photo: Philip Sayer, courtesy Marsden Woo Gallery

of high flat archive cases running down one side of the room made me decide to include the woven braids, and to treat some of the more graphic plates and tiles rather as images. The three-dimensional jigsaw puzzle of arranging all the work in the cases, on the low plinths and on the walls, was a process of finding a shape, to look right but also drawing out categories and themes, from an array of possibilities. The shape inherent in my choices was finally expressed by their display. I decided to start with the three Leach drawings that show his thinking about pots rather than the pots themselves, though a simple coffee pot nearby is part of a varied group of tableware, which I see as the basic alphabet of ceramics. Alphabets on paper follow the Leach drawings on the same wall, including the original artwork by Edward Johnston for the typeface for the London Underground drawn in 1916; it is the typeface used in this exhibition catalogue.

Colour was crucial in deciding the display; so many of the historic and modernist pieces are either brown or white, 'natural' colours so-called, and many kinds of each. One of the most recent objects is Tord Boontje's *Screen*, which is white and brown, the laser leaving a brown edge on the branching foliage, cut in white silk. Iron and deep blue indigo feature strongly in the palette of 1930s textiles too, powerfully basic as printed on unbleached grounds. I had chosen pieces with vibrant colours which brought in essential patches of brightness here and there: the yellow glaze on a mug, or the yellow-dyed goat hair of a carpet, green copper glazes on ceramics or as the patinated surface of metal, turquoise glass, a crimson silk lining inside a jacket. The synthetic colours of deck chair canvas are part of the vivid composition of Aust's wall hanging, and resonate more strongly in the calm context of the dominant palette.

I decided to illustrate this introductory essay with a few black and white photographs of artists's studios, or workshops, from the 1930s to the present. I wanted to allude to the determined fabrication, the hands, tools and materials, the cold buildings and long hours, the doing that has brought into being this entire exhibition. Think of the actions revealed in the work included here: drawing, cutting, painting, printing, creasing, weaving, press-moulding, modelling, glazing, beating, soldering, carving, grinding, scrumpling, gilding, trailing, stitching, threading, slabbing, inlaying, coiling, blowing, scorching, turning, laser-cutting, dying, knotting, spinning, sawing, tying, pattern-cutting, pricking, throwing, scratching, pouring, dipping, engraving, incising, patinating, spraying, scrubbing, assembling, and so on....

In these times when people increasingly sit in front of screens clicking through their intangible contents, you could read this list as an invigorating invitation and reminder to *do* something with stuff you can feel.

1. Ernst Gombrich, *The Sense of Order: A Study in the Psychology of Decorative Art*, Phaidon, 1979, p.1.

Andrew Lord

Ceramic Review 247, January/February 2011. Review of solo exhibition *Andrew Lord*, MK Gallery, 24 September–28 November 2010. Andrew Lord's retrospective was an exhibition of sculpture in clay, plaster, bronze, mixed media, drawings and video. British-born, he went to live in Holland not long after studying and has worked in New York for most of his career.

'When I started to paint the fall of light onto objects, to use light and shade as a tool for building, I was working in a bright studio in the Netherlands, but when I built *Sixteen Pieces. Angled* my studio was a dark cellar on the Lower East side of New York, so out of necessity my work changed.' This quotation from Andrew Lord's interview with the director of the MK Gallery, Milton Keynes, suggests a few background things that matter. Lord is a British artist who has worked abroad for almost his entire career, and though clay has been a major material of his expression, he is a sculptor who understands ceramic but has no interest in ceramics. His work through the last four decades has explored light, gesture, touch, interior and exterior, other artists, poetry, and recently landscape and recall. *Sixteen Pieces. Angled* (1986) is one of the earliest, sharpest, complex works on show in Milton Keynes, where the intention has been to reveal the phases of the whole story. This exhibition is paired with one in the Santa Monica Museum of Art, California, and there is a joint publication of a beautiful and extensive monograph that includes installation shots from both exhibitions. The form of a pot has an inherent inside and outside, and Lord has pushed the metaphorical possibilities with his great conglomerations of objects, still life gone mad, as in *Eighteen Mexican Pieces* (1993), a throng of fleshy turquoise-glazed forms, including a couple of books, and all with the rapid restless fingermarks of working in soft clay.

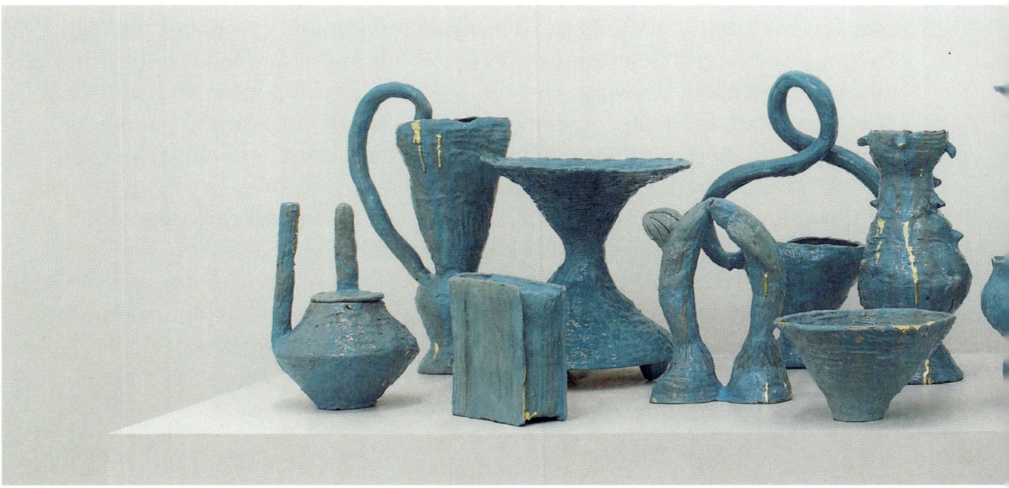

From the late 1990s, *Watching* is a group of three embodied pot forms with deep pokes and bumps formed by pressing clay into, presumably, his eye socket. Impressions of the space between hands, in the mouth, or nostrils, also exist on their own as hanging sculpture, wired together, or as elements of larger works as in the *Profile vase* series, and as plaster relief on canvas.

The new work, however, has moved outdoors and is full of a different thought and energy. Often made in plaster with a beeswax surface, Lord is now evoking running rivers, Blackpool Tower, a bay window, sheep on a bank, or a small Lancashire valley. He has filmed bits of landscape, meaningful in childhood, with characteristic elegiac looseness. These, as well as framed drawings and a series of sketchbooks, and poems, are the subtexts of this show. The plaster under-wax has a beautiful luminous quality that hints at a ceramic surface but wins. Evidence of the clay finger-strokes still dominate his final surfaces; now clay may be the mould and plaster the final substance.

The English outdoors is a huge departure as stimulus. A transitional piece is called *Second Avenue, No 3* (2007) and is the interior form of a jug shape, the narrow core space made solid, with a lyric sweeping handle. The title refers to a long poem by Frank O'Hara. The poems of Walt Whitman and O'Hara have been his companions and inspirations over the decades as much as Paul Gauguin, Pablo Picasso, Marcel Duchamp and Jasper Johns, seen in the *Profiles*.

Poetic intensity combined with looseness is Lord's great achievement over a long span of constant making. I hope to see a lot more of the Spodden river through his vigorous drawing and pale plaster forms springing with life.

Andrew Lord, *Eighteen Mexican Pieces*, 1993, photo: Andy Keate, courtesy MK Gallery

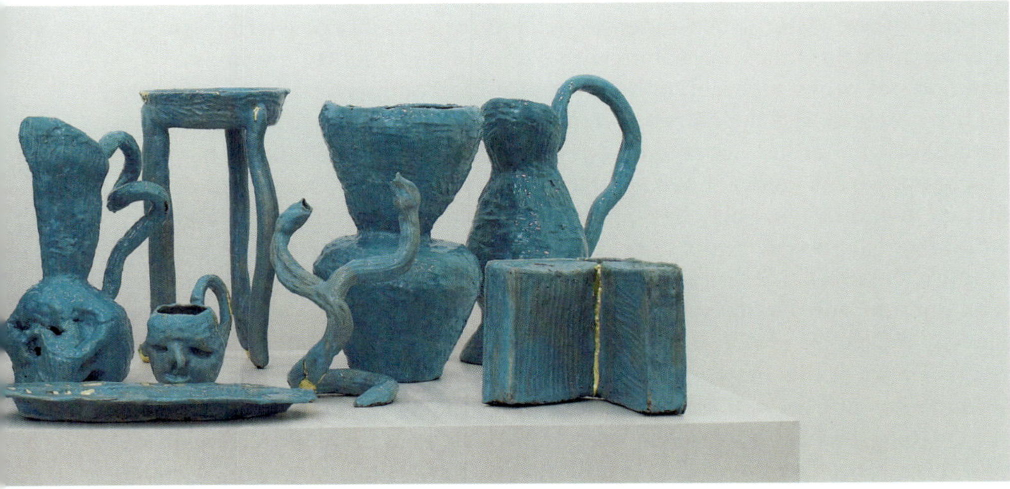

Making, Drawing, and Time

Gallery leaflet, *Introducing: Nao Matsunaga*, Marsden Woo Gallery, London, 24 March–30 April 2011. Nao Matsunaga was born in Osaka but came to England at the age of 12 to join his brother at a progressive school. Almost all his education has been in Britain, therefore, but his roots in Japanese culture seem uncompromised.

Nao Matsunaga doesn't bother much about colour in his recent work – the actual colour of clay, some black or white glaze, and stripped wood are his material vocabulary. At the moment he says terracotta is 'too red'. The putty colour of white stoneware and the pallor of a barkless twig articulate form without fuss. And what of the forms?

Some of these graceful awkward objects are just clay, some are just wood, but the core of this new body of work engages these materials with each other. Not suggesting any function but evidently hollow, apertures draw attention to themselves by being sharply rectangular, architectural you might say, well-finished, points of focus in the loose, slightly bulbous, weighty clay shapes. Perhaps the body as well as the building are in Matsunaga's imagination, but the content remains elusive and unspecific and this is his strength. The juxtaposition of familiar objects, across a range of scales, is in play. Storytelling implications, beasts, towers, caves, treehouses, a reclining woman – things alluded to but not followed through. There is danger in going straight for the figurative, he says, an oblique route is preferred. Proportions are tantalising, a big and bulky appearance achieved on a tabletop, a work like a miniature, perhaps, of something much bigger; there is a whiff of the absurd.

Matsunaga studied on the mixed media course in Brighton and worked in wood and clay, and his work speaks strongly for the possibilities of that course. After graduating, he worked for a couple of years in an architectural ceramics workshop with traditional terracotta methods, banging out press-moulded units for restoration and new buildings, working on big projects. Big things reenacted small, furniture, and architecture, have long been part of his visual language and field of reference. Over the years I have known his work, I have seen small flights of steps, seats you can almost use, a big raw clay bath, pots on tall wooden tripods of builders's wood from skips. He made a great arch you could walk through of pressed tile/bricks with a pub-green glaze. A rectangular structure with a small door as a point of entry in its seemingly huge wall was a memorable piece from his Royal College of Art years. It was made of terracotta with rapid diagonal finger marks across its surface. Playing with scale is a theme, articulated through surface as well as form.

There has been a gradual transition in his mode of making, though it would be fair to say that building skills are part of his everyday life, in and out of the studio. But regarding clay, his skills evolved through press-moulding in the factory, slabbing at Royal College of Art during his MA course, and coiling now – the slowest method so far....

Slowness makes its contribution. Matsunaga starts coiling in the middle so all options are kept open. His return to hand-built imprecision, intuition, and unprescriptive form-making is because he wants sufficient time to put the right kind of control into his making, and to find form. He works on two or three at once so they can influence each other, and spread the same mood over several pieces. Wood then makes its impact on the clay after his soft coiling: he beats them with wooden tools when the forms are leather hard, and then come the repetitive marks of wood – the scrape of a wooden modelling tool cutting a surface like fish scale across the form, which is 'capturing movement in a still object', he suggests.

Matsunaga started raising his clay forms on structures of twigs or small branches while on a residency at Cove Park in Scotland in 2010. He wanted to see how the weightiness of the clay form would seem stuck up in the air – the *made* encountering the *found* which brings its random nature. The wandering lines of a stick found in a woodpile of thinnings in a cemetery or a park has the movement of growth. The sticks need to be co-opted into the work;this is done by carving, also slow. Time almost doesn't matter, he says. Much as he admires the rapid gestures of Japanese calligraphy and brush painting, at this stage he needs to spend slow time with work, giving it his inattention as much as his attention. 'In order to make the branches

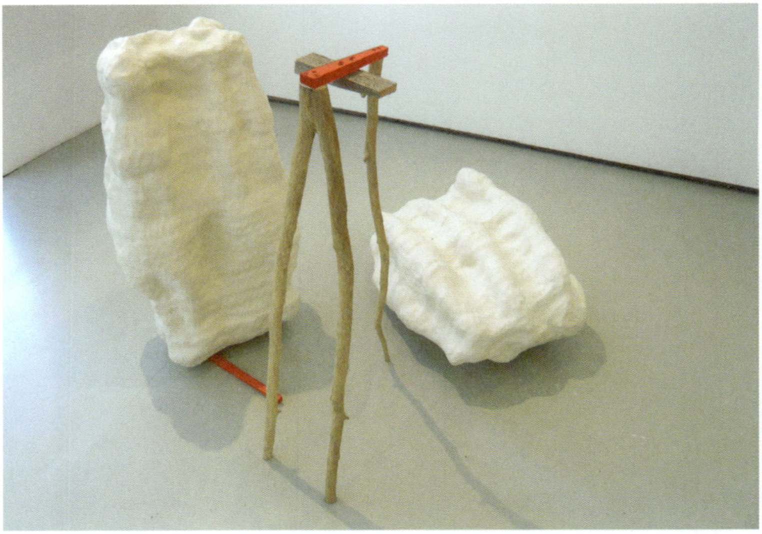

Nao Matsunaga, from left, *Standing Stone or Lost; Man, Woman, Child or Astute; Rest of My Life or Found,* 2011, photo: Philip Sayer, courtesy Marsden Woo Gallery

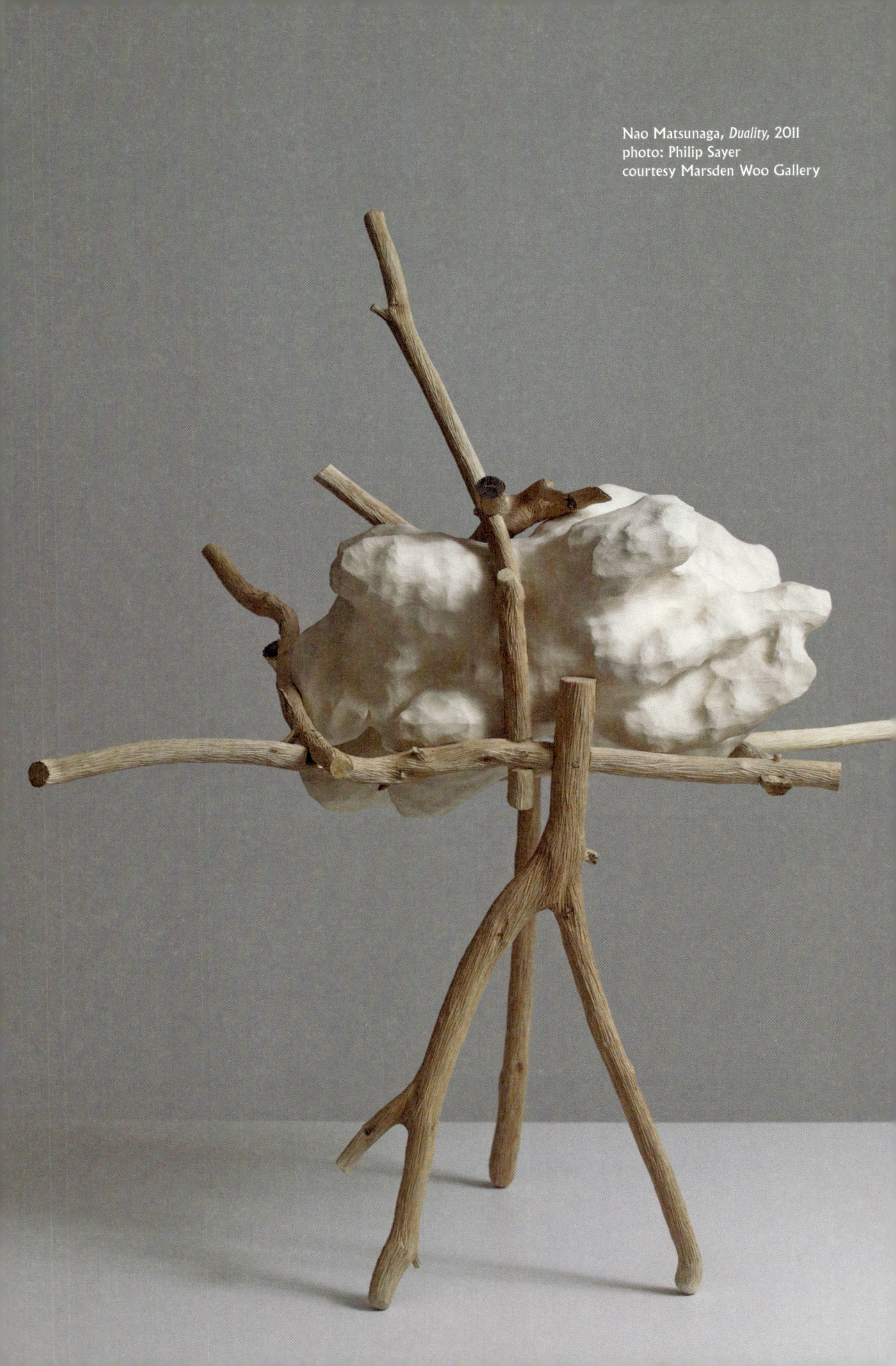

Nao Matsunaga, *Duality*, 2011
photo: Philip Sayer
courtesy Marsden Woo Gallery

"my own" I started to carve their surface to resemble tree bark (to create a kind of caricature of a tree) and also to echo brush and pencil marks that appear on my drawings.' He had wild deer in mind while he was working at Cove Park as well as submarines, beasts and built containers, cohabitants of the bare West Scottish coast.

In the current body of work his loose approach is further developed, in the open dialogue between wood and clay. He half-makes the stands before deciding which clay object will go on them, whether they will be support, signifier of nature and artifice, or cage. Ambiguous collisions of formal reference arrive at a final appearance when Matsunaga has defined their surfaces. The carved twig surface connects with the scraped clay surface, although their textures are different. They are comparably restless. He works all over with a V-cut chisel on the sticks, the tool that would have been used on a block of cherry wood for Japanese printmaking. The very fine texture produced means you can't quite focus on it, and perhaps this brings you closer to look. Marks of both kinds, the wooden scrape on leather-hard clay and the chisel gouge through wood, imply the human hand and this is important. The marks are also directional and steer and persuade the eye, echoing the idea of drawing, doodling even, all over a form. If it could be described as drawing, it is far from decoration; perhaps animation posed against the mass or bulge of clay.

In the past few years, an important encounter has been running at the back of Matsunaga's mind. Asked as an interpreter on an architectural research trip in 2008 for an exhibition at the V&A, he met the architect Teranobu Fujimori, whose buildings defy contemporary expectations, are rich with material qualities, and play with scale. Subsequently Matsunaga helped to develop Fujimori's project in the group exhibition *1:1 – Architects Build Small Spaces* which opened in the museum in June 2010. Matsunaga helped find the timber yard for hefty planks, scorch their surfaces, translate to the British workforce, and was then, to his delight, physically involved in getting the small building winched up.

Isanu Noguchi is another very important reference for Matsunaga. Noguchi is known across the Eastern and Western hemispheres. With a broad visual practice across architecture, sculpture, design and craft, this is form-making in the widest sense. Matsunaga spoke of his envy of the straightforwardness of working the 1930s, as modernism spread its influence across the world, of the ability to make something new without irony or appropriation or inverted commas.

Matsunaga's whole concern is rooted still in visual language: we need to eat with our eyes without verbal explanation and conceptual supremacy. Visual language for him has survived in German painting, in work he deeply admires such as Fujimori's buildings and the sculpture of Thomas Houseago, and, Matsunaga says, 'here, it survives in work in craft.'

Old Stuff – New Life – Still Life
The Lure of Junk

Essay, *Thing Tang Trash: Upcycling in Contemporary Ceramics*, exhibition catalogue, Permanenten West Norway Museum of Decorative Arts, Bergen, 17 September 2011–8 January 2012. This book of six essays was launched in October 2011 at the conference that concluded *Creating Art Value, a Research Project on Rubbish and Readymades, Art and Ceramics* funded by the Research Council of Norway. The project was directed by Jorunn Veiteberg, Bergen National Academy of the Arts, and ran from 2008 to 2012.

Most of the artists and designers I know like to go to flea markets and second-hand shops, rummage and linger in jumble sales and carboot sales on a regular basis. Some have even become junk dealers. This seems to be a passion that is most consistently sustained by the art community rather than 'normal' people. Why do we treasure old thrown-out objects, and wander for hours in their pursuit? Because of the open-ended random nature of what we might discover.

Second-hand

Material evidence of things made for human need, objects now in the limbo of disuse because people move house, or die, or change, is compelling to people who make things. History is a hook to artists who want to be informed, understand objects, and surprise themselves. We may like finding old techniques and manufacturing processes, like engraving, that usually decorated early industrial ceramic tableware. There is pleasure in recognising the luxury of so many layers of process on a 19th-century plate, for instance, a lost extravagance of skill. The cobalt blue print transfer, raised paste relief, hand-painted colours, acid etching through glaze as another tactile band of pattern under the final firing of gold; this sequence of accumulating ornament is far removed from the decorative norms of the tableware industry today.

There is a dogged economy in junk shopping too – the opposite of decadence and excess. Junk buying can be seen as rescue and repair, making a stand for resourceful adaptation and less consumption. Frugality is a virtue, an *unwasting*, beloved of the just-postwar generation with their careful parents and the last years of rationing.

An old restraint has been strengthened by a deep new sense of waste, both from decades of commercial pressure to acquire new things, and from diminishing world resources. We could see bric-a-brac as resistance – just a *find*, not a thing endlessly advertised and sold to us. Junk is outside the normal chain of commerce; we have not been coerced.

Clare Twomey, *Monument,* installation at mima Middlesbrough, 2009, photo: Dan Prince

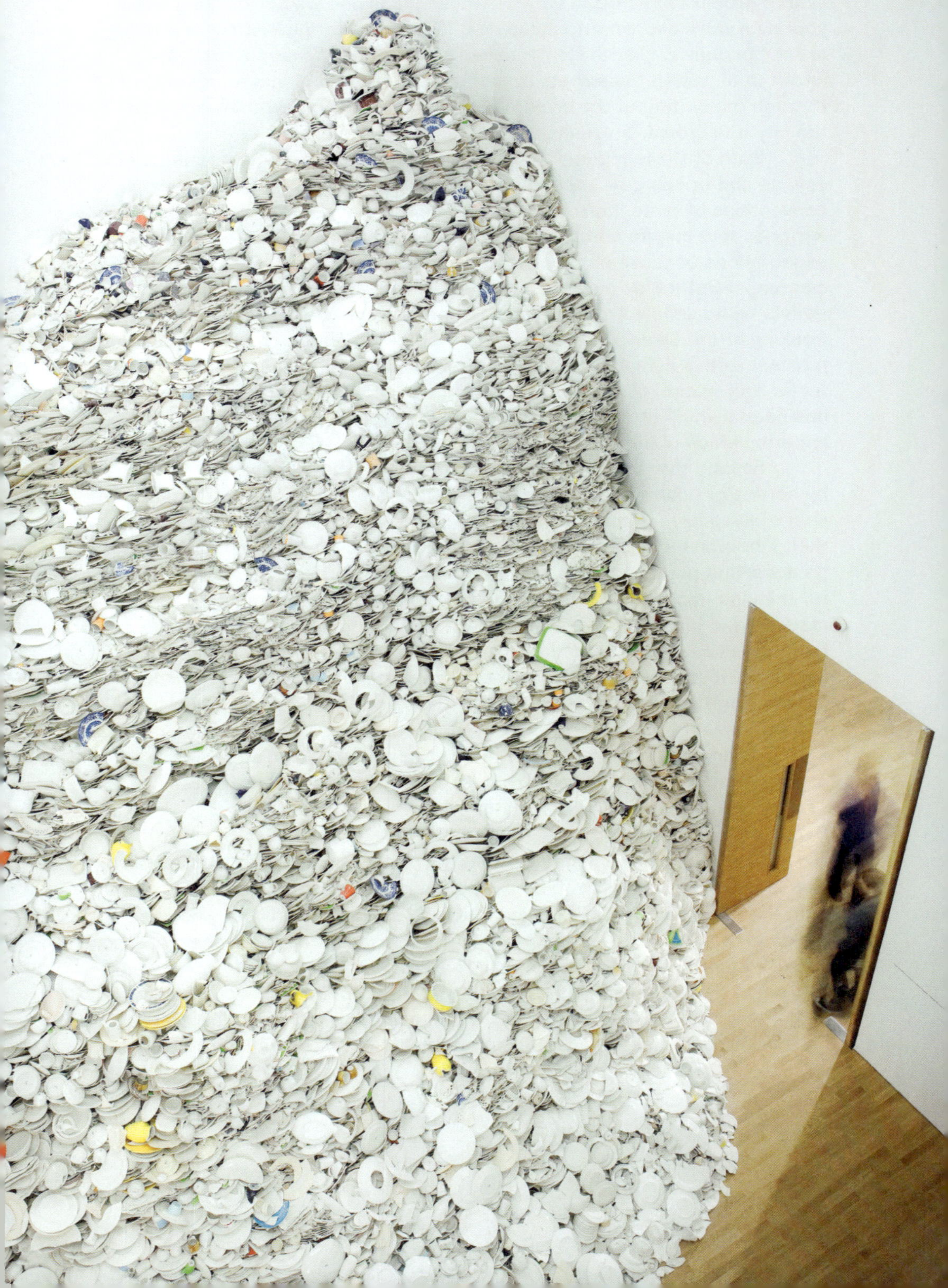

Beyond the considerable charm of the bargain, I think the roaming search process satisfies in various ways, and is one way of thinking about your own work and what to make next. Perambulatory quest has a distinct artistic pedigree. French Romanticism's idea of the *flâneur*, a restless intellectual pacing the streets at night like Charles Baudelaire, resonates through the writing of the critic Walter Benjamin with new thinking about the city, the crowd, Surrealism and Cubism.

Both of these modernist art movements celebrated the found object, collage and bricolage – aspects of freedom breaking away from academic conventions of taste. Leftovers, digressions, the random, these are modern intrigues that inspire and provoke. Every junkshop could confound your expectations because *anything* might be there, hidden in residues of house clearance. But it also matters that these things are thrown away, detritus, resists being seen with fresh eyes and perhaps remade. The searcher is *Looking at the Overlooked* [1], to quote the title of a book on still-life painting, relevant to this human sifting habit of accumulating ordinary things. The table, fruit, game, plates, glasses; still-life in the huge history of painting has been a small thread of connection with the everyday, and with the impermanence of life.

Finding the right object, seeing something that speaks to you, unseen by hordes of others, makes a creative path. And an insight into the material past of lived lives. People in junkyards may look for a thing that fits with their inner idea – but an unpredicted fit, a jolt too. The random object may be a starting point as things are sifted and used, actually and conceptually, for thinking into making. Finding old furniture, ornaments and crockery in markets and junk shops: few artists are immune to the pull and most find themselves collecting some kind of stuff. In three progressive phases of response, there is collecting, then the more engaged process of simulating or incorporating found objects in your work, and lastly, letting adaptations of found objects *be* your work.

Using objects in art is not a new practice, but as an apparent focus of the past decade in ceramic art, it is a phenomenon to be explored.

Bricolage

For two of my most eminently bricoleurial ceramic colleagues, the quest for junk is meaningful enough to be described in their biographies and books published for retrospective exhibitions in 2003. Carol McNicoll and I used to spend most Sundays in the early 1970s searching for old evening dresses in Brick Lane (then far scruffier) in London's East End, that we could wear to work in the ceramics department at the Royal College of Art. McNicoll uses the search in her current practice as a version of travel, which artists have always done as a way of finding fresh ideas. As Tanya Harrod writes:

.... she was keenly aware of developments in other disciplines in the 1990s, particularly the odd interactions between material culture studies, anthropology and the fine art world. Her compulsive wanderings around flea markets and junk shops went hand in hand with her strongly nuanced sensibility concerning things and their odd trajectories from high social value to ambiguous status to the category of rubbish.[2]

Harrod also describes McNicoll's decor in her flat and studio in an old piano factory as manifesting the same work ethic, a found-and-adapted style:

> The two interiors she created at Apollo Works ... were in themselves works of art; a scaled up version of her pattern-making, collaging and salvaging activities. They remind us of the woman herself and her endlessly inventive spirit, in which the magus artist's tabula rasa is set aside in favour of playful experimentation with what already exists. As we shall see, this tendency to trawl, drift and wander through urban space was to come into its own in the late 1990s. But these predilections had always been apparent in her appearance – her clothes being an exquisite extension of herself.[3]

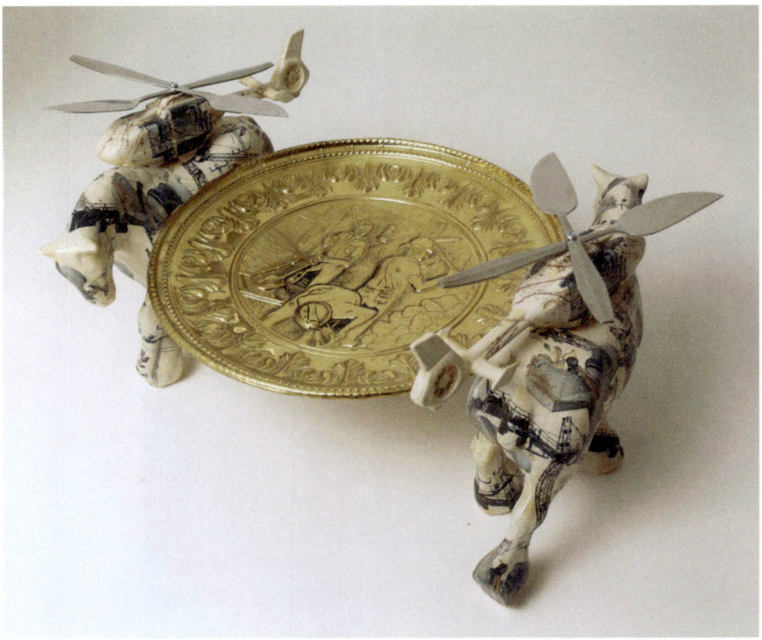

Carol McNicoll, *Subtext*, 2010, photo: Philip Sayer, courtesy Marsden Woo Gallery

Cathy Courtney writes in the biography of Richard Slee: 'By the late 1990s found objects began to appear in the work. Many were collected by his young daughter when she accompanied him to car boot sales searching for treasures. When his daughter reached adolescence and presented him with a bin-bag full of the china ornaments she no longer wanted, Slee found himself unable to throw them away and gradually began to subvert them by creating new contexts for them, ... In a typical Slee amalgam of practicality and commentary, *Wheelbarrow of the Medusa* (2001) is not only a gesture towards Théodore Géricault's *The Raft of the Medusa,* but brings this sequence to a close by loading the remaining figures from Pearl's bin-bag into a modelled wheelbarrow.'[4] And in his catalogue for the Tate St Ives showcase exhibition of 2003, Oliver Watson wrote of the emotional charge that can be felt from the autobiographical, as well as daft and comical, use Slee has made of the cheap figurine: 'To be interested in ornaments is inevitably to be interested in ceramics; ceramic history at one level charts the fluctuations of taste of just the level of culture in which he is interested. Slee knows the power of the Toby jug, the Staffordshire flatback, the ceramic basket-of-flowers, the mantelpiece knick-knack. It is his talent to be able to appropriate these, and re-present them to us, in a way that lets us into his secrets.'[5]

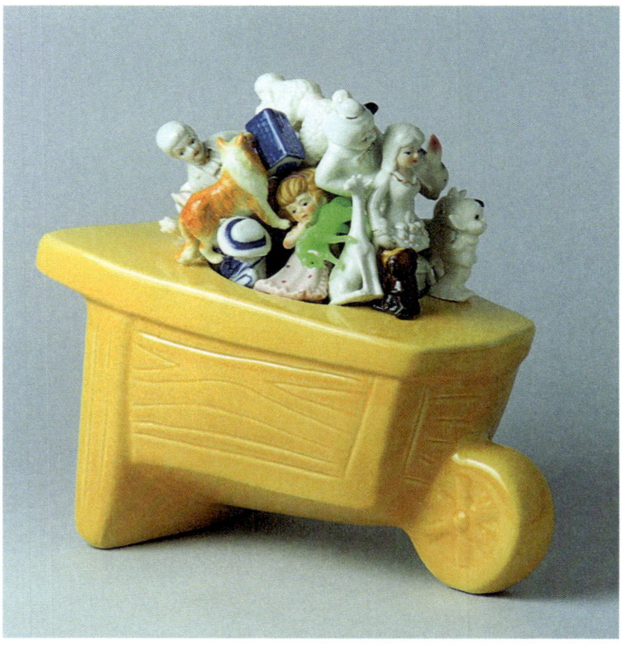

Richard Slee, *Wheelbarrow of the Medusa,* 2001, photo: Philip Sayer courtesy Marsden Woo Gallery

Materials

I want to turn now to a consideration of material. Ceramics sit apart from other media because it cannot be remade. Ceramic as a material is irreversible, we are stuck with it – it cannot go back to being clay. Through the transformations of heat in firing it, has changed chemically and irrevocably. Thus, unlike metal and glass that also thread through the utilitarian history of human life, it is not stuff for *actual* recycling. The fact that discarded metal and glass objects can return to their molten material state is spectacular. Good for the rapid realisation of cash, as in stealing the lead from church roofs, scrap-dealing and pawnbroking, but dangerous to historic certainties of style.

Melting down has been the cause of gaps in art history because metals, in particular, have been so precious. It is understood that many historic ceramic things, vessels mainly, across the world have aped the shapes of more expensive things made in metal, and have been cheaper versions of these high-class things.[6] Clay is a splendidly imitative material, and while the metal objects have been recycled when tastes and fortunes changed, the ceramic versions have survived despite being more fragile and less valuable, because they can't revert.

In the present time, recycling is seen as a norm of good behaviour; most materials are reclaimed in recent years of 'sustainability' conscience. In our earlier domestic culture of make-do-and-mend, knitting can be unravelled, clothes have always been unpicked and re-stitched, or made into rags or felt. Think of the folkart history of quilts, patchwork and rag rugs. Furniture gets adapted and remade, the old timber a precious advantage. But not ceramics. When you smash crockery you get shards, leading maybe to ingenious repairs with metal staples, an add-on beaten metal spout or neck, or glue, none of which entirely restores the object.[7]

There is a long record of the shard, enduring fragment of the midden and the rubbish tip, informing art history and anthropology, and social and technical histories. The shard has a place, too, in contemporary art. Fragments may say more than wholes; Clare Twomey installed a huge pile of reject crockery and shards in the exhibition *Possibilities and Losses: Transitions in Clay*, which she curated at Middlesbrough Institute of Modern Art in the North of England in 2009. In the same year, Grayson Perry included a room full of archive cases containing shards of his pots in an exhibition at Victoria Miro Gallery in London.

When you smash crockery and bricks you also get rubble, bits of hardcore, the bulk of stony fragments laid under a road, path or floor, which leads us to building.

Building and Rebuilding

The history of human living has building at its core, and once depended on rocks and trees, stone and wood, which can be used countless times.

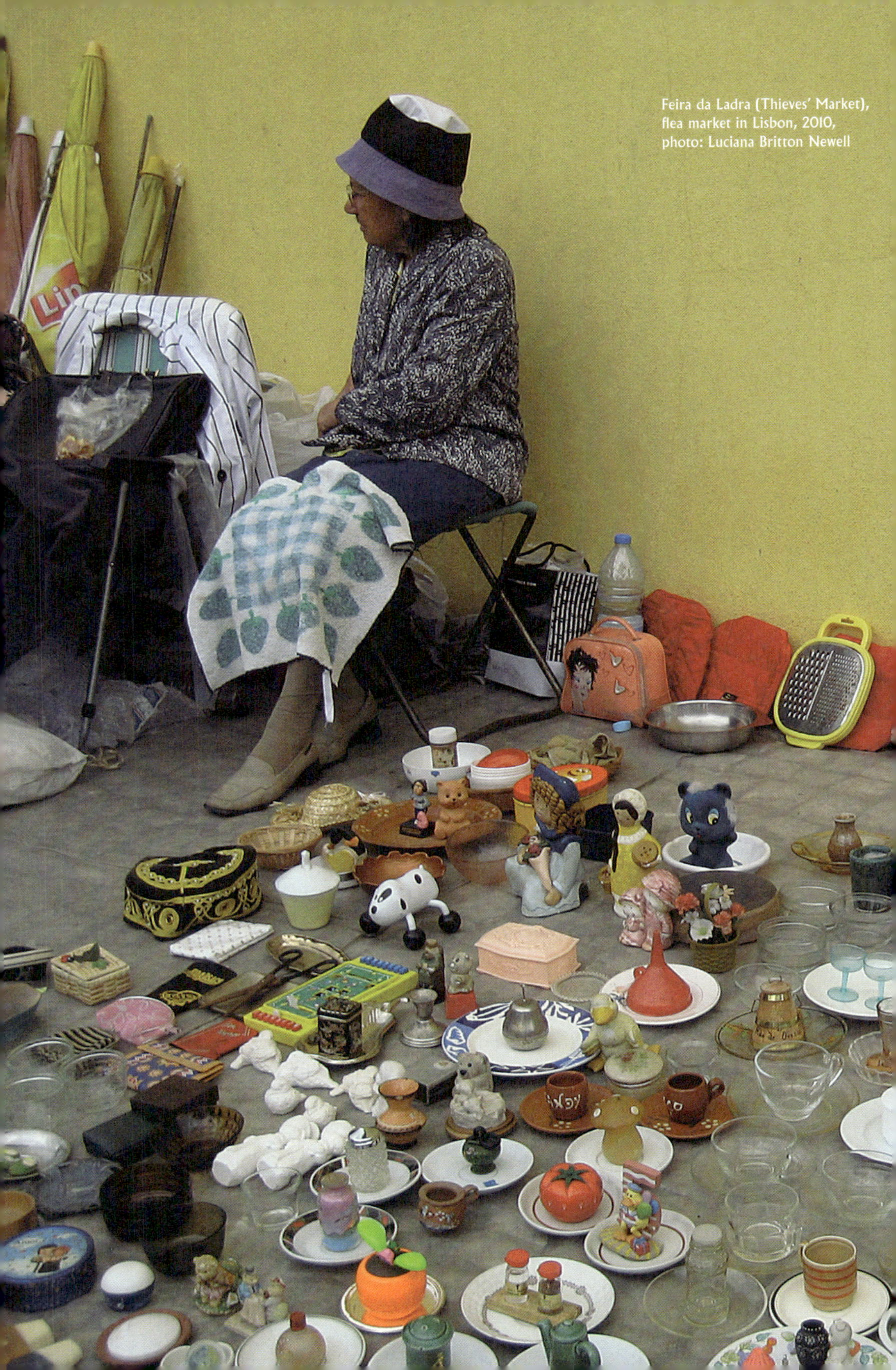

Feira da Ladra (Thieves' Market),
flea market in Lisbon, 2010,
photo: Luciana Britton Newell

Building is a good model of an essential process of reuse and repair seen in everyday life. There is such obvious sense in rebuilding because of the durability of traditional materials – pilfering from ruins. Timber improves with age; a beam or a stone lintel has intrinsic strength and can be carted away from a ruined cathedral and used in a barn. Slates for roofs, fired clay as bricks: these are modules, transportable, rebuildable, adaptable. To stray from ceramics for a moment, the artwork which won the Turner Prize for Simon Starling in 2005, *Shed Boat Shed*, is in my view a wonderfully bold, energetic and skilful revelation of reuse and adaptation, un-building and re-building on a large scale. He found an old shed near the river Rhine, took it to pieces and made a boat out of most of it, carried the rest of it down the river to Basle, where he rebuilt the shed in a Swiss museum.

Building is also a way of working with clay. Hand-building was a prominent technique in post 1960s ceramics and clarified a decision not to throw, and often led to making sculpture or pots for looking at rather than functional pots. But there was also new studio use in this period of the industrial technique of slip-casting from plaster moulds. Moulds could be taken from intentional designed shapes, but also from found objects. A lot of energy in the modernist and postmodern context went into recycling forms in a new material, for multiples and repetition, replication, simulation, and assembling complex sculptures from piles of cast elements. Allusion, quotation and reference have appeared across all art forms in the postmodern era and reward a knowing audience with a frisson of recognition.

Practice: Borrowing and Taking

Any surveyor of contemporary ceramics will notice that the plunder of forms and actual objects from demotic and popular culture is an aspect of new work over the last decade. Simulation, the reuse of an object's shape in a new medium, has been taken further into appropriation and incorporation, the inclusion of real found objects rather than replicas. The artists I have already referred to, McNicoll and Slee, have explored that transition in their different ways.

I think there are two main types of appropriated ceramic form: ornaments and crockery. Both of them are cheap and found in flea markets, and working with them raises questions about high and low culture, class, taste and value in general. (It is noticeable that precious ceramics are rarely re-appropriated in the crafts; this is the province of the upper reaches of fine art. It is hard to forget that Ai Wei Wei dropped a Han dynasty vase in 1995, an act recorded in a triptych of photographs, and he dipped a lot more in paint. Presumably a less exalted potter finding a piece of Sèvres in a carboot sale would take it to auction and make some money? Only the famous and rich can destroy ancient and priceless things, with a thousand times more provocation and pause for thought.)

The first ceramic appropriation type is kitsch, the cute figurine, toy, souvenir, or mantelpiece ornament. These have been seen in the UK in the work of the sculptor Tony Hayward, Barnaby Barford, and in Slee for those few years of the purposeful disbursement of his daughter's trinkets. The second ceramic type is the everyday functional object, tableware, especially the plate. The flatness of plates has great potential as image as well as object. This has been beautifully explored in Scandinavia for instance, in the work of Irene Nordli, Kjell Rylander and Caroline Slotte; and Kari Skoe Fredriksen, who used the title *Still-life* for a composition of plates that synthesised an old photograph of women engaged in needlework. Slotte takes appropriation to creative heights in the pure finesse of her craftsmanship, like a jewellcutter she carves back through the glazed surface of a plate. In a series made in 2009, called *Unidentified View*, she took plates decorated with a typical 'chinoiserie' engraving, so beloved in Europe and a tableware norm in the 19th century. It is a scene of a river, a man carrying a fishing rod near a bridge, with pagoda towers. When she has finished, after painstaking hours with a fine grinding drill, a sandblaster and a final sanding by hand, we have sculpture instead of painting (via the printed image). The little man, or a pagoda, is in perfectly nuanced relief on a bare white plate.

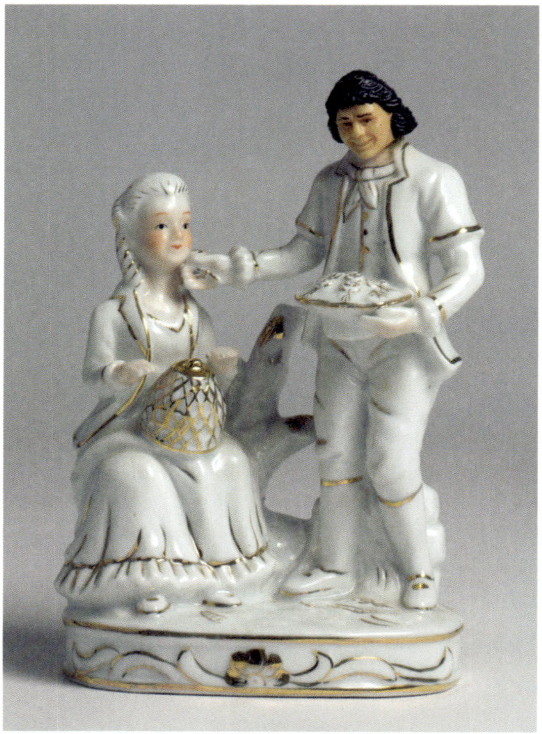

Tony Hayward, *Bearing Gifts*, 2010, photo: Philip Sayer courtesy Marsden Woo Gallery

The figurines in a McNicoll piece may be cast from souvenirs but are often figures modelled by her, like the dumpy tourist who appears in her polemic anti-capitalist pieces. Printed images that crowd across the surfaces may be appropriated too, or based on her own drawings. Her pieces with three-dimensional additions have usually brought in other media, such as glass vases (fake cut glass cast with geometric facets) or brass plates and trays, and the assembly is often threaded together on a metal rod for solidity. For McNicoll it has been a chance to mix media. Also for Slee, whose broader sculptural range and scale now includes large additions like broom handles and spades.

He too has lifted print images from familiar sources, like the generic graphics that advise the public – how to put litter in a bin and so on. So what is most important about the practice of reuse and are there any drawbacks? The questions I would ask of this way of working are these:

- Might extraordinary skill exclude the need to appropriate – do you take what, and when, you cannot make?
- Is categoric ambiguity, allusion, and openness to interpretation, less likely in work that incorporates actual and recognisable things?
- Could we be looking at the advance of cliché and nostalgia? And is that a problem?
- In the digital age when every image and fact is so accessibly replicable, is regurgitation of the past more, or less, likely?

Though a ceramic artist, I am an outsider in this field, but I imagine that the following nouns could be interesting reasons to cajole old objects into new ceramic art. Perhaps they could be made into strings of words like a concrete poem:

mimesis, quotation, replication
simulation, distortion, repetition,
homage, narrative, humour,
surprise, irreverence, satire,
politics, synthesis, possession:
making it yours.

For me there are three special qualities that show up in these rebuilt objects that all begin with 'A': *Absurdity* is part of humour, and is a strong trait of English work as seen in the juxtapositions of Slee and McNicoll; *adaptation* is a way of understanding changing conditions, play, rethinking objects into the present, the opposite of a controlling pursuit of clear concept into perfect form; and lastly, *Accommodation* is the opposite of imposition, the negotiation of awkwardness and disjunction in finding new roles for objects. A truly contemporary skill for the complexity of our times.

Reused

I will finish this essay by returning to the idea of the collection as a prop for thinking. Walking the dog day by day, I pick up shards of blue and white china that I come across in the woods, more appearing after heavy rain. I collect stray cups, mostly white, many bought abroad (no repeats), which are in daily use. I have a teapot from Afghanistan, a reused Chinese teapot, broken on purpose and riveted together with a new metal base so you can boil tea on the fire with milk and sugar in it. I have had it since the 1970s and I think of it as an artwork, a beautiful hybrid, and an enlightening adaptation. Recently I have realised I am collecting unfinished crockery, left semi-decorated by the factory because of flaws. The strangeness of this half-baked emptiness is often striking. The unfinished is another version of the fragment, leaving room for the mind's eye to run.

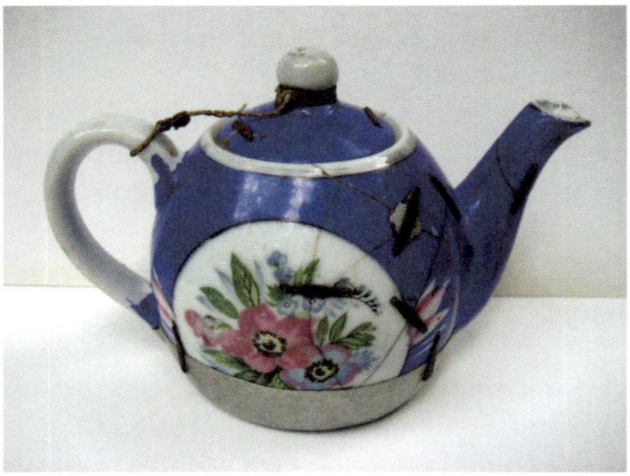

Afghan teapot, 1970s, photo: Alison Britton

A few years ago I was given £50 to spend on junk and write about it for a design group's magazine giving thought to the secondhand. I will end by reusing part of that text, appropriated from the recent past:

> Like words in a sentence, it is the relationships between objects that make them mean something to the eye. It was the forming of tableware groups, like fantasy/mundanity still lives, that made sense for me. Buying junk in a street market like the Waste in Hackney, the great piles of dross you wade through to find a gleam of interest, the chanciness of what you might or might not find, is appealling: most of the tableware, for instance, is thick, ugly and ill-proportioned and was not worth manufacturing in the first place. Objects with character shine through very directly, like seeing a face in a crowd. On a Saturday at the Waste when it rained all day I sloshed through plastic boxes of old crockery like sinks of washing up, looking for quirks ...

Tableware is everyday stuff, but it has the formal joys of verticals and horizontals, upright jugs, flat plates. What is visual wit? Part of the impulse to put things together is a small drama with improvisational humour, or play, behind it. Then there is the appeal of making patterns out of chaotic jumble – a simple human inclination. Old stuff/new life/ still-life.[8]

I find no way to *make* with my pile of cobalt-printed shards, though perhaps some echoes of the 'unfinished' begin to appear in my own work. I don't want to make or reuse tableware, but am drawn into its realm of thought, its human connection, its ordinariness, its verticality and horizontality, its offer of containment, for the dry, the wet, or just air.

1. Norman Bryson, *Looking at the Overlooked*, Reaktion Books, 1990.
2. Tanya Harrod and Roselee Goldberg, *Carol McNicoll*, Lund Humphries, 2003.
3. (ibid).
4. Garth Clark and Cathy Courtney, *Richard Slee*, Lund Humphries, 2003.
5. Oliver Watson, *Richard Slee Grand Wizard*, Tate St Ives, 2003.
6. Oliver Watson, at the time curator of Ceramics at the V&A, gave a paper on this subject *Pottery, Form and Status* at the Vessel conference for the Gulbenkian Foundation in Birmingham in 1987 – see essay above.
7. The new display of the Ceramics Galleries at the V&A includes an interesting case full of breaks and repairs.
8. *The Companion* (2009) magazine, A UBM Live Publication in conjunction with Designersblock for Interiors Birmingham 2009.

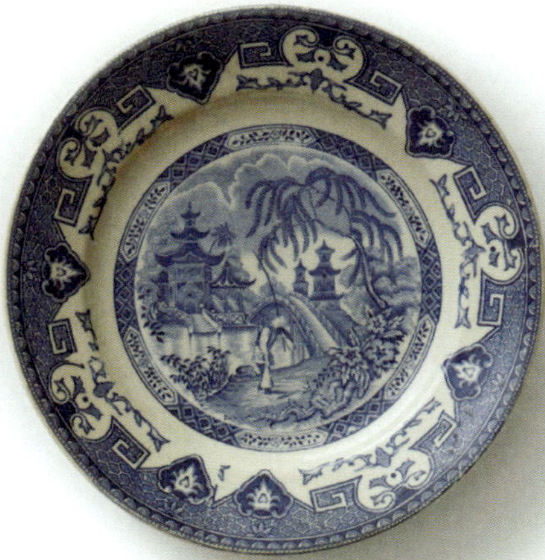

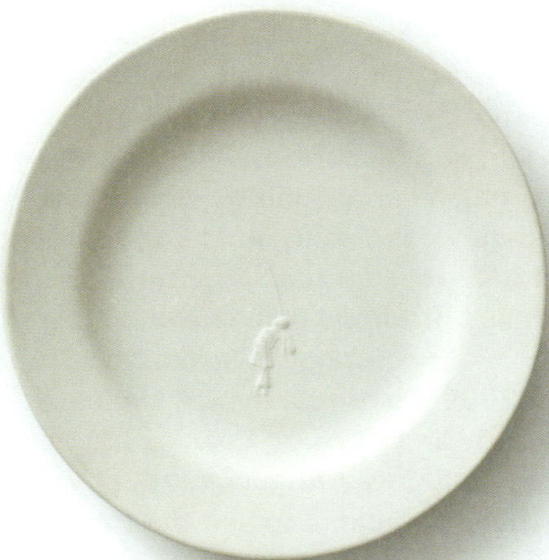

Left: Caroline Slotte, second-hand plate photographed before working on it
Right: Caroline Slotte, *Unidentified View*, 2009, photo: Oystein Klakegg

Things and Work

Introduction, *Life and Still Life*, exhibition catalogue, Crafts Study Centre, 2012. Following the idea of collection, this was an exhibition (Crafts Study Centre, UCA Farnham, 16 October–22 December 2012) in which I showed a hundred things that belong in my house or studio, alongside a group of new pots. These included crockery, paintings, drawings and photographs, and stray objects like a relief mould and a pencil case.

Everyone has things, but artists do something else perhaps with the objects they own, in using them to think with. This thinking happens of course in the studio, but also at home, where most of the things reside. In my case, the studio is not at home but ten minutes' drive away in Hackney, London. I make pots in the studio and write at home in an 'office' on the top floor. I think in all my rooms, and eat and use my cups, plates and spoons in the kitchen/living room. Some of the objects shown here have been brought from the studio but most from home. Always a home includes objects that furnish your life beyond function; other needs are met: stimulus, self-representation, sensuality, recollection. All objects can be symbols of something, especially if you became used to seeing the symbolic strength of things as a child, through toys or things in habitual surroundings.

As part of my teaching at the Royal College of Art, I have sometimes been part of an exam board in another department, Design History for instance. For one such occasion, I read a dissertation about the growing artisan/merchant class in Holland in the 16th and 17th centuries having developed a large, centrally important, chest/cupboard/wardrobe (called a *Kussenkast*) as the key piece of furniture in which most of the protectable possessions of a family could be stored – there were that few of them. Usually an inventory of everything in the house was made; another powerful idea, and seen from the present as a rapid insight into a way of living, as so much is revealed by simply reading the list. For me this was an enviable image of the past, and I hoped to find a rationale for making an inventory of the things that really mattered in my house, but could not begin: too many things. Perhaps this exhibition is a slim version of such a list, made visible.

In curating the exhibition *Three by One* for the Crafts Study Centre in 2009, I had found such treasures and insights in Ethel Mairet's Balkan braids and Bernard Leach's pot collection, including the 14th-century English jug, dull grey with a splodge of vivid green glaze, and his East Asian bowls. After this I came to see the things I have scavenged, swapped, bought, and gathered around me in a slightly more serious light; they were my 'study collection' also.

For an object to belong in a study collection, though it sounds a bit pompous, means it might have an impact on what you make, be part of a kind of growing tactile vocabulary. You don't always know why you bought or kept a thing until its moment arrives and it seems suddenly to promote an idea needing to be made. You change your mind; relevance can shift. If you have enough space or can put up with clutter, then you hold onto things even when they are not currently exciting. As with all imaginative engagement, you need the sustenance of different things as time passes and work evolves. I love the comment from Michael Cardew about objects from far afield and from the past working as models of aspiration, in writing 'We do not want to make Chinese, or Korean, or primitive pots. But we have seen clearly what they have which our own so badly lack, and having seen it we are not likely to lose sight of it again.'[1]

Twenty years ago, after an early retrospective exhibition, I wrote in *Ceramic Review* about getting a body of work started, and how I might jolt myself out of the normal early phase of indecision by looking at other objects – and you don't always have to actually possess them:

> The sight of another object is often a trigger. I might go and look for it or come across it incidentally. The greater the translation needed, the more comfortable I feel. I am very puritanical about influence, the filters of absorption must be thick. The object that excites will be recognisable, will in some way, because of its three-dimensional shape making a relationship with things that I have already made, already belong to me.

I gave the example of a small Indonesian rice bowl/plate in what was then the Museum of Mankind, a thin curved wooden plank, with straight sides added. A small compartment was boarded off in one corner, for some other sauce or ingredient needing to be separate. Like both a boat and a plate 'it fell into my context.'[2]

The contents of this exhibition are a so far uncounted number of objects I have collected, seen mostly in groups, because objects do things to each other and make new kinds of sense. This to me is what still life is about, putting things in contexts, holding them 'still' for a moment to take them in.

In life, in use perhaps, they are on the move. The collected things are in glass cases, as a kind of loose frame of reference for my own pots shown in the open, nearer the floor. I could not say which objects have had a direct connection with the way I want to make – it is less specific than that. They have all impinged with some spurring connective impulse, or spark, and it has been a gradual honing process of a subliminal kind to decide which ones to bring when there are a lot of them. Sometimes the drive comes not from an object on its own but how it sits with others. The way they reach out to each other is a clincher, whether through colour, strangeness, relief, form, pattern or content.

Crockery is a fundamental category, a baseline of ceramic understanding, and perceived through touch and use as well as sight:

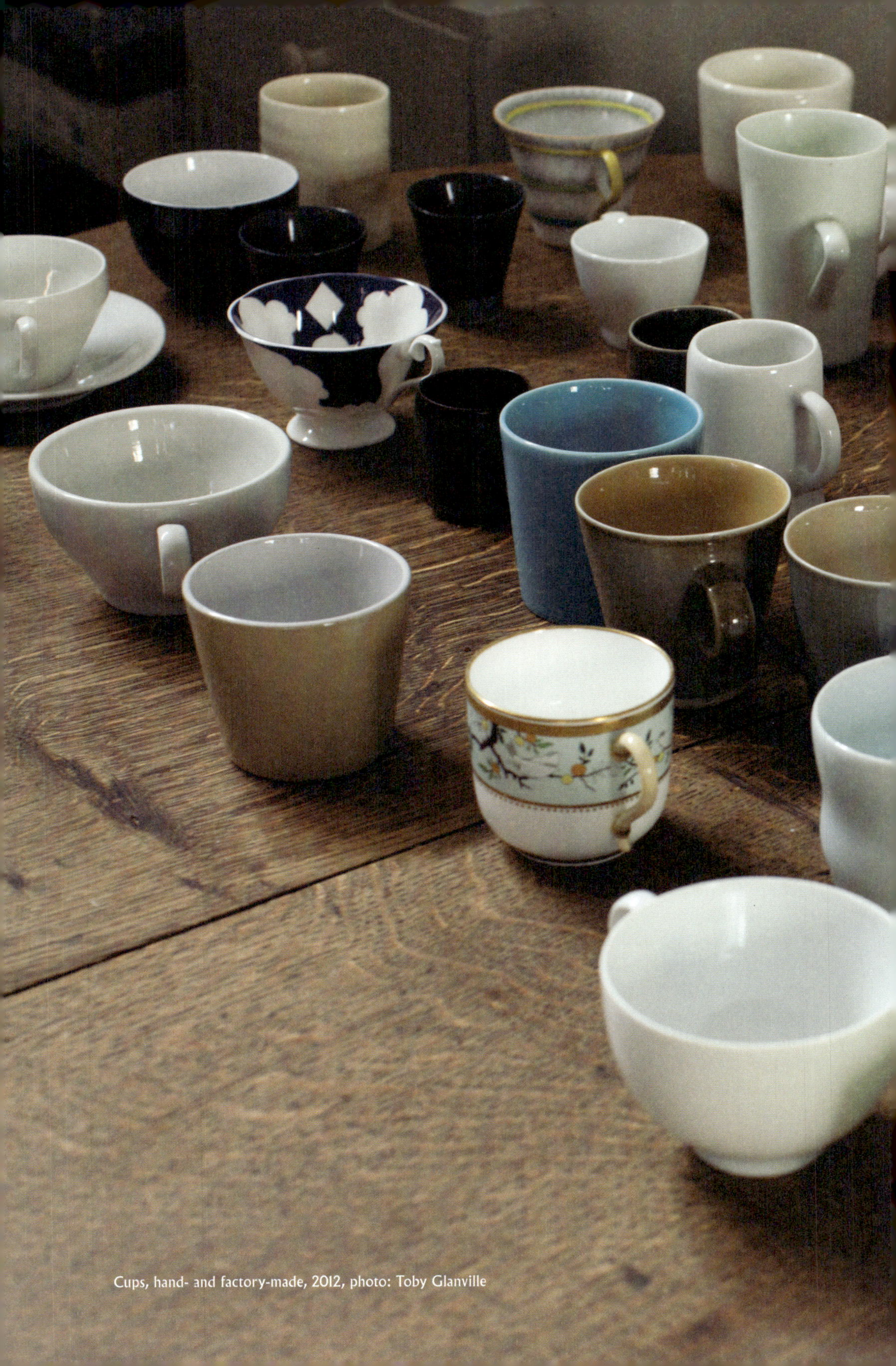

Cups, hand- and factory-made, 2012, photo: Toby Glanville

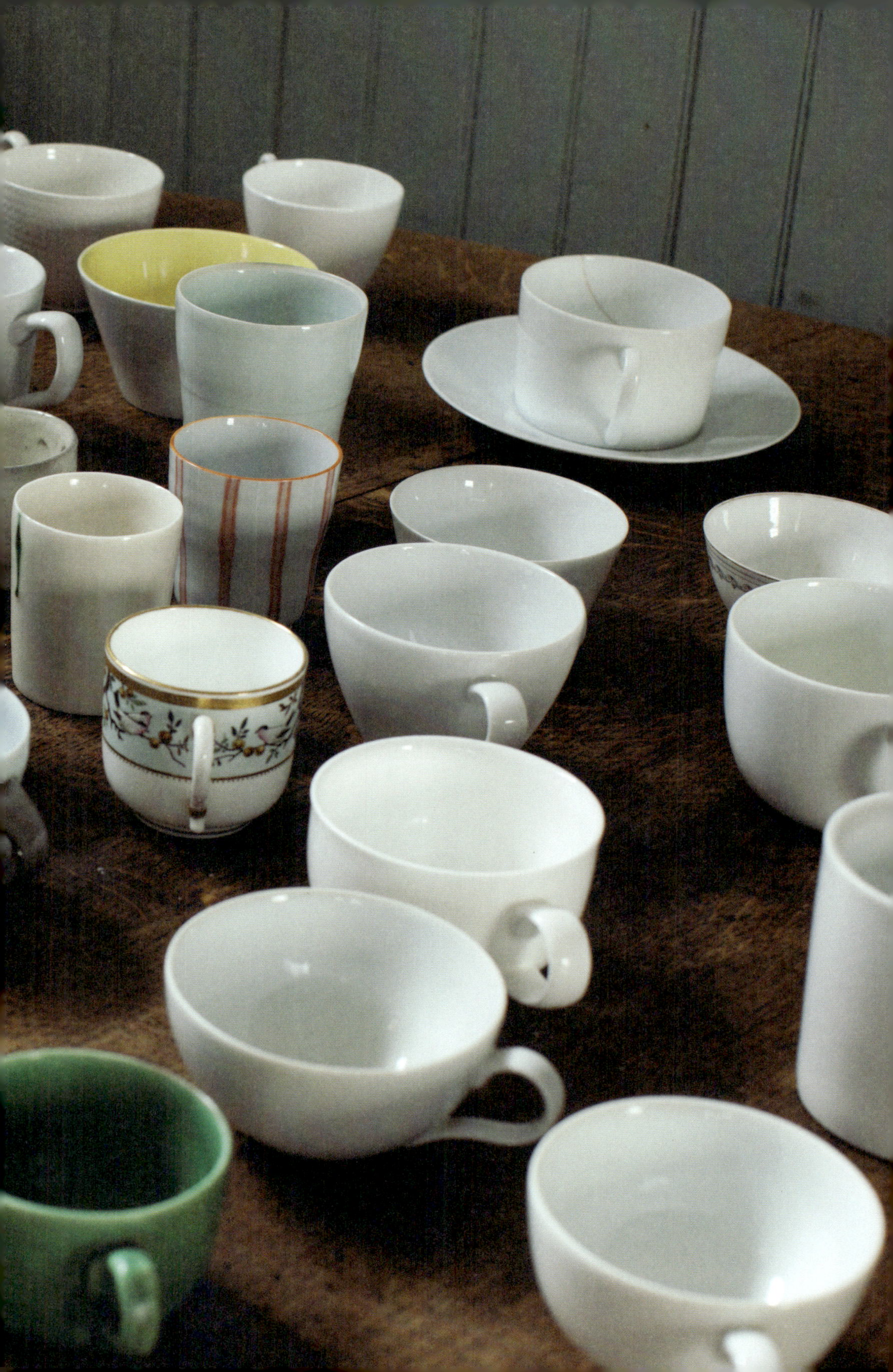

> Tableware is everyday stuff, and everyone eats, so everyone understands the basis for these forms – pots, bodies and eating are entwined. The ordinariness of the object field of table, cup, plate, bowl, jug, and the habitual rhythm of getting up, washing, drinking, eating, going out to work, and returning to eat again, give us, in the history of ceramic forms, an assimilated sense of bedrock understanding. There are good pots and awful pots, but we know where they are coming from.[3]

For decades I have looked for a white high-fired cup in almost every place I have travelled to, and bought in hardware shops and flea markets and fine china showrooms across Europe and in Japan. These I collect on purpose, while the rest of my objects find their own way into my need for them. There are cups from fellow artists too, the one-off and the studio production line, the industrial and the hand made in communication. The jug and the plate are other important types, verticals and horizontals, profiles and picture planes.

Closer to my own practice, I am showing clay works and small sculpture made by friends; including Bryan Illsley, who shares my studio, and Jacqueline Poncelet and Richard Slee whom I have known since college. Apart from ceramics, I am exhibiting things made of many other materials, as well as drawings, paintings and photographs. Some of these are images of 'still life' in an overt way, though everything brought here is, casually, within that paradoxical pairing of my exhibition title.

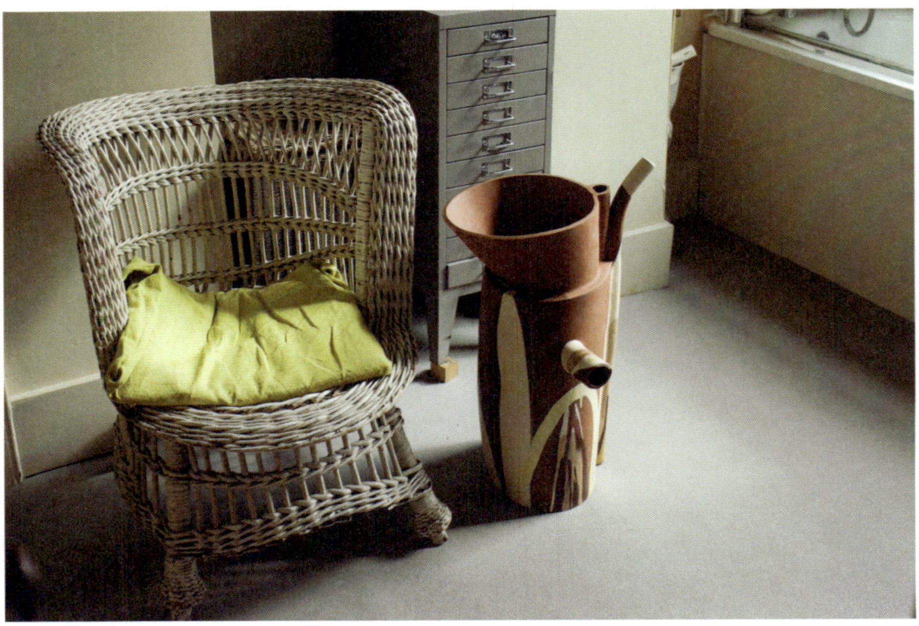

Alison Britton, *Still*, 2012, photo: Toby Glanville

As for my work, extending the slight archival tendency I am showing new and older pieces. Since 2007, I have reformed the way I deal with surfaces, no longer spraying a clear glaze everywhere over an entirely slip-painted external surface. Re-learning the immediacy and risk of pouring and dipping was a liberation with messy beginnings. During a short working period in Japan at Shigaraki in 2010, I re-found red clay, having used it a lot at school, and the beauty of its unglazed colour led me to make new sorts of surfaces exposing quite a lot of it unglazed. This feels very daring. My pots always held water in the past, although that was generally the only function on offer.

A couple of the pots are older white pieces; not many have been so colourless. *Squirl* is from the 2009 exhibition I shared with the Norwegian artist Marit Tingleff, where she used the wall and I used the table, but undercurrents of domestic reference were in both bodies of work, at very different scales. In the recent pieces I find myself making more symmetrical pots to accommodate the wildness of pouring slip and glaze, and flat and upright forms more simply than before, as if the plate and the jug were, in my case, inescapably in the background. What we perceive and what we produce are not the same thing, but both engage imaginative energy, the *intake* and the *outpour*, which could be titles for pots.[4] I am still not going to make tableware, though I am 'drawn into its realm of thought, its human connection, its ordinariness, its verticality and horizontality, its offer of containment, for the dry, the wet, or just air.'[5]

Taking these things, my habitual context, out of the house and into the exhibition; bringing the pots from the studio to the house to be photographed on the bathroom floor in daylight; seeing them brought together at the Crafts Study Centre is a special opportunity. The archives and holdings of the collection have inspired me to formulate an active response, to put the long gestation of a particular attention to things and what they may communicate more evidently into a public space.

Letting the everyday shape thought, the slight subversion in thinking of the house as a place of practice, it is only a small step further to recognise and celebrate *the intrusion of living into work*.

1. Michael Cardew, *The Maker's Eye*, Crafts Council Publication, 1981, p.20.
2. Alison Britton, 'The Story So Far', *Ceramic Review* 129, 1991.
3. Alison Britton, 'Laying the Table: synthesis, continuity, and the everyday', in *The RJ Lloyd Ceramics Collection: Artist as Collector*, ed. Simon Olding, Burton Art Gallery and Museum, 2010.
4. Michael Foley quotes the philosopher John Dewey from his 1934 lectures 'Art as Experience' thus: 'Perception is an act of the going-out of energy in order to receive, not a withholding of energy... We must summon energy and pitch it at a responsive key in order to take in' (*Embracing the Ordinary*, Simon and Schuster, 2012).
5. Alison Britton, 'Old Stuff-New Life-Still Life', see above, p.224–235.

Postscript
Freeing the Object from its Place

My selection of writing from the 2000s has more on ceramics and fewer essays on other things, which is not to say that my interests have narrowed, but is an accurate reflection of what I have been commissioned to do in the past decade.

The first text is a review of a performance by the Japanese ceramic artist, Satoru Hoshino, which added to his exhibition of several large black ceramic sculptures in the V&A at the time. Performance and installation have become widely recognised phenomena within the applied arts – ceramics and textiles[1] especially – since the 1990s, though its roots reach much further in fine art practice. Installation work in textiles and ceramics has been an avant-garde practice of the last decade.

Though I have seen and admired the evolution of this 'expanded field'[2] it is not a territory I was often invited to review or write on. Maybe I am seen to have a stronger sympathy with the object on its own, like the jar in Wallace Stevens's short poem, which 'took dominion everywhere'.[3] The great expansion of work in the installation genre happened in the generation after mine, and these artists are articulating it, as they should; in ceramics, Edmund de Waal and Clare Twomey have a strong record. Neil Brownsword, born and raised amid the Stoke-on-Trent factories, made ceramics that memorably evolved, or dissolved, from whole sculptures to horizontal planes of fragments, like an archeology of the declining potteries, in the exhibition *Close* at the Crafts Council in 2000. This new beginning led to a PhD in 2006 that was historical and archeological, and archived remaining craft skills in the industry. His work in clay for the PhD was a narrative of British post-industrial scattering.

Keith Harrison and Phoebe Cummings have been outstanding too. Harrison used the spectacle of unconventional firings with ad hoc electric appliances as performance.[4] Cummings builds minute detail into unfired clay scenarios of organic growth. The curator Alun Graves explores the work of these two and other V&A related projects in his essay *Beyond the Collection: the V&A and Ceramics in the Expanded Field*, a paper given at the first symposium of the Westminster research project in 2012.

An early work by Twomey was in *The Secret Life of Clay* at Tate Liverpool in 2004. *Consciousness/Conscience* was an installation in which gallery visitors performed, steered by the exhibition layout to tread a path through a passageway of dry, barely fired bone china tiles. These had a hollow box-like form that crunched and crumbled unnervingly under your feet. Work made with Wedgwood's blue jasperware clay body made her more widely known[5], last used as fired clay dust that was sifted over a formally laid dinner table in *Epoch*.[6] Her gigantic pile of shards, *Possibilities and Losses: Transitions in Clay*, is mentioned in my essay from the other end of the decade, written for the Norwegian research project on value and rubbish in ceramic art.

Works like these imply that artists are thinking a great deal more about context, what surrounds things, frames and underpins them, how and where they are to be seen, than they did in the early postmodern days. But in both cases the spectacular is emphasised. In 1986, I had written that the five pots were chosen 'for sticking out rather than fitting in'.[7] A pursuit of the spectacular was a reaction to norms of the Bernard Leach tradition in the shift from a modernist aesthetic to a postmodern one. Likewise, the radical momentum of early installation, the ephemeral conditions of being shown for a short time in a public space,[8] needed architectural scale and a sense of theatre, of eye-catching spectacle.

An interesting question for me is whether the spectacular and the ordinary must be separated, which I will return to later.

I have a longstanding sensibility for 'the everyday'. The ceramic cup has had my attention since I was an undergraduate and began to think of it as a symbol of the ordinary, a key word. I began making a collection of saucerless cups in street markets like London's Brick Lane in the early 1970s. At around that time, I made fireplace tiles for the psychoanalyst Marion Milner and then read some of her books, those written for a wider audience, like *On Not Being Able to Paint*. In *A Life of One's Own*,[9] a sort of diary, she attempts to write down as honestly as possible her stream of consciousness, all the phenomena that flit by under the radar, as it were. For the everyday observer, the bus ride is the experience as much as the destination. Walking the city streets noticing, not intervening but paying attention, is a lifelong practice. Thinking about the habits of home is also fundamental, and linked to objects seen subliminally in daily use.

And how does work in clay relate to this awareness? My determination to work with earthenware, because it is not precious, is noted in the wandering radio conversation with Michael Rosen. I wanted to include this speech transcript among the written texts as a truer representation of the normal, slow uneventfulness of making with materials. It gradually articulates the kind of mindless craft practice, rolling out a sheet of clay and getting the air bubbles out of it, that is generally beneath notice. Further, my persistence with the pot as an ongoing subject, pots small enough to lift, seen in domestic places, in different lights – all these are ordinary considerations that stay in the back of my mind.

And so it has been both stimulating and reassuring to discover (at some point in the new millennium for me) that *the everyday* was a field of research, an idea initiated by the Marxist social theorist Henri Lefebvre in

Paris in 1947, explored in greater depth by him and others between the 1960s and the 1980s, and taken up by modern literary France at the same time. Georges Perec's novels were all written in this period; he also stands out for his connections with the sociologists. The Paris street was *the* location in the first phase of social theorising of the everyday. Both the theory and the literature were largely masculine domains. The domestic, home, is another powerful place for the everyday, and in the postwar period still predominantly female in its negotiations: '... women 'undergo' the everyday – its humiliations and tediums as well as its pleasures – more than men'.[10] And here one would runin to the ordinary craft and design objects and containers, cups chairs and spoons. *Dwelling* was another early category of French research.

Internationally, visual art practice seems to have made the most use of the idea of the everyday since the late 1990s, explored for instance in *Everyday*, the 11th Biennale of Sydney in 1998.[11] This was an early location for the wonderful work of Vladimir Arkhipov, who began in the 1990s to archive an unnoticed Russian heritage of tools and gadgets improvised from the bits of other things, reflecting the paucity of buyable products in the USSR and the ingenuity of humans, the strategies of making do and mending. Some of his collection appeared in a book in 2006.[12]

It might be assumed that studio craft practice, the modernist tradition Leach epitomises, with its quiet integrity and restorative intent, fits well with the idea of the everyday. But its self-consciousness excludes it. The *everyday* of French theory was far more spontaneous and elusive and would flee a modest domestic stoneware bowl constructed on purpose – its ethical proposition a truly bourgeois concept. For this reason found material, *recognising* such qualities rather than inventing them, relates better, like Arhipov's TV aerial adapted with forks.[13]

These tensions were explored in *Out of the Ordinary: Spectacular Craft* in 2007,[14] where one of the spectacles was a great diversity of scale. Long sweeps of red paper-cut motifs cascading out of a suspended book, by Lu Shengzhong,[18] contrasted with minute carved wooden weeds inserted into cracks in the architecture by Yoshihiro Suda. Another spectacle was the very high level of craft skill. These tiny weeds, and the immaculate embroidered stains on dustsheets on the floor in Susan Collis's installation, whispered of the everyday and the overlooked, and indeed some of the audience didn't notice them. In the essay Glenn Adamson wrote for the catalogue, he says the artworks here are 'a recognition of the state of play', and 'are not fragments of the spectacular or the everyday; in their thoughtfulness and internal conflict, they are more akin to the many books written about those subjects. Like the writings of Henri Lefebvre or Guy Debord, these artworks create a space for consideration, where opposing qualities are summoned into uneasy existence'.

So where is the everyday in craft, in this book? Flashes of quotidian thinking have fed my interests for years; they are there in Thomas Eisl's use of old inner tubes and scrap metal, for instance, or Tony Hayward's ordered cardboard boxes of detritus made into sculptures. These he called 'a new world created from the mundane and ordinary at hand'. But in the 2000s more frequent references to the still life, the domestic, crockery and cutlery, reuse, and an awareness of routines and unconscious patterns of doing, emerge.

In the letter to Doffy, casual writing, both her questions and my answers, say more about *living* and working than is necessary. My essay on Eglin, remarks on the plastic packaging salvaged to make moulds for body parts. And my base in the ordinary is apparent in 'browsing with apparent idleness, like window shopping, sidling up to the ideas, keeping it open-ended,...' in describing my approach to curating *Three by One.*

A sense of the everyday is more overt in my last two essays. *Old Stuff*... explores reuse, common practice across visual culture. I took the opportunity here to write more about later work of Carol McNicoll and Richard Slee, longstanding colleagues from New Ceramics times, in a maverick context of indeterminate thoughts about materials, methods and junk.

A recent book by Michael Sheringham surveys the field of everyday thinking, and its subversion of any fixed definition, through French social theory, wider responses in cultural studies, and the arts. He asks,

> Do specific genres or media have particular virtues in granting access to, or purchase on, the everyday? Or does the everyday seem to slip between the fingers, so to speak, of established genres and, by virtue of an inherent elusiveness, seem to escape the purview of, say, narrative fiction, lyric poetry, drama, film, photography, pictorial art, reportage, thriving rather on the indeterminacy offered by the transgression of generic boundaries? [15]

With an increasing awareness of a quieter scale, random events, intimacy, private space, the changeability of a known object when lived with over time, in my final essay *Things and Work*, the idea of the everyday drifts closer to home, and finds my new pots sitting in the bathroom for photography.

Not theatre then, more the habits of daily life. If craft thrives ambiguously in the interstices between art and design, then it slips well, almost beneath notice, into the idea of the everyday.

1. E.g. Caroline Broadhead moved from making jewellery to conceptually clothing more of the body in semi-visible materials like muslin and tulle, using the garment as an idiom, in the early 1980s. Early clothing pieces were seen as distinct objects hung on the wall. Some of her work with light and shadow, and thread rather than cloth, became site-specific and others were performed by dancers in constructed textile spaces.
2. *Ceramics in the Expanded Field* is an AHRC-funded research project at the University of Westminster, co-led by Clare Twomey.
3. Wallace Stevens, *Anecdote of the Jar*, Faber, 1953 p.36.
4. Keith Harrison *Last Supper*, performance in Raphael Cartoon Court, V&A, 29 September 2006. 13 unfired clay blocks were matched to the colours of Christ's robes in Leonardo's painting. Cooker elements embedded in the clay slowly fired the blocks in front of the audience.
5. *Trophy* installation at *Clay Rocks*, V&A, 29 September 2006.
6. *Epoch* was exhibited in Ceramic Biennial, Stoke-on-Trent, 2009.
7. *5 Pots on the Horizon* in 'Our Domestic Landscape' catalogue, Cornerhouse, Manchester, 1986. This had also a feminist connotation. In 1980s thinking, the relation of craft to art was compared with the female relation to male.
8. Not all installation is temporary. Edmund de Waal's *Signs and Wonders*, 2010, for instance, is a permanent work in public view. A red steel channel runs around the circumference of the dome 11m above the V&A ceramics galleries, housing 425 porcelain pots.
9. Marion Milner, *On Not Being Able to Paint* (1950) and *A Life of Ones Own* (1934), both originally published both under the name Joanna Field.
10. Kristin Ross, 'French Quotidian', in *The Art of the Everyday: The Quotidian in Postwar French Culture*, ed. Lynn Gumpert (Grey Art Gallery, 1997), pp.19–30.
11. See 'Everyday', Jonathan Watkins's introduction to the Biennale, reprinted in *The Everyday, Documents of Contemporary Art*, ed. Stephen Johnstone, Whitechapel and MIT, 2008, pp.61–68.
12. Vladimir Arkhipov, *Home-made, Contemporary Russian Folk Artifacts*, Fuel, 2006.
13. ibid., p.149.
14. *Out of the Ordinary: Spectacular Craft*, V&A exhibition curated by Laurie Britton Newell; exhibition catalogue, V&A Publications and the Crafts Council, London 2007.
15. Michael Sheringham, *Everyday Life, Theories and Practices from Surrealism to the Present*, Oxford University Press, 2006, p.15.

Glossary

an iron	a blowing iron, hollow pipe; or a punty, a supporting metal rod, used in glass blowing
bandsaw	an electric saw with a rotating steel belt with serrated edge
batik, wax-resist	a decorating technique to make patterns on dyed fabric
black basalt	a black vitreous clay body used by Wedgwood
burl	flattened knotty growth on a tree
burr elm, oak	a tree defect caused by insects, used decoratively
cut off the bat	a pot might not be thrown directly on the wheel head but on a disc of wood, a bat
electroplating	superimposing a layer of metal on glass or another material by chemical means, electric current through acid in a plating tank
engine-turned	a ceramic decorating device using a lathe with an eccentric motion to make incised bands of geometric or fluted pattern on pots
Flatback	a type of Staffordshire figurine, for mantelpiece display
forging	forming metal by heating in a furnace and hammering on an anvil
glazed chintz	cotton furnishing fabric treated with a hot roller to give a surface sheen
ground-lay	a decorating technique with oil and powdered enamel colours to create a flat area of solid colour, eg. on Sèvres porcelain
hand-building	in ceramics: pinching, coiling, and slab building
kiln-formed	glass casting – glass fragments fired in a kiln in a plaster mould
lacquer	East Asian technique of layering paper with paint
lathe, machine	for shaping wood, metal, plaster, etc., a rotating spindle where the wood or plaster spins round and can be profiled against cutting tools
leather-hard	a clay state between plastic and dry – right for joining slabs, or refining form by scraping with serrated tools etc.
malleable	in metalwork, formable by hitting with a hammer. Inappropriately used for clay to mean plastic or flexible.

oxidised/reduced, porcelain or stoneware	a normal firing is oxidised; to affect the colour of a glaze, the atmosphere of the kiln is robbed of oxygen so the colour changes: brown becomes green in the case of iron oxide; celadon is a reduction glaze with iron in it.
papier mâché	a paste of water-based glue and paper for moulding forms
pâte de verre	a paste of fine particles of glass used in kiln casting
porcelain, stoneware, earthenware	are clay categories – clay bodies have different temperatures of maturation; porcelain and stoneware are high-fired to a vitreous state, terracotta and other earthenwares are lower-fired, porous, and need glaze to be waterproof
press moulded	pressing plastic clay into a plaster mould, or section of a complex mould, to make a form
raised paste	a hand-painted decorating technique to build relief texture in parts of a pattern
sandblast	a way of removing the surface of a material by directing a jet of fine abrasive sand at it.
sgraffito	a decorating technique of scratching through one layer of slip or glaze to reveal another
silk-screen, used in printing	a fine mesh in a frame, supporting a resist pattern/image/text, from which inks are pulled through with a squeegee
slip	clay and water; pigment can be added to make colours
slip cast	manufacturing process; slip poured in and out of plaster moulds
sprig	a pot-decorating technique where small press-moulded motifs are applied to the pot surface, eg. white cherubs on blue Wedgwood
underglaze	pigments, stains, decorating colours, derived from metal oxides
veneer	a thin sheet of exotic wood glued onto a basic wood for decorative purposes
Viewmaster	device to effect stereoscopic vision with rotating cards of colour photographs, introduced in 1939, popular in 1960s
wedge	a kneading process to de-air clay
welding	to join pieces of metal by fusing; in this case fire-welding, getting the metal to white heat and merging the pieces by hitting them

Index

Alison Britton

Since the late 1970s, Alison Britton has written about other peoples' work in contemporary practice across a range of art, craft and design, though the core of her writing has been about ceramics. Her essays, articles and reviews have mainly appeared in magazines and exhibition catalogues; this is the first book of her writing.

Born in the London suburbs in 1948, Britton was part of a radical group of Royal College of Art graduates in ceramics in the early 1970s. Working from a London studio over four decades, she has an extensive history of exhibitions, here and abroad. She was awarded an OBE in 1990. Her retrospective that year toured the UK and concluded at the museum Boijmans van Beuningen in Rotterdam. In 1996, a solo exhibition travelled to museums in Australia. Since 1998, her work has been represented by Marsden Woo Gallery, London, (originally Barrett Marsden) and she exhibits there biennially. In 2007, the exhibition *END*, a collaboration with six other ceramic artists from England, Norway and Denmark, was at the Danish Museum of Art and Design, Copenhagen, and Bomuldsfabriken Kunsthall in Norway. In 2011, she contributed to *Postmodernism, Style and Subversion 1970–1990*, at the V&A, London.

Britton has also curated exhibitions, such as *British Ceramics* for the British Council in former Czechoslovakia in 1984; and *The Raw and the Cooked* in 1993, working with Martina Margetts, for Modern Art Oxford, which toured in the Far East and Europe. In 2009, she curated *Three by One, a Selection from Three Public Craft Collections* for the Crafts Study Centre, UCA, Farnham, and worked there again on *Life and Still Life*, an exhibition that combined her new work with collected objects, in 2012.

She is a senior tutor and research coordinator in Ceramics and Glass at the Royal College of Art in London.

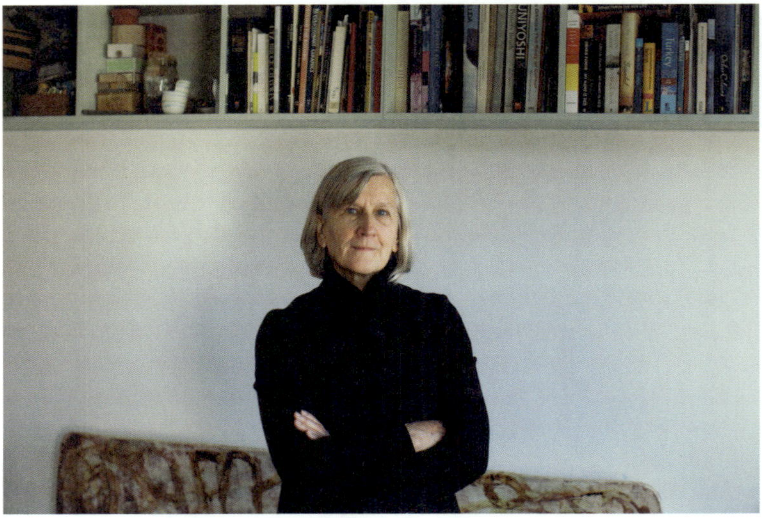

Alison Britton, 2012, photo: Toby Glanville

Seeing Things: Collected Writing on Art, Craft and Design
Alison Britton

Published by Occasional Papers
Copy editing: Antony Hudek
Design: Sara De Bondt studio
Printing: Die Keure, Bruges

Blue images on opening spreads:
1980s: Glass Workshop, Victoria Glass (detail), photo: Philip Sayer, courtesy Marsden Woo Gallery
1990s: Jim Partridge's wood workshop (detail), photo: Alison Britton
2000s: Emma Woffenden's studio (detail), photo: Philip Sayer, courtesy Marsden Woo Gallery
Cover: Alison Britton's studio (detail), 2010, photo: Philip Sayer

The author would like to thank first of all Occasional Papers,
for working with her with such focus, vision and speed on this book.

Also, for their attention, response and encouragement:
Glenn Adamson, Jeremy Aynsley, Myra Barrs, Celia Britton, Brigit Connolly,
Annie Fewlass, Jamie Gilham, Tanya Harrod, Martina Margetts, Tatjana Marsden
and Marsden Woo Gallery, Ruth Pavey, Alida Sayer, Philip Sayer, Linda Sandino,
Martin Smith, Oliver Watson, and her daughters Laurie and Lucy Britton Newell.

In addition to those listed above, Occasional Papers would to thank all
the original publishers for granting consent to reprint these essays,
as well as Sam Baldwin and Katie Morrell.

With the support of the Royal College of Art Research Development Fund.

© 2013 The author, artists, photographers, publishers and Occasional Papers.

All rights reserved. No part of this publication may be reproduced,
stored in a retrieval system or transmitted, in any form or by any means mechanical,
photocopying or otherwise, without prior permission in writing from the publisher.

Occasional Papers has made every effort to trace copyright holders,
but if any have been overlooked, they will be pleased to make the
necessary accreditations at the first opportunity.

ISBN: 978-0-9569623-5-5

www.occasionalpapers.org